D1566511

A WAR OF IMAGES

A WAR OF IMAGES

RUSSIAN POPULAR PRINTS,
WARTIME CULTURE, AND
NATIONAL IDENTITY,
1812–1945

Stephen M. Norris

NORTHERN

ILLINOIS

UNIVERSITY

PRESS

DeKalb

© 2006 by Northern Illinois University Press

Published by the Northern Illinois University Press, DeKalb, Illinois   60115

Manufactured in the United States using acid-free paper

All Rights Reserved

Library of Congress Cataloging-in-Publication Data

Norris, Stephen M.

A war of images : Russian popular prints, wartime culture, and national identity, 1812–1945 / Stephen M. Norris.

p.   cm.

Includes bibliographical references and index.

ISBN-13: 978-0-87580-363-0 (clothbound : alk. paper)

ISBN-10: 0-87580-363-6 (clothbound : alk. paper)

1. Prints, Russian—19th century. 2. Prints, Russian—20th century. 3. Printed ephemera—Russia. 4. Art and state—Russia—History—19th century. 5. Art and state—Soviet Union. 6. Art and war. 7. Nationalism in art. I. Title.

NE675.3.N67 2006

769.947'09034—dc22

2006001579

To Melissa

CONTENTS

ILLUSTRATIONS

PREFACE

• On 9 May 2005, thousands of Russians commemorated the sixtieth anniversary of the victory in the Great Patriotic War. President Vladimir Putin gave tribute to the struggles that the Russian people endured and the high price Russians paid for defending their motherland against the Nazi invaders. According to their president, Russians today had a duty to remember the heroism of the war. Young people, in particular, needed to be taught the "patriotic spirit" [*dukha patriotizma*] and "devoted service to the fatherland" that the wartime experience produced. Countless television series, documentaries, feature films, books, magazines, and other mementos commemorated the victory in a similar fashion. Throughout Russia, wartime posters and images reappeared, while television channels replayed Soviet wartime movies, visually reinforcing the dominant narrative of the Great Patriotic War, one that stresses the Russian people had won because of their spirit.

The events of 2005 and the revival of the war myth in contemporary Russia revitalized a patriotic culture that has its roots in the Patriotic War of 1812. When Napoleon's Grand Army invaded Russia, Russian artists responded by visually depicting concepts of Russianness in popular prints, focusing especially upon Russians who defended their native land. These prints, alongside the memoirs and other reminders of the war that appeared after 1812, presented an image of a "people's war" that subsequent wartime culture expanded. To be "Russian," as this patriotic culture articulated, meant possessing a "Russian spirit" that manifested itself in the defense of the motherland. Such a concept of Russian nationhood survived the fall of the empire in 1917, and artists revived it again in the civil war and particularly during the Great Patriotic War. The celebrations of 2005 represent one more expression of national identity that connects the experience of war to what it means to be Russian. *A War of Images* traces this process of nation building by focusing on the popular images that artists produced during the wars of the nineteenth and twentieth centuries. By examining the visual world of Russian nationhood between 1812 and 1945, this book affords a glimpse into how concepts of Russianness that developed during 1812 evolved for over a century. The celebrations of 2005 indicate that this patriotic culture still has resonance in contemporary Russia and still is used to articulate a sense of Russian nationhood.

| | |

This book could not have been completed without the support and assistance of a number of people and institutions. *A War of Images* began as a dissertation idea at the University of Virginia, and my advisor there, Robert Geraci, deserves a great deal of credit for helping me think through my project and its arguments. Bob has been the perfect blend of advocate, critic, mentor, friend, and colleague, and I thank him for all his help over the years. I also wish to acknowledge two other members of my dissertation committee, Jeffrey Rossman and Alon Confino, for their help and support at UVA, as well as the final reader, Matthew Affron, for his timely suggestions about images and history.

After graduation, Richard Stites and David Schimmelpenninck van der Oye did more than anyone else to help me turn the dissertation into a book. Richard graciously agreed to read the entire dissertation and offered useful suggestions, while Dave introduced me to Mary Lincoln and Northern Illinois University Press. I thank them both and also thank the numerous scholars who have made similar criticisms and provided me with valuable materials, particularly Richard Wortman, Hubertus Jahn, Karen Kettering, Mara Kozelsky, Marc Raeff (who read the book for Northern Illinois University Press), and Charles Ruud.

All projects of this kind require financial help, and I would not have been able to conduct the research necessary for the completion of this book without the following institutions: the University of Virginia Center for Russian and East European Studies (and its director, Allen Lynch), the United States Department of Education for its generous funding of FLAS Fellowships, the Graduate School of Arts and Sciences at UVA, the Corcoran Department of History at UVA, the College of Arts and Sciences at Miami University, and the Havighurst Center for Russian and Post-Soviet Studies at Miami. The director of the Havighurst Center, Karen Dawisha, deserves particular thanks for her constant support of this project. This funding allowed me to conduct research on three separate occasions in Russia and once in Palo Alto, and I thank the staffs at the Russian State Historical Archive (particularly Serafima Vaekhova), the State Public History Library, the State Museum of Vladimir Mayakovsky, the Museum of Folk Graphics, the Museum-Apartment of I. D. Sytin, the Central State Historical Archive of Moscow, and the Hoover Institution on War, Revolution, and Peace at Stanford University. Most importantly, I must thank the archivists in the Graphics Department of the State History Museum in Moscow. My team of "*lubok* experts" at the museum, who not only showered me with countless prints but also answered all of my questions about the images and their production, consisted of Elena Itkina, Nadezhda

Miniailo, and Nina Pyrova. I also thank Eteri Tsuladze and Elena Churina for helping me secure the images from the State History Museum that appear in this book and to Carol Leadenham and Heather Wagner for the posters from the Hoover Institution. The staff of the Special Collections in King Library at Miami also assisted in securing two of the illustrations that appear in this book. In Moscow, the Rezaev family hosted me and provided me with good food and good conversation.

This book and my life at graduate school benefitted a great deal from conversations with my "dissertation support group" of Andy Morris, Amy Murrell, Josh Rothman, and Andy Trees, as well as the later version of the Monday dinner club with Taylor Fain and Robert Ingram. Other friends and colleagues who provided tremendous support include Ed and Amber Anania, Allison and Mik Genovese, Matt and Susie Johnson, Chris Mizelle, Christof Morrissey, Mike O'Brien, Tim Schroer, Scott Taylor, Bob and Delores Tingley, Jamie and Laurie Van Hook, and Lara Diefenderfer Wulff. At Miami University, where I have been fortunate to work for four years, I thank all my colleagues in the History Department and also at the Havighurst Center for making Miami such a wonderful place to work, but particularly Charlotte Goldy and Mary Cayton (the two chairs of the department during my time) and Karen Dawisha. Thanks are also due to Drew Cayton, my faculty mentor, who not only read the manuscript and offered excellent advice but also has provided a steady stream of encouragement. My colleagues Shel Anderson, Renee Baernstein, Wietse de Boer, Venelin Ganev, Mathew Gorden, Scott Kenworthy, Carla Pestana, Doug Rogers, Ben Sutcliffe, Bob Thurston, Zara Torlone, Allan Winkler, and Judith Zinsser have also provided particular help and useful suggestions.

My parents, Tom and Lucia Norris, have been a constant source of love and support over the years and deserve a special thank you, along with my brother, David, and sister, Sarah. My grandmother, Marie Laird, has also lent her support. Thanks are also due to my in-laws, Fred and Danna Cox, and the entire Cox clan for similar reasons. I also want to acknowledge Dr. Julian Fagerli and especially Dr. Stefan Gorsch and the HOPE Center at Martha Jefferson Hospital for their help in 2000–2001, when I wrote the first draft of this work.

Several people fueled my interest in history over the years—my great aunt, Ruth Laird (1911–2002), deserves much credit for inspiring my historical studies. Ron Webb, twice my teacher in grade school, first made history fun for me. Most importantly, though, J. Graham Provan (1931–2001), my advisor at Millikin University, inspired me to pursue a career in history. I wish he and Aunt Ruth had lived to see me realize my dream.

Finally, I must thank my wife, Melissa Cox Norris, and my son, Jack William Norris, who arrived as I finished the edits for this book. Jack did not help with the editing very much, but he made it more interesting and more fun. Melissa has enriched my life in more ways than I could possibly list. Melissa has been my best friend and biggest supporter for seventeen years. I dedicate this book to her, although it still does not seem enough.

A WAR OF IMAGES

THE *LUBOK* AND
RUSSIAN VISUAL NATIONHOOD

Introduction

- In May 1945, Joseph Stalin gave a reception for the Red Army commanders who had defeated the Nazi troops and captured Berlin. The Soviet leader asked that everyone raise their glasses to the Russian people, who he stated, "are the most outstanding nation of all the nations in the Soviet Union." By placing the Russians over other ethnic groups in the USSR, Stalin confirmed the predominance of a Russocentric national identity within a multiethnic empire. Stalin's victory toast gave voice to a process that had been under way for over a decade, a process in which Stalin and his advisors—responding to unsuccessful efforts to mobilize the Soviet population through appeals to international communism—began in the 1930s to build loyalty to the Soviet Union by promoting Russian national identity.[1]

Stalin had always doubted whether Russian peasants and workers could be motivated by purely socialist principles. In a Bolshevik Party congress held in 1919, after he had been appointed the commissar for nationalities, Stalin argued that the vast majority of Russians would not fight for abstract ideals in the ongoing civil war, but could be inspired to fight against clearly defined enemies.[2] Despite Stalin's doubts, most Bolsheviks believed that Russian peasants and workers could be educated in the utopian ideals of socialism and transformed into the "new men and women" demanded by the events of 1917. Less than two decades after the Russian Revolution, Stalin called a halt to this effort. In order to prepare the Soviet Union for war and to build loyalty to the socialist state, he decided to appeal to Russian nationhood. The creation of what one scholar has termed "national Bolshevism" marked an important turn away from the internationalism promoted by Lenin and other Bolsheviks and toward a particular ethnocentric view of national identity.[3]

In making this turn, Stalin tapped into a long-standing cultural tradition that up to now has been little studied—the visual nature of Russian nationhood before and after 1917. The Bolshevik "propaganda state" created after the October Revolution used posters, films, and other visual sources in an attempt to mobilize the population to support the socialist experiment.[4] The Bolsheviks made use of images modeled on the tsarist wartime *lubok,* a Russian print that first appeared in the seventeenth century and over time became the primary visual source in Imperial Russia. When Stalinist propagandists began to promote Russian nationhood in the 1930s and again when Nazi Germany attacked the Soviet Union in World War II, posters that compared the German invasion of 1941 to the Napoleonic invasion of 1812 sought to reassure Russians that the Germans would meet the same fate as the French. Stalin's attempt to build a sense of belonging to the Russian nation thus reappropriated myths, symbols, and icons from the tsarist past.

|||

In Russia, the image known as the *lubok* (plural *lubki*) occupied an important place in Russian visual culture and in the articulation of national identity. These popular prints can best be described as lively illustrations similar to posters or European broadsides with short texts, usually at the bottom of the picture.[5] The term itself, as well as its adjective *(lubochnyi),* derives from an old Russian word meaning "bast," which is the soft layer of wood taken from trees in the spring and then used to make baskets, shoes, and other containers. In early modern Russian culture, artists often used these pieces of bast in place of expensive parchment, and thus the crude woodcut images painted on them became known as *lubochnye kartinki* (or "bast pictures"). The technique used to make these prints was as simple as the finished product. The artist placed a watery tempera on a slight pencil design, and then painted an illustration using pigments diluted in egg emulsion or sticky vegetable substances. When the *lubok* artist painted these materials onto wood blocks and pressed them on cheap paper, the result was a combination of a watercolor and a hand painting that gave the finished image an improvised look.[6] Russians eventually came to refer to these cheap prints as *lubki,* and even as *narodnye kartinki,* or "popular pictures."[7]

From its inception, the *lubok* served a propagandistic function in Russian culture. Although the word "propaganda" carries exclusively negative connotations today, the term itself comes from the seventeenth century and initially had more neutral meanings. In 1622, Pope Gregory XV established the Congregation for the Propagation of the Faith (Congregatio de Propaganda Fide) in an effort to combat the ideas of the Reformation. From its first use, "propaganda" was used simply to describe the propagation of beliefs within a given society.[8] When they first appeared in the seventeenth century, *lubki* performed such a role—originally all of the images were cheap icons, manufactured for city dwellers who used them to understand their Orthodox faith. Leonid Ouspensky, who has written extensively about the icon, argues that in Russia, Orthodox theology primarily expressed itself through imagery: "the holy image . . . transmits not human ideas and conceptions of the truth, but truth itself."[9] Because of this stress on the visual nature of religious faith, most Russians kept an icon in their homes. The *lubok* business developed as a result of the demand for icons and their ability to propagate messages about the Orthodox faith.

Like most other aspects of Russian culture, the *lubok* was transformed by the reforms of Peter the Great (tsar, 1682–1725). Peter I oversaw a revolution in the visual arts, one that changed the nature of the *lubok*.[10] No longer confined to religious subjects, *lubki*—beginning in Peter's reign—illustrated government reforms, folktales, and historical events. Thus, Peter and his image makers used the prints to propagate a new set of beliefs for those who bought them. At the same time, opponents of Peter, particularly the Old Believers who had broken with the Orthodox church in the late seventeenth century, issued their own *lubki* that criticized Petrine policies. By the end of the Petrine era, the *lubok* had become "propaganda" in the sense most understood it before 1914, simply a means to promote particular ideas.[11]

Because of its functions, propaganda has always been connected to war. The changes in the *lubok* established under Peter inevitably paved the way for the prints to be used to illustrate Russia's wars. The genre of war *lubok* first appeared during the Seven Years' War (1756–1763). "The Russian Cossack Strikes the Prussian Dragoon" (Figure 1.1), from 1759, illustrates the cultural traditions that nineteenth-century Russian artists and publishers drew upon.[12] This *lubok* features a single Cossack on horseback dispatching two Germans, one firing a musket vainly at the Russian, the other succumbing to the Cossack's pike. Images such as this one, however, did not appear in great numbers—only twenty were produced during that conflict, a testament to the fact that these propagandistic prints remained an urban product with limited distribution.[13]

By the turn of the nineteenth century, however, this situation changed. Prior to 1812, Russian elites and artists had started to form a sense of national consciousness that included many components. Over the course of the eighteenth century, an antipathy toward foreigners (particularly the French and their manners, which many Russian elites embraced), the belief that authentic Russianness lay in the peasant village and the Russian soul, a renewed interest in national mythology and history, and the idea that Russia possessed its own national character developed among Russian artists and cultural figures.[14] It took an event like Napoleon's invasion, however, to crystallize this early national consciousness. The war against Napoleon and the emotions that it produced led to a proliferation of the *lubok*—over two hundred images appeared between 1812 and 1814. The growth of nascent national identity, the uses of images for propaganda, and the increased production of the *lubok* as a form of Russian popular culture were parallel developments that converged when war began in 1812.

This change occurred in part because as the content of the *lubok* became more secular over the course of the eighteenth century, the audience for these prints in 1812 became more "popular" in the broadest sense of the word.[15] By the early nineteenth century, peasants, city dwellers, and

1.1 "The Russian Cossack Strikes the Prussian Dragoon" An early example of the war *lubok* genre, this image from the Seven Years' War depicts a Cossack fighting with two Prussian dragoons. Although only twenty images appeared during this war, they helped to establish the Cossack as an important icon of nascent Russian national consciousness. Source: Vladimir Denisov, *Voina i lubok* (Petrograd, 1916)

members of the small middle classes all purchased *lubki,* while the artists were mostly townspeople, who depicted government regulations and listened "to the buzz of the marketplace" in coming up with themes.[16] Russians could buy these prints at the shops set up by publishers, at booths located in most large towns, at the various fairs held throughout the country, or from traveling peddlers. As *lubki* became more and more accessible to Russians of all classes, their importance as disseminators of information and their persuasive power continued to grow. The publishers and artists who captured the events of 1812 in their imagery tapped into the growing importance of the *lubok* as a disseminator of information.

The *lubok* artists of 1812 also used their knowledge of European caricature and Russian folk traditions to exhort their countrymen to defend the fatherland. These artists were part of a general movement throughout Europe in the eighteenth and nineteenth centuries that came to recognize the power of images in shaping national sentiments. During the seventeenth and early eighteenth centuries, monarchs such as Louis XIV, Frederick the Great of Prussia, and Peter the Great used images as a means of making their power visible. In doing so, these kings helped to initiate the use of culture and imagery to articulate ideas about the nation to its people.[17] In France, a "cult of the nation" developed before the revolution, fueled in part by popular imagery.[18] After 1789, popular images depicting the "new France" were everywhere, and contributed to the redefinition of French nationhood.[19] British popular prints also articulated a sense of

British identity throughout the 1700s and 1800s, largely one that set itself against Frenchness.[20] The age of nationalism, in other words, witnessed an explosion of popular images designed to provide symbols and themes to forge a national community.[21]

The visual aspects of European nationhood represented just one part of the development of national identities that dominated the early nineteenth century. While countless scholars have debated how nations, nationalism, and national identities have come to be so significant in the modern world, this book does not seek to answer such queries. Instead, my focus on the production and reception of Russian war images allows for a glimpse of the ways in which publishers, artists, and consumers attempted to answer their own questions about Russian nationhood.[22]

In the scholarly debate over Russian national identity, the dominant historiographical argument stresses that before 1917 Russia "was not a nation"[23] and had a weak or "inarticulate" sense of national identity,[24] that the tsarist regime's attempt to foster an imperial identity prevented a national one,[25] or simply that Russia lacked a viable national identity.[26] The events of 1917 may constitute the major proof for this school of thought, for Russia alone among the First World War combatants experienced massive upheavals that toppled the old regime. In this view the Bolshevik seizure of power can partly be explained by a weak sense of Russian nationhood. Many of the scholars who take this position argue that Russian national identity only emerged under Stalin or during the Second World War.[27]

A War of Images challenges this paradigm and instead seeks to find moments when Russians have attempted to articulate a sense of nationhood, beginning in the Napoleonic era. Nowhere has this process of negotiating identities been clearer than during wartime. Wars, William Rosenberg notes, "are always about unsettling boundaries and picturing enemies." Defining one's enemy, a crucial component of war, remains "more than a simple matter of who one is fighting against. It necessarily involves some formal definition as well of who one is, provided symbolically by uniforms, hymns, and banners, as well as, and more importantly, of who one is not."[28] In this sense, the war *lubok* serves as an ideal source for understanding the "enmification" of Russia's wars—that is, how Russians both created and understood their foes.[29] During the wars of the nineteenth and twentieth centuries, wartime culture also identified several concepts of Russianness that, while undergoing redefinition to fit into changing circumstances, remained remarkably stable over the course of a century. The wartime *lubok* represents one very important medium through which artists and publishers attempted to define Russian characteristics and contrast them with Russia's enemies.

Russian artists and publishers articulated personal beliefs about national identity in a genre designed to attract large numbers of consumers.[30] *Lubok* artists in 1812 drew on established traditions, emblems, and myths to illustrate what "Russianness" was in the Patriotic War, and their successors continued to reappropriate these themes in future wars as a means of articulating *Russian* national identity. The stress on "Russian" is necessary here, for the patriotic culture of Russia's nineteenth-century wars emphasized Russian national traits in a multiethnic empire.[31] Each successive war that Russia fought in the nineteenth and early twentieth centuries built on the commercial success of the images from 1812. By the time of the Great War in 1914, publishers printed hundreds of images in editions that reached into the hundreds of thousands.

The images produced from 1812 to 1917 represented an evolving defin-ition of Russian patriotic and national identity that drew on past concep-tions about Russia while placing these conceptions in a contemporary per-spective. In the process, the *lubok* publishers and their artists helped to establish new myths and symbols of Russian identity, reinforcing the no-tion that national consciousness is an evolving process.[32] The wartime *lubok* represents just one of the ways that Russians defined their own sense of identity during the "long" nineteenth century, and it is one that cap-tures how nations are built "bit by bit."[33]

The war *lubok* not only reflected attitudes of the time but also simulta-neously helped to shape them. Images have undeniable appeal both for people who see them when they are created and for scholars who study them later. However, people who view posters, art works, and other visual sources rarely write down their reactions—in many ways, the inability to capture the essence of an image in words is part of its power. In the case of the wartime *lubok,* however, many Russians did attempt to record their thoughts. This book captures the records of these eyewitnesses and uses them to discuss the "learned experience" of a Russian's "visual world."[34] Ultimately, as the cast of characters reveals, the Russian wartime *lubok* acted as a powerful means through which Russians could articulate and discuss a sense of Russian nationhood.

These "acts of eyewitnessing," to use a term developed by Peter Burke, provide a deeper understanding of how Russian nationhood was dissemi-nated and received. The *lubok* publishers and artists played the most im-portant role in articulating the patriotic expressions found in their images, but at the same time they had to deal with the pressures of censorship and market demand. Though the *lubok* proved difficult for the imperial gov-ernment to control, censorship during wartime did influence its themes. The perceptions voiced by the *lubok* audience proved equally important in the expression of the war *lubok's* patriotic themes. Still, the articulation of national identity found in the war *lubok* did not come simply from gov-ernment propaganda or an elite effort to mobilize popular support for the wars (although these interpretations are certainly valid). It sprang from a complicated mix of market demand, popular reception, government ac-ceptance, and publishers' attempts to define "Russianness."[35] In other words, the national and patriotic identities espoused in the war *lubki* represent both an elite attempt to inspire loyalty to symbols and myths of the Russian nation and a popular attempt to understand them.[36]

The Russian government, through censorship, ensured that the war *lubok* contained themes deemed appropriate. Publishers and artists, who derived these themes both from the pressures of censorship and from what had proved popular in the past, in turn made an important contribution to constructing a Russian national identity. Russians from all walks of life bought the prints, discussed them, and interpreted them in personal ways. The evidence available suggests that while we can never know every way in which a consumer understood these patriotic exhortations, we do know at a basic, more general level that most Russians who came into contact with *lubki* found them to be inspiring. At the same time, some Russians who encountered the wartime prints believed that they promoted false ideas about Russia and Russian national identity. The response to these images of war, as the chapters that follow indicate, prompted a war over the use of images in fostering nationhood.

The wartime *lubok* also illuminates the relationship between commerce, wartime propaganda, and ideas of Russianness. Russian ethnographers who recorded peasant life in the nineteenth century noted that peasants bought contemporary images of religious scenes, folktales, and wartime events. Most of these prints, by the turn of the century, came from the companies run by Ivan Sytin and P. A. Glushkov, prominent Moscow businessmen who specialized in the *lubok* trade.[37] The peasants in the Russian heartland purchased products from traveling salesmen known as *ofeni* that illustrated a shared sense of culture and belonging to a nation. Russians like Sytin, a former peasant who had started a publishing business in Moscow after working as a *lubok* peddler, produced goods such as the popular print for consumption throughout Russia. Ultimately, the images that decorated the walls of peasant huts represented a product created by Russians for other Russians to understand and interpret their own culture. Peasants, in other words, took part in the creation and consumption of Russian culture. They actively bought images and discussed their meanings. They kept these images for years afterward, and in doing so they retained both a historical memory and a means to visualize what it meant to be a Russian. Ethnographers throughout the Russian heartland in the last years of the nineteenth century recorded an overwhelming presence of *lubki*—from Smolensk to Saratov, from Orel to Orenburg—for the peasants in all these provinces loved to decorate their homes with pictures of wars and other events.[38]

These ethnographers witnessed a process that had started decades before and one that would continue for decades more, for after the events of 1917, the Bolsheviks employed *lubok* artists to help create a new visual culture that built on the propagandistic elements of the old. When Nazi troops invaded Russia in 1941, many of the original Soviet poster artists, some of whom had worked for tsarist publishers during the First World War, again turned to visual sources as a means to articulate Russian national identity. The images these artists created made explicit references to the war against Napoleon and its importance within Russian memory. Stalin's victory toast in part acknowledged the success of these historical connections—once again, war and the visual culture it produced provided the impetus for a refashioning of Russian nationhood.

2

IMAGES OF 1812

The Patriotic War in Russian Culture

> They [Russian peasants] all know Suvorov and Kutuzov from
> pictures, and they have a great interest in the war of 1812.
> —F. E. Kutekhov (1898)

• Napoleon's invasion of Russia in 1812 triggered an unprecedented outburst of popular patriotism within the Russian Empire. As a result of both the French presence and Mikhail Kutuzov's scorched-earth policy, thousands of Russians died, fled, or suffered in other ways.[1] Kutuzov himself told a French ambassador that after June 1812 the ordinary Russian equated the French with the Mongols, and could not help but treat the invaders as such.[2] As soon as the French left Moscow, the invasion itself, the battle of Borodino, Kutuzov's decision making, and the subsequent French retreat became the stuff of legend in Russian culture. In the modern era, only the Second World War, known as the Great Patriotic War in contrast to the Patriotic War (of 1812), as Russians called the conflict, has remained a more powerful source of national identity than the Napoleonic invasion.[3]

Two of the monumental and lasting creations of Russian culture, Tolstoy's *War and Peace* (1865–1869) and Tchaikovsky's *1812 Overture* (1882), attest to the significance of the Patriotic War in the nation's cultural history. The memory of the invasion and the subsequent victory over Napoleon remains strong in Russia. Monuments and other cultural reminders of the war, including the museum near Borodino, dot the Russian landscape today. During the winter of 1998–1999, to cite just one recent example, the Central Museum of the Great Patriotic War held an exhibit of images from the Napoleonic Wars, thus reinforcing the links between the two most "patriotic" conflicts in Russian history.[4]

The war with Napoleon came after the gradual deterioration in Franco-Russian relations following the Tilsit alliance of 1807. On 22 June 1812, Napoleon led an army of nearly 600,000 men across the Nieman River and into Russia. Containing troops from allied and occupied countries throughout Europe, the French army outnumbered the Russian three to one. The two sides first clashed at Smolensk in August, where Russians under the command of Barclay de Tolly and Bagration suffered heavy losses, abandoning the ancient city to the French. Although Napoleon's army also sustained significant casualties, the Russians retreated, and command of the army fell to the aging Mikhail Kutuzov, a disciple of the legendary

Russian commander Aleksandr Suvorov. Kutuzov pursued a policy of gradual withdrawal, burning crops and villages along the way to deny supplies
to the invading force. The French lost a large number of troops from disease and intestinal illnesses as they advanced toward Moscow in the late
summer of 1812.

The next encounter between the two sides has entered into the realm of
legend in Russian memory. Seventy-five miles west of the former Russian capital lay the village of Borodino, where just over 130,000 French troops fought
against a slightly smaller Russian force on 26 August. The battle claimed as
many as 100,000 men, and no one emerged victorious, prompting Kutuzov
to retreat into the Russian heartland. Shortly after Borodino, Kutuzov decided
to abandon Moscow to the French and make further stands, if necessary,
deeper in Russia. Napoleon entered Moscow a week after the battle, but soon
discovered that the city was largely abandoned and his victory a Pyrrhic one.
Faced with the possibility of these endless Russian retreats and the prospect
of spending a Russian winter without supplies in Moscow (particularly after
the city was razed by a fire, allegedly started by Fedor Rostopchin, the governor), Napoleon left Moscow after thirty-five days.

Forced to withdraw along the same path by which they had come—
thanks to the efforts of Russian partisans and Kutuzov's troops—the
French army stumbled along the war-scarred route back to Smolensk. The
combination of guerillas, cold weather, hunger, sickness, and Kutuzov's
decision to avoid major battles while gradually chipping away at the
French in small skirmishes took its toll on Napoleon's grand army. By the
time the French left Russian territory in December 1812, around 20,000
French soldiers crossed the Berezina River.[5] The next two years witnessed
the gradual ramifications of Napoleon's Russian campaign, culminating
from the Russian perspective on 31 March 1814, when Tsar Alexander I
marched in triumph at the head of Russian troops in Paris.

The impact of 1812 on Russia proved enormous.[6] Despite the significance of the war against Napoleon and the subsequent mythologizing of
the conflict in Russia, historians have paid scant attention to the popular
culture produced during Napoleon's Russian campaign.[7] Russian schoolchildren continue to visit the Borodino panorama in Moscow and the museum dedicated to the battle in the former village itself, learning how the
war and Napoleon's invasion triggered an outpouring of patriotic spirit in
Russia. The "myth of 1812" taught that Russians of all classes united
against the French enemy and by their determination ultimately saved the
Russian homeland.[8] Yet what forms did this patriotism take and how did
it take hold? These are questions left largely unexplored by scholars, and
ones for which this chapter offers some answers.

The chapter explores the cultural legacy of the Patriotic War by examining the *lubki* produced during the conflict (1812–1815). The *lubok* enjoyed
a "boom" during this period and established itself as an important source
of national identity in Imperial Russia. Found in markets, bazaars, and

shops, and sold by peddlers throughout Russia, the images from the Patriotic War represented one of the first attempts to redefine Russian national identity during the Napoleonic era. From 1812 to 1814, the *lubok* artists responded to the unfolding events as they understood them, and endeavored to depict both the meanings of the war and what defined "Russianness" in their images. Artists such as Ivan Terebenev, primarily inspired by a sense of personal patriotism, focused their caricatures on the French enemy, particularly Napoleon, who was contrasted with what can be termed a Russian "spirit" and the emblems of Russian identity: the tsar, church, peasant, and Cossack. Initially stressing the heroism of Russians and lampooning Napoleon, the *lubok* artists began in 1813–1814 to focus more on the roles of the tsar and the Orthodox church in bringing about the victory over the French. The depiction of Russian national identity and the patriotic culture that would appear in later Russian wars grew out of the culture of 1812, and the themes of the *lubki* themselves became permanent features in Russian culture.[9]

The images from this war also helped to establish a dominant myth in Russian culture that has lasted until the present day: that the war against Napoleon was a "people's victory" that "proved" Russian cultural superiority over a devious foe. Russians view the war of 1812 as a watershed in their own history, and the *lubki* from the war attest to the beginnings of the myth surrounding the conflict.[10] While the artists who produced images during the early stages of the war certainly could not be sure of victory over the French, the *lubki* composed in 1812 and 1813 stressed the heroism of Russian soldiers, peasants, and Cossacks in the fight against Napoleon. By the middle of 1813 and throughout 1814, when Napoleon's army had been driven from Russia and as Russian troops pursued them across Europe, war images began to stress the role of the tsar, Alexander I, as the architect of the "people's victory" over the French. The images from the period reveal the beginnings of the myth of this victory as a significant event both in the history of the Russian Empire and in the history of its people, and show how the Russian tsar, church, and peasant (in a sense, autocracy, Orthodoxy, and *narodnost'*) served as sources for a revitalized national identity after 1812.[11]

The two main themes present in the war *lubok* were images of Napoleon and the French enemy and illustrations of "Russianness." Although the artists who produced these images shifted their focus from lampooning Napoleon to depicting the Russian tsar as the supreme architect of victory, all of the images from the years 1812–1814 contrasted the French enemy against what made Russia "Russia."

Defining the Enemy: Napoleon and the French

The war against the French in 1812 came to be viewed by Russians largely as a battle against the French emperor, Napoleon. The popular pictures devoted to the war were dominated by Napoleon's image. They satirized Napoleon and depicted French culture in general as degenerate. In defining both Napoleon and the French in such a manner, the images of war served as a means by which Russians could vent their frustrations with the costs of the invasion. Caricatures of Napoleon also served as an "other" against which Russians could assert their own cultural strengths. Historians have described how wars against a clearly defined enemy function as a source for redefining national identity,[12] and in this respect the war of 1812 proved to be a watershed in the history of Russian nationhood.

Three artists in particular produced the largest number of images during the war: Ivan Terebenev, Aleksei Venetsianov, and Ivan Ivanov. The most famous at the time was Terebenev, who produced forty-eight caricatures of the Patriotic War between 1812 and 1814.[13] Terebenev learned sculpture at the Russian Academy of Fine Arts in St. Petersburg from 1785 to 1800 and even designed part of the decorations for the Admiralty. Napoleon's invasion, however, prompted Terebenev to produce caricatures in which he drew on the *lubok* tradition. In producing these images, he followed events through word of mouth and the newspapers, and then designed caricatures to illustrate some of the heroic feats of Russians in defending their homeland.[14] Terebenev paid particular attention to the image itself and the figures within it, which could be easily understood by anyone. For him, the text only served as a means of deepening the meaning of the print for a literate reader.[15] The earliest reference to Terebenev's images appearing in the two Russian capitals was in February 1813, when a merchant in St. Petersburg advertised a group of these images for one and a half rubles.[16] From then until his untimely death on 16 January 1815, Terebenev produced *lubok* images that could be found in the traditional markets for popular pictures.[17] Like his well-known counterparts, Terebenev emphasized the exploits of the Russian peasant and Cossack and often took his themes from contemporary Russian journals such as *Son of the Fatherland* (founded in response to the invasion and a mouthpiece for patriotic exhortations to defend Russia).

Next to Terebenev, Aleksei Venetsianov stood out as the second most important producer of popular pictures during the Patriotic War. Born the same year as Terebenev, Venetsianov had already attempted to establish the political caricature in Russian culture before Napoleon's invasion. He founded the *Journal of Caricature,* but it soon ran into trouble with imperial censors, who forbade its printing on 18 January 1808.[18] Venetsianov's frustration, however, found an outlet in 1812 when he turned to the *lubok* tradition and produced a number of images designed to appeal to a wide audience.[19] He too followed the unfolding events and made use of actual episodes to illustrate his images, which attempted to portray the patriotic response to the French invasion. Venetsianov's popular prints appeared at the same time as Terebenev's, and often drew on the same legends and events.[20] His images, along with Terebenev's, sold well and helped to launch Venetsianov's later career as an artist, when he became famous for his contributions to the realist tendency in Russian art and for the schools he established to teach serf artists.[21]

Born in 1779 in Moscow, Ivan Ivanov studied art from a young age after entering the Academy of Fine Arts in St. Petersburg. After his first exhibition in 1806, Ivanov began work for the Imperial Glass factory, where he designed images for china and glassware. In 1813, he was appointed librarian at the Imperial Public Library, and from this position produced a number of patriotic images during the war.[22] Influenced by the work of Terebenev in particular, Ivanov turned to the war *lubok* as an outlet for his artistic talents and newfound patriotism, and by the final victory over the French he had produced over twenty prints. While not as widely known now as Terebenev or Venetsianov, Ivanov was at the time just as popular, and his work helped to define the patriotic culture of the era.

Numerous other *lubki* appeared alongside the images of these three artists, images about which there is less information, but ones that further reflected the patriotic explosion resulting from Napoleon's invasion. In total, over two hundred images appeared between 1812 and 1814, by far the greatest total of *lubki* ever devoted to a single event and in such a short space of time (by comparison, about twenty images appeared during the Seven Years' War devoted to its battles). The artists focused initially on Napoleon, whom they regarded as "mad" to have invaded Russia. In doing this, they helped to capture the mood of the time.[23] The popular pictures of Terebenev, Venetsianov, Ivanov, and others thus represent the first visual attempts to define "Russianness" in the wake of Napoleon's invasion.[24]

Terebenev's *lubok* "Treating Napoleon in Russia" depicts three Russian soldiers who have stuffed the French leader into a barrel marked "*kaluzhskoe testo,*" or "Kaluga Dough," after the route Napoleon took to leave Russia.[25] Dressed in the uniform of the regular Russian army, a soldier to the right of Napoleon is force-feeding him a large loaf of gingerbread marked "Viazma," while a Russian to the left pours over him a can of liquid labeled "boiled in the Moscow Fire." A third Russian soldier stands over the French leader, brewing tea to pour over him. Around Napoleon's head, the three have draped *bubliki,* the thick, ring-shaped bread rolls so popular in Russia. The message of the *lubok* is clear: Napoleon may have invaded Russia, but here he has received a "proper" Russian welcome, complete with the snacks one would normally offer such a preeminent guest, thus transforming food as nourishment into food as punishment.[26]

The unidentified *lubok* "Smashing of Napoleon's Power" portrays Napoleon vainly fending off a double-headed eagle, while French troops cower in fear.[27] Emblazoned on the eagle's chest is the letter *A*, the imperial letter for tsar Alexander I.[28] More crudely made than the Terebenev prints, this image nevertheless identifies one of the sources for the victory over Napoleon. In this example, the symbolic head of Russia, the tsar embodied in the figure of a double-headed eagle, brings about Napoleon's demise.

2.1 **"Russians Teaching Napoleon to Dance"** Ivan Terebenev's image from the Patriotic War of 1812 focuses upon the peasant partisans who defended Russia. Two Russians have captured Napoleon and force him to perform a Russian dance—the caption reads: "Don't leave us to tune your melody: Dance, infidel, to our pipe!" Source: A. Kaganovich, *I. I. Terebenev* (Moscow, 1956).

"Russians Teaching Napoleon to Dance" by Terebenev also turns to the theme of peasant partisans and Napoleon's defeat. This image (Figure 2.1) depicts two Russian peasants forcing Napoleon to dance for them or face a whipping.[29] One bearded peasant dressed in traditional clothing holds a whip in his right hand. Beside him sits a second Russian who plays a lute to provide the tune. Napoleon in this image was made to do a *Russian* dance by his captors, a response to Napoleon's attempts to force Russia to accept his ideas, a fact captured in Terebenev's short text, which states, "Don't leave us to tune your melody: Dance, infidel, to our pipe!"[30]

Although satirical in nature, the *lubki* reminded Russians of the devastation Napoleon wrought in their country while inspiring them to defeat the French invaders. Napoleon gets what he deserved and is portrayed as a small, insignificant figure next to Russian soldiers and peasants. Above all, however, these examples reveal the extent to which Napoleon served as an indirect source of Russian patriotism—*lubok* artists from this period also depicted Napoleon as a henchman of the devil,[31] and others poked fun at Napoleon's speeches and his reentry into Paris.[32]

Russian artists also illustrated Napoleon's inability to cope with the Russian winter. One such image, "Napoleon's Winter Quarters" (Figure 2.2), has the French general and his army covered in a bed of snow.[33]

2.2 "Napoleon's Winter Quarters" This image pokes fun at Napoleon's inability to cope with the Russian winter. The French emperor and his army, buried under the snow, question whether they should retreat. A Russian landowner named Pokorskii taunted his French captive in 1813 with this image. Source: *1812 god v karikature* (St. Petersburg, 1912).

Napoleon, his small stature emphasized, discusses the situation with two of his marshals. One complains that they will die from the cold, and the second asks whether Napoleon should order the troops to Paris.[34] Behind this comical scene, the entire French army (or what was left of it by winter) lies buried under the snow, the top of their helmets jutting out from under large drifts. In this and other images that featured Russia's wintry landscape, Russian artists helped to establish the Russian land as a source of national identity, much like other European artists (particularly English landscape artists) "nationalized nature" at the same time.[35]

As these examples demonstrate, Napoleon acted as the lightning rod for Russian anger at the French invasion, a fact illustrated by the sheer number of *lubki* depicting the emperor—he appeared in nearly half of the wartime images.[36] Yet the French emperor did not shoulder all of the ridicule in the popular pictures from 1812. The French troops and their culture also served as a target and became the foreign "other" against whom Russians defined themselves.

Ivanov's *lubok* "Napoleon Forms a New Army from Various Freaks and Cripples" suggests that the French army and its leader are weak opponents.[37] Among the "freaks" depicted in the *lubok*, which features the French leader placing weakened troops on horseback amidst a host of other unfit soldiers, are two large figures labeled "Polish Cossacks."[38] The subject resembles that of another Terebenev caricature, "The Retreat of the French Cavalry Who Ate Their Horses in Russia,"[39] which illustrates a group of ill-fed French troops shuffling behind their leader, who pretends to be on horseback. Bringing up the rear of this motley gang is a Mameluke dressed in a woman's coat to keep warm and carrying a horse's leg to eat at home.[40] Forced to eat their horses and shamefully flee Russia, this image suggests that the experience of war has emasculated Napoleon and his troops.[41]

Lubok artists also contrasted the French troops, often starving and weak, with Russian women defending their homeland. Venetsianov's "Hungry French Rats, Under the Command of the Old Woman Vasilisa" depicts three French "marauders" captured by Russian peasant women under the guidance of a woman on horseback.[42] The three French troops attempted to forage for food in a Russian village and were captured by Vasilisa, who now has them lassoed. One of the marauders kneels before his new commander and is distinguished by his *konfederatka* (the Polish national headgear of the time, known for its rectangular shape and lack of peak), while the other two French soldiers stand despondently, seemingly emaciated. To the right of Vasilisa are a group of three peasant girls and one boy, all waving pitchforks at the French would-be thieves. At the bottom of the image a rooster bites at the top of a staff adorned with the golden eagle, Napoleon's symbol. The image implies that Russia has transformed the French troops, once seen as virtually invincible, into a pitiful, begging lot that even Russia's women could defeat.[43]

This visual illustration had a factual basis. During the French occupation of Smolensk, an old peasant woman named Vasilisa decided to stand up to the invaders occupying her homeland. She came across two drunken French soldiers in the street one day. Inviting them into her *izba*, Vasilisa got the two drunk. With the Frenchmen thoroughly inebriated, she then burned her hut to the ground.[44]

The 1813 *lubok* "French Crow's Soup" suggests more trauma faced by French soldiers after their unsuccessful attempts to conquer the Russians.[45] This *lubok* shows three disheveled, emaciated French soldiers gnawing on a "meal" of dead crows (the adjective "black" *[voronii]*, also suggests the word for carrion-crows *[voron'e]*), while a fourth soldier lies sprawled across the background. The three lament in the text that accompanies the picture:

> To our misfortune under our great Napoleon!
> He fed us in the campaign from broth made of bones!
> In Moscow he feasted and smacked his teeth at us!
> Right here! Now we gulp down on black soup![46]

Forced to "eat crow," the French troops, who have been deceived by their leader, find themselves in desperate straits as a result of their invasion. These tales of French soldiers eating crow spread widely by 1813—

Ivan Krylov, the famous Russian fabulist who lived through the invasion, included in his fable "Crow and Fowl" accounts of French soldiers in Moscow using crow to make soup.[47]

While *lubki* such as "French Crow's Soup" satirized and ridiculed the French troops and their leader, other images ridiculed the French people in general, including those living in Russia. The print "French Teachers and Artists Leave Moscow," also by an unknown artist, depicts six French residents of Moscow leaving the city in the wake of the destruction their former countrymen have wrought.[48] From left to right in the image, a cook, coachman, wine-merchant, musician, and a fashionably dressed woman take leave of their city, imploring, "Forgive us, Moscow!"[49] Other *lubki* ridiculed the French for following Napoleon, for their artistic and commercial culture, and for their perceived attempts to dominate Europe.[50]

Much like the image of Vasilisa above, these *lubki* illustrate actual events of the time. Foreign residents were deported throughout Russia as Napoleon's army approached Moscow, and again after it left. In Moscow, the city administration expelled thirty-nine foreigners (Germans, Austrians, Swiss, and Prussians, as well as French), including Armand Domergue, the stage manager of the Imperial Theater. Many of these deportees had lived in Russia for a long time, while three of the French held Russian citizenship. Similar events transpired in Kaluga, Kozel'sk, and Borovsk.[51]

The *lubki* of 1812 show how Napoleon and his French troops ignited a nationalistic explosion in Russia when they invaded in 1812. The images made soon after the French had given up Moscow (and in some cases before they had even arrived) placed the French emperor at the center of the conflict. Napoleon and his soldiers, as well as all things French, met with derision and ridicule, and served as rallying points for most Russians.[52] The experience of the invasion and subsequent Russian winter rendered Napoleon and his troops powerless, and the *lubki* illustrated this view by depicting the French leader and soldiers as impotent when confronted by peasant men and women, and Cossacks. The popular pictures made during the period 1812–1813 ensured that Russians who bought them would remember the destruction Napoleon had brought to Russia, and reassured viewers that the French had paid a high price for what they had done.

Defining "Russianness"

If Napoleon proved to be the dominant symbol of the images from the Patriotic War, he also served as a catalyst for defining what made Russia truly "Russian." In this respect, Napoleon's invasion triggered an outburst of popular images that helped to illustrate Russian cultural, military, and social superiority, which contrasted with the inferior French. The *lubki* of the time produced concrete expressions of what "Russianness" consisted of, and established the contours of imperial wartime culture for the rest of the century. Images from the Patriotic War depicted the strength of both the Russian peasant and the Cossack, who became enduring symbols of Russian distinctiveness.[53] The images of 1812 defined Russian identity in terms of the institutions and persons that helped to win the war against Napoleon; namely, the tsar, the Russian army, and the Russian "spirit." The French emperor's invasion of Russia triggered this response, however, and thus Napoleon deserves credit, however unintentional, for helping to bring Russianness to Russia.

Artists such as Terebenev and Ivanov included the Cossack and Russian peasant as iconic figures of Russian national identity in their patriotic prints. An untitled image from 1812 depicts two Cossacks disposing of four French soldiers, two of whom lie dead along with their horses.[54] The first Cossack promises to destroy the French invader with his sword, while his victim begs to be pardoned even as he dies. The second Frenchman, who is about to be driven through by a pike, also dies with the words "pardon, pardon" on his lips, while his assailant informs him that now "you know the Cossack."

The Terebenev caricature "The Russian Hercules Drives Off the French" (Figure 2.3), depicts a gigantic Russian peasant wrestling with five puny French troops who cower in fear of this Greek god.[55] A French general, possibly Napoleon himself, crouches behind a bush to the left of the gargantuan peasant, also trembling before the strength of the Russian. Terebenev's image stresses the willingness of the Russian peasant soldier and partisan to fight any number of French troops. In this example, the artist symbolizes the strength of the Russian peasant over the French invaders by casting the partisans as a Hercules figure.[56] The text notes that the Russian Hercules "crushed [the French] like a man *[davil kak muzh]*,"[57] and the size of the Russian peasant evokes the idea of Russia's own vast size as a source of its strength.[58] Because of the popularity of this image and another image with the same name by Venetsianov, the Russian public began to refer to the partisans as the "Russian Hercules."[59]

This glorification of Russian heroism also found expression in an unidentified *lubok* from 1813, divided into two parts, of the "warrior" Ivan and the peasant Dolbil.[60] The top section of the image shows a Russian soldier, identified as Ivan, attacking a Frenchman armed with a rifle. Nearly decapitating the enemy with a pike, the "warrior Ivan," according to the text of the *lubok*, "bashed the infidel *[basurman]*."[61] The bottom portion of the image illustrates a Russian "peasant militia-man" about to club with the butt of his rifle a French soldier who is begging for mercy. Again identified as an "infidel," the Frenchman is about to be "finished off" by the Russian peasant.[62] The image also emphasized the "people's victory" that had occurred by the end of the period 1812–1813. The combination of Cossacks, regular peasant soldiers, and partisans had helped to defeat the "infidels" who had invaded the Russian homeland.

Finally, the *lubki* from 1812 to 1815 also gave examples of what one might call a "Russian spirit" that came to define a unique quality of Russian identity, and was a trait that continued to be articulated in future war

2.3 "The Russian Hercules Drives Off the French" Terebenev casts the Russian peasant as a larger-than-life symbol of Russianness in this image, which depicts one Russian partisan dispatching many French soldiers. Because of the popularity of this image and others like it, the Russian public began to refer to the partisans as the "Russian Hercules." Source: *1812 god v karikaturie*

images. Ivanov's "Spirit of the Fearless Russians" illustrates this theme best.[63] This image shows a solitary, bearded Russian peasant standing with his hand over his heart as a French firing squad, commanded by Napoleon himself, takes aim. To the right of the image a larger group of Russians awaits the same fate. The image proves even more striking in its setting, for these events transpire in Cathedral Square inside the Moscow Kremlin. The text states that the scene depicts "the exemplary firmness of spirit in twenty Russian peasants, whom Napoleon inhumanly [*bezchelovechno*] sentenced to be shot for their love of faith, tsar, and the fatherland [*liubov' k vere, gosudariu i otechestvu*]."[64] The peasant about to be shot cries out, "Remember me, Lord! Forgive me, good people!" as he faces his executioners.

This image had a factual basis. The journal *Syn otechestva* (Son of the Fatherland) published an account in 1812 that described actions taken by Napoleon in response to numerous guerrilla activities of Russian peasants around Moscow. French troops who marauded through the towns near Moscow for food and supplies met with resistance from the Russians, prompting Napoleon to order a large number of peasant men to be rounded up and executed in Moscow as a warning against future disturbances.[65]

2.4 "The Russian Scaevola" Ivan Ivanov's 1813 *lubok* is one of dozens from the war that celebrated a "Russian spirit." Ivanov took his subject from a legend circulating throughout the years 1812–1813 about a Russian peasant who had been captured and branded with the letter *N* (for Napoleon) on his arm. Rather than accept this outrage, the peasant took an axe and chopped off his arm. The caption praises the "glory of the Russian *[Rossian]* in 1812." The tale also captivated Russian sculptors, who cast statues of the "Russian Scaevola." Source: *Ivan Ivanovich Terebenev.*

Other *lubki* offered further examples of the heroism of Russians in equally dramatic forms. Many of the *lubok* artists, drawing from their education in the academy and the emphasis on classical patriotism, cast the events of 1812 and the actions of ordinary Russians in the form of Roman history.[66] "The Russian Scaevola" (Figure 2.4) recounts the legend of a Russian peasant captured by the French and branded with the letter *N* (for Napoleon) on his forearm. Based on the legend of Mucius Scaevola, a Roman famous for his courage and patriotism,[67] the *lubok* depicts the interior of a peasant hut, where this striking Russian peasant, clad entirely in white, is in the process of cleaving his branded arm in half with a small axe.[68] Five French soldiers shy away from the peasant, intimidated by his superior strength and determination. The text states in a matter-of-fact fashion that Scaevola would rather lose an arm "in order not to serve Napoleon, the enemy of the Fatherland," while praising the "glory of the Russian *[Rossian]* in 1812 during the French invasion of Russia."[69]

Ivanov's 1813 *lubok* "The Russian Curtius" depicts a solitary Russian soldier fending off six Frenchmen, one of whom is poised behind the Russian soldier about to deliver a deathblow to the defender.[70] In the background of the *lubok* one can make out the Kremlin's cathedrals, easily identified by their golden onion domes. This print, like "The Russian Scaevola" discussed below, used a legend from Roman mythology to illustrate an episode from 1812. A Moscow militiaman, as the text explains, saw a Polish colonel, whom he thought was Napoleon. The militiaman attempted to assassinate the colonel but was himself killed. The *lubok* concludes that this "warrior *[ratnik]* of the Moscow militia is sacrificing his life for the purpose of saving the fatherland *[otechestvo]* from the malicious enemy, Napoleon."[71] Although faced with such odds, this image cries out, the Russian soldier fought until the very end to defend his homeland, symbolized here by the Moscow Kremlin. His actions clearly inspire fear within the Napoleon look-alike and his troops, cowering to the right side of the action.

Artists depicted Russianness also in terms of the clever actions performed by Russians against the French invaders. The image "Heroic Firmness of the Eighty-Year-Old *Starets*" shows an elderly Russian peasant outside of his *izba* standing up to four French soldiers.[72] The *starets,* the text of the *lubok* explains, "is pretending to be a deaf man to save his comrades" from the clutches of the French bandits. The old peasant tells a Frenchman leaning over to him to "say what you like, old chap, I can't hear well in this ear, please talk louder," while the rest of the villagers escape as a result of his cleverness.[73]

The native intelligence and wit exhibited by the Russian peasant were also contained in images of Russian peasant women. Many *lubki* artists stressed the heroism exhibited by Russian peasant women in terms of their fighting prowess. The popular print "Hungry French Rats, Under the Command of the Old Woman Vasilisa," discussed above, inspired a second image from an unnamed artist, published on 20 January 1813. "The Russian Woman—the Heroic Girl, Daughter of the Old Woman Vasilisa" shows a young peasant girl stabbing a prone French soldier through with a pitchfork.[74] The young peasant girl, identified as the daughter of Vasilisa, the "commander" of the French troops in the previous image, tells the Frenchman not to "fly away" as she runs him through.[75]

These depictions of Russian peasant women reveal that in the iconography of the years 1812–1813, the heroic deeds of the Russian people—both in the cleverness exhibited by Russian peasants and in their fighting prowess—were not defined exclusively by masculine characteristics. Russian peasant women also showed their native intelligence in fooling the French invaders, and their military strength in killing the enemy. The *voennye lubki* from the Patriotic War defined the "people's victory" over the French as one that included all Russians, women as well as men. While the association of bravery and heroism with the Russian peasant and Cossack continued in the images of future wars, the depiction of Russian peasant women (and Russian women in general) changed somewhat.[76] While a scant number of *lubki* continued to stress the cleverness of Russian peasant women, and even their military prowess, after 1812 the peasant woman usually appeared as a plump *baba,* and more and more pictures began to depict Russian women as either the helpless victims of the enemy (first the Turks, then the Japanese, finally the Germans) or as nurses aiding their heroic menfolk.

While the vast majority of war *lubki* included representations of heroism, intelligence, and military strength, a few images associated Russian patriotism with certain figures and institutions that symbolized Russian culture. Foremost among these were the tsar and the Orthodox church. Religion, and particularly the dominant role of the Orthodox church in Russian daily life, has long been associated with Russian national identity, especially its popular variant. The images of 1812 made subtle references to this religious identity and associated it with the emerging definitions of Russianness that characterized the iconography of the Patriotic War. *Lubki* such as "The Spirit of the Fearless Russians" described how Russian peasants, captured and then executed by Napoleon, died because of "love for their faith, tsar and fatherland," thus linking these three concepts as components of national identity. Moreover, the peasant at the center of this popular picture dies asking, "Remember us, Lord," words meant to imply that the heroism and spirit of this brave Russian defender come from his faith.[77]

Other images offered more subtle reminders of the importance of Orthodoxy in defining Russian national identity and patriotism. The war *lubok* made frequent reference to the French as "infidels" *(basurmany)* who had to be expelled from Russia. Above all, however, Orthodoxy and its association with patriotism in the 1812 images could be seen in the background of the many war *lubki* that featured Russian Orthodox churches.[78] This visual association of Russianness with the Orthodox church not only reinforced the descriptions of Russians willing to die for their faith, but also made it possible for all Orthodox Russians to identify with the patriotism illustrated in the *lubki* of 1812. Virtually every Russian town and village had an Orthodox church or was near one, and Russians throughout the empire could define themselves and what made them different from the French by focusing on their faith. Future images of war continued to make this association while also stressing even more explicitly the role of the Orthodox faith in defining patriotism, particularly during the Crimean and Russo-Turkish Wars, which *lubok* artists largely depicted as holy wars.[79]

While the victory over the French and the subsequent celebration of the forces that made this triumph possible continued to be the dominant message of the images of 1812, *lubki* from 1813 and 1814 increasingly stressed the role of the tsar, Alexander I, in bringing about "divine victory." Although in 1812 the tsar made no appearance in war-related caricatures, representations of him in 1813 were accompanied by the mythologizing of Kutuzov in Russian culture. The general, who had commanded Russian forces at Borodino, died in April 1813. Terebenev and other artists immediately began to immortalize Kutuzov in their images of 1813 and 1814, and then turned to glorifying the tsar.[80] One of Terebenev's images from this period, "General-Field Marshal Prince Golenishchev-Kutuzov in Smolensk Accepting Command of the Russian Troops in August 1812," was widely copied in other prints. Terebenev based his portrayal of Kutuzov on a legend that circulated throughout Russia at the time. The legend claimed that when Kutuzov first reviewed his troops after receiving command of the army, an eagle soared above him, symbolizing the great future in store for him.[81] This omen became a standard element in other *lubki* depicting Kutuzov and marked a shift away from caricatures of Napoleon and illustrations of Russian bravery toward an identification of the heroic leaders of the war.[82]

When Leo Tolstoy wrote his characterization of Kutuzov for *War and Peace*, he had this Terebenev *lubok* in mind. Tolstoy published "Some Words about 'War and Peace'" in 1868 and intended the piece to be a companion for the novel and its historical claims. Tolstoy wrestled with the difficulties of an artist describing actual events and how to capture a person such as Kutuzov. An artist, unlike an historian, should try to portray an historical person in his entirety, not just as someone engaging in significant poses. To illustrate this difference, Tolstoy made reference to the *lubki* of 1812: "Kutuzov did not always hold a telescope, point at the enemy, and ride a white horse."[83] The author believed that historians too often fell victim to the portrayal of historical personages as the larger-than-life heroes that artists such as Terebenev captured in their prints from 1813 and 1814.

After 1813 and the Kutuzov images, *lubok* artists placed Alexander I at the center of Russian heroism. "The Battle Near Paris" depicts a scene with close hand-to-hand fighting between the French and Russians, who are led by Alexander I.[84] Describing the way the Russian tsar "perfectly smashed" the French, this 1814 *lubok* by an unidentified artist illustrates the tsar as the force behind victory over Napoleon. Other images reinforce the message. "Napoleon's Defeat near Paris by the Russian Emperor Alexander I" (Figure 2.5) also describes the tsar's final triumph over his French counterpart,[85] while the Terebenev *lubok* "The Liberators of Europe" depicts Alexander parading through the streets of France with thousands of Europeans cheering their liberator. Alexander I's entry into Paris also formed the subject of several other *lubki*, among them "The Ceremonial Entry into Paris of the Sovereign Emperor Alexander I," which depicts a majestic Alexander on horseback parading through the streets of the French capital as a crowd cheers. The text of the *lubok* stresses the divine nature of the tsar and his triumph, stating "the hands of all the people clap" for Alexander, while "glad voices praise the tsar," who "pacified" Europe. Describing the Russian emperor as "all-powerful," "Godlike," and a "divine being" [Bozhestvo], this *lubok* proclaims not only that Alexander "is worthy of his throne," but also "the highest of all thrones."[86] A number of other *lubki* extolled the virtues of the tsar, who by 1813 was being depicted as the principal architect of the victory over Napoleon.[87]

2.5 "Napoleon's Defeat near Paris by the Russian Emperor Alexander I" By late 1813 and well into 1814, as the Russian armies slowly approached Paris, *lubok* artists began to celebrate the role of Alexander I in the war, casting him as the "divine inspiration" behind the victory. In this print, Alexander I (in the foreground) orchestrates the victory as Paris awaits him in the background. Reprinted by permission of the State Historical Museum, Moscow [GIM]

Lubok artists also began to link Alexander's victory with his faith, reinforcing the connection between "faith and tsar" in Russian national identity.[88] The *lubok* "Public Prayer in Paris in 1814" depicts the tsar being blessed by Orthodox priests, a scene clearly meant to illustrate the "superiority" of the Russian church and leader over that of the French enemy.[89] A similarly titled *lubok*, "Public Prayer in Paris on the Day of Our Lord, Sunday, 10 April 1814," shows a massive Russian army led by Alexander I being blessed on a Parisian square, while another image depicts Alexander leading his two allies, Frederick Wilhelm of Prussia and Franz I of Austria, in a prayer after defeating the French at Leipzig in 1813.[90]

As Richard Wortman has demonstrated, the apotheosis of Alexander I as a popularly perceived divine figure occurred around the years 1813–1814, when the tsar's image became associated with the "divine victory" over Napoleon.[91] The war *lubki* from this time reinforce Wortman's argument, as Alexander I was lauded for his "all-powerful wisdom and abundant strength, like a God."[92] While the Patriotic War continued to be celebrated as a "people's victory," a theme that the *lubki* of the period 1812–1813 made clear, later images began to stress the role of the tsar as the architect of this triumph. The *lubok* "Alexander I Leads Russian Armies into Paris on 19 March 1814" illustrates the ways in which the tsar came to be praised in the popular literature of the time.[93] Accompanying this image of Alexander triumphantly leading his army into the French capital as crowds bow before him are the words:

> Extol Him as a deity;
> He is a Tsar worthy of altars,
> His throne is above all others,
> And he is asked for laws,
> By all peoples and a throng of tsars.[94]

Wortman's assertion that Alexander replaced the "people's victory" as the primary visual message of Russian victory after 1813 does not hold entirely true, however, for the *lubki* celebrating the heroism of the Cossack and Russian peasant continued to be distributed throughout Russia. Although the Russian patriotism depicted in the war *lubok* showed a "divine" emperor whom viewers could contrast with the "insidious" Napoleon, the patriotism espoused in the images of 1812 also stressed the deeds of individual Russians, as well as the influence and guidance of their tsar.[95] This relationship between tsar and people was emphasized throughout the nineteenth century, but by the wars of the early twentieth century it had all but disappeared from the *lubok*.[96]

Cultural Borrowings: The World of Visual Nationhood in the Napoleonic Era

The Russian image makers who produced their *lubki* during the Patriotic War took part in a European-wide effort to depict nationhood. The Napoleonic era witnessed an explosion of popular images that attempted to react to French preponderance in Europe and simultaneously articulate a sense of cultural differentiation between "us" and "them." In England, artists such as James Gillray and Isaac Cruikshank gained fame through caricatures that mocked Napoleon and the French while visually depicting ideas of Englishness. In the German states, particularly Prussia, artists also had a field day attempting to rally their countrymen around a common hatred of all things French.[97] Russian *lubok* artists such as Terebenev and Venetsianov, therefore, contributed to a larger process of visual nationhood in the early nineteenth century. While all of these artists drew inspiration from French caricature and from English pioneers such as William Hogarth and Thomas Rowlandson, they also borrowed ideas from each other and ultimately helped to disseminate their works to ever-increasing audiences.

English caricaturists proved particularly adept in their depictions of Napoleon, the French, and concepts of Englishness. The art of caricature had exploded in Hanoverian England, reaching an apogee during the reign of George III (1760–1820). Satirical prints that acted as an important source for understanding English politics, social mores, and news from abroad "formed a living part of everyday experience in Georgian

Britain."[98] Widely distributed across England by the turn of the nine-teenth century, British caricatures "permeated the national consciousness" of England, while continental artists even adapted them for their own po-litical messages. Caricaturists such as Thomas Rowlandson and James Gill-ray became known across the English Channel and their works proved nearly as popular in Europe as they had in England.[99] The early Georgian print focused mostly on domestic issues, but the French Revolution and Napoleon's rise to power provided the English artists with subjects that could be used to articulate national differences.

During the spring and summer of 1803, for example, images that warned their consumers of a potential French invasion flooded the English markets. Part of a "propaganda effort perhaps unprecedented in its scope," popular prints focused British fury on the figure of Napoleon.[100] British caricaturists depicted Napoleon's alleged treachery, cast him as a devil, la-beled him a criminal, and declared that his character reflected French de-generacy. Artists such as Isaac Cruikshank even suggested that the English had lost a sense of their identity and thus become more like Napoleon by slavishly copying French manners and fashions. His 1803 print, "The Phan-tasmagoria—or a Review of Old Times," features Napoleon arranging a meeting between two generations, Francophile Englishmen from the eigh-teenth century and Francophobe Englishmen from the nineteenth. The image conveys a sense of danger by suggesting that earlier adoption of French manners contributed to a "physical decline in English charac-ter."[101] Only by shedding their French manners, caricaturists such as Cruikshank suggested, could the English become truly English.

The proliferation of popular prints in 1803 England, many of them warning against a different sort of invasion than the cultural one depicted by Cruikshank, led to a backlash. While some images boasted that England "looked forward to Napoleon's landing" in order to teach the upstart a les-son, others created a sense of panic by spreading the notion that Napoleon and his mighty army were "coming to Ravish your Wives & your Daughters." Alarmist prints led James Gillray to create images that featured "English" characteristics of stoicism and bravery in the face of an enemy. One of Gillray's images featured John Bull standing next to a wall covered in alarmist prints telling an audience he does not fear Napoleon: "Let him come and be D—n'd!"[102] Gillray's "Bounaparte, 48 Hours after Landing" contains John Bull hoisting Napoleon's head on a pitchfork, while the artist's 1805 print "St. George and the Dragon" casts George III in the role of the English national saint and Napoleon as a beast threaten-ing the maiden Britannia.[103] Gillray's caricatures, along with those by Cruikshank and other artists, formed an important part in the articulation of British nationhood during the Napoleonic era. These images of war ini-tiated widespread discussion about what it meant to be British and how Napoleon and the French threatened the fabric of the nation. By invoking icons such as Britannia, St. George, John Bull, and even Queen Elizabeth (who in one imaginative print appears as a ghost brandishing an image of the Spanish Armada's defeat before a frightened Napoleon), British artists sought to invoke a visual language that could convey to consumers a sense of nationhood.

The British propaganda campaign against Napoleon bears a striking resemblance to the Russian reaction to the French invasion. Moreover, Russian artists such as Ivan Terebenev found inspiration from their British counterparts. Terebenev's interest in caricature sprang from knowledge of both the Russian *lubok* tradition and the influence of Georgian prints in England. Terebenev fused the style of Rowlandson, an artist he particularly admired, with the traditions of the Russian popular print. This cultural borrowing was reciprocated—George Cruikshank, Isaac's son, copied Terebenev's print featuring Napoleon being forced to dance and titled it "Russians Teaching Boney to Dance."[104] The world of visual nationhood that Napoleon unleashed thus found outlets across Europe—from England to Russia, the French emperor acted as a lightning rod for delineating national differences.[105]

Cultural Reception and Russian Memories of 1812

While British caricatures in the Napoleonic era relied on markets and distribution networks already firmly established, Russian popular prints helped to create a broader market for visual goods. In a tantalizing glimpse of the cultural reception of the wartime *lubok,* the *Saint Petersburg News* discussed the popularity of one of Ivan Terebenev's caricatures, "The Russian Scaevola." The unnamed author of the account states that the artist "presented an unforgettable memory of the incident," and "has rather successfully and perfectly expressed that minute when the peasant, rejecting Napoleon's service and scorning fear . . . suddenly seizes upon the brand on his hand and deprives himself of it with an axe."[106] The article claims that the image proved to be "very popular" in its illustrations of Russian heroism during the war against Napoleon. In a similar vein, an 1815 journal account from Perm reported, "peddlers trading engravings and *lubok* pictures supply the city and the village population with thousands of portraits of the Russian emperor and the distinctive heroes (including Kutuzov) of the war with Napoleon."[107] Other accounts of the *lubok* trade during the Patriotic War note that the images of Terebenev, Ivanov, and others could be found in Petersburg stores, newspapers, journals, and from street peddlers who specialized in the *lubok* trade.[108] While one can only guess at the ways in which the audience for these images received them, these two accounts offer a brief glimpse into their dissemination and popularity.

The images that spread to the Russian provinces offered a chance for consumers to use them in creative ways. In 1892, commemorating the eightieth anniversary of Napoleon's invasion, the Russian journal *Russkaia starina* published the memoirs of a French doctor who had been captured during the Patriotic War.[109] Taken captive after a battle, the Frenchman, de la Fliz, found himself imprisoned in the western provinces of Russia, where he often visited the homes of local landowners. One particular visit remained in de la Fliz's memory, an encounter with a landowner named Pokorskii, whom de la Fliz described as "a very rich person," and "a 40-year-old provincial man with simple manners."[110] Noticing that de la Fliz was interested in the portraits that adorned his walls, Pokorskii told the Frenchman that he had a number of other images he wanted him to see. Pokorskii then gave him a few *lubki* that mocked the French, including the image "Napoleon's Winter Quarters" (Figure 2.2). According to de la Fliz, these images depicted "all the disasters of the retreat from Moscow," and though they exaggerated their subjects, they "represented the bitter truth."[111] He angrily noted that Pokorskii laughed heartily at the despair these images aroused within his captive. Overall, the Frenchman found the experience "extremely insulting."[112]

De la Fliz was not the only Frenchman to remember the war and its images. When the Marquis de Custine made his famous journey to Russia in 1839, the resulting letters he wrote became a bestseller throughout Europe. Custine's vivid account of Nicholas I's Russia helped to confirm European perceptions of Russia as a despotic, barbaric land that conditioned its people for slavery. Although Custine's *Letters from Russia* has largely been remembered for these descriptions, the author also offered detailed accounts of the architecture and people that he encountered. When he first saw a Russian peasant in St. Petersburg, the countenance of the serf brought back certain unpleasant memories for Custine: "the most charming face [of the peasant] reminds me, in spite of my efforts to banish such ideas, of those caricatures of Bonaparte which were spread all over Europe in 1815."[113]

The war years, as Custine's account attested to, transformed the popular prints into commercially viable products. Many of the pictures from the war appeared for sale before they had officially passed the censorship committees, such was the demand for the images. Terebenev's *lubki* in particular sold so well that several publishers engaged in a bidding war for the artist's services. Initially Terebenev sold his prints exclusively to Ivan Glazunov, a publisher with stores in St. Petersburg. Glazunov in turn distributed the prints through his various shops and through the peddlers employed to disseminate the prints throughout the country. In March 1813, however, because of the tremendous sales of the Terebenev *lubki*, the artist signed a new contract to work with a different publisher, who would pay the artist more and who had offices in Moscow as well as St. Petersburg. Because of the intense competition for the prints, publishers began to denounce one another—in particular, the Petersburg publisher Glazunov issued a statement that he was not related to the publishers of the same name in Moscow (Ivan and Matvei Glazunov, two brothers). Particularly galling to the Petersburg Glazunov was the fact that his Moscow counterparts had seized on the popularity of the *lubok* and used the traditional markets, which were located in Moscow, to their advantage.[114] In the competition over the products of the patriotic culture, Moscow and its publishers defeated St. Petersburg.

These examples suggest that the experience of 1812 served as an important point of reference in the memories of Russians, establishing a "myth of 1812" as part of the renewed national identity in the wake of Napoleon's invasion. For Russians of all backgrounds, 1812 became a defining moment in their lives and helped to create a sense of belonging to a Russian nation in the making. The works of A. G. Tartakovskii and A. V. Buganov in particular have demonstrated how Russians of all classes remembered 1812, and in the process have added to the sense of national identity constructed by the wartime images.[115] Tartakovskii's work illustrates that the Napoleonic Wars helped to usher in a new sense of "Russian memory" after 1812, when Russians from Nikolai Kotov, a wealthy aristocrat, to Khristian Khristiani, a poor peasant, recorded their memories of the war.[116] For Tartakovskii, 1812 played a "special role" in the shaping of popular memories, as Russians struggled to understand the historical meaning of the invasion.[117]

Buganov concentrates more specifically on the memory of Russian peasants in the nineteenth century, and how historical events such as the war against Napoleon shaped peasant national consciousness. He notes that the Patriotic War spawned an incredible amount of folklore among the peasants, who also contributed substantial monetary sums to the war effort. The war produced the last great cycle of historical songs, which Buganov argues helped to place the event in a prominent place within peasant memory. He also notes that peasants retained specific knowledge about the events of 1812 and its heroes such as Kutuzov long after the war, passing on their memories to future generations and in the process furthering the national self-awareness that the war had brought to the countryside.[118]

One of the ways in which the myths and memories of 1812 spread throughout Russia involved both veterans of the war and the *lubok*. The *raek,* or peep show, an important and popular attraction at Russian fairgrounds, featured *lubki* that were placed in a box and viewed with a magnifying glass. Peep-show storytellers, known as *raeshniki,* provided explanations about the images that helped to make popular prints come to life. Much like the *lubok,* the *raek* "catered to the audience's curiosity," and wars featured prominently in these entertainments.[119] After 1812, peep shows featuring wartime *lubki* became increasingly popular.[120] Many of the *raeshniki* were veterans of the war against Napoleon, and they helped to propagate stories about the heroes of 1812 (including their own deeds) to whoever listened. The *lubki* of the Patriotic War, therefore, became the source for popular entertainments for years afterward, and in the process furthered the historical memory of the war itself.[121]

Several Russian scholars and cultural figures also left accounts of the role that the *lubok* played in defining national identity during the Patriotic War. Foremost among these figures is Leo Tolstoy, whose *War and Peace* remains the most famous account of the Napoleonic invasion. Tolstoy's research on his book led him to conclude that the victory over Napoleon came as a divine triumph largely engineered by the Russian people.[122] In addition to the musings about Kutuzov, Tolstoy's account of the events of 1812 also includes references to the war *lubok,* which the writer tended to view as unofficial government propaganda.[123]

Tolstoy refers several times in his account of Moscow in 1812 to "Rostopchin's broadsheets," after the governor-general of the city, and suggests that these images aroused uncertainty among the population about the war and its destructiveness.[124] One of the images later identified as approved by Rostopchin was "The Warrior Ivan and the Peasant Dolbil," discussed above.[125] For Tolstoy, this and other images from the war confused Muscovites more than exhorting them to resist. In the novel, Rostopchin's broadsheets, which contained images of resistance to Napoleon and implied that the Grand Army would never enter Moscow, caused residents of the old Russian capital not to take the French approach seriously. Tolstoy mentions a particular image featuring a Moscow burgher named Karpushka Chigirin, who had abused the French after hearing they wanted to take Moscow, and he claims that this *lubok* aroused a great deal of interest among Russians who discussed it.[126] Most residents who viewed this and other "Rostopchin broadsheets" in the novel remained convinced that the French would never reach Moscow. When Napoleon's army entered the city and panic ensued, Tolstoy attributed this panic in part to the false sense of superiority promoted in the popular pictures of the time. In his words, Russian resistance and the eventual defeat of Napoleon came "despite all the nonsense Rostopchin wrote in his broadsheets."[127] Although the author's assessment of the *lubok* was largely a negative one, Tolstoy's novel attests to the widespread appeal that the *lubki* had during the invasion.

Rostopchin himself provides an interesting case of the ways in which Russian elites attempted to describe the patriotism in Russia during the war. A political conservative, Rostopchin feared that talk of a "people's war" in 1812 could lead to a serf uprising, and sought instead to manipulate the masses.[128] While he understood that the nature of the war made it an unprecedented event in recent Russian history,[129] Rostopchin wanted to deflect popular hatred away from the nobility and serfdom toward Napoleon and the French by appealing to xenophobic attitudes in his broadsheets. Above all, the governor of Moscow sought to convince Russians that loyalty to the tsar and to the country, as well as its social system, was the duty of all Orthodox Russians.[130] Admitting that the mood of the populace was extremely anti-French, Rostopchin stoked these beliefs by publishing images claiming that the French had desecrated Russian churches and that Napoleon had converted to Islam while in Egypt.[131] After the Russians had driven the French out of the country, Rostopchin later claimed that he had "succeeded perfectly in making the peasant despise the French soldier," thus saving the empire.[132] Although he admitted that the common people of Russia displayed great patriotism in 1812, Rostopchin continued to fear the repercussions of depicting the event as a "people's war," just as he continued to believe that he had used his popular pictures to teach the masses how to hate.

Other scholars provide more favorable assessments of both the *lubok*'s popularity and its impact in Russia during the Napoleonic invasion. Dmitrii Rovinskii's unsurpassed five-volume collection of *lubki*, first published in 1881, listed a large number of the images from 1812, which Rovinskii viewed positively.[133] Rovinskii, a well-known jurist who played an important role in drafting the judicial reform of 1864, began collecting popular pictures at an early age. He believed that before 1839, when the tsarist government passed a new censorship law that clamped down on *lubok* artists,[134] the popular print truly reflected the everyday experiences and beliefs of the common Russian. In particular, Rovinskii found the images from the Patriotic War interesting, and while they tended to exaggerate the history of the time, they also helped to establish a popular memory of the victory over Napoleon.[135] He catalogued over 150 *lubki* from 1812, listing their texts and the artists who created them in cases where this information was known. Rovinskii wrote that "patriotic *lubki*" were a particularly popular form of these Russian images and believed that popular pictures from the Patriotic War inspired Russians to victory and helped them form a lasting interpretation of Napoleon's invasion.

Vladimir Denisov, whose succinct work *Voina i lubok* appeared during the First World War, also attested to the importance of the *lubki* of 1812. He wrote that "the Patriotic War left deep traces in Russian life," and that the *lubok*'s depiction of the ultimate victory over Napoleon was "involuntarily" impressed "in the memory of past Russian army successes."[136] Denisov asserted that the *lubki* of 1812 marked the first time that the patriotic *lubok* came into its own as a carrier of nationhood in Russia, and that its significance rested in its popularity and the lasting impressions it made in future images of war.[137]

One cannot conclusively state that the images from 1812 helped to foster a popular patriotism that took hold throughout Russia, but they certainly contributed to the rethinking of national identity that occurred throughout Russia in the wake of 1812. The images from the war against Napoleon left a lasting mark. The *lubki* from the Patriotic War not only illustrated the "visual world" of the time; they also revealed a great deal about how the artists who produced them defined "Russianness" in 1812.[138] In the years immediately following Napoleon's defeat, for example, Terebenev's images were reproduced in newspapers, on sets of fine china sold to Russia's elites, and even in an illustrated children's book for learning the alphabet.[139] A generation of Russian schoolchildren thus learned to associate the letter "*v*" with the word "*vorona*," or "crow," complete with Terebenev's *lubok* "French Crow's Soup." Terebenev selected the images for his alphabet himself, and even included works by Venetsianov and Ivanov. He wanted to leave a gift to his countrymen that would help to continue the memory of 1812 in the years afterward, and again believed that the wartime images were the best means to do so. The *Azbuka 1812 goda* eventually became more popularly called "Terebenev's ABCs."[140]

The French emperor and his troops, who provided the means by which Russians defined themselves and expressed patriotism throughout this war, continued to be depicted in *lubki* from later wars. Every successive Russian war, beginning with the Crimean conflict and including the Great War, gave rise to images depicting the French emperor, reminding Russians of the source of their "popular" patriotism. The Russian government officially commissioned a reprint of all of Terebenev's Patriotic War images in 1855, during the siege of Sevastopol, in order to inspire its residents and all Russians to defeat the new adversary.[141] Russian ethnographers working for the Tenishev program in 1898 found that the war and the deeds of famous generals still resonated with the peasants in the Riazan region. One concluded: "They all know Suvorov [Catherine the Great's general] and Kutuzov [the commander of Russian forces in 1812] from pictures, and they have a great interest in the war of 1812."[142] During the Russo-Japanese War the *lubok* "Regarding Russia's War with Japan in 1904: Napoleon Visits the Japanese" depicts a ghostly French emperor standing in front of a table full of surprised Japanese officers.[143] The text of the image has Napoleon warning the Japanese about the dangers of provoking the Russians into an attack.[144]

Napoleon's image appeared in Soviet visual culture as well, particularly during the Great Patriotic War. Several TASS windows, *lubok*-style posters produced by the Russian news agency between 1941 and 1945, drew comparisons between Napoleon's doomed invasion and the Nazi attack on Russia, reminding Russians not to forget the "people's victory" of 1812 in the midst of the crisis of 1941–1943.[145] The TASS window No. 841, "Before and Now," depicts two panels of Russia's enemies departing along a wintry road strewn with the rubble of war. Napoleon stands at the head of the first column of departing soldiers, Hitler at the head of the second. As this and other Second World War images make clear, the themes first established in the *lubki* of 1812 left a lasting impression on Russian visual culture and became important components of Russian national identity.

If Napoleon served as the source against which *lubok* artists defined Russian national identity, by and large this definition consisted of praise for the Russian spirit and identification of the two figures in whom this spirit resided—the peasant and the Cossack. The male or female peasant defender and the heroic Cossack became fixed components of the visual landscape of future Russian wars. Moreover, the institutions and figures that inspired the "Russian spirit" and "people's victory" of 1812, namely the Orthodox church and the tsar, established themselves as important components of wartime culture. Although the representations of Russian peasants, Cossacks, the tsar, and the church changed over time, these basic themes remained a constant in the war *lubok,* and owed their importance in Russian popular culture to the *lubki* of the Patriotic War.

The Russians, as the images of 1812 reveal, would not forget Napoleon's invasion. By launching an attack on Russia in 1812, the French emperor helped to awaken a redefinition of Russian nationhood that would continue to find expression over the course of the century. In the process, the artists who produced these images of war formed one of the first cultural expressions of what became a dominant myth within Russian society, the myth of the "people's victory" over Napoleon. Although the interpretations of this victory underwent changes in the years after 1812, the basic premise that the Russian people responded to Napoleon's invasion by rallying around their shared Russianness persisted. Other cultural legacies of the war stressed this myth in a variety of ways, from the monuments built to celebrate the victory to Tchaikovsky's famous overture. The *lubki* of the time represent one of the first expressions of this myth, and images from later wars continued to draw on it liberally. In doing so, the images of 1812 may have been too influential, as the remaining chapters indicate. Future publishers attempted to capture the essence of later wars by using the themes evident in the prints from 1812. No other war of the nineteenth century, however, would match the intensity of the Napoleonic invasion.

REGULATING WARTIME CULTURE
Government, Laws, Censorship

[S]ometimes, and rather frequently, the government used
lubki as a way for the promulgation of useful information and
even for suggestions of courage to protect the fatherland.

—**Dmitrii Bludov** (1851)

• On 1 September 1816, just one year after the wars against Napoleon
had ended, Count Sergei Uvarov, the superintendent of the St. Petersburg
Educational District, wrote a letter to the St. Petersburg Censorship Committee about the proliferation of popular images in Russia. Uvarov noted
that a large number of lithographic and other prints during and after the
war did not bear the censor's stamp. He wrote to warn the members of the
censorship committee that they needed to be more vigilant, and called on
them to "oblige" image makers to submit their work to the preliminary
censorship required by law. Uvarov's letter circulated among the members
of the Petersburg Censorship Committee in the following weeks, along
with a note from the chairman of the committee endorsing Uvarov's call
for greater vigilance in censoring popular images.[1]

With this letter, Uvarov, later Nicholas I's minister of education and author of the doctrine of "official nationality," initiated a government examination of the influence of popular images on the Russian population. His
call for greater surveillance, as he made clear in his letter, came because he
believed that the *lubok* played an important part in inspiring Russians to
defend their homeland during the Napoleonic invasion. Many of these
images from the years 1812–1815 appeared throughout the Russian countryside and in Russian towns without having been properly vetted. Uvarov
and other tsarist officials grew concerned about the influence that these
uncensored images appeared to have on the Russian population (even if it
was positive) and demanded that the St. Petersburg committee do its job
better in the future. By articulating this concern in his letter, Uvarov began a decades-long process of forcing the producers of popular images to
submit their work to government supervision. As a result of the *lubok*'s
popularity during the Napoleonic Wars, the imperial government began
to take its images very seriously.

While many scholars of Russian popular prints have asserted that the final measure in the government's quest, an 1851 law governing *lubok* production, fundamentally changed the nature of this production, in reality

the series of laws passed after Uvarov's letter did not really do so. Nevertheless, the laws passed after 1816 illustrate the ways in which the imperial government had come to realize that the *lubok* represented an influential source of information for many Russians. The Russian government feared that images made by Old Believers would fall into the hands of Orthodox citizens, and officials called on censors to prevent this from happening. The laws passed in the wake of the Patriotic War culminated in the 1851 law, which required all existing *lubok* plates to be destroyed and all new ones to be registered with the imperial censors. This act, while changing the themes of the popular prints very little, nevertheless paved the way for entrepreneurs such as Petr Sharapov and his student Ivan Sytin to dominate the *lubok* market after midcentury. While the war *lubok* never troubled censors after the 1851 law, the new law's greatest impact on the *lubok* came from the commercial aspects of the act. The themes of the wartime images from the Crimean War and after continued to be acceptable to the Russian authorities. Thus, the imperial Russian government played an important, if somewhat indirect, role in the articulation of national identity and patriotism depicted in the war *lubok,* helping to turn its images into semiofficial propaganda during wartime. Equally important, the presence of governmental censorship led to a culture of self-censorship on the part of *lubok* publishers, and established a mutually reinforcing relationship between censor and publisher.[2]

Regulating the *Lubok* Before 1812

The *lubok* first made its way into the laws of the Russian Empire as early as 1674, when a decree from Patriarch Ioakim attempted to outlaw the appearance of "sacred images" on "German (or foreign)" sheets.[3] Responding to the increasing number of cheap, paper icons that had found their way throughout Russia, the 1674 decree noted that "many tradesmen, having cut on boards and printed on paper sheets the sacred images of icons" have in turn "corrupted the image of the Savior and our Lord Jesus Christ." Making use of the imagery of the Orthodox church, the decree made clear, remained solely within the realm of the church itself. *Lubok* artists who violated this premise, largely "German heretics with their accursed opinions," assaulted the "reverence of the Orthodox church" and its "icon worship." Warning both the producers of popular pictures and "the ranks of peasants" who bought them, the decree promised "extreme punishment," destruction of the printing presses that produced the profane images, and a substantial fine to anyone who continued to trade *lubki.*[4] This law reflected the early themes that the *lubok* depicted, largely religious in nature, as well as the limits of the church's toleration. Engraved icons and prints copied from religious manuscripts formed the basis of early *lubki,* which were either printed from woodblock or, after the mid-1600s, from copper. Both the court and the church encouraged the production of these cheap icons,[5] but clearly the Orthodox church discouraged the production of religious imagery that did not reflect Orthodox values, as the 1674 law made clear.

While the church staked out its position regarding the production of "paper icons," the *lubok* nevertheless continued to flourish, and by the time of Peter I, it had become increasingly secular in its tone and content. Peter the Great, however, began to see the importance of *lubok* images in shaping attitudes, and his Holy Synod attempted to control production and sale in an effort to channel *lubok* religious themes.[6] In a 1721 *ukaz*, the Synod reaffirmed the 1674 law on *lubki* and decreed that religious imagery could appear in the popular prints, although only under certain conditions. Most importantly, the 1721 decree concerned itself with the dissemination of the images, which could be found all over Moscow's streets, markets, and other public places. The law required *lubok* publishers, who had largely produced the images on their own to sell in Russia's markets, to register their printing houses with the authorities.[7] Although the attempts to regulate the production of *lubki* proved difficult at best (*lubok* publishers infrequently registered their businesses), Peter's reign witnessed a shift in Russian popular imagery from religious to secular content.

The two best-known *lubki* from the time of Peter the Great illustrate both the transition to secular themes in popular imagery and the difficulties the Russian government had in regulating these prints. The *lubok* "How the Mice Buried the Cat" depicts a large cat being carried to his grave by a procession of mice. The cat's whiskers clearly resemble the moustache of Peter I, while the mice are labeled with the names of areas Peter had conquered. The print "The Barber Wants to Cut Off an Old Believer's Beard" features a clean-shaven barber wearing European clothes (who might represent Peter I), grasping the beard of a large Old Believer wearing traditional Russian attire.[8] The barber, holding a pair of scissors, is preparing to trim the beard of the Old Believer, while the text states that the intended victim of Peter's policies replies, "Listen, barber, I neither want to cut my beard nor shave. Watch out, or I will call the guards to teach you to behave."[9] Both prints, which were produced by Old Believer communities and were thus intended to be critical of Petrine policy, illustrate the changing role of the *lubok* in Russia. No longer just "paper icons," *lubki* could now depict current events and even satirize government policies.[10]

That these two *lubki* were produced by Old Believer communities proved quite significant. After the schism within the Orthodox church in the mid-seventeenth century, Russians who defended the old liturgy and traditional culture were hostile toward the Russian state.[11] Old Believers held the Russian government partly responsible for the change in Orthodox liturgy after Patriarch Nikon's reforms, and during the time of Peter the Great their suspicions again came to the fore. Peter's revolution, particularly his cultural reforms and the high-handed way the tsar pursued them, came to be seen by the Old Believers as another challenge to their carefully preserved culture and way of life.[12]

The *lubki* discussed above represented a way for Old Believer communities to articulate their contempt for Peter's policies, and to instruct other Russians about the nature of the Petrine state. As one prominent historian of the Old Believer community has noted, "Old Belief was a photographic negative of official society,"[13] a characterization that also applies to the Russian government's attitude toward Old Believer *lubki*. Immediately after the schism, Old Believers used "pictorial representations," including *lubki* like the two mentioned above, "outside the realm of iconography to bolster arguments against the state and the established church."[14] The imperial government remained fearful of the potential influence of these Old Believer images among the Russian peasantry, and attempted to quash their proliferation whenever possible.[15] Doing so remained difficult, for Old Believers printed hand-colored images of saints and other religious subjects and sold them to the itinerant peddlers who wandered throughout Russian towns and villages.[16]

The Russian government's inability to control the content of Old Believer images—and its inability to control the *lubok* in general—was made clear in a series of laws passed after the 1721 Synod decree. In 1744, the Russian government forbade engravings with "unskillfully made portrayals of saints," while a 1745 decree required images of saints to be examined by a bishop and made with properly registered materials.[17] *Lubok* publishers, however, continued to produce their images, which now mixed secular and religious themes. The religious nature of some of the images again met with official disapproval in a Senate *ukaz* of 6 November 1760.[18] The *ukaz* noted the increasing popularity of *lubki,* which could be bought throughout Moscow (particularly near the Spassky Bridge) and in St. Petersburg. While the secular themes of the images did not concern the government, the number of religious themes did. Russian officials noted in the *ukaz* that the 1744 and 1745 Holy Synod decrees concerning the publication of crude images of saints had not been obeyed, and the Senate authorized bishops to place official seals on religious images they deemed to be appropriate. Local policemen would aid the church officials in their efforts to curb production of "unskilled work" (a reference to prints made by Old Believers). This more active role in controlling the quality of the *lubok,* coupled with the trend toward more secular images noted earlier, saw the *lubok* disappear from Russian decrees for almost a half century.

By the turn of the nineteenth century, the issue of censorship began to occupy an increasingly important place in the minds of Russia's lawmakers, and their concern eventually affected the *lubok* as well. The effects of the French Revolution and Catherine II's caution regarding publishing meant that by the nineteenth century, "all printers and publishers in Russia remained in servitude to the empire and in sufferance to the autocrat's whims."[19] Alexander I, who became tsar of Russia in 1801, in response to these domestic questions, issued a new censorship decree in 1804. Although the decree has been characterized as "the most liberal censorship statute ever to appear in Imperial Russia,"[20] it ratcheted up the regulation of *lubki*. According to the statute, no book or image could be put on sale in Russia without having first been reviewed by the censor. Similarly, no foreign image could be sold in the Russian Empire without bearing a seal of approval from the censor. Local censorship committees were to be set up to monitor all written and visual materials within individual districts.[21]

The new censorship law, then, represented the culmination of over a century of governmental attempts to monitor and regulate the growing *lubok* trade in Russia and formed part of the establishment of a "well-ordered police state," as Marc Raeff has characterized the imperial system.[22] On the eve of the war with Napoleon, government control over the contents of Russian popular images had proven shaky at best. Despite attempts to control the themes of the *lubok*, particularly religious imagery, the *lubok* publishers continued to meet the obvious demand for images with a variety of themes, both secular and religious. Alexander I's censorship law and censorship committees, largely set up to meet the perceived threat from revolutionary France, marked a new, if failed, chapter in the history of governmental regulation of the print industry.

After Napoleon: Government Regulations, 1815–1850

The invasion of Napoleon in 1812, as the previous chapter indicates, provoked a wide variety of responses to the French invaders. *Lubki* by Ivan Terebenev and other artists had not always been officially censored, making them illegal in the eyes of the imperial administration, yet they also by and large depicted acceptable themes of Russian patriotism.[23] The years after Napoleon's invasion witnessed Russian officialdom's attempt to harness the popularity of the war *lubok* for its own purposes, though once again with mixed results.[24]

By the end of the war against Napoleon, even the caricatures of Terebenev ran afoul of the imperial censors, who deemed his depictions of Alexander I and the battles outside of Russia too sensitive to publish.[25] Russian officials frowned at descriptions of actual battles, number of troops and casualties involved, and other technical details of warfare included in later *lubki* from 1812, and as a result all of Terebenev's images were banned temporarily by 1815. Russian officialdom, while embracing most of the themes of the images from 1812, also remained uncomfortable with the freedom that Terebenev and his compatriots had enjoyed in producing them. At the same time, it is possible that censors made these charges in response to the fact that some of Terebenev's images had not properly been submitted to the censor when they first appeared. Regulation of wartime images thus had reached a crucial juncture by 1815, as censorship laws began to pay more attention to the dissemination of all information about the war, including information conveyed in popular images.

The resurgence of censorship may have been a result of pressure from publishers. The Patriotic War *lubki* were successful from a commercial standpoint, and various publishers attempted to take advantage of their popularity by copying the images of Terebenev and others. Publishers who distributed these prints tried to win the market for themselves, a practice that led to the illegal reproduction of some of the most popular prints.[26] Commercial rivalry over the *lubok* trade, in other words, contributed to the rise of censorship after 1812. This competition in turn may have led to greater self-censorship on the part of publishers, who would have incentive for not running afoul of the imperial censors and losing potential profits.

In addition to this rivalry, the Russian government remained concerned with regulating popular culture after the war. Although Alexander I's censorship law remained relatively liberal in theory, in practice its application, particularly in the wake of 1812, was generally conservative. The increasingly religious outlook of the tsar made its way into the implementation of his censorship statute, and Russian censors began to promote the Orthodox church, the tsar, and the fatherland after the invasion.[27] Russian censors treated anything that opposed Orthodoxy and autocracy as suspect and even rejected a translation of Walter Scott's "On the Eve of St. John," a highly religious work by the Scottish author, as "contrary to morality, religion, and the good purposes of the government." In the words of one historian of Russian censorship, by the end of Alexander's rule, "the church had emerged the victor in an out-and-out political struggle over censorship."[28] Moreover, Russian conservatives grew concerned with the state of learning among the lower classes, particularly after 1812. Government officials and conservative publishers alike hoped to create an Orthodox, Christian state through censorship and education.[29] The implications of this trend in censorship and its impact on the wartime *lubok* would become quite clear in the remaining wars of the century, which as mentioned earlier, tended to be depicted as holy wars.

It is within this context that one should interpret Sergei Uvarov's letter of September 1816 to the St. Petersburg Censorship Committee. Uvarov himself had experienced the defeat of Napoleon firsthand, but he also understood the nationalist forces that Napoleon had unleashed throughout Europe. Like many of his educated contemporaries in Alexander I's Russia, Uvarov initially supported proposals for liberal change in Russia.[30] Later, however, he became influenced by such German romantic thinkers as Friedrich Schlegel, whom he had met in 1808.[31] From Schlegel, Uvarov adopted the belief that religion formed the center of a spiritual life, writing to a friend that he was impressed by Schlegel's cultural-religious approach to understanding man.[32] During the Napoleonic invasion of Russia, however,

Uvarov seems to have undergone a profound philosophical crisis.[33] He published six essays reacting to the Napoleonic threat between 1813 and 1816, and even helped establish patriotic journals such as *Son of the Fatherland*,[34] which published Terebenev's caricatures. When Napoleon's defeat became evident, Uvarov composed a "hymn of praise" to Alexander I entitled "L'Empereur Alexandre et Bonaparte."[35] In this work, Uvarov portrayed Napoleon as satanic and Alexander as "God's instrument" who had liberated Europe. He emerged from the war espousing ideas heavily influenced by Schlegel and the romantics, who also developed their philosophy in the wake of the French Revolution and Napoleonic invasions. Uvarov now believed that the Russian people should be taught nationalistic principles that stressed their spirituality and love for their native land, and his letter of 1816 reveals that he believed popular images could serve as an important vehicle for promoting patriotic ideals.[36] He hoped that the years after 1812 could be fruitful ones that would spread patriotism throughout Russia.

Uvarov eventually got his chance to spread these ideals. Alexander I's death in 1825 brought with it not only a new tsar, Nicholas I, but also a reevaluation of the censorship law. Generally speaking, the mystical component of the post-Napoleonic period and its consequences for imperial censorship gave way to the "exaltation of Orthodoxy and nationalism" in the realm of Russian regulations. Uvarov's 1832 policy of "official nationality" eventually began to force its way into official thinking, and its tenets found their way into imperial censorship, which Nicholas himself viewed as a means by which to instill "official nationality" nationwide.[37] Censorship under Nicholas also came under the jurisdiction of a new entity, the Russian secret police (the Third Section), who would help to ensure that anything viewed as insulting to the Orthodox faith, the throne, or the morals of Russian subjects would be banned.

Prior to the publication of Uvarov's doctrine, certain conservative trends made their way into the new censorship charter of 10 June 1826, a law that also regulated what could be depicted in popular imagery. This decree laid out several polices regarding the *lubok* and other lithographic images, stating above all that they had to be submitted to censors for approval. In addition, all images had to have "a moral use or at least a harmless purpose," while also remaining inoffensive to the government or "any estate in general or any person in particular." Depictions of the royal family also were subject to strict censorship by the tsar himself, who threatened to reject any portrait of himself or his family that did not meet with his approval. Finally, humorous caricatures, if deemed too offensive to Russians, could be censored. In addition to these concrete recommendations governing the production of *lubki* and other images, the 1826 censorship statute gave more power to the censorship committees, the Third Section, and, in cases of religious imagery, the "spiritual censorship" of the church.[38]

In this law, the tsar ensured that he would retain control over the use of his own image. As Richard Wortman has demonstrated, Russian tsars guarded the use of their images quite carefully and used representations of themselves in attempts to define their individual "scenarios of power." For Nicholas, "the parade ground, the court, [and] the meetings in the Kremlin" became identified as symbols of the nation.[39] During the Turkish campaigns of 1828, for example, Nicholas I appeared in a few *lubki* commanding his troops, discussing strategy with his advisors, and crossing the Danube in a *bogatyr'*-like pose. Although the campaigns did not end in a military debacle, Nicholas's insistence on laying siege to the Turkish forts of Varna, Silistria, and Shumla—sieges that were portrayed in these images—amounted to "the capital blunders of the campaign."[40] Because of this characterization, in the years after 1828, Nicholas tended to use his image more carefully. Paintings and engravings that featured the tsar alongside his family became the standard image of Nicholas as a means to promote a sense of domestic harmony as a symbol for the nation.[41]

Overall, therefore, Nicholas's censorship law of 1826 took a defensive stance toward the dissemination of visual information in the Russian Empire. It sought to "defend" Russians against the moral decay of western European culture even as it promoted the superiority of Russian culture. Napoleon's invasion, which had witnessed the beginnings of a redefinition of Russian national identity vis-à-vis the West, also prompted a rethinking on the part of Russian officialdom about how to promote "Russianness" throughout the empire. As a result, the myth of 1812 and its components—especially the moral strength of the Russian people, their tsar, and church—became the cornerstones for imperial censorship under Nicholas I.

Aleksandr Nikitenko, a former serf who had gained his freedom and attended university, became an imperial censor during the reign of Nicholas I. In his frank diary he recounted the concern he felt when he accepted the post in 1833: "I am taking a very dangerous step."[42] His supervisor gave him explicit instructions on how to perform his job, stating that Nikitenko was to work "in such a manner that you not only base your judgments on the censorship code, but also on the particular set of circumstances with which you are faced and the course of events. Also, you must work in such a way that the public has no cause to conclude that the government is hounding culture." Over the course of fifteen years as a censor, Nikitenko was jailed twice for allowing subversive materials to pass through his department, and he constantly wrestled with his role in suppressing Russian writing. When Nikitenko discussed the government's policy behind censorship, he wrote: "the basic principle behind the current policy is very simple: only an administration based on fear can be strong; only a people that does not think is a peaceful people."[43] In 1842, after his second incarceration, Nikitenko mused about the life of a censor in Nicholas I's Russia:

> Censors are treated like little boys or smooth-faced ensigns; we are placed un-
> der arrest for trifles not worthy of attention. At the same time we are saddled
> with the responsibility of protecting minds and morals from anything that
> might lead them astray, of safeguarding the public spirit, the laws, and finally,
> the very government itself. What kind of logical activity can be expected of us
> when everything is decided by blind whim and arbitrary desire?[44]

Nikitenko's characterization of censorship would only grow more extreme in the years ahead. By 1848, Nicholas had grown even more reac-
tionary in his convictions, largely as a result of the revolutions that swept
across Europe that year. The tsar ordered his censors to forbid anything
"conceivably dangerous," and Prince Platon Shirinskii-Shikhmatov, who
replaced Uvarov in 1849 as the main official responsible for censorship,
ruled that all materials marked for consumption by the common people
had to be "filled with the living spirit of the Orthodox Church and with
loyalty to the throne, state, and social order."[45] This increasingly reac-
tionary mood resulted in two new laws passed in 1848 and 1851 on the
production and sale of *lubki*.

In 1848, the tsar formed the Buturlin Committee, which became in the
words of historian Charles Ruud, "one of the most striking embodiments
of the tsar's obscurantism."[46] Set up because Nicholas I believed that even
Uvarov had become too soft, the Buturlin Committee (also frequently referred to as "the committee of 2 April 1848") became Nicholas I's hard-
line censorship body in the last years of his reign. In its work on popular
pictures, the committee castigated Uvarov and the Ministry of National
Education for their inability to censor the *lubok* and recommended in 1848
that all pictures should bear a seal attesting to their acceptance in the eyes of
Russian officials.[47] According to Dmitrii Rovinskii, the well-known collector
of popular pictures, the work of the committee "led to the absolute destruction of this branch [*lubki*] of national village" art. For Rovinskii, the new laws
passed in 1848 and 1851 represented the final step in the effort by the Russian
government to establish complete control over the production of the *lubok*:
"so ended the uncensored people's pictures."[48]

According to Aleksandr Nikitenko, who remained an imperial censor at
the time of the formation of the Buturlin Committee, the mystery and rumors surrounding the creation of this new censorship body placed Russians on edge: "people were gripped by a panicky fear," and "terror
gripped everyone who thought or wrote."[49] Writings that rejected everything European and stressed the superiority of Russia came into vogue.
The fear that was felt by the educated classes also took hold of Nikitenko,
who resigned his posts as censor and as editor of *The Contemporary,* a journal that had come under suspicion for "liberalism."[50]

In the wake of the recommendations of the Buturlin Committee,
Uvarov lost his job, and Prince Shirinskii-Shikhmatov became minister of
education. The new minister had also witnessed the Napoleonic Wars first-

hand, having been commissioned as a naval lieutenant in 1813.[51] Under
his leadership, the ministry began to rethink the laws regarding *lubok* publication. In a letter echoing the thoughts of Uvarov's 1816 letter, Shirinskii-
Shikhmatov wrote on 23 May 1850 about *lubok* censorship. His ideas,
which influenced Russian censorship officials, foreshadowed the major
law on popular pictures adopted the following year. Shirinskii-Shikhmatov
noted, "Pictures known in our industry under the name *lubochnye kartinki*
ordinarily do not follow censorship rules," and he indicated that such a
situation was unacceptable to the government.[52] Noting that the *lubki*
were influential in disseminating information and that past attempts to
censor them had been unsuccessful, Shirinskii-Shikhmatov advocated giving more power to local police chiefs so that they could censor them.[53]

Shirinskii-Shikhmatov also invoked the threat posed by Old Believer
communities, which continued to produce images. After decades of toleration, Russian officials in the time of Nicholas I again cracked down on Old
Believers, viewing them as a threat to stability.[54] In addition, the letter
noted in detail that the *lubok* could be found in virtually every town and
city in the Russian Empire. However, the minister of education noted that
these pictures produced a number of interpretations that could have
"harmful influence, in particular, on the uneducated village inhabitants."
For this reason, their content had to be better regulated.[55] In particular,
Shirinskii-Shikhmatov noted that the content of *lubki* "quite often concern subjects of spiritual matters"[56] and stated that "dissenting sects" produced a number of images, a reference to the continued production of
popular prints by Old Believer communities.

Long associated with the production of popular prints—including the
satirical images "How the Mice Buried the Cat" and "The Barber," mentioned above—Old Believers produced religious images well into the nineteenth century. Although they were not widely distributed and circulated
mostly within Old Believer communities in the north, censorship officials
such as Shirinskii-Shikhmatov feared the potential influence of non-
Orthodox prints.[57] Hand-drawn images often referred to as "schismatic"[58]
continued to bedevil the censors, who found the *lubki* produced by Old
Believers difficult to control. Moreover, rumors that Old Believers both
supported Napoleon in 1812 and worshiped him since that time circulated among Russians of all classes.[59] Finally, the perception that Old Believers acted traitorously during 1812 may have increased the government's desire to control all popular pictures in the decades that followed.

Shirinskii-Shikhmatov's letter and the ideas in it found support in the
person of Dmitrii Nikolaevich Bludov, the head of the Second Section of
the tsar's chancellory, which was responsible for lawmaking in the country. Shirinskii-Shikhmatov wrote to Bludov personally to persuade him to
adopt the ideas proposed in the 23 May 1850 letter. Stating that he had
"come to know the meaning of *lubok* pictures" and their "profound cho-
rus in the hearts of the Russian people," Shirinskii-Shikhmatov requested

that Bludov pass a law regulating the contents of popular pictures.[60] Shirinskii-Shikhmatov stressed that the *lubok* played an important role in cultivating the "spiritual substance" of the Russian people, and he warned that uncensored images by religious dissenters or other "harmful" elements of society could negatively influence Russia's uneducated rural population.[61] Shirinskii-Shikhmatov's letter had its desired effect. On 2 January 1851, Bludov wrote back to the minister of education that he had thought about the proposals to censor the *lubok* and had prepared a draft law regarding its production.[62]

By the end of 1850, then, the Russian government fully recognized the role of the *lubok* as a popular source of information among a wide range of Russians. Moreover, the Ministry of Education and other government agencies admitted two important facts. First, the popular picture could contain potentially harmful ideas, but also served as a means by which useful information could be transmitted to the wider population. Second, Russian officials acknowledged that censoring the *lubok* in the past had proven difficult. In reaching these conclusions, Russian officials responsible for censorship paved the way for a law that would affect the commercial production of such images.

The Law of 1851 and *Lubok* Production

On 2 January 1851, after informing Shirinskii-Shikhmatov of his intent, Bludov submitted a draft for the most comprehensive law governing *lubok* production in Russian history. Passed in March, the 1851 law remained in force until 1917. The law itself was divided into four parts.[63] The first part explained the current situation and the decisions on censorship made in the previous years (since 1848). Bludov and his ministry agreed with the Buturlin Committee's recommendations for regulating the popular picture and the role of local police chiefs in implementing more effective censorship. In addition, the 1851 law agreed with previous laws that stated police chiefs should defer to regional dioceses in regulating images dealing with spiritual matters. In essence, the Second Section and its head concurred with the attempts to regulate the *lubok* that had been passed since the Buturlin Committee was formed, and they agreed with the means by which to censor these images, but still expressed doubts over the ability of the police to control all production of the popular picture. Something needed to be done in order to regulate the *lubok* properly.

In the second part of the 1851 law, Bludov and his department assessed the origins, content, and production of the *lubok* in order to get to the bottom of the difficulty surrounding its regulation.[64] In a brief yet revealing assessment of the role of the *lubok* in popular culture, the law stated that the origins of the term *"lubok"* were shrouded in ambiguity, but probably referred to the bark *(lub)* from which artists produced the woodblocks and paper used to make images, the wooden holders in which peddlers carried them, or even to Lubianka Square in Moscow (so named because of the proliferation of *lubki* sold there). These pictures could be found anywhere in Russia, even as far away as Siberia, where peddlers carried and sold them. Noting that their contents were sometimes religious, sometimes moral, sometimes historical, and at times allegorical, the government also made an admission of the functions these popular images served in the past. While recognizing that distribution and production of the *lubok* had proven difficult to regulate, Bludov wrote, "on the other hand, sometimes, and rather frequently, the government used them as a way for the promulgation of useful information and even for suggestions of courage to protect the fatherland."[65] In particular, the images from the Patriotic War were held up as excellent examples of unofficial propaganda that had served the interests of the government. What Bludov and his ministry essentially wanted was to ensure that all popular pictures, both during military conflicts and in peacetime, served the same purpose.

The second part of the new law adopted a broad definition of the term "*lubok*," stating that it meant all kinds of rough engravings, images, and lithographs. The center for this trade, as the government noted, had always been Moscow and its environs, although Novgorod and Kiev also had thriving *lubok* production centers. The third part of the 1851 law summarized all the decisions regarding the regulation of these popular images taken by the Russian government up to that time. Above all, Russian officials stressed that the production of *lubki* "had remained hitherto without any supervision."[66] Moreover, the Russian government suspected that its people believed anything contained in the *lubok* to be true—surely an unacceptable situation to the administration of Nicholas I. In assessing the previous laws regarding *lubok* production, the Second Section concluded that fines, short-term imprisonments, and other punishments had not stopped artists from producing religious and other images deemed inappropriate to the Russian government. The specter of religious and spiritual images appeared in the law once more—a reference again to the Old Believer images. If the prints of 1812 represented the positive aspects of the *lubok*'s influence, the Old Believer and other prints of a spiritual nature represented the negative side.

The fourth and final part of the 1851 law addressed what should be done in the future to better regulate the content of *lubki*. In particular, the Second Section and Bludov made two recommendations. The government noted that recent attempts to regulate the content of the *lubok* had proven relatively successful since 1826. An 1839 law forcing all images to bear the names of the publishers and artists as well as the censor who had approved them contained effective suggestions that needed to be better enforced. In addition, the powers given to the local police to monitor popular prints had also proven effective in the eyes of the government. Thus, Bludov and his department did not feel the need for any changes regarding the nature of censorship. Their first recommendation, therefore, was that previous regulations be implemented throughout the Russian Empire. Police chiefs and local censorship committees—particularly the Moscow Censorship Committee, which was responsible for regulating popular images in the old Russian capital, the center of the *lubok* trade—had their powers of censorship over the *lubok* reaffirmed and slightly increased in 1851.

Bludov and his officials believed that the majority of images in circulation in 1851 were harmless and reflected the demands of a wide population, and that the 1839 law had established the foundations for insuring that their contents reflected official views. However, the difficulty in controlling the production of the popular picture in the past stemmed mostly from the ease with which they could be made. Virtually any enterprising artist could make a crude woodblock and paper from which he could produce posters, and the longevity of the woodblock meant that popular pictures could be reprinted over and over again, then sold by peddlers.[67] Moreover, the availability of copper plates from which one could make posters and popular prints had increased in the nineteenth century, and this meant that potentially harmful elements of society (particularly Old Believers) could obtain old plates and produce images. Thus, the Second Section recommended that any previously existing plates should be destroyed, with all new woodblocks and copper plates used for making *lubki* subject to control by the censorship committees and police chiefs.[68] The 1851 law gave the tsarist police the power to destroy any production materials not bearing the stamp of the censor, ensuring that all aspects of manufacturing popular pictures came under regulation. Both the State Council and Ministry of Education approved of Bludov's ideas, and on 12 March 1851 they became law.[69]

The 1851 law only changed the commercial aspect of *lubok* production. Requiring all previously existing plates to be destroyed and new ones to be inspected meant that the last vestiges of the *lubok* as a purely folk art and cottage industry disappeared in Russia. In Moscow, the governor-general, Count Zakrevskii, personally oversaw the destruction of copper and wooden plates used to produce *lubki* and then returned the pieces to their owners.[70] In the wake of such measures, village artisans and *lubok* artists who had produced images in the past no longer could compete with larger, more centralized companies devoted exclusively to the mass production of images. Companies and entrepreneurs with more capital and better relations with censors began to dominate the market, for they had the means to make new plates with which to create *lubki*. Forced out of business, many former village artists came to Moscow and other centers of the trade to work for entrepreneurs like Petr Sharapov in the 1850s. One of these men, Ivan Sytin, later became the dominant force in the *lubok* industry and built a publishing empire on the profits from his popular prints.[71]

Furthermore, by 1851, when the law came into effect, the lithographic process of making prints had begun to take hold in Russia. In comparison with the labor-intensive and therefore expensive copper-engraving process, lithography proved to be quite advantageous, for the materials used in the lithographic process remained unspoiled by repeated use and could be purchased rather cheaply. Introduced in Russia during the 1820s, lithography improved the quality and increased the number of *lubki* that could be made from a single engraving. Although more prints could be made using the lithographic stone, "production of the prints still retained a handcraft character."[72] Entrepreneurs such as Sharapov and Morozov took advantage of the 1851 regulations to establish their dominance in the *lubok* market by utilizing the lithographic process. Just as copper plates had displaced the older woodblock, so now the lithograph rendered copper plates obsolete. In sum, the law of 1851 and the government intent behind it ran parallel to the technological innovations that changed the *lubok* industry. The former merely reinforced the latter process.

I. A. Golyshev, who worked for the Moscow *lubok* publisher F. E. Efimov, later identified the 1850s as an important moment for the Russian publishing industry. For Golyshev, the most significant development in the decade was not the 1851 law, but the introduction of the lithographic process. During the Crimean War, while working for Efimov, Golyshev had the job of transferring all prints from the old copper plates onto new, lithographic ones. Efimov, according to Golyshev, ordered the original copies of all prints, while Golyshev printed them using the new process. Golyshev's work ensured that the number of images produced during the war increased. Golyshev commented that Crimean War *lubki* appeared throughout Moscow and even in the provinces, where his parents bought them.[73] Notwithstanding Dmitrii Rovinskii's later lamentation, Golyshev's reflections suggest that the 1851 law merely reinforced trends taking place within *lubok* publishing. Its most significant effect proved to be commercial. Although Rovinskii believed that the images had lost their association with "the people," the publishers who benefitted from the 1851 law already knew the trade.[74]

Moreover, the themes of the wartime *lubok* did not prove unsettling to the imperial censors, and remained a positive, albeit now more strictly regulated, kind of propaganda. To summarize, the 1851 law paralleled many of the gradual changes within the production of Russian images and reflected many of the government's concerns about the regulation of images. As Jeffrey Brooks has argued, however, publishers continued to issue traditional pictures after 1851, while "the folkloric, religious, and literary subjects that had characterized the uncensored *lubki* remained the hallmark of the prints in the second half of the nineteenth century."[75]

Producing popular pictures became the domain of publishing companies, some of which specialized exclusively in imagery. A give-and-take relationship developed between the government censor, on the one hand, and the publisher, on the other—a relationship that determined what would appear in *lubki*. This association, one that continued to be renegotiated in the years after 1851, remained generally static nonetheless.

Through this relationship, Russian publishers eventually self-censored their images, and in doing so made them acceptable in the eyes of government censors.[76]

In the wars that followed the 1851 law, the war *lubok* never troubled the censors.[77] Each image produced in the wars after 1851, beginning with the Crimean conflict, bore the stamp and name of the censor who had approved it. This fact attests in part to the impact that the law of 1851 had on the production of Russian imagery (for fewer publishers produced war *lubki* after 1851), but also in part to the success of the images of the Patriotic War. The new entrepreneurs who began to dominate the *lubok* market by midcentury readily submitted their images to the censor. These *lubok* producers adopted the visual themes of 1812 in their own work, adapting them to the context of the time. Russian officials had noted since 1816 that the wartime *lubok* first produced during the Patriotic War represented the most positive example of the influence of popular imagery, and *lubok* publishers after 1851 consciously copied the themes of 1812 (the fact that the Russian government reprinted all of Terebenev's caricatures in 1855 to inspire the defenders of Sevastopol probably influenced *lubok* publishers of the time). Although censorship laws underwent several changes in the years after 1851, most notably during the reigns of Alexander II and Nicholas II, the regulations of the 1851 law remained in place. Publishers such as Ivan Sytin had established a stranglehold on the production of popular pictures and maintained it for decades.

Concurrently, although the actual significance of Old Believer *lubki* continued to decline, government officials perceived this influence differently. Their perception helps to explain why government officials expressed constant concern about censoring the "people's pictures" and remained vigilant about enforcing the 1851 law despite the fact that most of the images differed very little from previous ones. As soon as war broke out in the Crimean peninsula in 1854, tsarist censors immediately began to concern themselves with the activities of the Old Believers. Ivan Snegirev, a leading Moscow censor responsible for *lubok* production, recorded in his diary on 3 August that he discussed "the affairs of the schismatics *[delam o raskol'nikakh]*" with several government officials and then asked for God's strength to deal with them.[78] After discussing with Bludov three days later the role of the *lubok* in spreading information, Snegirev returned to the Old Believer activities three more times before the end of the year.[79] He even met with the minister of internal affairs, Dmitrii Bibikov, who personally thanked Snegirev for his work in shutting down the publications of Old Believers. Bibikov told Snegirev that the tsar himself would hear about his vigilance, thanked the censor, and asked him to continue his good work.[80] With war raging in the Crimean peninsula, Russian officials clearly considered the Old Believers to be unreliable and even potentially traitorous. Censors such as Snegirev insured that the prints made by religious dissenters no longer circulated.

I. A. Golyshev, who helped one Moscow publisher make the transition to a lithographic press, also remembered the government's concern with Old Believers during the Crimean War. Efimov, the publisher, submitted all his wartime prints to the local censor, P. S. Delitsyn, who stamped his approval on such *lubki* as "Recruitment," "The Sultan's Son," and "Battle at Sinope," among others.[81] While Efimov and Delitsyn received no complaints about these images, the Metropolitan of Moscow, Filaret (Drozdov), reproached the censor for failing to submit for his review the religious images made during the war. As Delitsyn later explained to Efimov (who then recounted the tale to Golyshev), the metropolitan stated, "at that time [1854], the schismatics *[raskol'niki]* made different interpretations, which opposed the doctrine of the Orthodox church."[82] In other words, during the war against the Turks, the government and its officials did not worry about the patriotic messages presented in wartime *lubki,* but they did grow more concerned about the influence of Old Believer prints.

The fact that the war *lubok* did not trouble the imperial censors after 1851 did not make the life of a censor during wartime any easier. In addition, the censors responsible for popular images also inspected other printed materials during Russia's wars and found many to be inappropriate. In most of these cases, imperial censors arrested and fined publishers simply for failing to submit their pamphlets and other materials to the authorities.[83] While the patriotic images did not run afoul of the censors, at times Russian princes and other aristocrats did seek legal recourse against publishers who used their portraits in print without prior consent.[84] But the most heavily censored (and most closely watched) materials were newspaper articles and brochures. During the Russo-Turkish War of 1877–1878, for example, imperial censors prosecuted Russians who circulated antiwar letters in the form of a brochure as well as the publishers of *Russkii mir* and *Sankt-Peterburgskie vedomosti* for reporting details of casualties.[85] Similar cases can be found in later wars also, as in the case of the manuscripts entitled "Trial of the Heroes (A Fantasy)," "The Good Word of the Russian People," and "The Japanese in Sakhalin"; all brochures referred to the Moscow Censorship Committee in 1905 that featured defeatist attitudes.[86]

Even Ivan Sytin, the publisher of vast numbers of *lubki,* had frequent run-ins with the censors, but none of these incidents resulted from his popular prints. Sytin's association with Leo Tolstoy in the 1880s, when the two men collaborated on the Posrednik series of cheap books for the lower classes, first landed Sytin in trouble with the authorities.[87] When Sytin set about to revolutionize the Russian newspaper business, absorbing huge financial losses offset by the continued sales of his images, he claimed that his paper, *Russkoe slovo,* represented "loyal opposition." At no time was this claim more evident than during the Russo-Japanese War. Sytin's daily paper featured numerous stories by V. I. Nemirovich-Danchenko that attacked the conflict as "the blind war," one rife with mismanagement and incompetence.[88] In taking this stance, Sytin's paper met with repeated fines from the Moscow Censorship Committee, although sales boomed. By October 1904, the minister of the interior, V. K. Plehve, suspended street sales of *Russkoe slovo* (subscribers still received their copies), a ban enforced until December.[89] Despite these restrictions, Sytin's paper became the most popular in all of Russia. He continued to have problems with the censors, however, during the First World War, when anything deemed "depressing" was rejected.[90]

These examples suggest some reasons why the wartime image did not feature in the records of the St. Petersburg and Moscow Censorship Committees. Perhaps most significantly, *lubki* took more time to produce than newspaper stories, pamphlets, or brochures. *Lubok* publishers had to commission a print, have it drawn by one of their artists, and then have another employee write the text. Although images that depicted battle scenes could appear within a week of the actual event, this time lapse provided more than enough for publishers to determine if any part of the print's content was likely to attract the attention of a censor. In Sytin's case, his frequent run-ins with imperial censors over the content of *Russkoe slovo* would have made the publisher aware of what information was too sensitive.

A second, equally important reason the wartime *lubok* did not trouble imperial censors may stem from the language of the 1851 law governing their production. The patriotic image that the government held up as examples of positive prints—that is, *lubki* that had sold well in 1812—in all likelihood established a model for later publishers to follow when making their own wartime prints. Compared to the Old Believer *lubki*, wartime images were far more likely to contain themes that were acceptable to the government. While the law may not have changed the content of the popular prints significantly, it did spell out quite clearly what kinds of images were appropriate, and this may have contributed to *lubok* publishers' increased self-censorship.

The censorship of *lubki* in nineteenth-century Russia took place within a mutually reinforcing system. At the top, the Russian government opposed anything that it considered potentially harmful, and regulated anything not firmly under its control. Russian censors attempted to "abolish ambiguity" present in any cultural product, and the thrust of tsarist policy was to hide anything that offended autocracy and Orthodoxy. Censors went after a cultural producer only when he deliberately attempted to publish subversive materials.[91] *Lubok* publishers, for their part, produced their images underneath this censorship system. In order to avoid trouble, they stuck with patriotic themes deemed appropriate in the past and avoided deliberately subversive materials. In a sense, though, this self-censorship, combined with personal patriotic beliefs, suggested a rough affinity between censors, publishers, and the government on the concept of Russian national identity. The government may have passed laws in an effort to control wartime culture and instructed its censors to enforce these laws, but publishers held similar views on what this wartime culture should promote.

What the law of 1851 did not do, however, as even Rovinskii admitted, was make popular pictures less "popular." The complete takeover of the trade by large firms—a change that represented a move away from *lubok* production as a trade to an industry—meant that *lubok* publishers could afford to make more images and employ more peddlers to sell them. By the time of the Crimean War and certainly by the Russo-Turkish War of 1877–1878, the countryside and cities were flooded with images of war. The Russian government had overseen a change in the production of the *lubok* and had turned these images into semiofficial propaganda (or perhaps "propaganda from the side"), but they continued to sell well. Uvarov's recommendations in his 1816 letter, in addition to his general belief that the Russian people were influenced by the information in the *lubok* and could continue to be influenced by the information in the war *lubok,* were accepted by many Russian officials by 1851. After decades of discussing how to regulate these popular prints better and after several laws that attempted to meet Uvarov's call for better surveillance, the imperial government had succeeded in bringing the *lubok* under official control by 1851, even if this control had in many ways come about gradually rather than suddenly.

CONSOLIDATING WARTIME CULTURE
Images of Crimea, 1853–1856

[T]he enemy troops were beaten by the Moscow graphic artists.

—N. V. Davydov

• In the summer of 1854, Count Leo Tolstoy, then an officer in the Russian army, decided that he had had enough of sitting on the "sidelines" in Bucharest. Tolstoy despaired that his fellow soldiers were fighting bravely against the British on Russian land. He petitioned Prince Gorchakov, one of the most prominent Russian generals leading the war campaign, to allow him somewhere—anywhere—near the action. On 19 July, Tolstoy's request proved successful, and the young, patriotic officer set off for the front. Tolstoy reached Kishinev on 9 September, where he unsuccessfully attempted to found a patriotic newspaper for the common soldier.[1] Once inside this border town, however, he again begged to be sent closer to the "real" action. In late fall his request was granted and he arrived in Sevastopol, on the Crimean peninsula, on 7 November 1854.

Tolstoy reached the fortress in the midst of what came to be known as the Crimean War. Sevastopol proved to be the defining battle of that war and its lasting image in Russian culture. Tolstoy's experience there precipitated a profound change in the young man's philosophical outlook. By the end of the war, this once patriotic soldier who had begged to go nearer to the action became disillusioned by warfare in general and the Russian government's conduct of the war in particular. Tolstoy's disillusionment did not change his admiration for the heroism displayed by Russians of all ranks at Sevastopol, however, and this admiration, coupled with his increasing dismay, appeared quite clearly in the *Sevastopol Sketches*, composed in the midst of the war.

Tolstoy's three sketches recreated three separate months of the siege. The first, "Sevastopol in December," discussed the bravery of the defenders in patriotic prose. The second sketch, "Sevastopol in May," picked up the story the following spring, when disillusionment had set in. At the end of this sketch Tolstoy wrote, "The hero of my story, whom I love with all my heart and soul, . . . is now and will always be supremely magnificent, [it] is truth."[2] His third sketch, "Sevastopol in August 1855," presented a town where collapse was inevitable, where "a general instinct of self-preservation and a common desire to escape from this terrible place of death" gripped all of the remaining inhabitants.[3] Although the mood of the sketches went from outright patriotism to dissatisfaction, Tolstoy never lost his admiration for the resoluteness displayed by Sevastopol's defenders, writing to his brother Sergei, "The spirit of the army is beyond all description. There wasn't so much heroism in the days of ancient Greece."[4]

Tolstoy's attitudes toward war and patriotism, captured in his *Sevastopol Sketches,* are not peripheral to this study of Russian images. Tolstoy's experiences prompted him to become a writer,[5] and he intended to develop his "hero," truth, in other works dealing with war and history, particularly in his masterpiece *War and Peace.* Tolstoy's experience of wartime and his disillusionment with the conduct of the war led to a personal pacifism and critique of the Russian government. The exposure to war and wartime culture influenced Tolstoy to denounce the war *lubok* as a pernicious means by which the government exhorted Russians to fight. Although the *lubok* did not appear in his *Sevastopol Sketches,* it did play an important, if negative, role in *War and Peace.* Tolstoy's characterization of the *lubok* as official and untrustworthy propaganda became the dominant view among Russian intellectuals for most of the nineteenth century. Thus, the wartime experiences of the young officer in the Crimea played an important part in shaping elite attitudes toward the patriotic image. Furthermore, the idea that the *lubok* represented government propaganda, a belief popularized by writers such as Tolstoy, serves as a window into further understanding one of the wartime image's functions.

Tolstoy's description of Sevastopol and admiration for its defenders also helped to further the image of that fortress as a "hero city," a concept first developed within the patriotic images produced between 1853 and 1856. The Russian army may have lost in the field, but Russians displayed admirable courage and heroism in defending their homeland, just as a previous generation had done in 1812. Tolstoy's sketches form part of what can be termed "the myth of Sevastopol," which turned the Crimean port into an important component of Russian national identity. The war changed Tolstoy's thinking about patriotism and helped to shape his negative attitude toward any form of government propaganda, but it also renewed the author's belief in the "Russian spirit," a concept developed and promoted within the patriotic images themselves.

In the midst of the Crimean War, as Tolstoy arrived at the front, the Russian government released a new series of Terebenev's images from the Patriotic War to inspire the defenders of Sevastopol. New *lubki* depicting Kutuzov and other heroes of 1812 also appeared. These pictures incorporated iconographic images of the Patriotic War, particularly the Russian peasant and Cossack, and placed them in the context of the war against the Turks, English, French, and Piedmontese. The artists and publishers who produced them drew upon the themes established by Terebenev and his contemporaries, but by the 1850s the role of Orthodoxy had begun to be stressed even more as a source of Russian patriotism. Moreover, the 1851 law meant that a few publishers, through their relationships with imperial censors, played a more important role in the articulation of national identity seen in the images from the Crimean War.

The war proved to be a turning point in Russian history, one that provoked the crises leading to the Great Reforms of Alexander II.[6] Despite the fact that Russia's army was the largest and considered the strongest in all of Europe, in reality it functioned better on the parade ground than in combat. Nicholas I and his ministers, however, retained faith in the Russian military and in the myth of superiority that had entered their strategic thinking after 1812. They thus were willing to provoke a war with Turkey and France over a relatively minor dispute about Orthodox and Catholic rights in the Holy Land. Russian claims in Jerusalem and other sites, which were then under Ottoman control, were based on an interpretation of a 1774 treaty and were tenuous at best. The arrogance of Russian diplomats sent to Constantinople in 1853 soon became evident to the Turks, who rightly believed that neither Great Britain nor France would idly stand by for Russian aggression in the Middle East. Turkish officials rebuffed Prince A. S. Menshikov, the tsar's envoy, after he had threatened and bullied the Turks into accepting Russian authority in the Holy Land. At the beginning of July 1853, Russian troops entered the Turkish principalities of Moldavia and Wallachia. Turkey declared war after several unsuccessful diplomatic moves, and France and Britain joined Turkey in the spring. The Crimean War, which one contemporary dubbed a "curious and unnecessary war," had begun.[7]

The war itself proved as curious and unnecessary as its origins. For nearly a year after Russia's entry into Turkish territory very little happened. Russia destroyed the Turkish fleet at the Black Sea port of Sinope on 18 November 1853, but then Nicholas I's military remained idle for the rest of the winter. This action provoked the British and French into action, and they officially declared war in March 1854. Over the course of the summer, however, both Russia and her adversaries attempted to reach a diplomatic solution, again to no avail. In September 1854, French and British troops landed on the Crimean peninsula and fought against the Russians in the battles of Alma, Balaklava (which featured the famous Charge of the Light Brigade), and Inkerman. Within a month the allies began a bombardment of Sevastopol, an action that became the symbol of the war's senselessness. Despite being outnumbered, the excellent fortifications at Sevastopol allowed the Russians to hold out for almost a year. Ultimately, however, the weaknesses of the Russian military and its transportation systems were too much to overcome. In the midst of the siege, Nicholas I died, leaving his son Alexander II to deal with the Russian losses, which amounted to over 500,000 men.[8] After ceding a large amount of territory and the rights to any naval bases on the Black Sea in the Treaty of Paris, Russia ended the war, yet its legacy proved immense. Alexander II, forced to deal with the realities of Russian inadequacies, embarked on a series of reforms designed to improve Russian military, economic, and social structures. In popular memory, however, the Crimean War became associated largely with the heroism of Russian defenders at Sevastopol, a memory in part fueled by *lubki* produced during the war.

This chapter examines the popular memory of the war by examining the popular images of the war. The changes the tsar and his officials embarked upon as a result of the Crimean debacle had not been advocated in the themes of Russian patriotism depicted in the war's images. However, it is plausible to suggest that the continued promotion of Russianness and its iconographic image of the Russian peasant, a depiction that had aroused a great deal of controversy after Napoleon's invasion, helped contribute to the general abolitionist culture in the wake of Crimea. Above all, however, the images from the period 1853–1856 articulated a specific Russian national identity and elaborated on the myth of 1812. Although the war was a disaster for Russia, it did not stop *lubki* artists from stressing the bravery of the Russian peasant and Cossack, and the spirit of Russians who defended Sevastopol, or from identifying Orthodoxy even more explicitly as a source of Russianness.

In addition, the popular pictures from the years 1853–1856 provided caricatures of the Turkish and English enemies that would reappear in later wars. The stereotype of the Turk depicted in these images of war became the standard one for all Islamic peoples in Russian popular culture.[9] Despite the apocalyptic losses in the war, the popular images presented the conflict as a triumph of the "Russian spirit" and its defining quality, the Orthodox faith, over the Turks. This chapter delves into how the wartime *lubok* functioned as propaganda, which in a broad sense the *lubki* certainly were, although not in the official sense that Tolstoy believed.[10]

Re-emphasizing Russianness

The Russian government reissued Terebenev's images in order to exhort Russians to defend their homeland again at the same time that new *lubki* appeared. Popular images from Crimea not only served as a means of defining the interpretation of that war; they also emphasized traits first made prominent in the myths and memory of the war against Napoleon. While individual artists such as Terebenev played the dominant role in articulating the themes in the images from 1812 to 1815, during the Crimean War the definition of Russian national identity within the *lubki* came from the major publishers of the *lubok*. Entrepreneurs such as Petr Sharapov took advantage of the commercial changes in the *lubok* industry aided by the 1851 law and created lasting images of the conflict.

The iconographic figures of the Russian peasant and Cossack again dominated popular pictures devoted to the Crimean War. The print "By Order of the Don Cossack Troops near Novocherkassk, 15 May 1855" depicts an impressive rank of troops near the Cossack capital.[11] The *lubok* features a formidable Cossack general on horseback reviewing his troops before a battle, with the background revealing a glimpse of the town of Novocherkassk and the rolling hills of the region. Reminiscent of the depiction of Kutuzov and other troops from the Patriotic War, this image and others like it reaffirm the Cossack as an important aspect of Russian patriotic identity.[12]

"The English Attack the Fisherman's Hut" emphasizes the positive characteristics of the Russian peasant in the Crimean War.[13] The *lubok* depicts a peasant's hut, or *khizhina,* with a prominent fireplace and a table. The interior is filled with over a dozen English soldiers, who harass the owners, a Russian peasant and his wife. One soldier is stealing goods from the mantle of the peasant, a fisherman, while a second soldier ties up one of the peasant's cows. Two more Englishmen visible outside the hut capture a second cow, while their comrades inside grab food off the table. Two soldiers detain the Russian, who stands stoically with his arms apart while the enemy ransacks his home. His wife stands to the left, leaning against a hoe, while their cat sleeps soundly near the fireplace. The image conveys a sense of the peasant's helplessness in the face of overwhelming numbers of marauding Englishmen, but also his pride and dignity in such a situation. The fisherman, as the text notes, passively yet heroically stands up to the enemy.

Unlike those of the Patriotic War, the images from Crimea did not feature the Russian tsar in an active role. Nicholas I appeared only in a handful of portraits, and they did not connect him to the ongoing war,[14] while Alexander II made only one appearance in an image entitled "The Emperor in Sevastopol Reviews and Blesses Sailors in October 1855."[15] The virtual absence of the tsar from the patriotic images of the war can be explained in two ways. First, the fact that Russia ultimately lost the war meant that the tsar did not want to be associated with Russia's defeat. Second, Nicholas I had personally approved a law that strictly regulated his image, and publishers were wary of this. As Richard Wortman notes, the effects of the 1825 Decembrist revolt played a significant role in the articulation of Nicholas's image to the rest of Russia. Stressing the family and the tsar's primogeniture signaled not only major innovations in the image of the autocrat, but also Nicholas's personal interest in its application. Oddly enough, although Nicholas desired to establish the image of the monarch as the most important symbol of the Russian nation, he remained more concerned with becoming the "embodiment of the nation" than with promoting his individual image, as his brother, Alexander I, had.[16] Nicholas preferred portraits of himself that stressed the figure of the tsar as a symbol of Russianness but did not have images made that showed him taking an active role in events. At the same time, Alexander II was linked only tangentially to the "victory" of Sevastopol. Nonetheless, the popular prints from Crimea marked an important departure from the patriotic themes of the war against Napoleon. The tsar, often considered the most important figurehead of Russian national identity, made only sporadic appearances in popular wartime imagery for the remainder of the nineteenth century.[17]

Though the Crimean War images left out the tsar, they did establish a new feature of the war *lubok* that would reappear in later wars. Popular prints praised individuals by name for their heroic actions in the war, and in the process furthered the construction of "Russianness" and its attributes begun in the images from 1812. "The Heroic Deed of Private Semen Kovalenko" illustrates this type of image. The print depicts a group of five Russian soldiers standing behind defensive fortifications. In the background one can see a Turkish fortress, distinguishable by the Muslim crescent moon on the tops of its minarets. A cannonball rests precariously close to the Russians, smoking ominously. The Russian soldier closest to the danger, identified as Private Kovalenko, has turned to his comrades, his arms outstretched. As the text of the print explains, this grenade landed near the Russian soldiers, and Private Kovalenko "quickly leapt over the embankment, grasped the shell, and threw it away." The text also quotes Kovalenko's commander, who praised his soldier's bravery and selfless deed in risking his life to protect his fellow soldiers, noting that Kovalenko's faith in God allowed him to perform this heroic act.[18] Much like previous wartime images, this one had a factual basis: Leo Tolstoy noted in a letter that "soldiers extract the fuses from bombs" at Sevastopol.[19]

Similar images appeared throughout the war. Another one produced at the same time as Kovalenko's, also near the fortress of Silistria, praised the actions of Stepan Tolstokorov,[20] while several prints in 1854 recalled the "victory of Andrei Siuzik," a Russian private who seized the flag from a fallen comrade and inspired his troops to continue the fight.[21] Two prints praised the "victory" of gunner Chilikin, who, despite suffering from a head wound, remained at his post during the siege of Sevastopol in 1854.[22] A second gunner, Ivan Ragozhin, also appeared as a popular hero in the images of the time.[23] Collectively, these images helped to link far-off battles with real people, and thus they highlight the *lubok*'s role in spreading a certain interpretation of the war, even if this information was glamorized. *Lubok* publishers recast the "Russian spirit," first discussed in the images from 1812, in terms of the heroic deeds performed by individual soldiers in battle. Like the actions of Russian soldiers and peasants during the Napoleonic invasion, the source of this heroism and selflessness often was attributed to the Orthodox faith all Russians followed and their love for their fellow soldiers.

Perhaps the most famous of these individual heroes of Crimea was Petr Koshka, a real-life Ukrainian soldier who fought in the war. "The Victory of the Sailor Petr Koshka" helped to make this sailor's feats legendary (Figure 4.1).[24] The *lubok* is set against the backdrop of the mountainous Crimean region. On the left side of the image, the Russian fortress of Sevastopol aims its cannons at English soldiers, who are approaching the city. Five Russian soldiers point in astonishment at the exploits of a sixth, who is carrying an injured comrade from battle. The hero is identified as Petr Koshka, a Ukrainian who had "constantly distinguished himself through bravery" over the course of the war. In this incident, Koshka volunteered to rescue an injured comrade trapped in front of the Russian lines of defense. After asking for God's blessing, Koshka set out to rescue his comrade and successfully returned with him. This feat not only earned him "general respect" among Russians,

4.1 "The Victory of the Sailor Petr Koshka" The *lubki* from the Crimean War (1853–1856) frequently celebrated the "Russian spirit" as embodied in individual Russian soldiers. Petr Koshka, depicted in this image rescuing an injured comrade as he dodges bullets, became one of the most famous heroes from the war. Reprinted by permission of the State Historical Museum, Moscow [GIM]

but "astounded the English" (Koshka, the text notes, successfully dodged five enemy bullets in the course of the action).

Koshka's deeds contributed to the catalog of heroism depicted in the images of war of the time. During the Soviet era, Koshka became an emblem of nascent Ukrainian nationalism, appearing in several accounts of the siege of Sevastopol as "proof" of the heroism displayed by non-Russians during the siege.[25] In the 1850s, however, Koshka represented just one of several "Russian" heroes singled out for praise in the *lubki* of the time. Russian heroism and selflessness became one of the defining traits of the "Russian spirit" that in turn illustrated Russianness. Popular imagery during the Crimean conflict again depicted Russian peasants and Cossacks performing "victories" and "heroic deeds," and used the themes of the Napoleonic images to illustrate these actions. Russian heroism served as the perfect foil for the Turkish enemy, the "other" against whom Russianness could be defined in this conflict.

Stereotyping the Enemy: The Turk

Defining the enemy has always been an important component of fighting wars, for the practice enables soldiers to fight and helps to rally popular support. The *lubki* from the years 1853–1856 provided this function in

4.2 "The Praiseworthy Deed of Ensign Kudriavtsev" Petr Sharapov's 1854 *lubok* contrasts the heroism of the average Russian soldier with the "true nature" of the Turkish enemy. The setting is inside a Russian Orthodox church, where a Russian soldier named Kudriavtsev inspires his fellow troops to kill the infidel who had violated the church and murdered its priest. Reprinted by permission of the State Historical Museum, Moscow [GIM]

Russia, although *lubok* producers made clear distinctions among Russia's enemies in the war. The English and French, while stereotyped in the war *lubok* as money-grubbers, were not the same as the Turkish soldiers, who were depicted as a savage, inferior people. Representations of the Turk dominated the Crimean War images devoted to the enemy. In many ways the *lubki* defined the war itself as a religious one, stemming from the origins of the conflict and the official culture under Nicholas I that stressed Orthodoxy as an important part of Russian identity. Images of Turkish atrocities, real or imagined, appeared throughout the war, as did numerous references to the Turk's "insidiousness." Above all, the *lubki* stressed that Turkish behavior stemmed from the Muslim faith, which artists contrasted with Christianity, the source of the "Russian soul."[26]

The print "The Praiseworthy Deed of Ensign Kudriavtsev" (Figure 4.2), from the firm of Petr Sharapov and approved by Ivan Snegirev on 6 June 1854, links the heroism of the common Russian soldier with the "true nature" of the Turkish enemy.[27] The image is set in the interior of an Orthodox church, easily recognizable by the icons that adorn its columns and the cross prominently represented on the altar. Three Russian soldiers, led by ensign Kudriavtsev, kill four Turks who have broken into the church and murdered its priest. The dead Orthodox clergyman lies on the left side of the image, his hand clutching at his heart. Two of the Turkish soldiers grasp items taken from the church, leaving little doubt regarding the reason for their entrance. The text of the *lubok* alleges that "several Turks" broke into a church within the war zone, intending to steal its icons and other religious treasures. Despite the murder of the priest, Kudriavtsev and his fellow soldiers have saved the church from Turkish attempts to defile it.

Alleged Turkish atrocities, usually committed within Russian churches, became a standard feature of images from the Crimean War and formed the basis for a wide variety of prints from the Russo-Turkish War of 1877–1878. The dramatic scene of the print above linked the ideas of Russian heroism from other images of war and contrasted this characteristic with the Turkish enemy, who did not shy away from murdering priests. In a similar fashion, the association of Orthodoxy with both Russianness and the Russian spirit clashed with the Muslim faith of the Turkish invaders, clearly portrayed as inferior and lacking morals in this and other images. While several *lubki* from 1812 referred to the French as "infidels," the popular prints from the Crimean War depicted a visual stereotype of the Turk as a savage infidel.

The images of war from Crimea also portrayed the Turks as weak and cowardly foes, recalling the characteristics attributed to the French in 1812 (and indeed an important aspect of emasculating one's enemy). The *lubok* "Turks Flee After the Turkish Pasha is Captured by Russian Troops" presents the Turks as timid.[28] This battle *lubok* features a Turkish pasha on horseback surrounded by three Cossacks. The pasha's exotic clothes and black horse provide a stark contrast to the Cossack uniforms and white horses of his captors. To the right of this scene stands an impressive column of Russian soldiers and Cossack troops, prominently displaying their banners, both Russian and the captured Turkish ones—thus visually linking the Turkish pasha's capture with the overall superiority of the Russian forces. The background of the image contains a Turkish fortress with the spires of its mosques clearly discernible, and a large number of Turkish troops fleeing toward the safety of the city. A smaller number of Cossack troops gives chase to the enemy, who have abandoned their leader in the midst of battle. The image contains no text other than the title and the names of the publisher and censor, yet the message of the print is quite clear. Despite having larger numbers and fighting on more familiar turf, the Turks have fled rather than fight Russian troops, choosing to run from a battle—and in the process leave their leader—to avoid loss of life. Compared to the numerous images that portrayed Russian soldiers willing to sacrifice their lives for the sake of other comrades, this popular print depicts a cowardly, inferior foe that lacked the spirit displayed by the Russians.[29]

A large number of images reinforced this sense of Russian superiority face to face with the Turkish foe even more strikingly. Popular prints such as "The Capture of the Turkish Fortress Kars on 16 November 1855" leave little doubt as to the differences between Russians and Turks.[30] This *lubok* portrays one of the great successes of the Russian army in the Crimean War. The Turks surrender to their Russian conquerors at the city gates. The right side of the print showcases the massed ranks of the Russian forces, whose tight formations and raised double-headed eagle banners convey a sense of military might. One Cossack general on horseback prominently leads Russian troops and oversees the surrender. A large number of Turks, both soldiers and civilians, kneel before their victors, recalling the images of 1812 in which French soldiers begged their Russian conquerors for forgiveness. Turkish leaders at the front of these kneeling ranks present the Cossack general with food and with their own symbols of authority. Most strikingly, a large Russian imperial banner bearing the double-headed eagle now dominates the fortress of Kars, which forms the background of the picture. The banner overshadows the minarets of Kars's mosques, conveying a visual image of Russian (and Christian) superiority. The text of the image reaffirms this claim, praising the "unshakeable heroism and bravery of the Cossack troops," who surrounded the city and cut off supplies to its residents. Confronted with hunger and the Cossack forces, the leaders of the fortress were "forced to give Kars" to their conquerors.

The acquisition of Kars became the subject for several other popular images of the time, all of which featured Turkish troops kneeling before their captors, whose banners fly prominently over the fortress.[31] Images of victory at Kars captured many of the themes of the popular images from the Crimean War. First, they celebrated one of the few actual victories of the Russian army in the war (although as shall be seen, *lubok* publishers presented the site of Russia's greatest defeat, Sevastopol, as a victory of sorts). This victory came against the "real" enemy, the Turks, who were no match for their Russian counterparts. The Turkish troops and leaders in the images of Kars display the cowardice prominent in other depictions of the Turkish enemy of the time. The contrast between the victorious Russians and the defeated Turks, reinforced by the visual image of the Russian flag flying above the Turkish mosques, conveys a sense of Russian superiority. These themes became the foundation of the images from the Russo-Turkish War of 1877–1878 and helped to establish stereotypes of Turkic peoples in Russian culture that remained well into the twentieth century.

The Holy War: Orthodoxy and Russian National Identity

While the popular pictures from Napoleon's invasion referred to Orthodoxy only marginally, the images from Crimea placed it at the center of the definition of Russian national identity. The *lubki* attempted to make clear that the source of bravery and the "Russian soul" stemmed from Orthodoxy, as a means of contrasting the Russian religion with that of Russia's most insidious foe. By stressing the role of the Orthodox faith as a source of Russian inspiration, the *lubki* served as an ideal means of reinforcing the inferiority of the Turkish enemy in visual culture. *Lubok* publishers depicted Russian triumphs as a victory for the Russian faith and simultaneously suggested that Orthodoxy was superior to Islam.

"For God a Prayer, For the Tsar Service Is Not Wasted" clearly attempts to link Russian identity with the Orthodox faith and trust in the tsar.[32] Russian troops and Cossacks stand near Kars. A group of eight Cossacks circle each other on horseback, preparing to enter into battle. They raise their swords and pledge their commitment to their God and to their tsar, into whose service they enter. The ground around these soldiers is littered with corpses of comrades who have sacrificed their lives for these ideals, while a group of fellow soldiers charges ahead toward the Turkish fortress. The resoluteness on the faces of these Cossacks reinforces the sense of calmness that the soldiers experience before entering into battle, a feeling stemming from their firm devotion to faith and their cause.[33]

A series of prints commissioned during the war and meant to provoke outrage among viewers clearly defined Orthodoxy as an important feature of Russianness. The *lubok* "Bombardment of the Stavropigial'nyi Solovetskii [Solovki] Monastery in the White Sea" portrays a tangential theater of the war. English vessels bomb a defenseless Orthodox monastery located in the White Sea. The spires of cathedrals located within the monastery are in the path of several shells about to fall inside the walls of the compound, while a line of the priests and monks who live there stands outside of the main cathedral. They clutch the valuable icons and other religious treasures now under fire, defenseless although resolute.[34]

Other images gave Russian priests a more active role in the conflict. The Sharapov print "The Victory of Father Savinov" (Figure 4.3) features an impressive battle scene comprising dozens of Russian troops engaged in hand-to-hand combat with their English counterparts in the Kamchatka peninsula, another remote (and often ignored) theater of the war.[35] In the midst of the Russian troops stands a priest, Father Savinov, who holds a cross toward the advancing army, blessing them before the battle. The text of the image states that the Russians successfully "threw the enemy out of the Kamchatka peninsula" in this battle, but only as a result of the "victory" of Father Savinov. The troops, initially afraid at the "onslaught of the enemy," were calmed by the actions of Savinov, who plunged into the fray and blessed each soldier with the words "the glory of God is with us!" Savinov also chanted Orthodox prayers, which "animated the troops," who then defeated the enemy. Like many of the images mentioned above, this one had a basis in reality, for soldiers such as Leo Tolstoy commented at the time on the role priests played in inspiring their soldiers.[36]

That the *lubki* from the Crimean War explicitly featured the Orthodox faith as the source of the "Russian spirit" and as an inspiration for Russian

4.3 "The Victory of Father Savinov" While images such as the previous one contained Russian soldiers hurrying to defend their faith, other prints highlighted the role of Orthodoxy as a source of Russianness. Here an Orthodox priest, as the text notes, calmed his soldiers by plunging into the battle and shouting, "The glory of God is with us!" Based on actual events during the war reported by Leo Tolstoy, among others, "The Victory of Father Savinov" connects the "Russian spirit" of previous wartime images with the Orthodox faith. Reprinted by permission of the State Historical Museum, Moscow [GIM]

troops is not surprising, given the culture of Nicholas I's Russia. As the last chapter showed, Russian officials viewed censorship as a means of instilling the principles of Uvarov's "official nationality." The prints from the Crimean War represented an ideal vehicle for promoting Orthodoxy as an important component of Russian patriotic belief and national identity. They are filled with references to the faith of the Russian troops, particularly in the numerous battle *lubki* of the years 1853–1856, images that stressed the notion that Russian heroism stemmed in large part from the Orthodox faith.[37] In addition, the examples above demonstrate the various ways in which *lubok* publishers attempted to link Orthodoxy explicitly to the "victories" that Russian troops enjoyed, from triumphant liberation of fellow Orthodox citizens to victories won on the battlefield because of the reassuring presence of Orthodox priests. Nowhere, however, was the link between Orthodoxy and Russian patriotism more explicit than in the images that depicted the siege of Sevastopol as a Russian victory, transforming the Crimean town into a "city of glory."

4.4 "Sevastopol" The Crimean War may have ended in devastating defeat for the Russians, but images such as this one cast the defense of Sevastopol as a "victory" of the Russian spirit. Residents, priests, and soldiers alike gather in front of the fortress to hear an inspirational sermon delivered by Archbishop Innokentii, who attempted to rally Russians around their faith during the war. Reprinted by permission of the State Historical Museum, Moscow [GIM]

Making More Myths: Sevastopol and Russian National Identity

The bombing of Sevastopol, a Russian port on the Crimean peninsula, proved to be the dominant symbol of the Crimean War, both in the war images from 1853 to 1856 and in later cultural expressions. War *lubki* depicted the English bombardment as an example of the heroism and faith of the Russian defenders, and in turn presented the defense of the fortress as a "victory." Sevastopol entered Russian popular culture as the defining term for this war, which came to be called the "Crimean" War largely as a result of this focus on Sevastopol—despite the fact that battles took place in the north, in Anatolia, and in Kamchatka. Moreover, the focus on Sevastopol in the popular prints of the war represented one of the first instances of labeling this city as an important site of Russian national identity. The city, which had only come under Russian control during the eighteenth century, became a "city of glory" after 1855, and entered the pantheon of names associated with Russian national identity, such as Borodino.[38]

The 1855 Sharapov print simply entitled "Sevastopol" (Figure 4.4) captures the themes present in a number of *lubki* devoted to the siege.[39] The detailed image features the city in the background, resplendent with picturesque houses and churches. To the left, in the Black Sea, four English ships approach, preparing to shell the fortress and destroy its beauty. Rather than inducing panic, this impending battle brings out steadfastness on the part of Russians of all classes, depicted by the action taking place just outside the city walls. These defenders of Sevastopol include the uniformed ranks of Russian soldiers on the left, impressive in their formations and displaying their standards. To the right stand more troops, fronted by their officers, their caps in their hands. The center features a number of Orthodox priests, who have removed the icons and religious objects from Sevastopol's cathedrals in order to lead a mass prayer service. Behind the priests townspeople are gathered, including men and women dressed in the clothes of merchants (or other people of the middle ranks) and a number of peasants. The uniform courage displayed by all Russians in Sevastopol became a defining feature of numerous images of the time, and in this print as well as others, Orthodoxy formed the source of this determination.

The lengthy text of "Sevastopol" adds further depth to its visual message. The action takes place on "Sunday, 26 June at seven in the morning," when the priests of the Mikhailovskii Cathedral, together with Russian leaders such as Gorchakov, decided to demonstrate their faith. The archbishop of the cathedral, Innokentii, "pronounced moving words regarding the present events." Turning to the generals and their troops, the archbishop then blessed all of them, stating "brave troops, Holy Russia prays for you, and as a blessed sign sends these holy icons, a sign of our strength." The troops then cried in "one voice": "God grant us council in our endeavor!" The text ends with a note that "the scene was very moving."[40]

This image summarized the role of the Orthodox church in promoting Russian national identity during the war itself. Archbishop Innokentii enthusiastically rallied Russians to the cause of church and state. His sermons were widely published during the conflict as a means to inspire Russians to defeat the Turkish enemy. One report claimed that Innokentii's sermons "served to raise spirits and to comfort the residents and to support the city with peace and order during an extremely grave time," while the tsar and the Holy Synod passed an ukase formally recognizing Archbishop Innokentii for "pastoral zealousness" during the bombarding of Odessa.[41] In the eyes of Russian authorities, Innokentii embodied the spirit of all Russians who fused their faith with their commitment to the Russian state.[42]

Two prints that depict actual battles on the Crimean peninsula featured priests playing a prominent role in the action, much like the "victory" of Father Savinov discussed above. "The Defeat of the Fourth Anglo-French Crossing along the Ochakov Cape, on the Black Sea" features a detailed battle scene on land and in the sea.[43] Several English and French ships assault a Crimean fortress, while enemy troops approach the land. The Russian defenders, who include a large number of artillerymen, work with their cannons. A Russian officer commands these troops on horseback behind the walls of the fortress, but in front of the commander stands a solitary priest.

Holding a cross aloft, the priest blesses the troops as they engage in battle, a contributing factor to the successful repulsing of the attack, as the title and text note. "The Operation on the Ochakov Cape" depicts the same event with one major change. In this *lubok,* which focuses on a group of nine Russian cannoneers, a priest identified as Father Golovachev in the text aids the soldiers more explicitly. Holding a cross in one hand, Golovachev hands a cannonball to a soldier with his other. The Russian then places the cannonball into the cannon, helped by the priest. The text explains that Golovachev, who had approached the Nikolai battery to bless and inspire them in battle, has come to the aid of an injured soldier while continuing to perform his priestly duties.[44]

The Iakovlev print "A Sortie from Sevastopol" further emphasized the patriotic behavior of Russian soldiers at the Crimean town.[45] The Russians have left Sevastopol at night in an attempt to gauge the strength of the enemy, but have stumbled upon a French squad. The heroes, clearly distinguishable by the imperial standard on their headgear, engage in a desperate struggle against the enemy in an effort to protect Sevastopol from further destruction. This battle scene stresses the fighting prowess and bravery of the Russian troops, particularly in hand-to-hand combat, long considered a strength of Russian armies. The text quotes an article from *Moskovskie vedomosti* that discussed the actual incident presented in the *lubok.* The skirmish, as the article noted, occurred during the night of 8–9 October 1854, when a small group of Russian troops set out on a nighttime reconnaissance mission near Sevastopol. The twenty-seven Russians who comprised this squadron stumbled upon the entire crew of the French Thirty-Third Fleet, also engaged in nighttime intelligence work. Despite the overwhelming odds, the Russians forced the Frenchmen back, preventing a potential surprise attack on the port. Recalling images from the Patriotic War, when Russian troops overwhelmed superior numbers of French invaders,[46] the text notes that the emperor, Nicholas I, became aware of this display of heroism and patriotic devotion and rewarded the troops with fifty silver rubles each.[47]

Several other prints of the time depicted large-scale battles around Sevastopol,[48] scenes of Russian cannoneers with labels explaining the famous sites of the city,[49] spectacular battle scenes between Russian Cossacks and Turkish troops just outside Sevastopol's walls,[50] and a view of the most spectacular lookout of the fortress, complete with portraits of the generals who led its defense,[51] among other examples. These images represented one of the first expressions of what Serhii Plokhy has termed "the myth of Sevastopol,"[52] which stressed the heroism of Russian troops in a conflict that resulted in defeat for the army but a "victory" for Russian heroism and the "Russian spirit." Because of such heroism, Sevastopol became a "sacred space," a site of patriotism and national identity that transformed the Crimean city into a "city of Russian glory" that represents a symbol of Russia's "glorious past."[53] As Plokhy notes, Sevastopol became a place of national veneration and "served as an important component of the new national mythology."[54] Much like Borodino, Sevastopol was celebrated as a victory, however dubious the claims, because Russian heroism had saved the homeland from foreign invasion. Part of this myth included the veneration of heroes of Sevastopol, such as the images celebrating individual acts of Russian heroism noted above.[55]

By the turn of the twentieth century, Sevastopol had become "one of the most venerated places of the [Russian] empire," with new monuments being added to the city and a museum of the defense of Sevastopol opened in 1890 as further examples of the enshrinement of the myth.[56] The Crimean city, annexed by Russian tsars only seventy years before the war, was now an important part of the Russia nation, a fact that continues to have present-day ramifications in Russian-Ukrainian relations.[57] In 1856, however, when the war ended, the "myth of Sevastopol" had already begun to take hold in Russian society, and the images of the Crimean War represented one of the founding sources of this myth.[58] Thus, the first expression of this myth came from the *lubok* publishers who produced images celebrating the defense of Sevastopol and the tsarist censors who approved them.[59]

Regulating Crimean Culture: Censors and Publishers

The journal *Otechestvennye zapiski* (Notes of the Fatherland) included a section entitled "Petersburg Notes" every month. Its author would record the major events, debates, trends, and goings-on in Russia's capital in every edition. With war raging in April 1855, everyone in Petersburg seemed to be discussing the defense of Sevastopol. That month's "Petersburg Notes" observed that everyone talked about the heroism of the Russian troops and the events of the war in general. Although many residents received news of the war from various journals, the author of "Petersburg Notes" also mentioned another source for news—the *lubok*. "The number of pictures devoted to wartime matters—a production of Moscow lithography—increases with every day."[60] Moscow publishers such as Rudnev and Efimov had produced so many images by April 1855 that they issued a collected album available in St. Petersburg's stores. The following month's issue again took note of the increasing number of popular images available in the capital, as did June's.[61] By July the author of "Petersburg Notes" simply stated in the column: "still more caricatures that have to do with contemporary events came out," including some that compared the events of 1855 with those of 1812.[62]

Sixty years after the Crimean War began, N. V. Davydov published his memoirs of childhood years, *Iz proshlogo* (From the Past). Despite the decades that separated him from the war, Davydov also vividly recalled the number of patriotic *lubki* in his hometown of Moscow. According to him, the pictures took the place of newspapers for many of the "simple public," who reveled in their depiction of the bravery and heroism of the Russian troops. Recalling one image that featured a caricature of the English, French, and Turkish enemies, Davydov labeled it and others like it "ultra-patriotic [*ul'tra-patrioticheskii*]." Although Russia suffered losses on the battlefield, Davydov wryly observed that the enemy troops "were beaten by the Moscow graphic artists."[63]

Davydov's recollections, alongside the documentation of the author of "Petersburg Notes," are an important starting point for discussing the role of the publishers and censors in developing the themes of Russian patriotic culture, as well as a way into exploring the images as propaganda. Although the 1851 law did not change the content of the wartime *lubok,* as the examples discussed above make clear, the relationship between governmental control and *lubok* production nevertheless remained an important one. This bond continued to be negotiated in future wars between different people, but in general a basic association emerged that lasted until 1917. Government censors approved the work of the *lubok* publishers who produced the images of war during and after Crimea, and an examination of their relationship sheds light on the nature of wartime culture.

Tsarist censors during the time of the Crimean War lived a precarious yet privileged life. On the one hand, the responsibility of approving materials for publication could land a censor in jail, as the life of Aleksandr Nikitenko illustrated. On the other hand, censors by and large came from the noble class, had access to a wide range of published materials that other Russians did not, and were considered invaluable servants in the eyes of the government. The career of one of the censors who regulated popular imagery during the Crimean War illustrates this point.

Ivan Mikhailovich Snegirev was one of the leading figures on the Moscow Censorship Committee during the 1853–1856 war.[64] Born in 1792, Ivan Mikhailovich attended the schools of the Moscow elite and graduated from Moscow University (where his father worked as a professor). By 1815, he had earned a master's degree from its language department. The following year, he accepted an appointment as a professor of Latin. Because of his interest in Roman antiquities, Snegirev began a series of studies on the folklore and national characteristics of his native land. In particular, he became very interested in Russian national architecture (particularly the histories of famous cathedrals), national holidays, and proverbs.

Snegirev was sixty-one years old at the start of the Crimean War, had risen to the rank of state councilor, and had received several imperial decorations for his service to the state.[65] He had distinguished himself as an effective censor since the 1830s, receiving high marks from his superiors and avoiding any trouble with the government during his lengthy career.[66] Snegirev in particular regulated popular images and developed an interest in the origins and cultural importance of the *lubok,* eventually publishing a book on the subject, *Lubok Pictures of the Russian People in the Moscow World,* in 1861.[67] Because of his high stature and the specifics of the 1851 law regarding *lubok* publishing, Snegirev's name appears on numerous prints from the war.

Snegirev became an important observer both of the images themselves and of their significance within Russian culture. The primary censor of *lubki* during the Crimean War, Snegirev personally approved their patriotic themes and contents (he also, interestingly enough, was an acquaintance of Archbishop Innokentii, one of the heroes of the war). His biographers, as well as his own yearly statements made to the Moscow Censorship Committee, testify not only to his great intellectual curiosity, but also to his unwavering support of the existing socioeconomic system in Russia.[68] His work on popular prints has earned him the label of a pioneer in Russian ethnography because of his zeal, intellect, and energy.

In the 1820s, when he had just become a censor, Snegirev startled educated society by declaring that the *lubok* was worthy of scholarly investigation.[69] Nearly forty years later, in 1861 and after he had written a series of books on Russian churches and their importance in developing a Russian national identity, Snegirev published the first serious study of the *lubok* in Russian history.[70] Dmitrii Bludov personally approved the idea for the book during the Crimean War, when Snegirev served as chief censor for pictures.[71] With its publication, Snegirev developed the first—and still predominant—interpretation of the definition of *lubok*. Already in an 1822 paper he had argued that it came from *lub,* the inner bark of the linden tree used to make crude paper upon which images were printed.[72] In his book, Snegirev traced the history of the genre in Russia, noting that it originally appealed to both upper and lower classes, who wanted a cheap alternative to icons. The *lubki* lost favor with the upper strata of society, Snegirev noted, but retained a broad appeal both in towns and villages. Snegirev established the first classification system for cataloging the themes of the *lubok* and grouped the images around five dominant subjects: religious and moral, philosophical commentaries on daily life, judicial topics, wars and past events, and legends or folkloric images.[73]

Especially valuable were Snegirev's comments on the importance of the *lubok* in daily life and on its general reception among its audience. In light of the lack of sources regarding the reception of these images, Snegirev's comments provide an important glimpse into the role of the *lubok,* and particularly the war *lubki* from the Crimean War, in Russian culture. Although Snegirev the author operated under the same constraints that Snegirev the censor enforced, he proved himself to be a dedicated scholar and ethnographer, a fact that even Soviet histories recognized.[74] Thus, his conclusions about the *lubok,* however biased, should be taken quite seriously.

In a letter to a friend written in 1844, Snegirev formulated the assessment of the popular prints that he would develop further in his 1861 book. He wrote that they represented "attitudes toward nationality *[otnoshenii k narodnosti]*" and an ideal means of understanding "the inner life of the people."[75] In his 1861 assessment, Snegirev noted that he had studied the popular prints for over thirty years and that he considered them a vital "display of Russian nationality [narodnost']" and a versatile combination of traditional applied arts.[76] He connected the *lubok* with national songs, holidays, and other expressions of daily life in Russia that represent "a close connection with history and national life."[77] For Snegirev, the influence of these pictures was immense, for they could be found "in the tsar's chambers, a boyar's mansion, and a peasant's hut," a fact that attested to their widespread appeal.[78]

Commenting on the images of the Patriotic War, Snegirev noted that the Russian government "used the caricatures as a means for exciting in the people an eagerness to protect the fatherland from a powerful enemy."[79] Snegirev documented the widespread appeal of the wartime images, which captured the "funny and the farcical combined with the awful and even disgusting" features of that war, particularly the French retreat from Moscow.[80] This popularity continued into the Crimean War, during which he claimed, "for the government, the caricatures continued to serve as conductors of useful information to the common people."[81] That they at least partly served this role in the years 1853–1856 largely resulted from Snegirev's job of approving the themes of the wartime images.[82] Snegirev, who certainly had a detailed familiarity of the Patriotic War images and their function as unofficial propaganda, ensured that the themes of 1812 imagery were refashioned to the circumstances of the Crimean War. Throughout the war, while he approved of print after print to be distributed, he expressed numerous hopes that the Russian people would rally around the tsar and his troops.[83] Snegirev concluded his 1861 work with the following statement:

> And so the *lubok* pictures represent not only subjects of entertainment and amusement in the tastes of the common people, but the spiritual, religious, and moral substance that they nourish in the people, as well as the feelings of belief and piety and love for the tsar and fatherland. They instill an aversion to vice and a fear of sins, and a respect for virtue as the purposes of life. One finds in them not just a single interest, but typical features from Russian life and its nuances, and also the religious, moral, and intellectual mood of the people, as well as its common and patriotic mood.[84]

For this imperial censor, the images he regulated proved to be an important tool for inspiring patriotism among the Russian population.

While the role of censors like Snegirev was vital in establishing the contours of wartime culture, the *lubok* publishers also played an important role in articulating their patriotic message. Understanding how publishers developed the themes for their wartime images requires some historical detective work and logical surmises, for there is no evidence of direct suggestions by censors to publishers. In fact, the records of the Moscow Censorship Committee during the Crimean War reveal that the *lubki* did not pose a problem at all. Censors such as Snegirev and his cohorts carefully recorded each image they approved for publication in lengthy lists, and while they cataloged any instances of problematic materials, not one *lubok* appeared on this list.[85]

The fact that the imperial government officially approved of a reissue of Terebenev's prints at the start of the Crimean conflict may have inspired *lubok* publishers to adopt the themes of the Patriotic War imagery. In addition, publishers in the 1850s would certainly have been familiar with the same traditions in popular imagery that had dominated prints in the past and most likely drew on them in their own work. While the law of 1851 helped to change the commercial production of popular pictures in Russia, it did not change the distribution of these prints. The *lubok* trade continued to be centered in Moscow, particularly near the Nikolskii Market (the Spassky Bridge had been destroyed after Napoleon's invasion), where publishers such as Petr Sharapov set up stores.[86] From these stores publishers employed *ofeni*, or peddlers, who then took the prints throughout Russia. These peddlers, often former *lubok* artists themselves, transported their goods to local fairs, cities, and villages.[87] Because of the nature of this distribution system, the publishers of popular materials retained close contact with their customers and were aware of what buyers demanded. As many as five thousand *ofeni* worked in Russia during the emancipation era, and they also acted as "bearers of news in the villages they visited,"[88] helping to interpret the images they carried to their audience.[89]

Entrepreneurs like Sharapov, the largest *lubok* publisher in Russia around the time of the Crimean War, remained acutely aware of the facts of the trade. Sharapov, as his most famous protégé, Ivan Sytin, recalled, was a deeply religious man who had been born a peasant.[90] Sharapov became a publisher soon after the 1851 law, and proved astute in adapting to the new conditions governing popular imagery in Russia. He used the lithographic process to produce more images and readily submitted his plates to the censors. He employed numerous salesmen and *ofeni* in his trade (eventually including the young Sytin, whom he took on in 1866 and treated like a son), and his humble origins ensured that he too remained close to the *lubok*'s audience, a trait his pupil inherited.[91] Sharapov's belief in the Orthodox faith and the tsarist system meshed perfectly with the desires of the imperial government and its censors such as Snegirev.

At the bottom of the *lubok* trade, it is important to note one other defining feature: the images sold increasingly well over the whole course of the nineteenth and early twentieth century. While it would be naive to assert that this sales pattern implied the *lubok* audience interpreted the images in the same manner, the fact that the Russian government did not distribute these prints for free in times of war meant that publishers relied on sales to promote their patriotic message, and thus the prints cannot just be considered mere government propaganda. Understanding how Russian peasants, townspeople, and nobles interpreted these images remains a difficult task, but the fact that the marketplace ultimately determined the success of the *lubok* is significant. *Lubok* publishers received no subsidies from the government in order to produce patriotic images, and had these images not sold well, businesses such as Sharapov's and later Sytin's would have disappeared. The images of the Crimean War by all accounts proved as commercially successful as the images of the Patriotic War—if not more so.

A War Made for Images: Crimea and British Visual Nationhood

Nikolai Davydov's recollections that the war had been won by the *lubok* artists serve as a reminder that the effects of the war and the concepts of nationhood depicted in popular prints contributed to a sense of dissatisfaction among certain Russians. The images of war that featured heroic Russian soldiers possessed of a brave spirit and guided by their Orthodox faith convinced Davydov that blame for the war's outcome lay with the artists who made these images or even, more importantly, with the government, which in his view promoted them.

The belief that popular images of war did not correspond to the realities on the battlefield did not exist just in Russia. In England, an explosion of imagery that initially stressed the pageantry of battle and the heroic exploits of British soldiers contributed to a widespread belief that the war could be easily won. When the siege of Sevastopol dragged on, however, dissatisfaction with the war grew. By early 1855, popular prints, illustrated newspapers, and other forms of visual culture began to depict the war in a different light. Eventually, the prime minister, Lord Aberdeen, resigned in disgrace, which prompted a series of crises in England.

Very early in the war *Punch* cast the conflict as one that featured heroic, "ordinary" English soldiers and officers who possessed the same sort of spirit as their Napoleonic-era counterparts. The cartoon of 25 February 1854, "Our Guards. They Can Play; and by Jove, They Can Fight, Too," features a young Englishman at a prewar ball gallantly asking a woman to dance in one panel and the same Englishman, now an officer, bravely leading his troops to fight in a second panel. The themes of this cartoon found expression in a host of popular prints, lithographs, and newspaper illustrations that flooded English markets in 1854 and early 1855. A press report in April 1855 observed, "there is not a village where there is not to be found . . . in almost every house wonderful prints of Alma, Inkermann, the charge at Balaklava, portraits of Lord Raglan, and others [the latter two referred to the famous Charge of the Light Brigade]."[92] The advent of lithography by the middle of the century meant that British image makers could produce a number of prints that contained heroic charges, brave British soldiers, and visually stunning sequences of battles. These images "served as the principal pictorial interpreter of the Crimean War's early, glorious phase," and "helped to shape public opinion" about the war in the process.[93]

As the war dragged on and casualties mounted, however, the visual nature of the war images shifted. *Punch* criticized the earlier images that boasted of glory, leading its writers to comment, "the English government seems to have declared war with Russia expressly for the benefit of the *Illustrated London News*." Fed up with what they saw as overly romantic visions of the war that appeared in the illustrated press, *Punch* artists began to produce images that blamed the generals and the war planners for mounting casualties in the Crimea. The cartoon of 3 November 1855, "Grand Military Spectacle," plays on the way in which previous images had depicted the war as a grand spectacle and reverses this concept—in the cartoon the "real heroes" of Crimea, the rank-and-file troops, inspect a group of old, overweight generals wearing their dress uniforms. An earlier *Punch* engraving entitled "The Queen Visiting the Imbeciles of the Crimea" showcased Queen Victoria inspecting another source of the war's failures—she stands before propped-up dummies labeled "Medical Department," "Routine," and "Commissariat." In these two images, ones that contrast with those that depicted the bravery of "our troops," a line is drawn between the average English soldier and the incompetent system that led him to death.[94]

Critical images such as these led the newly formed British government of Lord Palmerston to respond in kind, this time with a new visual weapon. By March 1855, the photographer Roger Fenton arrived in Sevastopol and used this new media to depict a different war, one that seemed more "real" and yet one that paralleled the pageantry of the earlier imagery. His 360 photos from the war mostly featured British soldiers at camp, on guard, or on parade, but Fenton avoided taking photos of the dead and wounded. As a result, his Crimean photographs have generated controversy ever since—for some, they showed "what the Crimean War was not like," while Fenton himself has been seen as a "royal photographer . . . dispatched to record a clean, ordered war."[95] Other scholars have stressed that Fenton "was a gentleman first and a photographer second" and thus chose to photograph officers and not the dead. In this view, Fenton avoided images that depicted death and disease because of a sense of personal tact, not because he acted on orders from the government.[96] Regardless of their intent, Fenton's photographs found approval among the British government and certain members of the public. For others, however, the photographs sanitized the war in a fashion similar to that of earlier lithographs. Alongside colorful prints and heroic photographs, *Punch* and other sources published images that remained highly critical of the war. In England, these images prompted a war over the images themselves —before Crimea, no formal censorship existed on how to depict war. In 1856, as a response to the war over Crimean imagery and the press coverage it generated, the British army issued an order forbidding future "information that might help the enemy," and this order established "modern British military censorship." The war over images produced a general belief in England that "the business of official propaganda and censorship" should be taken seriously.[97] For the government and educated citizens alike, wartime culture and particularly its imagery became a subject of intense debate.

The *Lubok* and Educated Russians

In the years immediately following the Crimean War, educated Russians, like their English counterparts during the war, began to pay attention to popular prints and their importance in disseminating information. For most, the *lubok* came to be viewed as government propaganda—cheap, vulgar, and lacking any artistic or cultural value. By and large, this attitude toward popular images dominated Russian intellectual life. Because of the general disdain most elites and radicals held for the peasantry—with the notable exception of the Populists—and anything considered to be "backward," the popular pictures were largely dismissed and rarely studied.[98] As Jeffrey Brooks has shown in his influential study of literacy in Imperial Russia, "critics, pedagogues, propagandists, and others concerned with popular education greeted the new literature [*lubok* chapbooks] with a combination of disdain and dismay."[99] The same statement could be made for the predominant view of the popular pictures in general and their wartime variant in particular.

Not everyone shared this attitude toward the *lubok*. As already seen, Ivan Snegirev viewed the *lubok* as a positive example of the Russian "national spirit." His assessment of the popular image, and particularly his approach in studying the importance of the *lubok* as a genuine artistic endeavor, paved the way for the most comprehensive study of this image ever conducted. Dmitrii Rovinskii, a legal scholar in nineteenth-century Russia, held a lifelong interest in the *lubok* and its cultural significance. Shortly after the Crimean War ended, he began to compile a collection of *lubok* images. At an early stage in his study, Rovinskii even consulted with Ivan Snegirev and compared ideas about the importance of the popular pictures.[100] Rovinskii's collection formed the basis for his magnificent five-volume work on the *lubok,* in which he cataloged various types of popular images and their significance in Russian culture. Far more nuanced in his attitude toward the *lubok* than most of his contemporaries, Rovinskii helped to inspire later Russians, in particular the avant-garde artists of the early twentieth century, to rethink the predominant stereotype of the *lubok* as popular trash devoid of any value.

Rovinskii, born in Moscow in 1824, played an important role in the judicial reforms of the 1860s and thus was what Bruce Lincoln would call an "enlightened bureaucrat."[101] Trained at the Imperial School of Jurisprudence, Rovinskii, who had studied criminal law, began his career in the Seventh Moscow Department of the Senate.[102] In 1853, he became the Moscow provincial prosecutor responsible for overseeing all police activities in the provinces, a position that would have entailed making certain the authorities enforced the 1851 law regarding *lubok* production.[103]

Rovinskii's experience working with the Moscow police initiated what became a lifelong interest in what the jurist called "people's pictures."[104] During the Crimean War, Rovinskii collected *lubki* and documented the government regulations that affected their publication. His research culminated with the 1881 publication of *Russkie narodnye kartinki* (Russian Popular Pictures).[105] For this Moscow jurist, the *lubok* prior to the middle of the nineteenth century represented a folk art that was "true to the everyday experience and requirements" of the Russian people, and Rovinskii viewed it as an accurate reflection of the tastes and attitudes of a wide range of Russian subjects.[106] As already noted, Rovinskii believed that the laws of 1839 and 1851 marked a time "when free national artistic creativity was inserted into the framework of official censorship."[107]

Rovinskii's assessment of the *lubok* appears on the surface to be similar to that held by other members of educated Russian society such as Leo Tolstoy, but underneath Rovinskii held a slightly different view. For Tolstoy, the ideas promoted in the popular prints obscured more than they revealed. As Tolstoy had written in his diary during the Crimean War, "the feeling of ardent patriotism that has arisen and issued forth from Russia's misfortunes will long leave its traces on her. These people who are now sacrificing their lives will be citizens of Russia and we will not forget their sacrifice."[108] A witness to the heroism at Sevastopol, Tolstoy personally saw the patriotic spirit throughout the Russian army, and blamed the disasters in Crimea on the government and its leaders, whom he labeled "lousy, shriveled-up heroes."[109]

In a sense, Tolstoy, Rovinskii, and Snegirev all believed that the *lubok* was propaganda, yet differed over how they interpreted this function of the image. "Propaganda" originally meant the systematic propagation of beliefs, values, or practices, and the use of the term originated in the seventeenth century.[110] In this sense, the wartime *lubok* was "propaganda," for propagandistic images are meant to convince the viewer or to help him make sense of political and social realities in a certain way. Propaganda, as other scholars have argued, is a social phenomenon that operates in several directions and contains messages that can be interpreted in a number of ways.[111] For Snegirev, the propagandistic elements of the wartime *lubok* represented a way to rally Russians around the system while disseminating information on Russia's wars. Rovinskii, who believed that the 1839 and 1851 laws had changed the nature of these prints, thought that the propagandistic elements of the *lubok* had compromised its ability to mirror popular tastes. Tolstoy, by contrast, viewed the wartime *lubok* as an expression of patriotism, and thus as government propaganda. His definition of propaganda, therefore, comes close to our twentieth-century understanding of the term, which has been affected by the attempt to mobilize the masses during the two world wars.

Tolstoy, for his part, began to rethink his assessment of the popular print after the publication of Rovinskii's massive collection. The 1880s marked an important turning point for Tolstoy. His lengthy novels such as

War and Peace and *Anna Karenina* lay in the past. At this stage of his life, Tolstoy wanted to provide inexpensive books and other materials to the great, illiterate masses of Russian society, particularly the peasants.[112] In order to carry out this task, Tolstoy and his "alter ego," Vladimir Chertkov, conceived of using *lubok* chapbooks as a means of instilling more "positive" ideas among Russians. For Tolstoy, this task meant introducing peasants to great works of literature as a means by which they could come to view themselves as part of a larger, worldwide community. Tolstoy had visited the Nikolskii Market and had even met Ivan Sytin there, and the young publisher impressed the author with his authenticity and connection to the common people.[113] By 1884, Tolstoy and Chertkov established the remarkable *Posrednik* (Mediator) series of popular books and prints, published and distributed by Sytin. Consisting of cheaply made and inexpensive renditions of Russian and European literary classics in a *lubok* format, the series lasted from 1885 until Tolstoy's death in 1910.[114]

Tolstoy's change in heart toward the potential function of the *lubok* did not alter the opinions of all educated Russians, and the popular prints continued to arouse disdain until avant-garde artists "rediscovered" the *lubok* in the early twentieth century.[115] Tolstoy's attitudes, however, reflect an important point about popular prints in the era of the Crimean War. As a young officer, Tolstoy, who had fought in this conflict, became interested in warfare and history as a result of his experiences. When he wrote his *Sevastopol Sketches*, Tolstoy furthered in many respects the construction of the "myth of Sevastopol" begun by the popular prints of the Crimean War. At first inspired by the heroism and patriotism of the soldiers in the Crimea, Tolstoy later began to view wartime culture and its patriotism in a negative light. Part of this view of war included its cultural products, and Tolstoy's negative attitude toward the *lubok* appeared most clearly in *War and Peace,* where he discussed the images. While his opinion about the potential usefulness of the popular print changed a bit by the 1880s, Tolstoy's assessment of the wartime *lubok,* one shared by a majority of educated Russians, always acknowledged that they exerted a powerful influence among Russians of all ranks.

The Crimean War images not only affected Tolstoy's view of the *lubok* in Russian life; they also crystallized the attitudes of the Moscow censor, Ivan Snegirev, and the Moscow jurist, Dmitrii Rovinskii. What is important to consider in these assessments of the *lubok* in general and the war image in particular, is that all three agreed that the *lubok* inspired Russians to fight and instilled patriotic ideals within a large number of them—though Tolstoy lamented this function.

However one interprets the accounts of Tolstoy, Snegirev, Rovinskii, and others, the images of the Crimean War undoubtedly represented the way in which the Russian government wanted patriotic notions to be portrayed. The stereotype of the Turk became a standard one within Russian culture after the war, and many of the themes that had appeared in the

Patriotic War images reappeared again in the years 1853–1856, recast in the context of the events in the Crimea. The irony in this "propaganda," however, is that it did not feature the tsar as an important component of Russian national and patriotic identity. In addition, the depiction of Sevastopol as a "city of glory," combined with the continued construction of this myth in the years after 1856, may have indirectly served as a means to criticize the government. Russians could be credited for their heroism at Sevastopol and depicted in images of the time, but the imperial government could be blamed for the eventual military defeat.[116] This fact opened up a "populist" patriotic discourse on the war, one that also appeared in the images of the time.[117] For many Russians, therefore, patriotism did not have to mean loyalty to the government or even to the tsar. In their role as propaganda, the wartime images were not limited to spreading information about the war and its heroes; they also offered different perspectives from which to view patriotic and national identities.[118]

DEPICTING the HOLY WAR

Images of the Russo-Turkish War, 1877–1878

> The picture of the crossing [of the Danube] made such a strong
> impression on me *[takoe sil'noe vpechatlenie proizvodila na menia*
> *kartina perepravy]*.
> —**M. Ch., Russian officer** (1878)

• Within Moscow's wooded Ilinskii Gardens, across from what served as
the Central Committee building in the Soviet era, stands a remarkable
monument devoted to Russia's armed forces. Dedicated to the grenadiers
who died in the 1877 siege of Plevna against the Turks, the monument
contains some startling bas-reliefs that reveal a great deal about the way in
which Russians remembered the war. Veterans of the Russo-Turkish War
planned and erected the memorial to comrades who had fallen in the numerous attempts to take the Turkish fortress, one of the most dramatic
events of the conflict and one that featured prominently in the popular
images of the time. After a successful subscription campaign, the Plevna
memorial, designed by Vladimir Sherwood—the architect of the Historical
Museum on Red Square—opened on 28 November 1887 in time to com-
memorate the tenth anniversary of the storming of the fortress.[1]

The monument itself is a small chapel, reopened in 1998. The fact that
the form of the memorial is an Orthodox church says a great deal about
the way veterans of the war wanted the conflict in which they had just
fought to be remembered.[2] The most striking feature of the monument is
the gold dome shaped like traditional Orthodox church domes. The cross
at the top rests on a Muslim crescent moon, a stark, visual reminder of the
Orthodox victory over the Turks. Just as striking as the cross are the four
bas-reliefs that depict the action of the war as well as the ostensible reasons for the conflict. The first features an Orthodox Balkan or South Slav
peasant in chains, a result of living under Turkish rule, with the figure of
Mother Russia standing over him. The second depicts a Slavic peasant
woman clutching her child, desperately trying to save him from the Turk
standing above her. The Turkish man, with distorted, animal-like features,
has a knife drawn above his helpless victim. The next features an old Russian
muzhik, Bible in hand, pointing toward the "action" of the previous bas-
relief and urging his son, who is kneeling and wearing a soldier's uniform,

to enlist. The last sculpture depicts a Russian grenadier striking a commanding pose over a solitary Turkish soldier who is begging for mercy. The words that accompany these images remind viewers of the heroism of Russian troops in the war against Turkey, a "vicious" enemy. Inside the chapel visitors are asked to remove their hat and pray for the memory of all Russian soldiers who died in this and other "holy wars."

The Plevna memorial proves to be a striking reminder of the importance of wars to Russian national identity. Its exterior and interior form, in addition to the cross and panels, parallels the representation of the "holy war" against the Turks that *lubok* publishers and newspapers developed in the midst of the fighting. The chapel serves as a permanent reminder of the victory of Russia over the Turks, and of the alleged superiority of Russian Orthodoxy over Islam, a crucial component of Russian patriotic culture in the nineteenth century.

The war against Turkey from 1877 to 1878 began after a period of rising Slavic nationalism in the Balkans combined with the growing influence of Russian Panslavism at home.[3] The Balkan region in the 1870s remained largely under Ottoman control, and Russian Panslavists such as Mikhail Pogodin, Ivan Aksakov, and Nikolai Danilevskii increasingly called on their government to unite all Slavs under Russian hegemony. Even Russia's ambassador to Constantinople, Nikolai Ignatiev, believed in the tenets of Panslavism, which reached the height of its influence by the late 1870s. The events of 1875 and 1876, which saw Herzegovina, Bosnia, and Bulgaria revolt against Turkish rule, led Serbia and Montenegro to declare war on Turkey in the summer of 1876. Turkish irregular forces massacred as many as 30,000 Bulgarians in the spring of 1876,[4] and Russian Panslavists called on the tsar to aid his fellow Orthodox Slavs against the menace posed by the Turks.

Alexander II initially tried to work with other European rulers to solve the crisis in the spirit of the congress system that still governed European diplomacy at the time. The major powers attempted to broker a reform program in the Balkans that Turkey could administer. Inside Russia, however, the enthusiasm for the Slavic struggle grew rapidly, inflamed by newspaper publishers such as Mikhail Katkov and by popular images that stressed the heroism of fellow Orthodox Slavs. Russian Orthodox Church leaders, in addition to the Slavonic Benevolent Committee, began to send aid to the Slavs fighting against Turkey. From Constantinople, Ignatiev called on the tsar to aid the Serbs, who had suffered a series of defeats and found their capital of Belgrade threatened. Alexander faced pressure from his wife, Maria, and his son, the future Alexander III, to intervene, and after several more failed attempts at diplomacy, he declared war against Turkey in April 1877.

Educated Russians cheered the declaration of war, and Fedor Dostoevsky wrote that Russia was fighting for a sacred cause that would help to unite Russia around Orthodox ideals, a declaration that would be repeated from various corners throughout the conflict. The war itself unfolded in three phases. The first featured Russian troops amassing in Wallachia, after which they successfully crossed the Danube River. The second phase, lasting from July to December 1877, brought a series of disheartening operations in Bulgaria, symbolized by the "time- and manpower-consuming siege of Plevna."[5] The third phase, which lasted from the middle of December 1877 to February 1878, witnessed a spectacular Russian breakthrough in the Balkans and a direct march from Kishinev via the Shipka Pass to San Stefano, about fifteen kilometers from Constantinople. The Russian troops forced the Turks to sign the Treaty of San Stefano in March.

By the terms of the treaty, Russia would have regained southern Bessarabia, a territory it had lost in 1856, and created a large, independent Bulgaria with a significant Aegean coastline, effectively a client state of Russia. Russia also would have received territorial gains in the Caucasus, long a contested region with Turkey, an indemnity from the defeated Turks, and a guarantee of Serbian, Montenegran, and Romanian independence. Quite clearly a sign of Russian assertiveness in the Balkan region and a desire to alter the 1856 Treaty of Paris, the Treaty of San Stefano set off alarm bells throughout European capitals. Fearful of what they saw as naked Russian aggression vis-à-vis Turkey, Austrian and British officials asked Otto von Bismarck to act as an "honest broker" and negotiate a new peace. Alexander II, facing the financial strain of the war, agreed.

The ensuing Congress of Berlin met in mid-1878 and resulted in the Treaty of Berlin. Its provisions reduced Bulgaria in size, while Austria-Hungary and Great Britain received territory in the Balkans to counter Russia. In Asia Minor, however, as well as in Bessarabia, Russia maintained its gains. Despite these real achievements, most Russian elites viewed the Treaty of Berlin as a blow to Russian pride and another betrayal by fellow Christian nations. Alexander II considered it one of the worst moments of his reign. The victory over the Turks, however, continued to be celebrated in Russian popular culture, and the concept of the years 1877–1878 as a war to free Orthodox Christians from the hands of Muslim Turks remained a component of popular culture for some time.

The idea that the war was a holy one gained wide currency in Russia. Dmitrii Miliutin, the minister of war at the time, wrote in 1877 that he could not believe European nations such as France, Italy, and England failed to support Russia in a war against the Turks, a war started over the deaths of "Balkan Christians, victims of Turkish barbarism." Mikhail Gazenkampf, a Russian officer, also thought of the war as one between a Christian nation and a Muslim one.[6] Even Francis Greene, a lieutenant in the United States Army who observed the war from within the Russian camp, absorbed the idea that the war was a holy one. He wrote in his reminiscences of Alexander II's attempt to "free his co-religionists from the intolerable oppression of the Turks. No more generous or holy crusade was ever undertaken on the part of a strong race to befriend a weak one. So all true Russians believe; so even a sceptical [sic] foreigner is forced to admit after seeing and appreciating the sacrifices which the effort entails, the enthusiasm with which these sacrifices are endured, and the small returns which it brings in material benefits."[7] Finally, A. Puzyrevskii, a member of Russia's General Staff during the war, began his military reminiscences by stating, "in 1877 the Bulgarian people were freed from five centuries of slavery by blessed Russia."[8] The Plevna monument mentioned above in many ways represented the construction of this myth about the conflict and a further elaboration of the Turkish stereotypes seen in the images of the years 1877–1878.[9]

The popular pictures from the Russo-Turkish War initially cast the war in a similar fashion. *Lubki* trumpeted Russian acts of heroism, including the siege of Plevna and other Turkish fortresses. These images helped to create a new hero, General Mikhail Skobelev, who appeared in numerous prints of the time and whose leadership became a regular theme in the Russian press. Skobelev became one of the most popular figures in the empire, and his legendary status grew when he led Russian triumphs in Central Asia after the war.[10] The "Skobelev phenomenon" began in the *lubki* of the Russo-Turkish War, and his presence in Russian popular culture remained vivid decades after his death right into World War I.[11] Most importantly, however, the images of the years 1877–1878 celebrated the Russian triumph over the Turks, and *lubok* publishers depicted this victory as proof of Orthodox superiority over Islam, firmly establishing the Russian faith as a source of patriotism and nationhood.

This chapter will examine the articulation of the "holy war" and will discuss the images of the Turk as a means of exploring not only Russian national identity, but also Russian attitudes toward the "Orient."[12] Finally, the description of the *lubki* in this chapter will highlight how these images functioned roughly like newspapers for much of the population. Containing valuable information about the conflict itself, and often appearing within a week of events, the *lubki* of this war, while certainly containing highly subjective renditions of the war's events, nevertheless remained the best means for a number of Russians to learn about the details of the conflict.[13]

The Holy War in Images

The popular images published in the midst of the Balkan events of 1876 foreshadowed the tone adopted by *lubok* publishers during the war itself. Russian images had never before appeared prior to a war in a manner designed to sway public opinion against the enemy. Serbian forces commanded by Mikhail Cherniaev, the "lion of Tashkent" (so named because of his role in capturing the Central Asian city for Russia in the 1860s), fight Turkish troops in the print "Slavs in the Turkish War Battle near Kaziak." Heroic troops on horseback engage in close hand-to-hand fighting, and the Slavs successfully repulse the Turks from the town. Highlighting this heroism, as well as the nature of the Turkish enemy, a young child stands transfixed before his tiny hut, watching the war around him. The text notes that Cherniaev and his Serbian troops "held up in the persistent battle with the Turks," who had brought war to their village.[14]

A second example stressed the religious nature of the conflict in the Balkans. Entitled "An Incident in the Balkan Peninsula before the Conclusion of the Armistice," the image depicts a large number of Serbian forces receiving an Orthodox blessing from two priests.[15] The priests stand behind a makeshift altar. General Cherniaev bows his head and receives a blessing for his contributions to the Serbian cause. The image, produced by an artist identified as N. Kulakov, clearly asserts that the Slavic cause in the Balkans is one that the Russians, symbolized by the Panslavist General Cherniaev, should take up. The religion shared by the Serbian troops and their Russian leader and the blessing given by the Orthodox clergy provide a powerful visual theme.

Russia's entry into the Balkan conflict brought an immediate outpouring of popular prints that contained similar themes. The print "Kishinev, the Racing Ground, 12 April 1877," illustrates events on the day Russia declared war.[16] This *lubok* contains most of the imagery that reoccurred throughout the war images, and features a large public prayer given for the departing Russian troops. An altar adorned by an Orthodox cross and around which several priests hold icons and other religious banners dominates the print. Alexander II kneels to receive a blessing at the shrine, along with the tsarevich. The rest of the print contains numerous Russian troops kneeling solemnly before their tsar and receiving the blessing of their Orthodox faith for the coming war. The text notes that these troops, about to embark for a long march through Turkey, kneel "in the presence of His Imperial Highness, the Emperor of Russia," who proudly "makes way for the ceremonial march of the troops." From the very first days of the war, then, the Russian tsar appeared in the patriotic images, alongside the notion that religion formed a prominent part in the meaning of the conflict.[17]

A second image provides a powerful attempt at defining what the war would be about. "Russia [Rossiia] for Faith and the Slavs" (Figure 5.1) appeared on 20 April.[18] The print, identified as the work of N. Kulakov, focuses on a bearded Russian peasant soldier defiantly holding his rifle aloft. The soldier stands atop a small knoll, while a large number of fellow soldiers march by, prominently carrying the imperial standard. A group of South Slav peasant women, dressed in traditional clothing, stand nearby and offer thanks to their "savior." A solitary male peasant kneels before the Russian soldier and offers his thanks as well. These peasants, probably Bulgarians or even Russians living under Turkish occupation, thank their hero for "rescuing them." Underneath the small mound lie the bodies of four Turkish soldiers slain by the Russians. The image contains a powerful series of visual references to Russian identity: Slavic background, faith, the

5.1 "Russia for Faith and the Slavs" This *lubok*, which appeared shortly after the 1877 Russo-Turkish War broke out, appropriates the peasant-soldier hero present in previous wartime images and situates him within the context of rising Panslavism. A solitary Russian soldier leads his comrades in a quest to "liberate" fellow Slavs from Turkish rule. The lengthy caption, written by the poet Fedor Miller, claims "the hour of retribution has struck for the Slavic blood" to "avenge the torture of Christians" suffering "abuses" from "the savage Muslims" *(svirepye musul'many).* Reprinted by permission of the State Historical Museum, Moscow [GIM]

peasant soldier, and the imperial banner all help to define what Russia fought for in the war, while the Turkish soldiers and the thanks of the liberated peasants remind viewers why Russia must fight.

The text of this *lubok,* attributed to the nationalist and xenophobic poet Fedor Bogdanovich Miller, contains language that reappeared throughout the images of the years 1877–1878. Claiming that the "hour of retribution has struck for the Slavic blood," Miller calls on "Holy Rus' [Sviataia Rus']" to "avenge the torture of Christians" suffering "abuses" from "the savage Muslims *[svirepye musul'many]."* Noting that the Turks had started the war on Russian land, Miller writes that "the tsar appeared" to declare retribution against the Turks, and that "the love of the father among his children" delighted everyone gathered to hear him, who called "Bless us, God" and asked for Russians to "stand up for the motherland *[rodnaia strana]."* Miller then appealed for God to "bless the Russian tsar," to "help us to victory" for "the fatherland and for Christ." The text refers to Russia as "Holy Rus'," a term that referred to the first Russian polity and a name that occurred countless times in the images of the Russo-Turkish War.

Other examples from the first full month of the conflict redefined the concepts of Russian heroism and Turkish cowardice that appeared in images from the Crimean War.[19] "The Passage of the Russian Army across the Danube" depicts impressive-looking Russian artillery, infantry, and cavalry marching across a makeshift wooden bridge or aboard ferry boats.[20] Accompanied by the same text by Fedor Miller that appeared in "Russia for Faith and the Slavs," this image became the source of other *lubki* also advertising the heroism of the Danube crossing.[21] Just two days after the first Danube-crossing print appeared, a *lubok* from Andrei Vasil'evich Morozov derided the cowardice of the Turks and their leader in the face of battle. The popular picture entitled "Possessed with Fear of the Russian Troops, the Turkish Pasha's Troika Leaves with a Message for the Turkish Sultan" portrays the Turk in traditional garb smoking in the back of his carriage.[22] His driver whips the three horses that carry him away from the action in a frenzy, both from fear of the advancing Russian troops and to warn the sultan of their prowess. Similar to *lubki* of the Crimean and even the Patriotic War in depicting the cowardice of the enemy just at the mention of Russian soldiers, this print adds to the stereotype of the Turk as both savage and cowardly.[23]

"The Capture of the Turkish Fortress 'Ardahan,' 5 May 1877" establishes a pattern of imagery devoted to the heroic sieges by Russian soldiers.[24] Turkish soldiers flee on horseback from Cossacks giving chase. The panic on the faces of the Turks contrasts with the raised sabers and heroic poses of their pursuers. The background of the print is dominated by the siege of the Turkish fortress, a depiction that includes numerous Russian troops scaling the walls of Ardahan. At the top of the walls, a single Russian soldier raises the double-headed eagle standard of Russia atop the fortress, dwarfing the other features of the town. The text reproduces a *Moskovskie vedomosti* article of the event in which the Cossack commander "congratulates our great Emperor with the taking of Ardahan, which has now been introduced to Russian authority."

The summer months of 1877 brought a variety of popular images that furthered the notion that the ongoing war was a holy war against the Islamic Turks. The print "Entrance of the Russian Troops into the Turkish Fortress of Machin" features the army marching proudly through a main street of the town, cheered on by its residents. The border town of Machin had earlier appeared in the popular print "The Entry of Prince Gorchakov into the Machin in March 1854," which celebrated the town's liberation during the Crimean War.[25] Having lost this territory through the Treaty of Paris, Russian armies returned in 1877. In the 1877 print, at the head of the column of soldiers rides General-Lieutenant Zimmerman, whose forces had crossed the Danube and "liberated" the Orthodox citizens in the Turkish fortress. Zimmerman's troops are welcomed by a group of local peasants and Orthodox priests bearing icons and religious banners, thanking the troops for freeing them from Turkish hands.

"God Save the Tsar" depicts Alexander II's appearance in a small town across the Danube. A shell explodes in the center, narrowly missing the tsar, whose horse rears back from the blast. Alexander is surrounded by Russian generals and troops that he is reviewing as the shell explodes. The text notes that the incident occurred when the tsar, after crossing the Danube, reviewed Russian forces at the village of Sistov. An unexploded shell "blew up near the tsar, who asked calmly, 'Is anyone injured?'" When everyone answered negatively, the tsar "crossed himself twice," then blessed his troops, who received him "with the usual enthusiasm and rapture."[26] The print attributes Alexander's narrow escape from death to the fact that God was on his side, a point further reinforced by the action behind the emperor, where Russian shells rain down on the spires of a Turkish town.

The summer months also produced a wealth of images that hailed Russia's gains in the war.[27] As the conflict moved into autumn, the war *lubki* glorified Russian victories and acts of heroism, and reveled in the demonstration of military prowess not apparent in the Crimean peninsula from the period 1854–1856. Near the end of August, the first image appeared in Russia that depicted the newest target of the Russian army, the fortress of Plevna. Simply entitled "A Battle near Plevna," the subject of this *lubok* was the fierce engagement of 19 August between Russian and Turkish troops.[28] Its features are typical of the battle *lubki* of the war: Russian forces impressively organized and urged on by stoic commanders and comrades proudly carrying the Russian banner face off against the less-organized Turkish troops easily identified by their fezzes.[29] Several Turkish troops lie dead or wounded in the foreground. One Russian soldier lies wounded nearby, clutching his heart with one hand and holding his rifle with his other. His face is turned toward two comrades behind him, beseeching them to carry on.[30] The crucial moment of the war began with this first engagement near the fortress of Plevna, which appeared in the background of the image.

The focus of the war images changed somewhat by September 1877, as the Russian army laid siege to Plevna and suffered through numerous hardships and casualties. In a style similar to the Sevastopol imagery from the Crimean War, *lubok* publishers focused on acts of heroism by Russian troops, lionized Mikhail Skobelev, and stressed the faith of the Russian troops and their tsar. From July until November 1877, the two sides fought a prolonged and bloody siege at the Turkish fort located halfway between Bucharest and Sofia. In the words of a leading military historian of the war, this event "set the stage for an epic confrontation at Plevna between Russian and Turk for Balkan hegemony."[31] After numerous attempts at taking the fortress, and over the course of three separate strategies at gaining control of Plevna, the Russians, guided by the ideas of a Sevastopol veteran, General E. I. Totleben, settled on a policy of starving the enemy into submission.[32] Despite massive losses, this approach proved victorious in late November, when Oman Pasha surrendered the fort to the Russian command.

Because of the casualty figures and difficulty in capturing Plevna, the five-month siege became the defining moment of the war in its popular images, and the subject of future myths and remembrances after the war, as the campaign to build a memorial to the soldiers at Plevna indicates. The ferocity of the siege, combined with the possibility of military failure reminiscent of Sevastopol, resulted in a wide range of images that depicted the bravery of the Russian troops (as in the *lubok* above).[33]

Other *lubki* published at the height of the Plevna campaign depicted the Turks as savage enemies, capable of committing incredible acts of brutality. Reminiscent of similar images from the Crimean War, the *lubok* entitled "The Russian Generals" features several leaders, including Mikhail Skobelev, all on horseback surrounded by their troops.[34] Illustrated by P. Shcheglov, this print focuses on the decapitated corpses in the center, alleged victims of the Turks. The Russian leaders and their troops stare solemnly at the bodies of their countrymen, reminding them (and the viewer) of the barbarous nature of the enemy. The text notes that "the seething battle was not long lost and the Turks ran," massacring Russian prisoners in the process of fleeing back toward Plevna. As this and similar images claimed, the Turks' savagery and brutality toward Russian soldiers and civilians necessitated the continued war and the capture of Plevna.[35]

The siege also furthered the growing stature of Mikhail Skobelev, who appeared in a number of prints in the late fall of 1877. The son of Dmitrii Skobelev, another prominent Russian general,[36] Mikhail Skobelev inspired an array of patriotic images devoted to his exploits.[37] In the *lubok* called "The Valiant and Heroic Victory of General Skobelev in Battle near Plevna," Russian and Turkish troops engage in close hand-to-hand fighting in a trench.[38] Skobelev stands with his left arm on his sword and his right pointing forward, unmoved by the shells exploding around him and inspiring his troops forward. Underneath the Russian general rests his dead horse, killed in the midst of the battle. Unaffected, Skobelev continues onward, and his troops respond. The print, drawn by N. Astashev, includes a text that claims that Skobelev inspired both his troops and the Turks, who "were already well aware of the White General."[39]

By the end of the fall, the siege of Plevna took its toll on the Turks. After three unsuccessful attempts to storm the fortress, the Russian troops isolated the Turkish fort and forced the Turkish army into the open. When the Turkish attempt to escape failed, the fortress fell into Russians hands in late November 1877.[40] The impending Russian victory prompted the reappearance of Alexander II in the wartime images. "The Visit of the Sovereign Emperor to Wounded Russian Soldiers" (Figure 5.2) depicts the tsar's concern with his soldiers.[41] This brightly colored *lubok* presents the interior of a field hospital, complete with thirteen beds, wounded soldiers, and several Red Cross nurses. Alexander II stands at the nearest bed, flanked by his staff and two nurses. A Russian soldier in the bed sits upright and is presented with a small gift from the tsar. Other soldiers look onward or receive treatment from the nurses. The text states that the tsar "appeared in the field hospital on August 21 with entire masses of gifts for the wounded," and personally "made his way around the chamber several times and gave every wounded soldier a present," thanking each one for his service.

With the war apparently won by December, the popular prints reemphasized the role that Alexander II had played in the victory, in a similar manner to the prints that lauded Alexander I as the architect of victory over Napoleon. In these prints, however, Alexander II not only appeared as the inspiration behind Russian bravery in the field, but also as a fellow soldier and a father figure concerned with the welfare of his troops. Alexander did in fact visit many hospitals during this time of the war, where Vladimir Sollugub recounted that he approached each soldier "not as a person who was insignificant before him but as a comrade in heroism, as a confrere in painful service." These visits, Sollugub wrote, transformed the injured: "sufferings were forgotten. Faces beamed with happiness, tenderness, and gratitude."[42] Both V. A. Cherkasskii, the chief of the Russian Red Cross, and S. P. Botkin, Alexander's personal physician, also remembered the positive effects of Alexander's hospital visits in 1877.[43]

With Plevna in Russian hands, *lubok* publishers in December 1877 turned their caricatures on the Turkish leaders while simultaneously celebrating the Russian fighting spirit. Sharapov's *lubok* "The News in Constantinople about the Capture of Plevna" ridicules the Turkish leaders for their lack of fighting prowess.[44] A Russian peasant triumphantly celebrates his victory over Turkey in "One, Two, Three!" (Figure 5.3). The *lubok* is dominated by a larger-than-life peasant, again reinforcing images from earlier wars that defined Russian identity in terms of the size of the

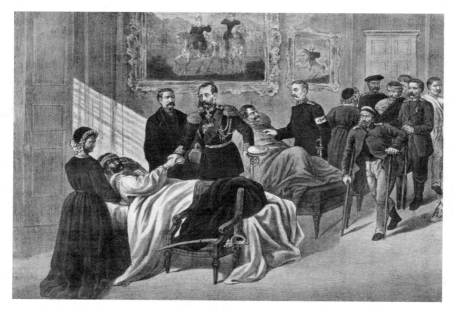

5.2 "The Visit of the Sovereign Emperor to Wounded Russian Soldiers" Alexander II's visit to wounded soldiers, depicted with a newspaper report, illustrates the way in which the tsar's image changed within wartime culture. Alexander II did not appear in *lubki* as the "divine inspiration" behind victory, but as a sovereign performing mundane acts such as distributing presents to his troops. Reprinted by permission of the State Historical Museum, Moscow [GIM]

country.[45] The peasant hops over the Danube River, his hands in fists as he easily performs the feat. Behind him are the smoking ruins of three fortresses (the "one, two, three" of the title), which the Russian has conquered. Labeled, from left to right, "Plevna," "Kars," and "Ardahan,"[46] the peasant strides toward three more cities in the distance marked "Sofia," "Adrianople," and "Constantinople." To the left of the giant, a small Turk in fear points out the onrushing conqueror to a Turkish woman. Abramov's text celebrates the Russian victories of 1877 as a manifestation of the Russian national spirit and assumes a light tone to convey a false sense of ease with which Russia defeated Turkey. Adopting the language of a folktale, the text recounts how the "Russian man snatched everything from the Turk." The peasant "leapt with one leg, and jumped over the Danube, strode with the second and crossed." The Russian then "flapped his arm," causing "Kars to shake" while another wave of his arm sent "Ardahan crumbling." Taking another step, the Russian "took Plevna captive" and now strode ahead toward his three next targets, asking the Turks, "well now, how are you getting on," and pausing to tell the woman, "I don't mean to bother you."[47]

5.3 "One, Two, Three!" The larger-than-life Russian peasant as a symbol of Russian national identity found further expression in this 1877 *lubok*. The title refers to three fortresses captured by Russian troops (Plevna, Kars, Ardahan) and the three Turkish cities the peasant hopes to capture soon (Sofia, Adrianapole, and Constantinople). Source: Denisov, *Voina i lubok*.

The new year brought new images that celebrated Russian conquests, beginning with the entry into Sofia. With Plevna captured, Russian troops had an easy path into the Bulgarian capital, then under Turkish control. "The Ceremonial Entry of the Russian Troops into Sofia" commemorated the arrival of the Russian soldiers on December 22, 1877.[48] General I. V. Gurko rides his horse at the head of a festive military band, behind whom march the Russian forces. Gurko and his men approach the entrance to an Orthodox cathedral in Sofia, where several priests stand with crosses and icons to bless their saviors. A solitary Bulgarian peasant kneels before the Russian general, holding a plate of bread and salt, the traditional Orthodox greeting for travelers. The emotion of the scene, which reinforces the idea that this war was a holy one designed to free fellow Christians from Muslim control, is strengthened by the faintly visible outlines of the mosques of Sofia in the background. The Russian general, his soldiers, and the Bulgarian townspeople celebrate in front of an Orthodox cathedral, with the Muslim mosques occupying a secondary position behind them.[49]

This triumphal tone continued in images that exalted the advancing Russian army. After the Russian forces entered Sofia and then Adrianople, the path to Constantinople lay open. Turkish diplomats began to press for negotiations in January 1878, as the Russian army slowly advanced toward the capital. The Russians halted at the village of San Stefano, also located on the Aegean Sea and a mere fifteen kilometers from Constantinople.[50] "A Solemn Prayer upon Hearing of the Concluding Peace in San Stefano (near Constantinople)" provides a final testament to the religious nature of the war.[51] A large contingent of Russian soldiers, including such luminaries as Skobelev and Gurko, kneel in prayer to celebrate their victories. Leading the service are four Orthodox priests, who bow in front of a large cross and two icons. Resembling the *lubok* that featured a prayer service in Kishinev on the day the war began, this print serves as an excellent bookend to the conclusion of the war.

With victory won and harsh terms imposed upon the Turks, *lubok* publishers in March and April produced popular images that reflected on the meanings of the war. A Glushkov print entitled "Skobelev's Pedigree" (Figure 5.4) featured an arresting portrait of the Russian hero on horseback, surrounded by pictures of a youthful Skobelev and his father. Further images recounting Skobelev's heroic acts during the war, particularly at Plevna, reaffirmed the position of the White General as the preeminent hero of the campaign, and furthered the construction of the "Skobelev phenomenon" that would follow the war. The Russian general became the most popular and well-known figure in the country, and his further successes in the conquest of Central Asia would be celebrated in newspapers and popular prints. Skobelev's death in 1882 at the age of thirty-nine only added to his legend, and the crowds that thronged his funeral procession were composed primarily of people of the lower classes who had embraced the general.[52] The Russian government commissioned an official collection of his orders in 1882, and the first call for a statue to celebrate the heroism of Skobelev was heard in the same year. By the time the project was finished in 1912, dozens of pamphlets, *lubki,* biographies, reminiscences, and fictionalized accounts of Skobelev had appeared, all part of the cult begun in the images during the war.

Other prints praised the Russian spirit that had brought victory against the enemy, a spirit embodied in the common Russian soldier. The Sharapov *lubok* "Soldier's Song upon the Capture of Plevna" reminded Russians of the major battle of the war and the Russian national character that had triumphed there.[53] A large number of peasant soldiers sing and dance in front of their field tents in the print. Four soldiers engage in typical Russian activities before a table: one stands on a bench, playing an accordion, while a second claps his hands and sings a folk song. A third dances a Russian dance, while a fourth seated at the table tends to the large samovar brewing tea. The soldiers gathered around do a dance, throw their hands in the air, or engage in conversation, while the text notes that the "brave Russians enjoyed themselves" at the expense of "Mohammed" [*magomet*] and the defeated enemy.[54]

5.4 "Skobelev's Pedigree" The major hero of the Russo-Turkish War was General Mikhail Skobelev, who was the subject of numerous images, pamphlets, and memoirs during and after the war. This 1878 *lubok* attempts to quantify his heroism by visually linking it to his background (portraits of his father and grandfather, both military men, are included) and his actions as a soldier throughout his career, acts that fueled his leadership in 1877 and 1878. Reprinted by permission of the State Historical Museum, Moscow [GIM]

While several images featured depictions of a "Russian spirit" that every soldier embodied, other prints reaffirmed the stereotype of the "cowardly Turk." One entitled "The Danube Army" was set during the bombardment near Kars, in the Turkish town of Rushchuk.[55] While Russian shells explode in the background of the print near the fortress of Kars, the foreground features Turks from all walks of life fleeing from the Russian advance. Two Turkish soldiers stroll nonchalantly through the town, their guns slung uselessly over their shoulders. Instead of defending their homeland—as popular pictures from the Patriotic War and the Crimean War showed Russians doing—these soldiers and townsmen flee. Like many other prints during the war, this *lubok* distributed at the end of the hostilities explicitly depicted the Turks as cowardly and inferior to the Russians.[56]

Two *lubki* best sum up the tone of the images from 1877 and 1878. The first, a Strel'tsov image approved in March, is entitled "In Memory of Russia's War with Turkey" (Figure 5.5). The print includes a number of Russian national symbols. In the center, a Cossack soldier stands proudly, holding a flag of victory adorned with an Orthodox cross, in the middle of the Kremlin. Behind him loom the cathedrals of Moscow, all physical manifestations of Russian identity.[57] Beneath Ivan the Great's bell tower one can glimpse the Tsar Bell. In the most striking part of the image, the Cossack is standing on a Turkish flag adorned with the Muslim crescent moon, a clear visual reinforcement of this war as a holy war with the superior Russian side emerging victorious. The text quotes a poem from Evgenii Gorbushin:

> Glory to the realm of the Russians
> Glory to the tsar-father
> Glory to the tsar's home
> Glory to the ancient Kremlin[58]

The second print appeared around the same time, and was entitled "Hurrah to Our Glory!"[59] It contains portraits of all the heroes of the war, on horseback behind Alexander II (Figure 5.6). Radetskii, Skobelev, and Gurko, the victorious generals of the conflict, ride before a large number of banners (Cherniaev had fallen out of favor). The Russian tsar, however, dominates the print, magnificent upon a white horse. Beneath the hooves of Alexander's horse is a crushed Turkish crescent moon. To the left is a broken set of chains, symbolizing the breaking of Slavic slavery under the Turks. The text lauds Alexander II as the architect of this great victory, stating, "Praise be to our mighty tsar! From all the humble Russians—you set in motion our awesome troops that fought for the oppressed Christians." Calling the tsar's leadership "powerful" and "accomplished," the *lubok* claims that on "liberating the Christians," Alexander II "has brought to its knees the arrogant moon *[slomil roga lune nadmennoi]*."[60]

5.5 "In Memory of Russia's War with Turkey" In 1878, after a victorious Russia had imposed harsh terms on the Turks, prints such as this one celebrated the victory. The *lubok* contains a number of Russian national symbols (the Cossack, the Orthodox cross, and the Moscow Kremlin), while the accompanying text promises "Glory to the realm of the Russians, Glory to the tsar-father, Glory to the tsar's home, Glory to the ancient Kremlin." Reprinted by permission of the State Historical Museum, Moscow [GIM]

5.6 "Hurrah to Our Glory!" With victory won, this image attempts to link Alexander II to the war's successful end in a fashion similar to Alexander I in the 1812 war. The tsar sits on horseback flanked by his generals while his horse crushes a Turkish crecent-moon beneath its hooves. The accompanying text praises Alexander for "set[ting] in motion our awesome troops that fought for the oppressed Christians," which ultimately "brought the arrogant moon to its knees." Reprinted by permission of the State Historical Museum, Moscow [GIM]

These two prints illustrate many of the dominant themes of the war against Turkey, a conflict that *lubok* publishers depicted as a "holy war" against the Muslim enemy. The symbols of Russian identity present in the war *lubki* since 1812 found redefinition in the years 1877–1878: the double-headed eagle, the Russian peasant, and the Cossack were visual reminders of a Russian spirit, the Orthodox church, and Russian heroism. Alexander II, the tsar of Russia, appeared as the architect of victory in this holy war, marking the first time since the Patriotic War that the tsar featured so prominently in the patriotic images. One prominent scholar has provocatively argued, however, that the images of Alexander at the front, not just in *lubki* but in newspapers as well, "only magnified [the tsar's] inability to affect the direction of the war and made his sacrifice appear an empty gesture and his suffering trivial compared to the privation and death around him." By contrast, Skobelev "struck a glamorous figure," forcing the tsar to "contend with a new type of hero—the general-adventurer who showed courage, abandon, and a contempt for the routine that constrained most commanders of the imperial army."[61] In other words, the presence of the tsar's image in the wartime *lubok* may have been just as detrimental to his place in Russian patriotic culture as his absence.

The War at Home, 1877–1878

The difficulty in gauging the response to the popular images of war has already been mentioned several times and still holds true for the Russo-Turkish War of 1877–1878. However, the way in which the Russian countryside understood the war can be detected in the reminiscences and evidence available. It is known that the war images of the time proved popular in Russia and helped to inspire a patriotic response throughout the country. The most prominent Russian historian to study the reception of the war among the Russian peasantry, A. V. Buganov, has argued that it created a feeling of national consciousness among the Russian peasantry.[62] Moreover, the *lubki* of the 1877–1878 war did not just appeal to the countryside. The future tsar of Russia, Nicholas II, then a young boy, enjoyed receiving the patriotic images as gifts and followed the war closely through them.

The most revealing window into the peasantry's response to the war comes through the letters of Aleksandr Nikolaevich Engelgardt.[63] Engelgardt was a member of the Russian landed nobility and a chemist who had studied at the leading schools of St. Petersburg. After years as a teacher and researcher in the capital, Engelgardt was sentenced in 1870 to internal exile when a Russian court held him accountable for a student uprising at the institute where he served as rector.[64] With few other choices available, he decided to return to the estate on which he had grown up: Batishchevo, in the Dorogobuzhskii district of Smolensk province.[65]

Engelgardt arrived at Batishchevo just ten years after the emancipation of the Russian serfs, and the effects of that momentous event were still being felt throughout the countryside. Once he settled at his estate, Engelgardt became an important eyewitness of the post-emancipation village. His keen eye for detail and intellectual curiosity led him to compose a series of letters about the successes and failures of the land reform, and his writings appeared in the progressive journal *Notes of the Fatherland* beginning in 1872. They were an immediate hit, and over the next twelve years, ten more letters from Engelgardt appeared in the journal, which tsarist censors shut down in 1884.

Most of Engelgardt's letters discussed the problems of the post-emancipation world of the Russian peasantry and the difficulties of gentry-peasant relations. The sixth letter gave his impressions of the impact of the Russo-Turkish War.[66] Above all, Engelgardt was struck by the changes apparent in his district during the war. "Seven years ago, that is the way it was: we followed our usual routine, we did what was required, and nothing else mattered to us. But now, even in our backwoods, a different current of air has begun to come through and gradually budge us."[67] Engelgardt observed that the "peddler Mikhaila," who usually sold scarves and colorful pictures on the estate, "suddenly is offering scarves with pictures of 'the leaders and heroes of the Serbian uprising in Bosnia and Herzegovina who fought for the Christian faith and the liberation of the fatherland from the barbarians.'" The former chemist noted, "Well, how could you not buy one!"

In addition to the colorful scarves sold by peddlers, Engelgardt noticed that gentry women, townsmen, and other residents of the district wore patriotic colors and traded in patriotic goods soon after the first images appeared. The whole district, according to Engelgardt, became acutely interested in the events of the war. At one point, the wife of Engelgardt's steward burst into the study and announced, "We've taken Plevna!" obviously joyous at the news.[68] When Engelgardt inquired about how she knew of the taking of Plevna, he observed the following:

> The peddler Mikhaila brought war pictures: "The Marvelous Dinner of General Skobelev under Unfriendly Fire," "The Storming of Kars," and "The Taking of Plevna." Mikhaila knows all the pictures in great detail, and just as he previously explained the merits of his cottons and scarves, so he now describes his pictures.
>
> "Here you have," he explains to the *babas* and day laborers who have gathered around him in the dining room, "here you have Skobelev, the general, he took Plevna. Here's the same Skobelev standing and pointing to the soldiers with his finger so that they'll run faster to take the gates to Plevna. Here, you see, are the gates, here are our soldiers running. Here they're taking the Osman Pasha by their hands—look how he's hunched over! Here our soldiers are taking Kars; do you see how our soldier has seized the Turkish flag?"

Mikhaila points to a soldier who has erected a two-headed eagle flag on the walls of the fortress.

"That is the Russian flag, not the Turkish one," I remark.

"No, it's the Turkish flag. You see, there's an eagle drawn on it, and there'd be a cross on the Russian one."

"Here you have Skobelev dining . . ."[69]

Engelgardt's account is a wonderful window into how the Russian peasantry viewed the war *lubki,* as well as the role these images played in inspiring the countryside to follow the events of the conflict. Engelgardt clearly expressed doubt at the ability of the peasants to understand the war, and later recounted that the peasants believed in rumors about the conflict inspired in part from the images.[70] He muses "knowing how ignorant the peasants are, knowing that they do not possess even the most elementary geographic, historical, and political knowledge . . . it is true that you cannot imagine that these people could have any kind of comprehension of current political events."[71] For Engelgardt, "it seems unlikely that one would be interested in something one does not know, that one could sympathize with the war, understand its significance, when one does not know what Tsargrad [the Russian name for Constantinople] is." To this member of the gentry class, the fact that the Russian peasantry did not know the historical background of the war or its aims excluded them from grasping the true significance of the conflict.

Yet one could look at the information presented by Engelgardt in a less patronizing tone. Engelgardt never doubted that the peasants and villagers in his district expressed a great deal of interest in the war and continued to follow events throughout. The fact that Mikhaila believed that a Russian flag should have a cross on it indicates that the peddler conceived of himself as Russian and that this identity revolved around the Orthodox religion, a point stressed in the war imagery of the time. His lack of knowledge about the double-headed eagle suggests that in his case, this symbol of Russian identity made less sense than religious imagery also present in the war *lubki.* In fact, in this case the peasant had it right—Russian troops went into battle with regimental flags, not with the imperial standard. Engelgardt may have believed in the iconography of the wartime imagery, but his peasants (who had to supply the troops to the army and thus knew far more about its workings) knew differently.[72] Far more instructive, however, is Mikhaila's ability to view himself and his audience as Russian, with a sense of patriotism and a clear ability to view the Turks as non-Orthodox—and thus non-Russian. Mikhaila's tales of Skobelev's heroism had an effect on Engelgardt's peasants too, for they later asked Engelgardt to join them in a toast to the White General (Skobelev).[73] The fact that the peasants around Batishchevo displayed a keen interest in the war and its events, eagerly gathered in the local tavern to discuss their views, and bought the pictures of Mikhaila indicate that they grasped the basic patriotic views depicted in the popular prints, however differently than Engelgardt did.[74]

This view of the Russian peasants' ability to see themselves as belonging to a Russian nation echoes the important and ultimately convincing argument made by A. V. Buganov. Buganov has researched the attitudes of the peasantry to the war of 1877–1878 in more depth than any other historian,[75] and in a larger monograph on peasant national identity in nineteenth-century Russia, he argues that the experience of the Patriotic War of 1812 and the Russo-Turkish War of 1877–1878 fostered a sense of national consciousness among the Russian peasantry.[76]

Buganov studied the records of nineteenth-century ethnographers who had examined the attitudes of Russian peasants toward the war both during the conflict and in the years afterward.[77] Through an examination of questions asked to peasants in twenty-three provinces in central Russia from 1876 through 1900, including those individuals accompanying the Tenishev program, Buganov concludes that Russian peasants understood the war in patriotic terms and had preserved a particular memory of the war and their role in it that formed a sense of "national consciousness."[78] In the midst of the war, several ethnographers noted that the peasants remained extremely interested in the news of the conflict and received their information, Buganov shows, through newspapers read aloud to them and from letters written to them by relatives at the front.[79] In addition to these sources, peasants also received news from the itinerant book and *lubki* peddlers like Mikhaila.[80] Even at the turn of the century, when ethnographers questioned surviving veterans and other peasants alive during the war, they all remembered "the national excitement of the time" and that "the whole world saw the strength of Russian troops." Many ethnographers even saw *lubki* from the war still hanging on the walls of peasant huts.[81]

Buganov further suggests that stories of Turkish atrocities that circulated in the Russian countryside before and during the war inspired a sense of sympathy with Balkan "brother-Slavs" suffering under "the Turkish yoke,"[82] an attitude recalled in several provinces years later. During the war, several peasants in the Pskov region noted that the Turks had started the conflict, and much like the events of 1812, the situation needed to be dealt with through warfare. Buganov argues that the memory of 1812 and all of its meanings had helped to form a national consciousness among the peasantry in the decades afterward, and 1877–1878 found this memory reaffirmed and recast in the war against the Turks.

Above all, Buganov concludes that Russian peasants conceived of the war as "a struggle for the Christian faith." Like many fellow correspondents for the journal *Etnograficheskoe biuro*, A. L. Grebnev wrote that peasants in the Viatka province believed the war needed to be fought after "the Turks began to restrict and torture their Orthodox citizens." E. A. Menzenkampf recorded that several peasants near Voronezh thought the war revolved around "the defense of Christians from the Muslim yoke *[musul'manskogo iga],"* sentiments echoed in similar reports from the Kazan, Penza, and Iaroslavl regions.[83] The idea that the war was a struggle against "infidels" or "un-Christians," Buganov argues, became the defining concept of the war as its participants remembered it.

Buganov also recounts the observances of ethnographers who recorded the popular reception with which Russian peasants accepted the "heroes of 1877–1878," particularly Skobelev and Gurko.[84] By embracing the exploits of these generals, Russian peasants created a memory of their own roles in the battles of Plevna, Kars, and elsewhere. One newspaper correspondent who visited the Orel region in 1899 recorded that peasant veterans still told tales of their exploits with Skobelev and Gurko. Buganov notes that through this "memory of 1877–1878," Skobelev entered into the pantheon of great Russian generals such as Suvorov and Kutuzov, whose exploits also continued to resonate in Russian culture.

In his conclusion, Buganov argues forcefully, "the attitude of the peasants to the Russo-Turkish War testifies to their high level of national consciousness *[natsional'noe samosoznanie]*. In wartime conditions, within the peasants' consciousness, patriotic, nationalistic, and religious feelings blend. Because of the specification of the present war as a struggle against 'infidels,' confessional feeling played an essential role in the attitude of the peasants toward the war."[85] Although Buganov only mentions in passing the popular images that flooded the Russian countryside, his argument is a convincing one.

Engelgardt's account of the popular images in his region, placed alongside the evidence presented by Buganov, suggests that the war *lubok* fulfilled an important function as a source of information about the war. The religious nature of the war presented in the war *lubki* fueled the memory of the war among the peasants as a struggle against infidels. For many, the images themselves served as a means to remember the conflict. In 1898, when a Russian ethnographer visited the Viatka province, he noticed the number of popular prints from the war that still adorned peasant huts. When he composed his notes later, he noted, "the peasants love to decorate the walls with pictures."[86]

The news of the war presented in the popular images of the time did not just attract Russian peasants, however. A second glimpse into the reception of the war *lubki* of the years 1877–1878 offers another tantalizing account of the popularity of these images. During the war, Konstantin Pobedonostsev served as the imperial tutor to the son of the tsarevich. His charge, Nicholas, later ascended the Russian throne as Nicholas II. Just ten years old at the start of the conflict, Nicholas displayed his father's feeling of "national pride and contempt for other nationalities" at an early age.[87] In a letter written to Nicholas's father (the future Alexander III) dated 12 January 1878, Pobedonostsev suggested that Nicholas had begun to form opinions about other nationalities through his excitement at receiving patriotic *lubki*. Commenting about Nicholas's education, the tutor noted, "today I saw your lovely children. I came to Nicholas Alexandrovich with the new *lubok* pictures about the war; he always waits for them with impatience and asks if some more are present."[88] Young Nicholas found it impossible to resist the images. While it is certainly hopeless to assert that the future tsar of Russia formed his later chauvinistic attitudes toward other nationalities solely from patriotic *lubki*, Pobedonostsev's letter offers a reminder that the *lubok* proved not just popular in the countryside, but in the cities as well.

In addition to city dwellers who bought *lubki*, Russian soldiers from a variety of backgrounds also encountered the popular prints at the front or imagined the scenes of war as depicted by *lubok* artists. A Russian officer who had participated in the crossing of the Danube on 21 June looked at the scene and imagined it as a *lubok*. Gazing at the Russian troops forging ahead across the "majestic Danube," the officer imagines that a "worthy artist" could have designed it. He then sees himself revealing the scene to the Turks and "show[ing] them this mass of people, pedestrians, horses, hundred of guns, and tell[ing] them: you see—this Russian force, which is as numerous as the sand in the sea, is flowing toward you, to make you carry out its wishes! Do you know, that what you see, is only a fraction of what there is? Would you like to suppress this force?"[89] After envisioning this encounter, with the Turks replying, "No, we surrender to you, spare us," the officer writes, "the picture of the crossing made such a strong impression on me *[takoe sil'noe vpechatlenie proizvodila na menia kartina perepravy]*."[90]

Lubki were "visual narratives" that made them a pictorial equivalent to the newspaper.[91] Visual accounts of Russian heroism in battle thus fulfilled a variety of roles, and during the 1877–1878 war enabled Russians to envision the action of the conflict and their place within the Russian nation. No less important than the reception of these images among a variety of Russian subjects, however, was the role played by publishers such as Ivan Sytin.

Ivan Sytin and the Articulation of Russian Nationhood

Wartime images certainly drew on existing stereotypes of the enemy in an effort to articulate Russian patriotism and cultural strengths. How did *lubok* publishers come up with their themes? A brief examination of the career of Ivan Sytin, who became the dominant producer of *lubki* in the Russian Empire shortly after the Russo-Turkish War, sheds more light on the commercial aspect of the *lubok* and why it proved so successful from a financial perspective. Sytin's life story serves as an ideal link between the popular prints from the Russo-Turkish War and the Russo-Japanese War of 1904–1905.

Ivan Sytin was born in 1851 in Kostroma province, a poor region located in what many at the time considered "the ancestral homeland of the Great Russian people and of Russian Orthodoxy."[92] The son of semi-literate peasants, Ivan went to the village school in 1861, the year of the emancipation of the Russian serfs. He lasted only two years in the school, which stressed religious and rudimentary knowledge, leaving in 1863 upon the birth of his brother. When he left, Sytin later admitted, he did so "lazy and with an aversion to books"[93] and had acquired only a rough semblance of literacy, much like other peasants of the time who spent only a couple of years in the village schools.[94]

The post-emancipation order proved difficult for the Sytins, and Ivan's father was forced to move his family to Galich, fifty miles south of Kostroma, to take a position as a clerk in 1864. The very next year, when Ivan turned fourteen, he made his first trip away from home. He traveled to the Nizhnii Novgorod fair to work for an uncle who traded furs.[95] At the famous market, Sytin saw for the first time the numerous peoples who made up the Russian Empire, and his experiences at the fair, according to his biographer, taught him "some basic tenets of profit-making . . .: know the tastes of your buyers, sell in quantity, [and] give credit,"[96] ideas that Sytin later used as a *lubok* publisher.

When Ivan Sytin returned to the Nizhnii Novgorod fair the following summer, 1866, he met another fur trader who also printed and sold popular prints, Petr Sharapov. Impressed by the young Sytin's energy, Sharapov arranged for him to begin an apprenticeship in Moscow. On 14 September 1866, Ivan Sytin arrived in the old Russian capital to begin work at Sharapov's shop near Ilinskii Gate. An Old Believer, Sharapov exerted a strong influence over his young charge, whose religious and patriotic upbringing in Kostroma meshed well with the views of the Moscow trader. Sytin proved an apt pupil, and Sharapov increasingly invested more and more responsibility in him, including operating the lithographic press Sharapov used to make his *lubki*.

As the apprentice learned the features of the *lubok* trade, Charles Ruud asserts, "now, as later, rusticity helped Sytin by making him easy with the country folk who were Sharapov's customers."[97] Sytin learned to run the press, color in the printed sheets, deliver them to customers, and even "forged good relations with the buyers of Sharapov's pictures and little books." Ivan also engaged in work as a peddler *(ofenia)*, traveling to outlying villages and local fairs to trade in the popular prints. In these years, Ruud notes, "the affable and quick-witted Sytin took careful stock of peasant tastes and interests, a commonsense method of market research that gave him grounds for urging Sharapov to forego certain pictures . . . or add new ones."[98] In sum, Sytin, a barely literate peasant, learned a trade that enabled him to focus on his own religious and patriotic views. His close connection to the peasantry, combined with the skills he learned in Moscow, allowed Sytin to develop *lubok* themes that sold well. Sharapov too possessed these skills, and "had no recorded run-ins with the censors,"[99] a relationship Sytin would continue in his own production of patriotic *lubki*.

The Russo-Turkish War of 1877–1878 was a momentous event in Sytin's professional career. Then twenty-six years of age, Sytin had opened his own shop the previous summer in 1876, after his marriage. Having thoroughly learned the *lubok* trade from Sharapov and having witnessed the *lubok*'s success throughout the Russian countryside, Sytin wanted to start his own business. He borrowed money from Sharapov to establish his firm on Voronukhinaia Hill in Moscow, where he employed *lubok* artists whom he believed could produce pictures that would capture the attention of potential buyers.[100] Initially struggling in a market that included his mentor, Sytin's relationships with his customers paid dividends in 1877. After experiencing difficulties in competing during the year since opening his shop, Sytin responded to the popular demand for maps of the Balkans with which to follow the unfolding events in the region. His detailed maps proved successful commercially and allowed Sytin to branch out and make patriotic *lubki* that accompanied them.[101] Sytin's images of war from the years 1877–1878, together with his maps, established the young businessman as an important personage in the publishing world. His experience in Sharapov's shop, together with his keen understanding of popular demand, were a formidable combination in the commercial world of Imperial Russia. Ivan Sytin had become a Russian entrepreneur, and the war *lubok* formed the foundation of his success.

Sytin himself acknowledged the fortuitous circumstances of the period 1877–1878 that paved the road to his later success. Embarking on a risky venture such as *lubok* publishing, he admitted "I hired the best graphic artists and first-class printers, did not bargain with them over wages, but demanded high quality work; finally, I followed the market and with the greatest effort studied people's preferences."[102] His success in carving out a niche for himself emboldened Sytin, who embarked on a series of other commercial ventures after 1878. In addition to his *lubok* pictures, Sytin also printed pamphlets, and these, together with his prints, "sold in the millions of copies."[103] By 1882, Sytin opened his first retail outlet near Sharapov's store at Ilinskii Gate, and in 1883 he formally founded Sytin and Company.[104] The career of the man who came to be known as the undisputed king of the *lubok* had indeed begun.

Over the next couple of decades, Ivan Sytin established himself as the leading publisher in Imperial Russia. Although exact figures on the number of popular prints Sytin's firm produced are difficult to obtain, even during the carefully regulated periods of wartime, other statistics attest to the staggering success of the semi-literate publisher. By the end of the century, Sytin had established two shops in Moscow, and one each in St. Petersburg, Kiev, Nizhnii Novgorod, Warsaw, Voronezh, Ekaterinburg, and Odessa.[105] In addition, Sytin employed a virtual army of nearly two thousand peddlers who distributed his popular prints throughout Russia in the 1890s.[106] A careful assessment of Sytin's business accounts in 1900 and after reinforces the importance that the publisher placed on his popular pictures: Sytin spent a great deal of money on paper, repairs, new machinery, artists, and other supplies to keep his *lubok* business running smoothly.[107] Despite the fact that Sytin lost money on other commercial ventures, including the journals he opened in the early 1900s and even his newspaper, *Russkoe slovo*, Sytin and Company still turned massive profits in these years, making the publisher a millionaire.[108] By the turn of the twentieth century, Sytin's company produced over fifty million *lubok* prints a year, available virtually everywhere in the vast Russian Empire.[109] This fact demonstrates that Sytin's publishing empire rested above all on his popular prints, and allowed him to take risks in other fields without the threat of bankruptcy. While Sytin's biographers, including Ruud, have often concentrated on the variety of Sytin's publications and status as a true entrepreneur (as well as the growing liberalism that got him into trouble with imperial censors), it is important to stress that Sytin's fame and fortune rested on his *lubki*, and that these images never incurred the wrath of the authorities.

In addition to his dealings with Leo Tolstoy mentioned in the previous chapter, Sytin became acquainted with a large number of cultural figures. In 1916, when his company celebrated Sytin's golden anniversary in the publishing field, luminaries at the banquet included Dmitrii Merezhkovskii, the famous poet, and Nicholas Roerich, the artist. The chairman of the jubilee commission, N. V. Tupolov, began the formal tributes to Sytin with the words: "Without exaggeration, in no Russian home, in no school, in no peasant hut is there a corner without some publication issued by Sytin."[110] Tupolov then read telegrams of congratulations and praise from Mikhail Rodzianko, president of the State Duma, and Georgii Lvov, soon to become the prime minister of the Provisional Government, among others. Following Tupolov's speech, Sytin was toasted at the Praga Restaurant by Ivan Bunin, the great Russian writer, and others.[111] Tupolov also celebrated Sytin's anniversary by editing *A Half-Century for the Book*, which featured a short autobiography from the publisher and letters of praise from people acquainted with Sytin's importance, including Maxim Gorky, Anton Chekhov, Leo Tolstoy, and Vasilii Vasnetsov.[112]

In his autobiographical account, Sytin reminisced about the fortuitous circumstances that had given him his start in the publishing world. In April 1877, soon after the declaration of war against Turkey, Sytin remembered buying a map of Bessarabia and Romania on the Kuznetskii Most. Having studied its outlines, Sytin worked through the night to produce better maps in order to meet a growing demand, and by "5 in the morning" had produced his first. "In the course of the next three months," Sytin wrote, "I dealt [in the maps] alone." Having found his first taste of success, Sytin turned to producing *lubok* prints, because as he put it, "I had studied the tastes of the people *[izuchal vkusy naroda]*. The result was brilliant. My pictures were the most sought after."[113] Later in the edited tribute to Sytin, A. Kalmykov contributed an article entitled "Russian *Lubok* Pictures and Their Educational Significance for the People during the Last 75 Years of Our Lives."[114] Kalmykov praised the role that Sytin and his mentor, Sharapov, had played in the lives of Russians, particularly in producing a sense of national consciousness. He singled out the importance of the Russo-Turkish

War *lubki,* which depicted the sufferings of fellow Slavs at the hands of the Turks and featured famous figures like Skobelev. The prints of the war produced by Sharapov and Sytin, wrote Kalmykov, proved popular indeed: "The entire war for the people was clear and aroused great sympathy."[115]

Ivan Sytin set off on his path of becoming a true "Russian entrepreneur" during the Russo-Turkish War of 1877–1878. The popular prints he produced, like those of his mentor Petr Sharapov, helped to construct the notion that the conflict was a holy war against the Muslim Turks. In producing images both during and after the war, Sytin drew on his close contacts with customers, a practice that allowed him to scale unprecedented heights in the publishing world. Sytin's first expansion near the Ilinskii Gate placed his images next to the Plevna monument dedicated to the bravery of Russian soldiers against the Turkish infidel, a theme first developed in Sytin's and fellow *lubok* publishers' images of the years 1877–1878. This theme continued to be emphasized in the years afterward, and not only in the building of the Plevna memorial: in his attempts to teach new converts to Orthodoxy about the faith and about Russia in general, the Kazan professor Evfimii A. Malov often showed his pupils the *lubki* of the Russo-Turkish War, including prints of the Danube crossing, because he associated Russianness with Orthodoxy.[116] Malov thought that Tatars would convert from Islam once they understood the superiority of Russian culture and religion. The "postwar mythology of national victory over Asian fiends"[117] in which Malov believed first found expression, as this example highlights, in the wartime *lubok.*

6 ILLUSTRATING the RACIAL WAR

Images from the Russo-Japanese War
of 1904–1905

> People of my generation will probably remember those wartime
> posters. They were meant to suggest the cheap prints of popular lit-
> erature . . . Alas, the posters . . . were distinguished only by their
> counterproductive passion to persuade. The Japanese were uni-
> formly portrayed as knock-kneed weaklings, slant-eyed, yellow-
> skinned, and for some reason, shaggy-haired—a puny kind of mon-
> key, invariably dubbed "Japs" *[iaposhki]* and "monkeys" *[makaki]*.
>
> —**Aleksandr Pasternak**

• In the midst of the Russo-Japanese War of 1904–1905, I. P. Belokonskii
wanted to see how Russian peasants understood the conflict. Aroused by
this sense of curiosity, he set off to the provinces to witness firsthand their
reactions. In a series of three articles published in the literary journal
Obrazovanie (Education), Belokonskii commented on the popularity that
the war *lubok* enjoyed in the Russian countryside, as well as its powerful
role in shaping public opinion. He noted that peasants eagerly awaited
news from the Far East and gathered around to hear the news read
aloud, often by a literate peasant or priest in a fashion quite similar to
what Engelgardt remembered of the war news from 1877. Popular prints
produced by such companies as I. D. Sytin's would be sold, discussed,
and passed through the hands of the audience gathered to hear the
news. For Belokonskii, the experience proved revelatory: he discussed
many images by name and lamented that their content proved all too
easy to understand. In particular, he noted that the wartime *lubki* were
popular among Russian peasants because they enjoyed hearing "stories
about monkeys and bears."[1]

Belokonskii's experiences help to illuminate not only popular attitudes
toward the war in the Far East; they also shed light on one of the major
themes of the Russo-Japanese War as it appeared in the wartime images.
War *lubki* stressed not only notions of Russian cultural superiority over the
Japanese foe, but also racial superiority.[2] Numerous prints referred to the
Japanese as "monkeys," "animals," "Mongols," "slant-eyed," and "yellow
faced dwarves." The pictures that accompanied this language proved

equally crude, as *lubki* featured Russian soldiers and Cossacks fighting against small Japanese pests with animal-like features. Thus, the war images from the years 1904–1905 bring to the forefront an important aspect of the Far Eastern conflict: its racial nature, and specifically Russian perceptions of the Japanese enemy.[3] While the *lubki* from this time served as a source of information in a means similar to those mentioned in previous chapters, they also highlight another important aspect of the wartime *lubok*: its historical importance as an illustration of Russian imperialist notions.[4] Finally, while the images of the war contained racist caricatures of the Japanese, their reception caused a backlash against such a characterization of the enemy. The portrayal of the Japanese as an inferior race had serious consequences, for the defeat at the hands of such a foe triggered profound crises throughout Russia.

Racism toward the Japanese undoubtedly played a significant role in the origins and course of the 1904 war.[5] Nicholas II, the tsar of Russia, privately referred to the Japanese as "short-tailed monkeys," a conception shared by many of the imperial elites who helped drive Japan toward conflict in the Far East.[6] The fact that the Russian army and navy were far from ready to wage war in the region, combined with the poor communications established in Russia's Asian colonies, did not bode well for success against the formidable Japanese, yet "inept diplomacy, great power rivalry, and corrupt political and commercial interests,"[7] all tinged with a contempt for the Japanese presence in the Far East, contributed to the outbreak of the war. As Bruce Menning has noted, "contempt for Orientals," along with a "basically racist conception of Oriental ineptitude" on the Russian side forced the hand of the Japanese.[8]

After years of provocative maneuvers on the part of the Russians in the Far East, Japanese troops launched a surprise attack on the Russia's Pacific squadron anchored at Port Arthur on 25 January 1904. In a sense the first "Pearl Harbor" of the twentieth century, the Japanese attack in 1904 was hailed by countries like Great Britain as deserved, such was the universal scorn with which western countries held Russia and her Far Eastern policies at the time. The conflict itself boiled down to two major features: the siege of Port Arthur and attempts throughout the Far East by the Japanese to gain a decisive victory over the Russians. Despite the surprise attack of January 1904, the Russian fort put up fierce resistance over the next several months, and the siege, much like Plevna in 1877 or even Sevastopol in 1855, came to dominate the popular understanding of the war. The Russian fleet, led by Admiral Stepan Makarov, initially proved a formidable foe on the Korean peninsula, but Makarov's untimely and martyrlike death aboard the battleship *Petropavlovsk* brought a stalemate in the port after March 1904.

The Japanese threw caution to the wind and hurled everything at capturing Port Arthur, as much for prestige as for military reasons. In territory that one attacker later recalled consisted of "steep mountain, kissing the heaven—even monkeys could hardly climb it,"[9] the repeated sieges around Port Arthur that dominated 1904 brought savage fighting, huge casualties, and thousands of corpses that lay for months where they had fallen. A Russian correspondent described the horror that became Port Arthur: "It was hardly a fight between men that was taking place on this accursed spot; it was the struggle of human flesh against iron and steel, against blazing petroleum, lyddite, proxyline, and melinite, and the stench of rotting corpses."[10] After repeated attempts and casualties that would only be surpassed at Verdun, the Russian commander, General Stessel, raised the white flag over Port Arthur on 20 December 1904.

Port Arthur exerted an enormous symbolic pull on both the Japanese and Russians alike. Its surrender certainly hastened the end for the Russians and boosted the morale of the Japanese immeasurably, but the war was not over. Outside of Port Arthur, in Manchuria, the failure of Russian generals, particularly the commander, A. N. Kuropatkin, contributed to the disaster. Kuropatkin had once been told by Skobelev, the famous "White General," "God keep you anytime from accepting the role of the principal commander because you lack decisiveness and firmness of will,"[11] an apocryphal comment that proved all too true in a war that lacked both qualities. Needing time for reinforcements to arrive from European Russia, Kuropatkin nevertheless failed to develop a clear plan for the large number of troops he had at his disposal, and defeats at Liaoyang, Sha-ho, and Sandepu sapped Russian confidence. The decisive blow came at Mukden in February 1905, when the Japanese commander, General Nogi, inflicted 90,000 casualties on Kuropatkin's forces. Two months later, when virtually the entire Russian fleet, which had made an around-the-world voyage, first to rescue Port Arthur and then to come to Kuropatkin's aid, was crushed at the Tsushima Straits, the humiliation was complete. Russia became the first European country to lose a war to an Asian nation. As one writer noted, "the coolies had become conquerors."[12]

The Racial War: The *Lubki* of 1904–1905

The popular prints of the war can be roughly divided into five categories: battle scenes (the most numerous), battleship prints, patriotic images, portraits of military leaders and heroes, and satirical *lubki*. War images depicted the Japanese in 1904–1905 as racially inferior, devious fighters, whose culture and religion did not measure up to that of Russia's. By contrast, *lubki* that featured Russian soldiers stressed their heroism, masculinity, and honor.

The print "Attack on Port Money" (Figure 6.1) powerfully illustrates many of the themes of the war imagery. Featuring a giant figure of Uncle Sam grasping a large moneybag, the American is surrounded by swarms of small, pesky Japanese soldiers attempting to take the purse. The text of the print labels the Japanese as "squint-eyed warriors fighting over someone

6.1 "Attack on Port Money" The Russo-Japanese War (1904–1905) produced a number of images like this one, which features pesky, insect-like Japanese soldiers attempting to take a moneybag from Uncle Sam. Attached copy pokes fun at the "small, squint-eyed warriors" who fight for money and not for honor. Source: Denisov, *Voina i lubok*.

else's purse,"[13] thus claiming that the Japanese attacked Port Arthur at the behest of their allies, the United States. The image establishes the Japanese enemy as small, animal-like pests who fought for money and not for glory. These attributes reappeared throughout the war *lubki* and provided a stark contrast to images that praised Russian heroism, masculinity, and solidarity.

The well-known patriotic *lubok* "Cossack Petrukha" (Figure 6.2) displays a similar message. In the print a large Cossack hurls several Japanese soldiers away from him. The enemy troops are again depicted as small pests with distorted features, in comparison to the stoic features of the Cossack. To the right of the hero another Cossack sits on his horse, laughing at the ease with which his comrade dispatches the tiny pests. Overlooking the scene are characterizations of John Bull and Uncle Sam, both of whom frown at the escapades of the Cossack. The text of the *lubok* promises "glory to the great life, smartness *[lovkost']*, and bravery of the young Cossack," who "straightened out the enemy." Noting that "the monkey arrived for a fight," the text reminds the reader of "the well-known fact" that the "glorious Russian Cossack" can teach anyone a lesson, whether "a Tatar, a Turk, or a dishonest enemy," concluding, "the monkey will not soon forget the Russian's lesson."[14]

The Sytin image "Fighting Song of the Don Cossacks," from February 1904, features a Cossack dressed in traditional clothing bending a Japanese naval commander over one knee. The Don Cossack warrior has one

6.2 "**Cossack Petrukha**" A Russian Cossack easily dispatches the animal-like Japanese enemy in this *lubok* from 1904. Reminiscent of the "Russian Hercules" from 1812, this image reappropriates the patriotic culture of the war against Napoleon and places it in the context of the war with Japan (and her "allies" Uncle Sam and John Bull, who look with consternation at the events unfolding below them). Reprinted by permission of the State Historical Museum, Moscow [GIM]

hand raised, clenching his whip *(nagaika)*, about to teach the enemy a lesson. In front of the pair a Russian cannon fires a shell at a distant Japanese vessel consumed in flames. To the right, Uncle Sam and a Chinese leader watch in dismay. The walls of Port Arthur, seemingly untouched by warfare, dominate the background of the print. The text, written by the well-known Muscovite Vladimir Giliarovskii (identified as "Uncle Gilly"), features the following "lyrics" to a fighting song: "Hey, Mikado [a reference to the Japanese emperor], you will feel badly when we destroy your vessels," "it is a shame about your yellow faces," and "then, yellow-skinned brothers, you will lose your sailors."[15] The word "mikado" in its plural form, "mikados," became a pejorative reference for the Japanese because of its continued use throughout the war, and was widely used as such in the images of the war.[16]

The print "Russo-Japanese Caricatures" (Figure 6.3), which appeared in early March from the firm of A. P. Korkin, illustrates the racial nature of the war most clearly of all.[17] The *lubok* features twelve postcard-style scenes that illustrate various satirical aspects of the war. The three center caricatures depict Japanese soldiers as animals, accompanied by a short text. The central image features the head of a Japanese soldier with a monkey's body crawling up the mountainous region near Port Arthur. To the left, a representation of Mother Russia pulls in her dog, which has the face of a Japanese soldier. On the right side, a solitary Japanese soldier bays like a dog at a map marked "Korea," salivating at the prospect of conquest. Other caricatures depict a Russian soldier grabbing a smaller Japanese counterpart by the ear, a Japanese soldier trying to ride an emaciated donkey, a Japanese soldier desperately trying to pull a large Chinese man, two Japanese soldiers running from bayonets (reminiscent of images from previous wars), an old Russian peasant pinching a small Japanese soldier on the cheek, and two images of younger Russian peasants easily defeating the enemy. The texts that accompany these caricatures reinforce the main theme of racial inferiority, often in parodies of Krylov fables. Language such as "yellow dog" is used to describe the Far Eastern foe, while other texts refer to the enemy as "snuggling in the corner, with clicking teeth and bristling hair" and having "eyes and teeth flare up."

Lubki that depicted battle scenes further highlighted the perceived racial differences between the Russians and the Japanese. Dozens of prints portrayed the Japanese as devious, unfair, and savage fighters, particularly those that described the attack on Port Arthur. One of the first prints of the war, entitled "Russia's War With Japan," shows the Japanese fleet retreating after its bombardment of Port Arthur, which "came without warning."[18] The text describes the Japanese fleet as devious, then depicts a bird's-eye view of Port Arthur before the shelling, reminding the viewer of the enemy's treachery. Several other prints reported the attack on the fortress in stark, terse imagery that conveyed a sense of outrage at the surprise bombing.[19] Two *lubki* explicitly labeled the Japanese attack as treacherous—

6.3 "Russo-Japanese Caricatures" This 1904 *lubok* casts the war as a racial one. Filled with postcard-like representations of the Japanese enemy, individual images depict a Japanese soldier as a monkey and a dog, while others have Japanese soldiers easily defeated by Russian peasants, women, Cossacks, and bayonet charges. Reprinted by permission of the State Historical Museum, Moscow [GIM]

one stated that the Japanese "brought war on the Russian tsar" because of their "insidiousness" and attacked Port Arthur "without a sound."[20] The second railed against the enemy who "treacherously attacked our squadron."[21]

A Morozov print from 10 March 1904 combines the battle *lubok* style with a satirical bent. Entitled "Well Done, Brave Japan!" the image mocks the Japanese attack on Port Arthur. At the center of the print, a lone Cossack on horseback corrals a Japanese soldier, whose features are distorted, by the ear. The Cossack runs two other Japanese troops through with his lance, easily taking care of the enemy. In the background, a single Japanese vessel shells Port Arthur, a reminder of the war's origins. The title satirically comments on the "brave" attack in the Korean peninsula, while the text claims that "the Japanese run around as if in a drunken state," before stating, "Hey, Japanese, it is a sin, it is a sin [to attack us]."[22] The *lubki* of the war like this one produced recurring images of the Japanese that in turn reflected certain stereotypes about the enemy. Other images suggested that given a "fair" fight, the Russians could easily deal with their foes.[23] In these prints, the Japanese method of fighting was implied to be a reflection of an inferior culture and inferior race.

These examples of war *lubki* correspond to the pattern of a racial war, outlined by John Dower in his influential work about the war in the Pacific from 1941 to 1945.[24] As Dower argues, visual images of racism are "invaluable for recreating the ethos which underlay the attitudes and actions of men and women" at the time. Dower links the outpouring of such images to poor military intelligence, planning, and performance.[25] His characterization of the American images of the Japanese as "subhumans" and the use of "apes and vermin" to portray "obedient" and "treacherous" fighters all parallel Russian images of the Japanese in the 1904–1905 war.[26] Just as Pearl Harbor served as the symbolic image of Japanese treachery in World War II to Americans, Port Arthur served the same purpose in Russia during the war with Japan. Similarly, the use of the term "yellow" to describe any attribute of the Japanese enemy, from his complexion (the Russian adjective "yellow" also means "sallow," but the term would not be lost on a Russian audience) to the colors on his uniform, echoes the use of the terms "yellow" and "treacherous" during the Second World War.[27]

Dower's work, in combination with the war *lubok,* brings to light an understudied aspect of the 1904 war with Japan—its racialized nature. In the case of the images of the Russo-Japanese War, the attempt to get an audience to understand the meanings of the war and to exhort Russians to fight, two important functions of the war image, were conveyed in racial terms. This characterization of the Japanese was so pervasive that the publishers of a new edition of the dictionary compiled by Vladimir Dal' added a reference to it. The term "monkey" *(makaki)* not only listed synonyms; it also stated that the word was a derogatory reference to the Japanese and referred to the text from a *lubok.*[28] Publishers thus dehumanized the East Asian foe, a characterization that gains more depth when one examines their popular prints for religious and cultural references about the two combatants.

Religion and Culture in the War *Lubok*

The popular prints of the Russo-Japanese War also treated the issues of religion and culture. The Konovalova print entitled "The Enemy is Terrible, but God is Benevolent" attributes the strength of the Russian soldier to his Orthodox faith.[29] A larger-than-life Russian peasant strides across Korea toward Japan, with Manchuria already behind him, a warning that the Russians could threaten the Japanese-controlled mainland because of the impudence of the attack on Port Arthur. Underneath the *muzhik*'s boots several Japanese battleships burst into flames, while two small enemy soldiers flee from the boot that threatens to squash them. The Russian clutches several more troops in his large mittens, having stuffed more Japanese in the sash around his waist. Like images from wars discussed in previous chapters,[30] this *lubok* visually exaggerates the size of the Russian peasant, a symbol of Russia's size as a nation, and contrasts it with the puny Japanese figures, suggesting that Japan should not be considered a serious country. Reinforcing this contrast, the text, written by D. Gusev, uses derogatory terms for the enemy, asking "where are you running to, yellow face?" and referring to the Japanese as "slant-eyed," "foul," "devils," "feline" and "snub-nosed." By contrast, the text lauds the courage of the Russian peasant, an attribute that stems from his "benevolent God," and concludes "don't be worried, mother Russia."[31] Here racism and religion overlap, reinforcing the dominant theme of the war images.

Other *lubki* claimed that the Orthodox faith of the Russians would carry them to victory in even more explicit references. A St. Petersburg print, "The Cross and the Priest before the Enemy," claims that the "strength of the Lord's cross" during a trial or "national calamity" will prove enough to overcome any defeats and produce ultimate victory.[32] The *lubok* "First Capture Them with Swords, Yes, with Swords They Perish; or, The Impertinent Attack on Christians by the Heathens" features a portrait of Kuropatkin, the commander of the Russian forces in Manchuria.[33] The text quotes Pushkin on the "Russian land" and adds that "our God is with us," leading the Russians to victory. A third *lubok,* "The Prophetic Vision of a Russian Peasant Man *[muzhichka]* and the Promise of Russian Victory," depicts a single Russian peasant inspired by a dream of victory, which takes the form of a religious experience promising that "Rus will celebrate," while the enemy who "invaded Russia's lands" will suffer from hunger and wholesale death.[34] Additional images featured a "ray of God's light" that would "cut through the darkness" of war to bring victory, while a final example depicted "a miraculous appearance of the Virgin" to Russian troops and her assurance of victory.[35]

Religion formed the theme of a print drawn by N. Bogatov that featured Nicholas II, one of only three *lubki* to appear in the war that depicted the Russian tsar. Entitled "The Sovereign Emperor Blesses His Troops with a Holy Icon before Departing for the War," a solemn-looking tsar on horseback holds an Orthodox icon in his hand.[36] Behind the Russian emperor stand several generals overlooking the blessing of the troops. Numerous soldiers, with their caps removed, kneel before their tsar and the symbol of their faith. A simple yet powerful reminder of Russian national identity, this *lubok* visually illustrates the reasons Russians should be prepared to fight and shows how this war, like ones that preceded it, also was portrayed as a holy war. That the Russian tsar, however, only appeared in three out of nearly three hundred patriotic *lubki* issued during the course of the Russo-Japanese War speaks volumes about the way in which the tsar's image disappeared from popular prints.

The reasons why the tsar did not appear in wartime imagery in 1904 are not readily discernible. As Richard Wortman has shown, the tsar used his image quite indiscriminately at times during his reign, most notably during the 1913 Romanov tercentenary. Nicholas II also allowed his image to be reproduced in prints that depicted him with his family, part of an attempt to stress "domestic virtues [as] a public sign of his supreme humanity." In addition, during the 1912 commemorations of the anniversary of Borodino, Ivan Sytin estimated that he printed over 350,000 copies of books and pamphlets that included the tsar's image. Finally, Wortman notes that Nicholas's likeness "embellished the material items of the everyday, associating him with the mundane."[37]

Most likely the reasons why *lubki* did not feature the tsar stem from personal choices made by publishers not to associate the emperor with a war that did not promise victory. In addition, the laws that required members of the imperial family to censor their own images may have led *lubok* publishers to stay away from using pictures of the royal family. Publishers may have avoided using the tsar's image during wartime without an explicit command to do so. Unlike his grandfather, Alexander II, Nicholas II did not become a recognizable figure through the Russian wartime image. Moreover, when he did feature in the wartime propaganda, Nicholas II only did so in mundane roles.

The tsar's relative absence from the popular prints did not make him a prominent symbol of the Russian nation, but wartime images continued to depict manifestations of the Orthodox faith. Recalling prints from the Russo-Turkish War, the print "Battle near the River Yalu" is dominated by intense hand-to-hand fighting. With mountains of Korea forming the backdrop, the massed ranks of both Russian and Japanese troops engage in bayonet charges. The Japanese hold their national flag, while many of the facial features of the Asian foe appear distorted. Russian troops charge heroically, bayonets firmly pointed at the enemy, holding the double-headed eagle standard. The striking part of the *lubok*, however, is the Orthodox priest in the center, standing prominently above the Russian troops in full regalia and holding a cross aloft, blessing the Russians as they charge ahead. The text lauds the actions of this unnamed priest, who entered the fray "with a cross; he was injured, but in his despair" he continued to inspire the Russian troops.[38] The message of the print comes across quite clearly: in all their military endeavors, the Russians had God, symbolized here by the priest, on their side, a stark contrast to the Japanese "heathens."

Lubki that featured Russian or Japanese cultural references contrasted Russian cultural symbols with images of Japanese savagery and exotic behavior. Unlike the images from the Turkish war, those of 1904 did not refer explicitly to Japanese religions, no doubt because of lack of knowledge about them. Instead, by focusing on the culture of the Japanese, *lubok* artists and publishers subtly furthered the construction of the Russo-Japanese War as a racial one.

Taking a different approach to satirizing Japanese culture, the popular print "In Pursuit of Money (A Japanese Song)," resembles the print "Attack on Port Money" in content. A tall, frowning figure of Uncle Sam reaching into a money purse dominates the scene. Surrounding the American both on land and in the sea behind are dozens of small, pesky Japanese troops and sailors, desperate to get at Uncle Sam's money. In this print, capital motivates the Japanese war effort, as well as a slavish attempt to be regarded by the Americans as "brothers." The "song" that represents the text, composed by the war poet Sergei Fedorovich Sulin, contains "lyrics" such as "Uncle Sam—rich with money and he counts us as brothers *[Diadia Sam'—bogat' den'gami i schitaet nas druz'iami]*!" The song then alleges that the Japanese went to war in order not only to please their "friend," but also to get paid by the Americans.[39] Illustrating strong Russian anti-capitalist moods, this print contrasts with those that portray Russians fighting for God, honor, and the tsar.[40] In this image, along with several others that lampooned the English and Americans,[41] Russian war *lubki* linked notions of cultural superiority vis-à-vis the West, which had come to be held as a source of contempt among many Russians because of the capitalism and secularism that predominated there,[42] with the concept of cultural superiority vis-à-vis Japan. To Russian *lubok* publishers, the fact that a nation such as Japan would chose to ally itself with decadent countries such as the United States was not surprising.

A Sytin print, "Regarding Russia's War with Japan," features allegorical representations of the Russian and Japanese nations. Set in East Asia, Mother Russia, adorned in regal armor decorated with Russian symbols, majestically looks across the Sea of Japan. A double-headed eagle perches on her shoulder, while an angel flying overhead points toward the Japanese mainland with a curved sword. Across the sea a large red devil, representing the Japanese, crouches in a sinister pose, flames shooting from its wings. The lengthy text notes that all the Russian troop ranks are "blessed by God," who "strengthened and developed all of Russia's defenders." Consumers were instructed to take comfort that God and his soldiers will "conquer the evil [Japanese]."[43]

Other *lubki* emphasized Russian cultural strengths, particularly the "Russian spirit" that had become a feature of wartime imagery. "How a Russian Soldier Cut Off a Japanese Nose" is a satirical print from Sytin based on an actual event.[44] The picture celebrates a successful naval maneuver in Port Arthur by Admiral Makarov, who blew the bow off a Japanese ship in March 1904, preventing a blockade. The *lubok* satirizes this event by poking fun at the Japanese and making use of a pun: the Russian word "nose" *(nos)* can mean the nose of a person and a ship's bow. The print features a robust Russian sailor, the brow of his cap marked "Rossiia," clutching a sword that drips blood. To the right, a smaller Japanese sailor falls backward over a cliff, blood pouring from the gaping wound where his nose used to be. The nose itself lies harmlessly on a plot of land marked "Manchuria." Two side panels depict the sailor standing behind Port Arthur preparing to slice the Japanese fleet, and the Japanese sailor sitting dejectedly, hand on his head as the blood pours from his nose, lamenting how the Russians had defeated him.[45]

Two final examples further illustrate the cultural strength of Russia as portrayed in the 1904–1905 wartime images. The first, a Sytin image entitled "Parting Words" depicts the interior of a peasant *izba* at the moment a young peasant soldier takes leave of his family for the front. The young peasant, dressed in his Russian uniform, is on both knees at the center of the hut, his father standing before him blessing him with the family icon. Around the father and son stand the rest of this peasant family, some of them wiping away tears. The walls of the *izba*, in a wonderful touch, are adorned with other icons in the corner, but also with several *lubki*—presumably more of Sytin's work. The text has the father telling his son to follow his oath of service and to show "devotion to his faith and truth to the tsar and motherland *[rodina]*," much as he did during the Russo-Turkish War.[46]

The second example, a print from early in the war entitled "Sitting by the Sea, Waiting for the Right Weather!" (Figure 6.4) depicts a giant, jovial Russian peasant with his arm draped around a large cannon. The peasant sits on territory marked "Manchuria," with Port Arthur labeled near his right boot and Vladivostok (resplendent with the imperial standard) looming behind the *muzhik*'s elbow. Across the bay, puny allegorical figures representing Japan, China, the United States, and England stare balefully at the bemused Russian. Again stressing the size of Russia and the lack of strength of the enemy, the print captures the themes of the cultural superiority of Russia, represented by the simple Russian peasant defending the motherland, vis-à-vis Japan, which depends slavishly on the help of England and America. The text serves as an ideal way to sum up the religious and

6.4 "Sitting by the Sea, Waiting for the Right Weather!" The Russian peasant as a symbol reappears in this image from 1904, this time as a representation of the Russian landmass itself. He protects the Far Eastern fortresses of Port Arthur and Vladivostok from Uncle Sam, John Bull, and their Japanese "puppet." The jovial expression of the Russian and the title of the image recalls images such as "One! Two! Three!" (Fig. 5.3). Reprinted by permission of the State Historical Museum, Moscow [GIM]

cultural themes present in the *lubki* of the Russo-Japanese War, concepts that reinforced the idea of this war as racial in nature: "Just look what kind of terrible freaks are visible behind the Japanese's back. I will prove to the yellow-skinned enemies that God helps us!"[47]

Images of Heroism and Masculinity

Images that dealt with heroism provided the most common theme running through the *lubki* of the war. Publishers often combined the definition of heroism presented in these prints with notions of masculinity that served as another reference point to the racial nature of cowardice, symbolized by the portrayal of the Japanese as small, subhuman foes. By focusing on the heroic deeds of Russian soldiers and sailors, *lubok* publishers hoped to convey to their public a definition of sacrifice for the motherland and the tsar, as well as expose future soldiers to these notions. The ways in which the war images from the years 1904–1905 portrayed heroism were varied, from valiant regiments grappling with the enemy to individual acts of heroism from leaders, soldiers, and civilians. The dominant theme in all of these deeds, however, was the connection between courage and masculinity, a combination that Russians possessed, but which their enemy allegedly lacked.

Often popular prints portrayed the heroism of Russian soldiers side by side with the cowardice of the Japanese. In a *lubok* discussed above, the print entitled "Russia's War with Japan," the Japanese fleet is shown retreating from their surprise attack on Port Arthur, defined as treacherous and cowardly. A portrait of Evgenii Alekseev, the governor-general of the Far East and commander of the forces at Port Arthur, accompanies the depiction of the Japanese fleet. Alekseev and his troops stand resolutely after the attack, providing a representation of Russian courage and masculinity that contrasts with the cowardly retreat.[48]

Other examples further define the manly courage of the Russian soldier.[49] One *lubok* featured an impressive March battle scene. In the midst of fierce combat, with Japanese bodies strewn everywhere, a wounded Cossack leads a charge to repel the enemy. The text takes the form of a telegram General Kuropatkin wrote to the tsar after the March engagement to inform him personally of the sacrifices for the cause made by the Cossack lieutenant Shil'nikov, who despite receiving wounds to the hand and shoulder, remained in formation and led his troops to victory.[50] A Sytin print from August 1904 entitled "Mukhortov's Victory" featured the exploits of a soldier in the Russian army who also received recognition from Kuropatkin.[51] The commander of the Russian forces pins a medal on Mukhortov for courage and bravery shown in battle, and then kisses him. Both of these prints demonstrate to the audience that the heroic deeds of Russian soldiers did not go unnoticed by the military leadership.[52]

Admiral Stepan Osipovich Makarov, who died in a naval battle near Port Arthur on 31 March 1904, appeared in numerous images that emphasized his courage and martyrdom for his country. The prints devoted to his memory helped to embellish his mythic status throughout Russia, and Makarov became the Russian hero of the war.[53] After the destruction of the Russian fleet near Tsushima in 1905, Makarov's legend grew, and many Russian military and civilian observers believed that had Makarov lived, the Russians would have won.[54] "In Memory of the *Petropavlovsk*" appeared just two weeks after Makarov's death. Featuring a portrait of Makarov in the upper left corner, the print depicts his battleship, the *Petropavlovsk*, being chased by three Japanese vessels in the moments before its sinking. The text asks for "eternal memory" to "pay the faithful sons of Russia" who lost their lives in service to their motherland.[55] A second print contains a solemn portrait of the dead Russian hero, with funeral flowers adorning the top of the print and a small Orthodox cross underneath his name at the bottom.[56]

Similarly, other images combined heroic exploits with explicit references to the racially inferior foe. A *lubok* simply entitled "The 1904 Russo-Japanese War," printed in July and illustrated by N. Kazachkov, featured fourteen separate images of battle that stressed the heroism of the Russian troops and the nature of the enemy. One scene depicted a battle between P. K. Rennenkampf's troops and Japanese soldiers who were drawn with animal-like features; it was accompanied by a text that described the enemy as "savages," with the Russians taunting, "Yellow-faced dog, just try to test the Russian's strength!" Other battle scenes were accompanied by texts that featured Russians expressing the wish to defend their "holy motherland" *(sviataia rodina),* calling "God is with us" before entering into battle.[57] A medieval Russian knight confronts more than a dozen small Japanese soldiers in a second print, "The Russian *Bogatyr'* in the East: The *Bogatyr'* and the Yellow Dwarves" (Figure 6.5).[58] In the background, several Japanese battleships fire their weapons at the knight, who remains unaffected. As Yulia Mikhailova has argued, "the message is evident: the Russian national spirit is stronger than modern technology."[59] The text of the *lubok,* in addition to calling the Japanese "yellow dwarves," also refers to the Japanese as "Mongols," while referring three times to the superiority of "Rus'" in this war.[60]

Expressions of Russian courage can be found in the images from 1904 that depicted Russian women. In the most poignant of these prints, entitled "The Selfless Russian Mothers: The Moving Case of How a Loving Mother Blesses Her Son for the War," a Russian peasant woman inside her *izba* blesses her son, clad in his uniform. The caption notes that the young man, named Ivan Kudriashev from Riazan, and his mother, "though saddened," must go and fight "for faith, tsar, and Russia."[61] "The Distribution of Christmas Gifts to the Wounded in the Far East" also features Russian women helping in the war effort.[62] This *lubok* is set inside a field hospital in which numerous wounded Russian soldiers are convalescing. Although the print depicts Russians wounded in the war, all of them appear cheerful and spirited despite their wounds. Five Red Cross nurses distributing gifts to the soldiers no doubt help revive the men, who appear grateful for the attention. In this *lubok,* like the previous ones mentioned above, the women add further meaning to the courage and masculinity displayed by Russian troops in the war. The *lubki* from the years 1904–1905 that featured Russian women represent a far cry from the images of the Patriotic War, when peasant women actively participated in the struggle against the French. In the Russo-Japanese War, the mothers, wives, and sisters of Russia stood behind their sons, husbands, or soldiers, providing them with the strength and inspiration to perform heroic deeds for their country and faith.

Courage and masculinity, vital qualities of military culture, found a variety of expressions in the popular prints of the Russo-Japanese War. The companies that produced these images encouraged attributes that expressed ideals of Russian heroism. By contrasting the Russian soldier and the Japanese enemy, they not only helped to define masculinity; they also provided a sharp juxtaposition between the subhuman, cowardly "other" who had savagely attacked Port Arthur and the brave, loyal soldiers who

РУССКІЙ БОГАТЫРЬ
НА ВОСТОКѢ
БОГАТЫРЬ и ЖЕЛТЫЕ КАРЛИКИ.

6.5 "The Russian *Bogatyr'* in the East" Another Russian national symbol, the *bogatyr'* (a medieval knight), is mobilized in this print. The modern technologies arrayed behind the knight may help to defeat the Japanese troops (referred to as "yellow dwarves" by the text), but this image suggests that ultimately victory will result from the timeless Russian spirit. Reprinted by permission of the State Historical Museum, Moscow [GIM]

defended the Russian Far East. The process of enmification frequently involves emasculating the enemy, and the wartime culture of the years 1904–1905 proved no exception.

One print entitled "Regarding Russia's War with Japan in 1904: Napoleon Visits the Japanese" aimed to portray the foolishness of the Japanese attack as an attempt to conquer Russia. The image features six Japanese generals sitting around a table, planning their next move in the war. All six stand up in surprise at the arrival of Napoleon's ghost. The text has Napoleon addressing the Japanese military leaders, warning them of their impending folly, stating, "Yellow monkeys, you took up arms against Russia—what kind of warriors are you?"[63] By linking the racial war to the war against Napoleon, this *lubok* not only reminded Russians of the patriotism demonstrated in 1812, but also exhorted them to display similar feelings in the present war.

Japanese Prints of War: Joining the World of Visual Nationhood

While Russian popular prints of the war sought to dehumanize the Japanese enemy, stressing the racial superiority of the Russians, Japanese popular prints depicted the Russian enemy as formidable in an effort to embellish the magnitude of their victory. After the Meiji emperor came to power in Japan in 1868 determined to "modernize" the country and make it more European, image makers began to turn their attention to promoting visual representations of Japanese nationhood. Official ceremonies and rituals created to bind the Japanese people together behind European concepts of patriotism and national identity included a flood of woodblock prints that drew on earlier myths and memories of the national past.[64]

The Russo-Japanese War, however, presented a unique opportunity for Japanese artists to depict the progress of this new sense of nationhood, and they seized the opportunity. Fusing representations of the warrior in traditional Japanese woodblock prints with western traditions of wartime imagery (particularly lithographs), Japanese artists helped to create an effective form of propaganda that "conveyed both nostalgia and Japaneseness to the Japanese viewer." The proliferation of Japanese triptychs during the years 1904–1905 reflected, as well as helped to shape, public opinion about the conflict.[65] Where Russian images stressed the alleged racial and cultural inferiority of the Japanese enemy, Japanese prints emphasized that the Russians were "sometimes villainous, sometimes failed heroes, but always formidable enemies."[66] These images lacked the racism present in Russian popular prints of the war.[67] By depicting the enemy as a worthy foe, they accentuated the importance of the Japanese victory over Russia and furthered the "visual dominance" of Japanese nationhood and thus Japan's entry into "modernity."[68]

The triptychs, which featured three sheets, each fifteen inches high by ten inches wide and placed side by side to form a horizontal image, "were produced by Japanese woodblock designers during the Russo-Japanese War to depict a formidable enemy defeated at every turn by the Japanese spirit [Yamato-damashii]."[69] From the moment the war began, Japanese prints proclaimed "the Japanese army's great victory" and stressed loyalty to the imperial institutions while emphasizing the necessity of enthusiasm for the war effort. The print "Destroying the Enemy Wire Entanglements, the Japanese Forces Capture Nanshan," published on 24 August 1904, for example, features Japanese troops heroically engaged in difficult combat near the Nanshan Hill. The text of the print reads: "The enemy tried desperately to fend off our ever-advancing Fourth Brigade. A death-defying corps of engineers was ordered to cut the enemy entanglements. Defying flying bullets, they crawled to the wires and accomplished their mission. Their exploit merits a special note in our war chronicle."[70]

As this and other triptychs stressed,[71] Japanese prints celebrated the courage and success of the Japanese military above all, while stressing that the Russian enemy remained a dangerous one. The April 1904 triptych "A Great Victory for the Great Japanese Navy, Hurrah" features Admiral Makarov on board the *Petropavlovsk* as it sinks. With water rising around him and two sailors vainly attempting to rescue him, Makarov stoically looks off to the distance, resigned to meeting a hero's fate.[72] Similarly, the print "Battle of the Liaoyang Peninsula" features an impressive-looking Kuropatkin leading his troops on horseback in the loss. Far from being a weak, unworthy adversary, Kuropatkin and Makarov, as the Japanese prints make clear, were deserving foes and served as "a foil for the celebration of Japanese victory. Pictures of a formidable enemy led by valiant officers and defeated by the home army were important tools in creating a new national image" in Japan, for they revealed "both the way the Japanese wished to be seen and the way they saw themselves."[73] By presenting the Russian leaders as brave and tough, Japanese images helped to enhance the performance of the Japanese military.

In striking contrast to the racist depiction of the Japanese so prevalent in Russian *lubki,* Japanese triptychs, perhaps in a deliberate attempt to combat widespread Russian beliefs about the Japanese as uncivilized Mongols, stressed the high ethical standards of the Japanese troops. The print "Picture of the Russo-Japanese War, with the Japanese Red Cross Helping and Healing Wounded People in a Field Hospital," a March 1904 triptych, shows Japanese medics treating wounded Russian POWs. The grateful faces of the Russian troops for the food and care given to them contrasts with an insert in the image featuring two Russian soldiers kicking and abusing two Japanese women.[74] By stressing the civilized traits of the Japanese, this print suggests that western notions of Japanese barbarity had no foundation, and again signaled the rightful place of Japan among the world's powers. At the same time, the image reminded the audience of the racism inherent in Russian attitudes toward the Japanese. For a Japanese audience, this and similar triptychs reinforced the importance of the triumph over the Russians, a significance captured later by the immense victory pageants that borrowed from "the triumphal ceremonies of the Western countries."[75] For Russians, who believed that the Japanese were a racially inferior, uncivilized opponent, the Japanese victory in 1905 helped to set in motion a variety of crises that would greatly affect Russian society, in addition to illustrating some ambiguities surrounding the entire notion of Russian imperialism in the Far East.

Russian Imperialism and the War *Lubok*

The differences between Russian and Japanese popular prints illustrate the varying ways in which artists and other cultural figures viewed their respective imperial missions. In the Russian case, the popular images of war represent an important source for examining ideas about Russian imperialism in its East Asian variant. Nineteenth-century Russian imperialism, as one historian has remarked, was always emblematic of a desire to become a European power, but equally ambiguous.[76] Russian imperialism lacked "a popular and catchy phrase to capture" its essence, and it tended to be explained through cultural products.[77] Because of this lack of clear definition, supporters of imperial expansion in Russia felt they had "to assert Russia's membership in the European community as distinct from Asian cultures." This attempt led many Russian elites "to overcompensate for the perceived inferior qualities of Russia's domestic institutions by extolling the superior qualities of its imperial mission."[78] In other words, Russian elites at times embraced a deeply ambiguous yet popular imperial mission that projected Russian inadequacies onto the "uncivilized" peoples of Asia, while they simultaneously developed an equally ambiguous "Asianist" vision of Russian penetration in the Far East.[79]

As David Schimmelpenninck has recently argued, the view of Asia as both an alien element and as part of Russia's own heritage led to a variety of opinions that advocated diverse roles for Russia in the region. "Asianists" such as Prince Esper Ukhtomskii stressed Russia's Asian heritage and destiny as a reason for the tsar to turn toward the east and welcome new subjects. According to this view (one shared by many Silver Age writers), the incorporation of Asian peoples into the Russian Empire would not be one based on inferiority, because Russian culture was neither wholly European nor Asian, but both. On the other hand, Sergei Witte, the finance minister, called for a Russian version of *pénétration pacifique* in the Far East as a means for advancing Russian commercial interests. Other Russians viewed the Far East as an object of conquest solely for the sake of conquest. Schimmelpenninck explains that these competing ideas about Russia's imperial role all helped shape the policies that Nicholas II and his statesmen pursued in Asia, as Russia's leaders accepted elements of one ideology at different times.[80]

For his part, the Russian tsar, having experienced an assassination attempt on a trip to Japan while still tsarevich, viewed his Asian neighbors with a mixture of contempt and fascination.[81] Overall Russian policy in the 1890s partly grew out of Sergei Witte's plans to build a Far Eastern railroad that would connect the Russian Empire with its newly acquired (and ever-expanding) lands in the region in an effort to construct a "road to power" in the Far East.[82] This railroad project brought the Russian Empire into direct dealings with the Japanese, a nation that had undergone significant transformations since the Meiji Restoration of the 1860s. Witte's motives proved largely commercial, for he wanted to transform Russia into an industrialized state partly by creating new markets in the Far East and by taking advantage of a weak Chinese state and its two territories, Manchuria and Korea. For the last two tsars and other officials, however, the expansion was not only commercially motivated, and opinions about a Russian "mission" in the Far East gained more currency.[83]

This notion of a Russian mission increased in popularity among educated Russians through several sources. One was the Russian explorer, Nikolai Przhevalskii, who claimed in the 1880s that many Chinese would gladly "become subjects of the White Tsar."[84] A group of Russian professors began to advance the idea in the same period that Russians, because of their status as a Eurasian people, could expand in the Far East not as conquerors, but as liberators. The Christian philosopher Vladimir Solov'ev put it more bluntly when he called for eastern expansion to defend against the "yellow power" and because inferior races should always submit to superior ones or risk disappearing from the face of the earth,[85] comments that paralleled Wilhelm II's well-known exhortations to his cousin, Nicholas II, to turn east and face the "yellow peril." Although not every educated Russian supported these views, very few spoke out against them.[86] Russian attitudes before the war toward Japan contained strange, vague notions of a Russian mission to civilize the region combined with a fear of Japanese expansion. By 1904, therefore, most educated Russians viewed Japan as a small, distant country that had only recently begun to emerge from barbarism, and this perception led to the exaggerated notions of Russia's ability to deal with the Japanese forces.

These ambiguities at the heart of Russian imperial expansion can be detected quite clearly in the wartime *lubki* both from the Russo-Japanese War of 1904–1905 and the Russo-Turkish War of 1877–1878. Although some Russian elites advocated expansion because of Russia's shared culture with Asia, citing geographic location as a source for positive relations, the wartime images betray the sense of superiority that also lay at the center of Russian imperialism. *Lubok* publishers who depicted the Turks and Japanese as culturally and racially inferior peoples saw Russia's "mission" as far from progressive and tended to illustrate it as a mission of conquest.[87] In defining the otherness of Russia's enemies, *lubok* publishers inadvertently helped to reveal one of the inherent "tensions of empire."[88] As a recent collection of essays that discusses imperialism makes clear, "colonial projects were fundamentally predicated on a tension between notions of incorporation and differentiation that were weighted differently at different times."[89] During wartime, as the popular images illustrate, Russian imperialism was portrayed in stark, racial terms that overshadowed notions of incorporation and pointed to a fundamental tension within the ambiguous imperial project. Although Russia's aims in the 1904 war consisted of defeating a foreign enemy, the characterization of the Japanese reflected a belief in Russian superiority over all Asian cultures. In a very real sense, then, the wartime *lubok* deserves to be considered an artifact of Russian imperialism.[90]

Understanding the Racial War

Wars tend to bring tensions to the surface of a society, and the Russo-Japanese War proved no exception. In addition to highlighting the tensions of empire throughout Russia, the conflict provided a momentous catalyst for change in several other arenas. Politically, Russia's Far Eastern failure was generally blamed on the incompetence of the tsarist governmental system, and the opposition to the fighting helped to bring about the October Manifesto of 1905. Economically, the war produced a widespread belief that both the Great Reforms of the 1860s–1870s and the industrialization in the 1890s had not gone far enough. More needed to be done if Russia truly was to be a European power, and in the years following the war, the Russian government adopted significant new reforms in the countryside and the cities. Socially, the war sparked the unrest that dominated Russia in 1905, and military failures fueled the revolutionary attitudes of wide swathes of the population.[91] Culturally, the war led to its own tensions too, and earlier feelings of superiority over the Japanese (and the Orient in general) began to be more widely questioned. Historians, while understandably devoting a great deal of research to the tensions in Russian politics, economics, and society after the war, have paid scant attention to the cultural ramifications of the Russo-Japanese War, although the tensions brought out in the cultural sphere proved no less important.[92]

Understanding how Russians interpreted the wartime *lubok,* combined with an examination of their wartime experience, sheds more light on how a subtle, but nonetheless powerful, change in attitudes toward the Japanese began to form. In some respects, the *lubki* from the Russo-Japanese War undermined the war effort. In its role as propaganda, these prints created a belief in the superiority of Russian arms that could not be matched on the battlefield. When Russia began losing to such an "inferior" nation as Japan, the catastrophe sparked unrest throughout the empire. Just as the images of the Crimean War provided people like N. V. Davydov with an opportunity to criticize the government, so too did the *lubki* of the Japanese War.

During the war itself, the recollections of I. P. Belokonskii, mentioned at the opening of this chapter, offer the most comprehensive account of the reception of the racist attitudes present in the popular prints of the time. A writer for the journal *Obrazovanie,* Belokonskii studied peasant responses to the *lubki* of the time in a three-part series. He began his meditations on the popular attitudes toward the 1904 war by noting that the demand for information on the events of the war, both in the cities and throughout the countryside, far exceeded that of previous conflicts, even the Russo-Turkish War of 1877–1878. For Belokonskii, however, this desire for information about a war "on the other side of the world" was tempered with "deep regret" about the "chief supplier" of news about the war, namely the *lubok,* which publishers produced "in many quantities" throughout 1904.[93]

In a visit to the Kharkov company of Iurii Gunaropol, a Ukrainian publisher, Belokonskii noted that the images produced and distributed with government approval came after the publishers "took it into their heads to dupe the public."[94] These "monkey and bear stories . . . exclusively belong to low-grade *lubok* literature." Belokonskii elaborates, "this name right away defines their content: of course, the monkeys are Japanese, and the bear is Russia [Rossiia]. First of all, they are backward, and they are funny, but second, they are powerful."[95] He noted that this publisher also included another caricature in his images, "the bulldog," which "craftily and naturally incited the monkey to violate the bear's rest." The *lubok* publishers such as Gunaropol, according to Belokonskii, wanted to make the contents of their images, as well as the reasons behind the conflict, "fully understandable" to their audience.

On his Kharkov tour, Belokonskii then examined and discussed in detail four images that he found had sold well in the region and that best captured the demand for "stories about monkeys and bears." The first was the print "Sitting by the Sea, Waiting for the Right Weather," the second "A Strange Enemy, but a Kind God," the third "The Fighting Song of the Don Cossacks," and the fourth "The Fighting Song of the Russian Sailor." In all the examples, Belokonskii cried that the images contained "all sorts of worthless exaggerations" that would lead one to believe "in this present war, both on sea and on land, that the Japanese court and army will perish like flies."[96] In examining the images themselves, Belokonskii notes the "disgraceful features and physiognomy" of the Asians, the "lack of culture displayed in the *lubok*, as in the previous war [against the Turks]," that "everything is founded solely on crude, brute force," while Russia's enemy "is confused because of its 'little stature,' that it will be enough to 'smash their cheek-bones,' 'blow away the blockheads,' 'rip out', etc.," in order to win the war.[97] Regarding "knowledge, culture, and the lawful conditions of the Japanese people," lamented Belokonskii, the *lubki* he bought threw out all attempts to examine the real nature of the enemy in order to focus on "rubbish." In conclusion, Belokonskii wrote that "if our current *lubok* literature really goes toward creating national ideals, as is true, they are nearly all terrible for the Russian people, but as we have already said at first, one notices among the masses a more heightened demand [for the crude prints], and intelligent publishers took care to satisfy it."[98]

While purchasing various prints on his 1904 travels, Belokonskii found other cultural expressions that also incorporated the crude caricatures present in the war *lubok*. In particular, the Russian journalist examined several pamphlets that discussed various aspects of the conflict. One of these pamphlets, entitled "Story of an Eye-Witness: How the Japanese Fight," from the Petersburg firm of A. A. Kholmushin, attempted to examine the nature of the Far Eastern foe through the eyes of a fictional Russian soldier fighting at Chemulpo (the present-day Korean city of Inchon). The soldier, named Bobra Rychagovii, observed the struggle between a Russian vessel and a squadron of Japanese soldiers attempting to overtake it. Although the "[enemy] throng made a hole in the vessel," "the sailors were capable right away of throwing the undersized enemy head over heels," a sight that proved "funny and terrible." After suffering such ignoble treatment, Rychagovii notes, "the monkeys savagely ran away, filling the air with their shrill cries." In terms of casualties, the pamphlet noted, "the number of Japanese dead turned out to be three times more than ours." Belokonskii, in a typical caustic aside, only noted, "no comment *[kommentarii, polagaem, izlishni]*."[99]

Other pamphlets Belokonskii bought carried similar messages. The war was blamed on the "deceitful and insidious Asian people" in one, while others stressed the physiognomy of the Japanese, commenting on their "narrow heads and brows." One pamphlet asked the question, "what is this Japan, what is the government like," and answered that the country consisted of "500 thousand civilized people out of 39 million, 500 thousand apes." The same circular went on to compare Russia, a "European, Christian" country, with Japan, a country that possessed "favorable conditions for civilization," but one that Russia needed to help by "waking up the savages."[100] Still more pamphlets contrasted the Russian Orthodox faith with the Japanese gods as a means of reinforcing the lack of civilization and culture in the Far Eastern nation.[101]

In the last part of his series, Belokonskii again discussed several *lubki* that enjoyed wide popularity throughout his travels. The first of these images, "Help for the War Needs,"[102] features an emaciated Japanese emperor begging before Uncle Sam and John Bull, both of whom ignore their ally with disdain. Japanese troops fleeing after a Cossack attack dominates a second image, "The Japanese Hussars," which also contains a text from Vladimir Giliarovskii that crows, "it is for the best, that the Cossacks have taken and chased on foot the poor monkeys *[chto poluchshe, zabrali kazaki i poshli peshechkom bednye makaki].*"[103] A third print Belokonskii discussed was "Attack on Port Money (Figure 6.1)," examined above, which featured animal-like Japanese pests attacking their ally, Uncle Sam, for his money.

The fourth print Belokonskii mentioned, "The Russian's Present," is dominated by a giant Russian *muzhik* dressed in traditional clothing and holding a whip, sitting patiently atop Port Arthur.[104] Behind the peasant the sun rises, while in the foreground smaller figures representing Japan, China, the United States, and Great Britain confer on how to approach the Russian, who waits to deliver his "present." The text has Uncle Sam, frightened to attack the peasant, chiding the Japanese sailor, stating, "Hey, you're a coward, monkey!"[105] Other images Belokonskii discussed include and "The Cossack's Breakfast," which features a caricature of a giant Cossack about to devour a small Japanese soldier for his morning meal and contains a text that notes, "the Japanese nature is to lie," while calling on the audience "to look as your skin tears on my teeth!"[106] For Belokonskii, who bought these images four months after his first foray into the *lubok* market, "no progress" in their themes "is noticed."

Belokonskii concluded his examination of the *lubki* of the war by complaining of "the amazing scarcity of ideas, the poor fantasies, roughness, monotonous facial images, horrifying ignorance and illiteracy" contained in the wartime images. At the same time, he reiterated that "to go into the market" at the time was to understand how popular these images were and to become aware of how much money *lubok* publishers made selling their images to "the ignorant buyer," who paid between fifteen and twenty-five kopeks per print.[107] Distressed at how influential he believed the *lubok* to be in promoting false ideas about the war in particular and national ideals in general, Belokonskii called on his readers to "engage in combat with the *lubok* literature" to defeat "the wide demand for this literature among the masses."[108]

Kh. Podborovskii, another journalist interested in the reactions to the war, also studied attitudes in the Russian village. He too noted the importance that the *lubok* played in shaping beliefs among the peasantry toward the Japanese enemy.[109] Podborovskii echoed Belokonskii's complaints about the nature of the information contained in the wartime images. After writing, "no less familiar [in the countryside] are the *lubok* pictures, which go to the people by the hundreds of thousands," he laments that the prints "don't stand on ceremony at all" in regard to facts. For this journalist, the wartime images present "the worst sides of the soul: cruelty and absurdity." After studying reactions among Russian peasants to the prints of Andrei Morozov in particular, Podborovskii presents a catalog of attitudes held in the countryside toward the Japanese, including the ideas that "the Japanese have no God," are "island braggarts," and are "weak people and not especially hardy, probably both from a physical nature and undernourishment." Throughout his account of the wartime countryside, Podborovskii notes the role that rumors and legends played in how the Russian peasantry conceived of the war, fueled in part by the information they received in the wartime *lubok*. Podborovskii, like Belokonskii, rued this fact, although he despaired of the Russian peasantry ever "truly understanding" the war because "the oppressive censorship" in Russia does not try to correct exaggerations contained in the *lubok*.[110]

Frederick McCormick, an American war correspondent who followed the Russian army throughout their Far Eastern campaign, also wrote extensively about the attitudes of the Russians toward their enemy. McCormick characterized the Russian perception of the war as a racial one between Occident and Orient. When he discussed the image of the Japanese held by Russian troops, McCormick mused: "from the misguided moujik to the Viceroy of the Eastern Empire, monkey was the favorite epithet" for the Japanese. For this American, "the war was a natural outcome of such opinions and ideas."[111] McCormick's coverage of the war reveals the extent to which Russian soldiers had accepted the popular stereotypes of their Japanese enemy so prevalent throughout Russian culture. For McCormick, this attitude carried over into the battlefield, in the form of atrocities, which Russians were more likely to inflict:

> In an army where even up to the Battle of Mukden generals regarded the Japanese as "monkeys" and continually applied the epithet, it was not strange that the ignorant peasant soldiers where they had the power, actually treated highly civilized Japanese soldiers as mere animals, and even in some cases as wild beasts.[112]

In other cases that McCormick observed, captured Russian troops begged the Japanese not to cut off their heads because they feared what the enemy would do.[113] For McCormick, this "great modern war was sorrowfully fought in the name of the Occident," and the "spectacle of Occidental mankind in his adventures in the promotion of the Eastern Empire has the most damaging animal aspect."[114]

McCormick's account of the stereotypes held by Russian peasant soldiers finds added support in a letter written by a Russian soldier to a newspaper during the waning months of the war. This letter also addressed the attitudes held toward the Japanese among the army. Appearing in the conservative paper *Rus'*, the letter was written by a Russian POW held in Japan, and illustrates how the experience of war may have changed the cultural assumptions held by many Russians about their foe:

> Monkey was the most frequent expression heard at the beginning of the war concerning the Japanese. The application of such a term to a brave enemy was both undignified and shabby. . . . That seemed to be the opinion at the outbreak of the war. But the English knew better, and making an ally of the "monkey" was on their part a master-stroke of diplomacy. All the stories told of the brutality of the Japanese have been shown to be unfounded. Our soldiers who have been prisoners and escaped are unanimous as to the kindness shown them by the Japanese. And the same feeling is expressed in letters coming from our soldiers, prisoners of war. Thousands of Japanese who have so heroically sacrificed their lives in front of Port Arthur have more than wiped out the first perfidious attack upon our ships. A feeling of mutual respect has grown up between ourselves and the Japanese with the common acknowledgment of the great sacrifices that each of us has made. Such sentiment has grown and become rooted. Our opinion of the Japanese has completely altered. Probably the opinion of our enemies toward us is also altered. Amid the horrors of war we have learned to understand one another, and it is earnestly to be hoped that the awful price we and the Japanese have paid for that knowledge will form the basis for future peaceful relationship.[115]

For this soldier the racist caricature of the enemy in which so many Russians believed around 1904 proved untenable after actually encountering the enemy.[116]

Other Russians reached similar conclusions about the East Asian foe without engaging in any personal encounters. Alexander Pasternak, the brother of Boris, also recalled his changing feelings toward the Japanese in his memoirs, particularly noting the importance of images in promoting ideas. Although only a schoolboy at the time of the war, Pasternak remembers how news of the war dominated talk in his school, and particularly recollects the "flood of boastful posters and jingoistic journalism" in early 1904.[117] For Pasternak, the war was an event that brought long-standing emotions to the surface of society, a process he described in the following manner:

In town everything kept step with the strut of the double-headed Imperial eagle. The nation may have seethed secretly, but the surface was calm; like a pond smothered over in duckweed, it was plastered over with posters in whose potency the state had intense faith. Those ubiquitous, monstrous posters! Who could ever have thought them up, and for what? I can swear with absolute certainty that they never fulfilled their intended aims. Oh, but they did achieve the reverse effects, as often as you could wish.[118]

As to the *lubki* themselves, Pasternak recounts their contents:

People of my generation will probably remember those wartime posters. They were meant to suggest the cheap prints of popular literature, with their bright, improbable colours, and strong salt of folk humor. Alas, the posters achieved neither the one nor the other; they were distinguished only by their counterproductive passion to persuade. The Japanese were uniformly portrayed as knock-kneed weaklings, slant-eyed, yellow-skinned, and for some reason, shaggy-haired—a puny kind of monkey, invariably dubbed "Japs" *[ia-poshki]* and "monkeys" *[makaki]*. Opposing them were the legendary heroes of our army, Russian stalwarts and the Manchurian Cossacks (distinguished by their yellow, rather than red, braided trousers). One poster, for instance, displayed a swarm of spider-like Japs, faces twisted with fear, vainly trying to struggle out from under a huge Caucasian fur hat. The caption read "catch them by the capful!" On another, an Olympian hand squeezed a fistful of macaques, legs and arms writhing in their last agony. The *chef d'oeuvre*, I remember, was a Cossack, riding at the trot with lance aslant his shoulder, a clutch of Japs skewered on it like rats on a spit, while another, in flight, was about to be transfixed. We knew the reality well enough! We knew that the Japanese won not only by heroism, but by their swiftness and skill in manoeuvre, their excellent new arms, and above all, their use of camouflage.[119]

While Pasternak claimed that not all members of his class believed in the patriotic exhortations contained in the images from 1904, he offered a slightly different view in another passage, when he noted, "naturally the general war-spirit found its way into our daily play." He recalled that the toys and games he and his friends bought and used in 1904 adopted patriotic themes, "with the intention of inculcating patriotism, veneration for Tsar and fatherland, and faith in the might of Russian arms." Pasternak claims that these calls did not work on him, but muses that they may have succeeded with other families.[120] In some respects, Pasternak's reminiscences speak volumes about the importance of the wartime *lubok*. His memoirs, written between 1969 and 1975, reflect more than sixty years of musings on the events of 1904–1905, and his negative memories of the wartime images may have been affected by the outcome of the war and subsequent revolution. Notably, however, Pasternak's reminiscences of 1904 deal almost entirely with the *lubki* of the war.

Although not every Russian experienced the same feelings as Pasternak or the unnamed officer who wrote to *Rus'*, their accounts reveal a number of important insights. First, both demonstrate that the themes present in the images of war gained wide currency among the combatants, who fought in the war, and civilians alike. The letter mentions that most soldiers thought of the enemy as "monkeys," culturally inferior, treacherous and unfair fighters, and capable of acts of savagery, all notions promoted in the war *lubki*. While Pasternak's memoirs claim that the *lubki*'s "intended aims" were not realized among his schoolmates, he does attest to the widespread proliferation of popular images in 1904 and later speculates that other Russians may have found them persuasive.

However, the letter—and to a certain extent, Pasternak's account—suggests that at least among some Russians, a change had taken place regarding the attitudes they held toward the Japanese. Armed with an image of a subhuman foe, many Russian soldiers eventually found their Japanese opponents to be just as human as themselves, an idea ironically promoted in the triptychs produced in Japan discussed above. The attempt to construct a human self pitted against a subhuman other dissipated amidst the experience of war for some. As Russian attitudes about the Japanese foe were changing, Russians turned to open questioning about the government's reasons for fighting the war in the first place. The reasons behind the war had never been explained in clear terms, and when the war was lost, its aftermath unsettled Russian society. Although what became the revolution of 1905 did not stem entirely from the defeat, the shock of losing a war to such an "uncivilized" foe played a crucial role in the culture of the time.[121]

Popular literature after the war portrayed the Japanese "with a mixture of respect, hostility, and fascination, perhaps as a result of the impression of the Russian defeat in the Russo-Japanese War."[122] In this comment, Jeffrey Brooks captures the ways in which the war came to affect attitudes toward Asians in general and the Japanese in particular throughout Russian culture. The complex mixture of hostility and humanity that had marked Russian expansionary policies in the Far East had found its way into popular culture. Russia's proclaimed role as liberator of the East and the belief that it had a significant role to play in Asia because of its Eurasian roots can be seen in a variety of sources, most notably the popular Russian detective stories featuring Japanese characters written after the war. While a growing cosmopolitanism may have contributed to less racist images of Asian peoples in Russian culture after 1905, some stereotypes persisted, and Russian attempts to define the Japanese after the war presented an amalgam of contradictory ideas, images, and themes.[123]

The popularity of detective stories among certain portions of the Russian population must also be viewed alongside the popularity of the stories about "monkeys and bears" that Belokonskii reported. In the aftermath of the war, it is hard to believe that all racist stereotypes toward the Japanese either disappeared or gave way to more nuanced depictions of the former enemy. Attempting to come to terms with such a surprising, comprehensive defeat proved difficult at best. As David Wells has noted in his examination of Russian literature after the Russo-Japanese War, "the war came to be seen as a symbol of powerful forces determining the destiny of humanity which were outside the control of humans themselves, whether these were conceived on a psychological, metaphysical, or eschatological plane."[124] The apocalyptic imagery present in Russian culture after 1905 suggests that the effects of the war were intellectual as well as strategic.[125]

The defeat at the hands of the Japanese, as Alexander Pasternak noted, suggests that the wartime propaganda succeeded in its characterization of the enemy because it illustrated the vast overconfidence throughout Russia. The war's end unsettled many. When Russia went to war in 1914, popular prints again utilized stereotypes of the enemy and again portrayed the foe as inferior. What may be termed a "crisis of Russian national identity" and a crisis in patriotic culture emerged after 1905 and became more severe in 1915.

7

THE **GREAT WAR** IN RUSSIAN IMAGERY, 1914–1917

> The successful operations of our troops within the first months
> of the war gave rich food for the *lubok,* and no event or feat was
> not reflected in one, and even several sheets. The victory of
> Kozma Kriuchkov, the valor of Russian and allied pilots, individ-
> ual episodes from the campaign in East Prussia, the sinking of
> enemy battleships, the expulsion of the Austrians from the
> southwest lands, the capture of L'vov, Peremyshl', the crossing
> of the Carpathians, Krakow under threat . . . all of this was
> picked up by the publishers, and the cheerful, colorful message
> was carried across the face of the Russian land.
>
> —**Vladimir Denisov** (1916)

• The Great War, as contemporaries called the First World War, has fasci-
nated historians ever since hostilities broke out in August 1914. Indeed,
perhaps no other event in the twentieth century has been so thoroughly
documented and analyzed as this war, the legacies of which continue to
cast a shadow over our contemporary world. Despite the fact that Russia
played a prominent role both in the diplomatic crises that led to war and
in the actual fighting on the Eastern Front, Russia's participation in the
Great War has until recently been widely ignored by historians.[1] The revolution that broke out in February 1917, followed by the Bolshevik seizure
of power in October instead led scholars to concentrate on these events.
This historiography came at the cost of coverage of the war, a conflict that
made the events of 1917 possible.

The collapse of the Soviet Union in 1991 produced a small group of historians who have reconsidered the importance of the Great War in Russian
history, a reexamination that has yielded several important works.[2] Despite this growing body of scholarship, most publications devoted to the
Great War continue to stress the Western Front, which has entered into
popular imagination as the dominant image of the war. Niall Ferguson's
The Pity of War, which caused a stir in 1998 and 1999 upon its release,
barely mentioned Russia in its controversial assessments both of the war's
causes and its effects upon soldiers and civilians alike.[3] Similarly, the lively
debate about the cultural legacies of the war that has engaged scholars such

as Modris Eksteins and Jay Winter, to name just two of the most prominent historians of the subject, concentrates on western powers such as
Great Britain, France, and Germany, despite claims by both authors for the
universality of their conclusions.[4] In sum, Russia's wartime experience
continues to receive short shrift from other scholars. Historians largely
persist in viewing the Great War and its legacies in a binary fashion: the
experience of the Western Front, which conjures images of trench warfare
and the "birth of the modern age" in its cultural legacies; and the Russian,
eastern experience (often called the "unknown war," after a term coined
by Winston Churchill), which brought Bolshevism to Europe.

This chapter examines the images of war produced in Russia from 1914
to 1917 through a broader lens. Russian wartime propaganda, and particularly the war *lubok,* exhorted Russians to fight and understand the war in a
fashion similar to all the other wartime belligerents. Drawing on themes
and stereotypes present in Russian visual culture for over a century, *lubok*
publishers articulated a patriotic culture that featured such "modern" elements as aviation alongside appeals to the Orthodox background of most
Russian citizens. These popular prints again enjoyed a tremendous popularity during the first two years of the war, as market sales exceeded figures
from the Russo-Japanese War of 1904–1905. Eventually, as Hubertus Jahn
has noted, the patriotic appeals present throughout Russian culture from
1914 to 1917 proved unable to prevent the whirlwind of revolution.[5]

At the same time, the February Revolution of 1917, while ending tsarist
rule in Russia, can be seen in many ways as a patriotic event. War, as this
book has argued in other chapters, can act as both a social cohesive and a
solvent at the same time, and nowhere is this fact more evident than in
Russia in 1917. While historians such as Jahn have viewed the events of
1917 as proof that Russians lacked a sense of national identity,[6] in many
ways, February 1917 can best be termed a patriotic—and nationalistic—
revolution. Russia's lack of a unifying national symbol to override social
antagonisms and questions about nationhood, moreover, may not be a
sign of lack of patriotism, but a strength. No doubt Russia experienced a
national identity crisis during the war, and 1915 did in fact prove to be a
turning point in cultural production during the war, yet this fact holds
true for most of Europe.[7] Ultimately, this chapter will challenge the prevalent view that Russia lacked a strong sense of nationhood in 1917 by situ-
ating the patriotic culture present in wartime imagery from 1914 to 1917
within the century-old tradition upon which it built.

The Kaiser's War

More than in any other war since the Napoleonic invasion, the *lubki* of
the years 1914–1917 focused on the figure of a national leader. During the
Great War, Kaiser Wilhelm II of Germany was vilified in numerous ways
and became the dominant image of the enemy against whom Russians

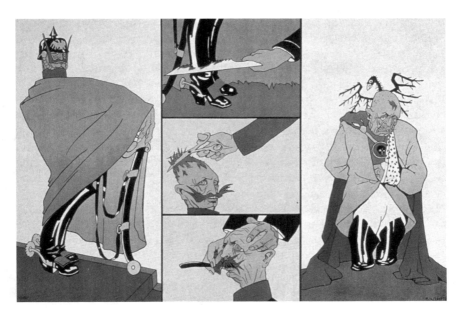

7.1 "So You Want to Be Napoleon" This 1914 Ivan Sytin *lubok* defines Kasier Wilhelm II by his mustache, the dominant feature of the German emperor in the wartime images. The center of the print features a Russian soldier "helping" Wilhelm become Napoleon, while the caption simply states: "So you want to be Napoleon? Well, then, we'll help." Reprinted by permission from the Poster Collection, Hoover Institution Archives.

could vent their frustrations. Although Franz Joseph of Austria and the Turkish leader, Mohammed V, appeared in several images themselves, they usually featured as pawns of the Kaiser, whom *lubok* artists explicitly compared to Napoleon in an effort to recapture the essence of 1812 in 1914.[8]

The print "So You Want to be Napoleon" (Figure 7.1) makes this comparison most explicitly.[9] In this 1914 Sytin *lubok*, Wilhelm is defined by his mustache, which became the dominant feature of the German emperor in the wartime images, standing straight up past the top of his head. The center of the print features an anonymous Russian soldier "helping" Wilhelm become Napoleon. The central part of the image depicts a sword chopping off Wilhelm's feet, scissors roughly cutting his hair, and a razor shaving off his mustache. The right side of the print depicts the new Kaiser, smaller and with his arm in a sling, thus resembling Napoleon. The text of the *lubok* is as stark as the imagery, asking, "So you want to be Napoleon? Well, then we'll help."[10]

Much like images from the Patriotic War, Great War *lubki* also featured Wilhelm as mad to have brought war to Russia. Two prints from 1914 place the Kaiser inside an insane asylum because of his plans for Europe. In the first, entitled "Wilhelm's Fantasies," the German emperor slouches on the floor, wearing hospital pajamas with his Prussian military helmet.[11] Wilhelm appears dazed, the bed behind him is unmade, and he sits with his finger in his mouth. To the right of the Kaiser, the arm of a Cossack grasping his whip prepares to disabuse Wilhelm of his ideas. The text quotes the Kaiser's "mad plans" of "breakfasting in Paris," then attacking Russia so he can "eat lunch in Warsaw, then eat dinner in Moscow." The second print, "From the Letters of a Lunatic," has Wilhelm in the same room of the sanitarium as the previous image, wearing the same clothing. The Kaiser is standing on his bed, one arm pointing upward as he dictates his plans for Europe. Behind Wilhelm, written on a chalkboard attached to his bed, one can make out the Kaiser's diagnosis: "megalomania" *(maniia velichiia)*. Wilhelm again spouts "mad plans" for himself in the text, claiming, "the emperor of Europe sits in Prussia! He has appeared! I am this emperor!"[12] The Kaiser's alleged plans for Russia and Europe have been placed in their proper context in these two images, which link the "insanity" of Wilhelm to that of Napoleon one hundred years earlier.[13]

Other *lubki* mock Wilhelm by depicting the Kaiser in various demonic forms. Wilhelm appears as a red devil, complete with hooves and a tail, in Sytin's "Enemy of Mankind."[14] Although his body is that of a demon, the Kaiser is recognizable by his face and Prussian helmet, as well as his mustache. Clutching a skull in either hand, the German emperor grins manically at the viewer. Surrounding Wilhelm are the towns that he has destroyed in the war. Banners provide short texts that explain why the Kaiser is the "enemy of mankind," proclaiming, "a great number of peoples furiously destroyed," "many cities furtively pulled down," specifically referring to Rheims in France and Louvain in Belgium as sites of Wilhelm's destructive nature. The tone of this *lubok,* which appeared after Russian defeats in the war, takes a much harsher approach to characterizing the German emperor and the destructive nature of the enemy, no doubt a result of growing Russian anxieties about the conflict.[15]

While some *lubok* publishers vilified the Kaiser as a devil, others ridiculed him in a way that employed traditional stereotypes of Germans in Russia. "Look Here, My Old Chap" features Wilhelm with his arm draped around an aged Franz Joseph.[16] Illustrated by S. Ivanov, the print exaggerates the size of both of Wilhelm's arms (despite the deformity of one of them), and shows an arm clenched in a fist, the other draped over his ally. Behind the two loom the Eiffel Tower, an English battleship distinguished by the Union Jack, and the Moscow Kremlin, all objects of Wilhelm's ambition that he is showing to Franz Joseph. The lower half of the print features the same pose from Wilhelm and his Austrian counterpart. A French soldier and British sailor join them and watch as a Russian Cossack cuts off Wilhelm's hand. Instead of blood spilling out, cockroaches spurt from the wound, and are trampled by four gleeful Russian peasant children. The *lubok* provides a visual depiction of the colloquial term for "cockroach" *[prusak]* in Russian, which sounds the same as "Prussian" *[prussak].*[17]

Several other popular prints from the war depicted the Germans as cockroaches, including *"Prussaki,"* in which three Cossacks spray insecticide on several smaller cockroaches, all of which have Prussian helmets and mustaches;[18] and a Vladimir Mayakovsky *lubok* that depicts a Russian *baba* disposing of *"prussaki,"* half of them German soldiers with Prussian helmets, the other half cockroaches.[19] These depictions of Germans as cockroaches not only served as a means to ridicule the enemy, but also focused hatred of the enemy on the person of the Kaiser, who became the symbol of long-standing clichés and stereotypes, "the convenient personification of the ugly German in general and the hated leader of the enemy in particular."[20]

In another respect, the portrayal of the Germans as vermin furthered the racism toward an enemy presented in the images from the Japanese War. As George Mosse has argued, "racism was a visual ideology based upon stereotypes," and while European racism was most often directed toward Africans, Asians, and Jews, it could also be used against other Europeans. In particular, the nationalism of the nineteenth century contributed to the idea that individual nations contained individual races. Because the French, for example, shared a common history, language, and emotions, all attributes upon which French national identity was built, nineteenth-century thinkers often talked about the "French race." Similar comparisons could be made for the German and Slavic races as contemporaries viewed them.[21] In short, racism and nationalism, as Mosse argues, at times reinforced one another, and in certain respects, as this study indicates, war tended to make all enemies into racial "others" through the use of stereotypes such as those employed in images of the Turks, Japanese, and Germans.

Overall, though, publishers presented this war as the Kaiser's war. In over one thousand images from the First World War located at the State Public History Library of Moscow, the State History Museum of Moscow, and the Hoover Institution at Stanford University, Wilhelm II appears in nearly one-third of all the caricatures of the enemy.[22] In the collections of the State Public History Library, which contain 350 *lubki* from the war, Wilhelm appears in thirty-three different images, while the tsar of Russia appears in only two.[23] Not since the Napoleonic invasion had popular prints focused on the enemy as personified in one leader.[24]

Russian Heroism and Masculinity: Recasting the "Russian Spirit"

Wartime propaganda frequently attempts to demean the enemy by presenting battle scenes that stress the heroism of one's own troops. In the Great War, wartime images and their producers once again recast notions of heroism and ideas about "the Russian spirit" that had been present in popular prints since the Napoleonic war, placing them in the context of the war against the Germans, Austrians, and Turks. During the First World War, however, *lubok* publishers personified this spirit by depicting individual acts of heroism.[25]

More than any other figure, the Cossack Kozma Kriuchkov became the embodiment of the Russian spirit in the *lubki* of the Great War. With the exception of Wilhelm II, Kriuchkov appeared in more prints than any other individual, and he also featured in numerous pamphlets, popular songs, short books, and even a film devoted to his heroic deeds.[26] Kriuchkov became the first soldier to be awarded a St. George's Cross in the war for an encounter on 12 August 1914 with the Germans, during which he allegedly single-handedly defeated eleven German soldiers. Despite suffering sixteen wounds (his horse was hit eleven times), Kriuchkov valiantly fought until the battle had been won and all the Germans were driven away.

Numerous prints recounted this legend, all of them contributing to the mythic status of Kriuchkov in particular and the Russian Cossack, a long-standing iconic figure of Russian patriotic culture. The print "Cossack Hero Kozma Kriuchkov" features a portrait of the hero, his hat rakishly tilted, with the St. George's Cross pinned to his uniform, a style reminiscent of portraits of military heroes from previous wars.[27] The *lubok* "Heroic Victory of the Cossack Kozma Kriuchkov" adopts a realistic style to illustrate the action of this "son of the Don." Kriuchkov fights at the center of the print upon his white horse, which bleeds from one of the wounds it has received.[28] Surrounded by seven German soldiers attempting to kill him, Kriuchkov heroically fends them off with his lance, knocking his cap off in the process. Around this scene lie the bodies of four Germans with whom the "Cossack hero" has already dealt.

Other *lubki* adopt a more playful style in recounting Kriuchkov's deeds, reminiscent of the style seen in images from earlier wars such as "One, Two, Three" from the Russo-Turkish War. Dmitrii Moor's poster, "The Heroic Deed *[bogatyrskoe delo]* of Koz'ma Kriuchkov" (Figure 7.2), features a larger-than-life-size Kriuchkov in the tradition of Cossack Petrukha from the 1904–1905 war.[29] The 1914 hero and his horse ride confidently at the center of the print, chasing three smaller Germans who flee. Kriuchkov holds his lance, on which the hero has run through two more enemy soldiers. Behind him, on three additional lances now planted firmly in the earth, seven other Germans are impaled.[30] The caricatures and smallness of the Germans harkens back to a tradition in wartime imagery of emasculating the enemy by suggesting his small stature and inability to defeat a single Russian.

Although Kriuchkov was by far the most prominent hero of the war, and the embodiment of masculinity and Russian military culture,[31] he was not the only soldier praised for these virtues. Other war *lubki* trumpeted the exploits of the Cossack Gumilov, who risked his own life to save that of a Russian officer about to be killed by an Austrian squadron;[32] the Russian

7.2 "The Heroic Deed of Koz'ma Kriuchkov" The first Russian soldier to win the St. George's Cross for bravery was a Cossack named Kozma Kriuchkov, who allegedly defeated eleven German soldiers by himself in August 1914. This image by Dmitrii Moor for Sytin's company features the larger-than-life hero in the tradition of Cossack Petrukha from the Russo-Japanese War (Fig. 6.2). Vladimir Denisov, the author of a 1916 study of the *lubok*, commented that images of Kriuchkov like this one were "carried across the face of the Russian land." Reprinted by permission from the Poster Collection, Hoover Institution Archives.

pilot P. N. Nesterov, who sacrificed his life to destroy an enemy craft;[33] and a Jewish soldier, Private Katz, who fought the Germans with such ferocity and commitment that he was carried from the battle by an officer and awarded the St. George's Cross.[34] In all these images, the exploits of individual Russian soldiers are used as a means to stress the heroism inherent within the Russian troops, their commitment to the cause, and love of their country.

As in previous wars against the Turks and Japanese, popular imagery from the Great War also made implicit (and explicit) connections between courage, race, and culture. As Karen Petrone has noted in her study of Russian war posters, cowardice had a racial and gendered nature. The Chelnokov print "Parade," for instance, featured Wilhelm II and Franz Joseph reviewing their officers, who are portrayed as little boys being supervised by nursemaids. Petrone writes, "the message that any nursemaid could deal with Kaiser Wilhelm created a gendered juxtaposition between a female nursemaid and a real, Russian warrior, implying that the Germans were so lacking in manliness that they were weaker even than women."[35]

In a similar fashion, the Sytin print entitled "The Old Woman is Not a Blockhead, She Can Capture an Airplane," recalls the actions of Russian peasant women portrayed in *lubki* from the Patriotic War against Napoleon.[36] In the image, a creation of Dmitrii Moor, three Russian *baby* wrestle with an Austrian officer, who vainly fires off his pistol. One of the peasant women gleefully raises her hand to spank the enemy for his bad deeds. Behind the three women is the Austrian's airplane, which had landed near the peasant women's village. Two more women stand before a subdued Austrian, their rakes slung proudly over their shoulders. Russian peasant children watch the action, adding further shame to the Austrian defeat. As Petrone argues, the print "suggests to the viewer that since the Austrians were beaten by uneducated and unarmed peasant women, they could easily be defeated by the real, male, Russian warriors of the Imperial Army."[37]

While the Austrians and Germans were depicted as unmanly and weak fighters, the Turks, recalling images from previous conflicts, were depicted in war *lubki* as racial and cultural inferiors to their Russian counterparts. Two examples illustrate this point quite clearly. The first, entitled "About Turkish Cowardice and Spirited Boldness," contrasts the stereotype of the "cowardly Turk" with the "Russian spirit."[38] In the print, a solitary Turk flees from a Cossack. The Turk's appearance conforms to the stereotypes present in wartime culture since the Crimean war: his large, swarthy face betrays his fear of the Cossack, while his fez, clothing, and slippers establish his quintessential difference from the Russian. The Cossack, although barely discernible, contrasts starkly with his enemy: handsome, determined, and brave, there is little doubt that he will capture his weaker opponent. The text of the print, written in verse, reinforces the cultural and racial differences between the Cossack and the Turk. Charging the Germans with "setting fire to the Turks" in order to invade the "Orthodox land," the Cossack promises to make "the infidel *[busurman]* know Plevna, Kars, and the Shipka" all over again, invoking Russian triumphs from 1877.[39]

The second print, "A Conversation Near Constantinople," also denigrates the Turkish foe.[40] The print features a young, cleanly dressed Russian sitting on a military drum, casually smoking a cigarette. He is talking to and laughing at a Turkish pasha whose small size contrasts with the giant Russian. While the Russian soldier smiles and sits patiently, the Turk, with a hook hose, swarthy complexion, and fez, stamps his foot and grimaces at the young man. Behind the two loom the magnificent spires of Constantinople, identified by the print in its Russian name, Tsargrad. The text is a song by M. Petrov, which reinforces the themes of the print. The Turk asks the Russian, "Where did you get so much strength?" The reply:

Oh my friend—though you are a Turk
And look like you're good at darting blows,
As for such a mind as yours,
It seems as if there's nothing there.

With my strength to fight against you,
You'll never be able to get even.
And your Turkish guns
Can't even reach me.

Many different foreigners,
I've beaten and will beat again.
I've pounded Austrians and Germans,
But on you I . . . sneeze.[41]

The Turk, because of his cultural and racial inferiority, simply cannot comprehend the source of the Russian's strength, just as he cannot defeat the Russian army.[42]

If Russian wartime culture denigrated the Turk as the weakest of Russia's enemies in the war, images presented the Germans as the strongest and the Austrians as German puppets. Several prints that appeared at the outset of the war charged the Germans with atrocities against innocent Russian citizens, echoing similar claims made throughout Europe in late 1914. Others that featured examples of the "Russian spirit" presented the Germans as dullwitted and easily fooled by Russian Cossacks and peasants.

Immediately after war broke out in August 1914, the allied belligerents began to level charges at the German army of committing a variety of atrocities. Used as effective propaganda tools throughout the war, films, posters, and other cultural products depicted the Germans as savage "Huns" who needed to be stopped at all costs.[43] Dozens of Russian war *lubki* also graphically dealt with the German atrocities. "An Innocent Victim in the Hands of the Cultured Butchers" (Figure 7.3) connects the savage nature of German troops to their perceived lack of culture.[44] The *lubok* is set within a nondescript house and features three German soldiers. One is seated at a table full of food, holding a mug of beer, while a second stands beside the first, also drinking beer and casually holding his rifle. The third soldier aims his rifle outside the door to the room, guarding his two comrades. The scene turns shocking because of the presence of a solitary Red Cross nurse lying dead or unconscious on the floor of the room. Her clothes are torn, while the crumpled bed she lies beside leaves little room in the imagination for what atrocities have been committed. One of the soldiers drinking beer stands on the hem of her uniform. The text reinforces the outrage that this image was designed to provoke among its audience, calling the event "a foul, bloody deed by the monster-Germans."

Other images provided equally graphic scenes of German bloodthirstiness. "German Bestialities" provided viewers with the most violent scene of all the prints made in 1914.[45] The action of the *lubok* takes place outside a burning building, from which run several Red Cross nurses, peasant women, and their children. The fact that all of the inhabitants of the building are obviously unarmed does not stop the four German soldiers from ruthlessly killing the women and children. One soldier stabs a nurse with his bayonet, a second holds his saber above his head, about to bring it down on a peasant woman and her child, while a third shoots a nurse. The foreground of the *lubok* is littered with the bodies of three previous victims, and their blood forms the dominant color of the print. Behind the scene, amidst more flames, the viewer can make out the silhouettes of other German soldiers, and they too are engaged in committing atrocities.

The popular prints from 1914 also depicted a squadron of German soldiers engaged in beer drinking, rape, and murder of innocent children;[46] still more *lubki* featured German firing squads executing Red Cross nurses,[47] German troops executing the mayor of Kalisz in Poland,[48] and a large number of German troops engaged in various despicable acts in a Serbian town.[49] In all of these prints, the German foe is depicted as inherently savage, uncultured, and capable of any outrage in the whirlwind of war. This characterization of the German enemy provided a stark contrast to the heroism and "Russian spirit" displayed by Russian troops, and in turn featured graphic detail exhorting Russians to fight or to support the war effort.

Images also depicted the Germans as foolish and easily duped by their Russian counterparts, while still more *lubki* highlighted the brutish nature of the German enemy by painting the relationship between the Germans and Austrians as one built upon unequal footing. The 1914 Sytin print, "Wilhelm's Cattle," illustrated by Dmitrii Moor, highlights the alleged relationship between the Germans and their allies.[50] Wilhelm II, adorned with his customary Prussian helmet and prominent mustache, rides atop his "cattle": Franz Joseph and Mohammed V. Their German counterpart has corralled both the Austrian and the Turk, a fact made evident by the harnesses around each man. This illustration provides a symbolic depiction of the popular perceptions in Russia—one obviously promoted by the wartime imagery—that the Kaiser had forced the Austrians and Turks into conflict against Russia, and that Wilhelm secretly pulled the strings behind the entire war effort. Behind the three leaders, however, a single Cossack and his horse peer at them, laughing at their ridiculous and pompous appearance, reassuring the viewer that the enemy could be dealt with easily.[51]

Russian *lubok* publishers also mocked the German home front. The print "Famine in Germany," illustrated by N. Remizov, ridicules the inability of the German nation to deal with the necessities of waging war—an ironic theme, given what befell Russia in 1917.[52] A small, emaciated cari-

7.3 "An Innocent Victim in the Hands of the Cultured Butchers" Russia and her allies in the Great War (1914–1918) all produced propagandistic posters that spread reports of German atrocities committed against civilians. In this Russian version of the atrocity-image genre, a Red Cross nurse lies dead or unconscious on the floor, a victim of a "foul, bloody deed by the monster-Germans," as the caption notes. Reprinted by Permission from the Poster Collection, Hoover Institution Archives.

cature of a German weeps over an empty plate, joined in his despair by his starving dog. With tattered clothes and holding a large spoon that has not been used, the print imagines what Germans behind the front lines of the war must be experiencing, given the ineptitude and national character of their troops. Highlighting the difference between Germans and Russians in this print is the presence of the sun over the eastern sky, representing Russia. This sun contains the face of a well-fed Russian Cossack, who smiles at the German's predicament.

"Hungry Michel" links the supposed weakness displayed by all Germans, from the emperor to the simplest peasant, even more explicitly.[53] Drawn in the style of earlier, cruder *lubki,* this image features the German Kaiser and a German peasant named Michel (an iconic individual that German cultural figures had created in the nineteenth century as a representation of the German nation).[54] The Kaiser, his face saddened by all that has befallen his country, is easily distinguishable by his mustache and helmet. The peasant Michel is dressed in traditional German clothing, much like his counterpart in the print mentioned above. Both are sharing a single loaf of bread, while the barren ground around the pair attests to the state of Germany in the midst of war. The text has both the Kaiser and his subject crying their desire for a single potato, a product unavailable in Germany because of the war. This print aptly sums up many of the themes in the *lubki* of the Great War: the Kaiser as the chief enemy, the alleged inferiority of the enemy, long-held stereotypes about the Germans, and the cultural nature of cowardice portrayed in images that dealt with Russia's foes in the war.

Religion, the Tsar, and National Symbols in the Great War

While a larger number of *lubki* focused on the inferiority of the enemy, a substantial number again recast notions of Russianness. In comparison to previous holy wars, however, the number of prints devoted to these themes provided a smaller percentage of the overall number of *lubki*. They still, however, represented an important part of the visual and patriotic culture of the Great War. Numerous prints featured what had become the traditional iconographic figures of wartime patriotic culture, the Cossack and peasant, while others featured symbols of Russian identity such as the bear and Mother Russia. Although religious imagery proved not as pervasive as in the *lubki* from previous wars, popular prints made in the Great War still appealed to Russian Orthodoxy as a source of identity.

An A. V. Krylov print from August 1914 depicted many of the traditional symbols of Russian patriotic culture while attempting to inspire a "spirit of 1914" among its viewers.[55] Entitled "Russia's War with the Germans: The Day of the War's Declaration," the print presents an idealized view of Palace Square in St. Petersburg (soon to be renamed Petrograd) on 20 July 1914, when the tsar announced mobilization. Before the Winter Palace, featuring the tsar's standard flying above it, stand masses of Russian citizens displaying their loyalty to the regime and their enthusiasm for the coming war. Among them one can see a peasant man waving his cap toward the palace; a well-dressed middle-class woman holding her son, both of them cheering the announcement; and a peasant woman with her son. Many of the crowd salute the Russian flag with its white, blue, and red stripes, all in an effort to display a united front to "repulse the impertinent enemy," as the text notes.[56] Designed as a means to exhort Russians to fight and to inspire a diverse population to rally behind the "war with the Germans," this image may have in turn furthered the construction of a "myth of the spirit of 1914" that spread throughout Europe after August.[57]

Other prints used the peasant and Cossack icons in humorous scenes that ridiculed the enemy in *lubki* reminiscent of images from wars since the Patriotic War. In the Krylov print titled "The European Criminals Caught Red-Handed," a huge Russian peasant is about to take on his enemies.[58] Caricatures of Wilhelm II, Franz Joseph, and Mohammed V clutch bags labeled "Belgium," "Bosnia," and "Armenia," respectively, alluding to the crimes the rulers committed during the war. Behind these three, a French and British soldier close the gates to the arena in which the "European criminals" find themselves. Ignoring these two soldiers, the three allies fearfully glare at the large Russian peasant who faces them, rolling up his right sleeve preparing to teach the three a lesson they won't forget. In a second print, a Russian Cossack also teaches his enemies a lesson. The untitled *lubok* depicts a Cossack, laughing at his fun, bending a scared Wilhelm II over his knee, baring his backside in the process.[59] In one hand the Cossack grips his belt and prepares to spank the German Kaiser for bringing war to Russia. Underneath his right boot the Cossack pins Franz Joseph down, and promises him that he too will "suffer like Wilhelm" once he has finished.

In addition to the peasant and Cossack, other traditional Russian symbols served as a means by which Russians who bought them could define Russianness. "The Great European War" (Figure 7.4) contains a Russian *bogatyr'*, or medieval knight, clad in chain mail armor and clutching a sword and shield, fighting a dragon.[60] The beast has three heads, each one representing one of the countries against which Russia is fighting. The central head of the dragon is Wilhelm II, while Mohammed V and Franz Joseph flank the Kaiser. Beneath the dragon one can make out the smoldering ruins of cities that the beast has laid waste in the war, the kind of destruction that the knight fights to prevent in Russia, while the caption announces that this scene represents "the great battle of the Russian *bogatyr'* with the German serpent."[61]

"Russia" could be visualized as a medieval knight in images, while "Russia and Her Soldier" features a visual representation of Russia as a woman, a depiction that illustrates the term *rodina,* or motherland.[62] Russia in this print is portrayed by a boyarina wearing a sarafan and a *kokoshnik,* the traditional Russian headdress, and seated on a tsarist throne embossed with the double-headed eagle. Holding a sword in her right hand and an imperial orb in her left, Russia gazes at a solitary soldier who stands at attention before her. Behind the two other Russian soldiers engage in battle with the Austrian enemy, capturing a small hillside from them in the process. The text has Russia exhorting her "kind son [and] stately soldier" to remember that "God is with him" in his fight against the Germans, who are "insidious and strong" but no match for the "strong spirit" of the Russians.[63]

Other prints depicted Russia as a bear. In the Sytin print "Franz Listened to Wilhelm," caricatures of the German and Austrian leaders flee from the fight they brought. The print is set in the woods, with the Kaiser and his Austrian counterpart scurrying up a tree in comical fashion. To their right a bear wearing a peasant's cap mocks the two, while a sign above the bear contains the imperial emblem and the word "Russia" on it. The text is written in the style of a rhyming *chastushka,* or traditional folk song: "Franz listened to Wilhelm, but Wilhelm put him in a spot—what a

148

7.4 "The Great European War" This striking *lubok* from 1915 features a Russian *bogatyr'* (see Fig. 6.5) fighting a dragon with the heads of Wilhelm II, Franz Joseph of Austria, and Mohammed V of the Ottoman Empire. Beneath this action one can make out the ruins of cities the "German serpent" (as the caption calls the beast) has laid waste, the kind of destruction the knight fights to prevent in Russia. Reprinted by permission from the Poster Collection, Hoover Institution Archives.

rascal! Look, the bear is already here, and the friends are kaput!"[64] Whether illustrating masculine or feminine ideas about the Russian nation (*otechestvo* or *rodina*), Russian images from the Great War presented a number of visual depictions of national symbolic figures.

Although *lubki* from the Great War did not feature religious imagery as often as did those of the Russo-Turkish War or even the Russo-Japanese War, Orthodoxy continued to be an important component of the prints expressing ideas about Russianness. The Orthodox church itself had upheld in 1916 the duty of its clergy "to use the symbols of the church to encourage and incite patriotic feelings for the war," and it responded by staging large communions for recruits, public prayers, and distributing religious emblems to soldiers. As Richard Stites has reported, "the front was well supplied with Orthodox chaplains who blessed and doused troops and weapons with holy water."[65]

Several examples clarify how *lubok* publishers made use of religious imagery in 1914. "Holy War" (Figure 7.5), depicts Russia again as a *bogatyr'*.[66] In this image, Nicholas II is depicted as a larger-than-life knight, astride a white horse and pointing his sword forward, exhorting Russian troops. Attired in emblems of Russia that include a double-headed eagle on his breastplate, a religious banner clutched in his left hand, and a shield embossed with the words "God is with us," Nicholas the *bogatyr'* rides with the sun illuminating the path behind him, alongside the silhouette of the Moscow Kremlin. Beneath the enormous figure, the Russian army marches steadfastly onward, their bayonets accentuating the steely look on the soldiers' faces. The caption calls on "mighty Rus'" [*moguchaia Rus'*] to prepare itself for war by "praying that the deeds of our highest God lead us to victory until the end," while calling on the same God to "let the accursed enemy perish" in the war that has enveloped Russia.

While this image recast the idea of Russia's wars as holy ones, a concept that dated back to the previous century, the print "Russia's War With Germany and Austria" involves an Orthodox priest in the action of war, again reminiscent of images dating from the Crimean War.[67] This *lubok* featured a battle between Russian, German, and Austrian troops on 8 September 1914. With the nearby river and town forming the backdrop to the print, complete with exploding shells, the image is dominated by Russian soldiers engaged in fierce hand-to-hand combat with the enemy, reinforcing the popular notion that Russian troops excelled in fighting with the bayonet. An officer on horseback exhorts his troops to fight by pointing his sword in the direction of the enemy troops. Just behind the officer stands an Orthodox priest, also inspiring the troops by blessing them in their battle. A flag bearer holds the imperial standard, and the priest's cross meshes perfectly with the chest of the double-headed eagle in a striking visual definition of Russian identity.[68]

If the previous two examples illustrate the ways in which *lubok* publishers used religion in their prints from early in the conflict, other *lubki*

7.5 "Holy War" "Holy War" appropriates the language and visual codes of prints from previous wars: Nicholas II appears as a *bogatyr'* on a white horse brandishing a sword and a shield emblazoned with the words "God is with us!" Behind him, a sun illuminates the Moscow Kremlin and inspires the Russian troops forward, while the caption calls on "mighty Rus'" *(moguchaia Rus')* to prepare itself for war by "praying that the deeds of our highest God lead us to victory until the end." Reprinted by permission from the Poster Collection, Hoover Institution Archives.

demonstrate the changes in religious imagery evident by the time of the Great War. "The Appearance of the Holy Mother from the Heavens before the Battle of Russian Troops, an Omen of Victory" depicts an alleged incident that took place earlier in the month on the front lines.[69] Set at nighttime, a dramatic apparition of the Virgin Mary holds the Baby Jesus, light streaming from behind them.[70] The heavenly apparition has a profound effect on the numerous Russian soldiers gathered at the edge of a forest, many of whom kneel and cross themselves. The text recounts the details of the incident, which supposedly occurred the night before a Russian victory on the Eastern Front and thus provided the inspiration behind this triumph. The appearance of the Virgin Mary in this print illustrates the degree to which spiritualism in general and Marian cults in particular had spread not only in Russia before and during the war,[71] but also throughout Europe. As Jay Winter has argued, "the popular art of all combatants included images of saints or Jesus on the field of battle, and a brisk business in religious bric-a-brac grew during the conflict."[72] Russia proved no exception to this phenomenon, just as Russian soldiers too told a variety of spiritualist stories and legends along with their European counterparts.[73]

The print "I Shall Manifest Myself to Him" also illustrates the growing spiritual nature of the wartime religious imagery.[74] The *lubok* depicts a dying Russian soldier lying in a wooded grove, wounded from a recent battle. The soldier shows both the scars of past battles and evidence of his courage in these episodes, for his head is wrapped in a bandage and he wears the St. George's Cross on his uniform. Surrounding the Russian are the bodies of other dead comrades and the discarded materials of war. Despite this somber tone, the message of the print is intended to be uplifting for its audience because of the appearance of Jesus before the dying man. Clothed in white, Jesus reaches his hand out to the dying soldier to comfort him, a gesture that calms the Russian. The text that accompanies the print consists of two Bible verses, both of them from the Gospel of John. The first verse, from chapter 15, states, "Greater love hath no man than this, that a man lay down his life for his friends," while the second, taken from chapter 14, claims, "he that hath my commandments and keepeth them, he it is that loveth me: and he that loveth me shall be loved of my father, and I will love him, and I will manifest myself to him."[75]

While Orthodoxy featured significantly in the popular prints of the First World War, images of the tsar figured barely at all. Of the hundreds of prints that form the source base for this chapter, Nicholas II appeared in only four. The first of these prints, a 1914 Sytin *lubok* produced soon after the war began, featured a panorama of all the European leaders of the time, divided into friends and enemies.[76] Another Sytin print from 1914 also consisted solely of a portrait gallery of leaders from the allied nations. Entitled "The Leaders of Europe in the Struggle with the German People in 1914," this *lubok* placed a portrait of Nicholas II in the center, surrounded in clockwise fashion by his allies.[77]

After his depiction as a *bogatyr'* in the image mentioned above (Figure 7.5), Nicholas's final appearance in a patriotic *lubok* also came from Sytin's plant, an untitled print from late 1914.[78] In a scene that had become typical to wartime imagery, Nicholas is shown visiting a field hospital in order to inspire his troops and reward them for their service. The tsar, surrounded by various army leaders, pins a St. George's Cross onto a wounded soldier who, despite the bandages covering his hand and head, proudly accepts the award. Behind the soldier, several injured comrades receive treatment from Red Cross nurses and Russian doctors, waiting their turn to speak to their tsar.

The relative absence of the tsar from the images of the Great War continued a trend in Russian visual culture present since the Crimean War. After 1812, only during the Russo-Turkish War of 1877–1878 did a Russian sovereign figure prominently in wartime culture. Thus, in the unofficial propaganda produced to help Russians define themselves during wartime as well as inspire them to fight, the Russian tsar did not form an important pillar of patriotic identity. The Russian monarchy, as one historian has rightly claimed, had long been uncomfortable with mobilizing mass opinion, a stance that created antagonisms between the tsarist regime and social groups that would have worked with the government.[79] Instead, the iconographic figures of the Russian peasant and Cossack, as well as symbols such as the *bogatyr'*, the Russian bear, illustrations of the "Russian spirit," and the Orthodox religion continued to define Russianness in the images of war produced after 1914.

Technology and the Russian Fighting Spirit in Wartime Imagery

In addition to stressing the "traditional" elements of Russianness mentioned above, *lubki* from the Great War furthered the myth of a Russian fighting spirit that stressed superiority in hand-to-hand combat. The bayonet, a symbol of this spirit, appeared in numerous images in a conflict that was defined by the machine gun. Battle *lubki*, particularly the Sytin ones, also continued to define the traditional fighting spirit of Russians through the figure of the Cossack. Alongside these images representations of the new weapons of mass destruction that one identifies with the Great War appeared, particularly prints that depicted airplanes and the tank, both introduced as fighting machines after 1914. In other words, in the midst of the first truly modern war, with its mechanized killing and reliance on technology, Russian images of war stressed elements of warfare that seemed anachronistic. Nowhere was this tension more evident than in the patriotic *lubki* that adopted a modern, avant-garde style yet depicted Cossacks and peasant cleverness.

Battle *lubki* remained the most abundant form of popular pictures in the Great War, just as they had in previous conflicts. For many Russians, these images represented the only form of information about the skirmishes of the war, and the best means by which to follow the events that involved loved ones. As in previous wars, however, the images from 1914 portrayed Russian soldiers as inherently superior to their enemy counter-parts, and particularly stressed Russian "victories," however insignificant or imagined. "An Unsuccessful German Offensive," for example, illus-trated an episode from 12 September 1914 that the Russian correspondent from *Rannoe utro* reported.[80] The incident involved a German attack on the Eastern Front that Russian troops successfully repulsed, and this *lubok* de-picts that victory in graphic detail (the skirmish should, however, be viewed in the larger context of Russian losses against the Germans in 1914). A Ger-man platoon runs from the field of battle, eagerly pursued by a large number of Russian soldiers. Prominent among the Russian heroes are an officer astride his white horse, reminiscent of the Skobelev imagery from 1877, and a Russian flag bearer, both of whom urge their comrades forward. The troops in the print are above all defined by their bayonet charge, and many among them are engaged in hand-to-hand combat with the Germans, a visual image that implies the "unsuccessful offensive" met its end against the Russian bay-onet. Several bloody corpses of German soldiers litter the battlefield, further testament to the prowess of the Russian bayonet.[81]

In addition to the depiction of Russian bayonet charges, several *lubki* defined the Russian fighting spirit as embodied in the Cossack. "In Battle near Warsaw: The Cossack Pursuit of the Defeated German Army" depicts a large number of Cossacks on horseback bearing down on the German enemy.[82] The Cossacks lay waste to the Germans, whose rifles and artillery prove no match for the lances of the Russian forces, all on horseback. Ger-man troops either flee before the Cossacks or lie dead, victims of the fight-ing prowess of their Russian counterparts.[83]

The war against the Turks, whom *lubok* publishers had ridiculed for their lack of courage and fighting ability since the nineteenth century, also produced patriotic prints that featured Russian military superiority in 1914. The *lubok* "Russo-Turkish War: The Capture of Baiazet" illustrated a Russian victory on the southern front in 1914. A Russian bayonet charge, promi-nently led by officers urging their soldiers forward, puts a larger number of Turkish troops to flight. Several Turks lie bleeding from wounds inflicted by the charge, while more engage in a fruitless struggle against the Russians. Above all, as even the text notes, the Russian fighting spirit, embodied by the bayonet, proved to be the decisive factor in this encounter.

Alongside these images that depicted hand-to-hand combat, however, *lubki* containing new technologies appeared, highlighting the tension be-tween constructing Russian strength as embodied in the bayonet charge and the ways in which warfare had changed by 1914. The image entitled "The Great European War: An Episode from the Great Battle Near Warsaw" bears a resemblance to the prints of Cossacks pursuing German troops mentioned above with one exception.[84] Russian soldiers chase a larger number of Germans away after an encounter near Warsaw. Like the prints examined above, a Russian officer on a white horse, saber raised, leads his troops, while a standard bearer also inspires his comrades to charge. In the midst of the retreating German troops, whose more modern weaponry has proven unsuccessful in warding off the Russians, a tank also flees from the scene. Hanging out of the tank is a single German soldier with a Prussian-style helmet discharging a pistol at the onrushing Russian troops. The guns of the tank are quiet, visually conferring the idea that this new technological wonder had proven no match for the Russian fighting spirit.

The 1914 Sytin print called "The War in the Air," however, stands in stark contrast to other battle *lubki* of the Great War.[85] This *lubok* featured allied planes engaged in a battle with German zeppelins, both new technologies introduced to warfare in 1914. As the text of the print notes, "our century is a century of achievements in the air," while the "technology of every country" has been affected, and the introduction of the airplane to the field of combat was almost inevitable. The juxtaposition between this new type of warfare and the kind of combat stressed in other battle images also appears in a Sytin print from 1914 entitled "Attack of the Austrian Positions near Tomashev."[86] In this *lubok*, Russian troops engaged in a battle from which Austrian troops flee alongside airplanes that race across the sky. Traditional, older means of warfare, particularly in the form of bayonet charges, coexist in a type of conflict that employs new technologies. Russian patriotic culture, in which *lubok* publishers had helped to construct a myth of Russian fighting spirit, now had to deal with the new type of warfare, a tension that proved unsettling not only in the *lubki* from the Great War, but also on the field of battle in 1915.[87]

If the continued stress on bayonets in the Russian patriotic culture of the First World War seems anachronistic, the appearance of numerous images that combined an avant-garde, modernist style with traditional patriotic icons such as the Cossack and peasant appears equally strange. The 1914 print from the publishing house The Contemporary *Lubok* entitled "Masses of Germans" featured a verse from Vladimir Mayakovsky and was illustrated by Aristakh Lentulov, both well-known figures of the Russian avant-garde.[88] In the years before the war, members of modernist art circles such as Mayakovsky and Lentulov had increasingly found inspiration for their own works in the *lubok*, and when war broke out in 1914, they quickly formed a patriotic publishing firm that produced war *lubki*.[89] This particular image features a group of Cossacks with lances engaging smaller German troops who ride in trains. Employing both a modernist style and traditional iconic figures such as the Cossack, this *lubok* suggests that the technologies of the Germans prove no match for the fighting spirit of the Cossack, a theme explored by Mayakovsky's rhyming verse as well.[90]

The print "Germans!" also from The Contemporary *Lubok* but drawn by Aleksandr Apsit and featuring another Mayakovsky ditty, stresses the strength of the bayonet charge in a similar artistic style to the *lubok* above.[91] Russian and German troops skirmish, with the Russians gaining

7.6 "What a Crash and What a Thunder the Germans are Making near Lomzha" The Great War imagery differed from that of previous wars through the influence of avant-garde artists who railed to the Russian cause. While it contains a radically different style, this *lubok* by Kazimir Malevich contains patriotic symbols present in wartime culture since 1812: a larger-than-life peasant drives off the enemy with his scythe in Malevich's use of this symbol. Reprinted by permission from the Poster Collection, Hoover Institution Archives

the upper hand by charging the enemy with fixed bayonets. German cannons explode harmlessly around the Russian soldiers, who are led by two officers, one engaged in battle and the other raising his sword to inspire more troops forward. A solitary Russian soldier fires a machine gun at the enemy, who are driven off by the force of the Russian fighting spirit. Like the image above, Mayakovsky added a rhyme in a style that he would develop further after 1917 in his ROSTA Windows (prints made for the Russian Telegraph Agency, or ROSTA): "Germans! You are strong, but you won't see Warsaw. Better to rush off to Berlin than for the present not move."

Kazimir Malevich, himself a prominent member of the Russian artistic community, also drew patriotic *lubki* for the same publishing company. His image "What a Crash and What a Thunder the Germans are Making near Lomzha" (Figure 7.6), with a verse by Mayakovsky, also employed traditional patriotic imagery in a modernist style.[92] Featuring a giant Russian peasant grasping a hand held thresher and wearing traditional clothing, the print also depicts numerous small German troops fleeing. Behind the giant peasant lay the bodies of Germans who have already crossed his path, while several Prussian-style helmets rest at the Russian's feet. Like the previous two examples, the contrast between the style of the print and the use of iconographic figures like the Russian peasant and Cossack is striking. Similar in subject matter to the more realistic *lubki* that featured Russian bayonet charges and Cossack troops outfighting enemy soldiers armed with new technologies, however, this contrast proves all the more unsettling.

While members of the Russian avant-garde eagerly joined in the production of patriotic images in 1914, massive Russian losses the following year produced a widespread disillusionment among these artists, and The Contemporary *Lubok* closed.[93] Most of the artists who produced these images did not turn away from making prints in the future, and used the skills they had learned in the Great War by producing posters for the Bolsheviks. The *lubki* they made in 1914, however, serve as an ideal means for viewing the tensions within Russian patriotic culture. Patriotic figures such as the Cossack and peasant, as well as their fighting spirit, simply did not hold up against the realities of the war front.

The Visual War in Europe

The declaration of war in September 1914 unleashed a wave of propaganda prints throughout Europe. Across the continent, the language of visual nationhood that had formed a vital part of the "age of nationalism" found a renewed outlet. Initially, posters across Europe called on citizens to defend their nation by depicting scenes of the homeland while other images promised swift victory. The French-produced "To Triumph, Subscribe to the National War Loan," for example, contained French soldiers marching beside the Arc de Triomphe toward certain victory. Joining them are Marianne and Napoleonic troops.[94] British poster art, by comparison, invoked ideas of British honor and fighting spirit, calling on men to "step into your place" or "be a man" and fight.[95] Even Hungarian posters tapped into cultural myths about Hungarian nationhood to promote easy victory— "The Beer from the Spring Hops Has Arrived; The Enemy is Surrendering" contains Allied soldiers (French, Scottish, British, and Russian) rushing toward German and Hungarian troops sharing beer, preferring Central European libation to actual fighting, a decision the Germans and Hungarians laugh about.[96]

By the middle of 1915, however, "the posters of all warring nations revealed signs that the first sweep of public enthusiasm was being replaced by a more sober resolve."[97] With earlier promises of a swift victory as a result of national character now increasingly irrelevant in the face of a long war, poster artists instead turned their visual propaganda to the task of "maintain[ing] the dislike and fear of the enemy" or producing self-images of sacrifice. British posters such as "Red Cross or Iron Cross" depicted all Germans, even Red Cross nurses, as inhuman barbarians ready to enslave the British, while one of the most famous French posters of the war, "They Shall Not Pass [*On ne passe pas!*]" warns French soldiers to remain vigilant against false German peace feelers. Among the Allies, a propaganda campaign that stressed German atrocities and thus the savage nature of the German people focused hatred on the enemy. The image of the "savage Hun" that dominated European posters after 1915 even led the German government to counteract with propaganda prints of their own. "We Barbarians!" from 1916 stresses German cultural and scientific achievements by placing portraits of Dürer, Goethe, Beethoven, and other luminaries alongside graphs that show Germany has fewer illiterates, prints more books, and spends more on social security than the Allies. Other German posters from 1915 and 1916 stressed that German soldiers loved to read, cared about their families, and longed for their hometowns as much as any other soldier in the war.[98]

Ultimately, European posters in the Great War followed a similar pattern to Russian wartime imagery. Initially boastful and emphasizing national traits that previous wartime images helped to articulate, posters flooded European markets. As two leading historians of the period have written, "the perfidious British shopkeeper, the impotent Gallic lover, the Bavarian sausage eater, and the savage Cossack all appeared in the graphic pandemonium of wartime villains and buffoons," and, "in imagery and imagination, they were easily bested in the field of battle by the propagandists' own heroes and demigods."[99] By the time the harsh reality of this war set in, the number of popular prints declined in some countries, while in others posters that stressed hatred toward the enemy (particularly Germany) or the necessity of defending a way of life replaced the images from 1914. In England, for example, the war over images that had appeared during the Crimean War returned with a vengeance. Prints and other forms of media that promoted hatred, promised victory, and cheerfully called on a British spirit in order to send young men to war produced a backlash and gave the word "propaganda" new meaning. Images of German savagery appeared so fanciful and masked other aspects of war so completely that many Britons even refused to believe truthful atrocity stories.[100] Before the war, as the 1911 *Encyclopaedia Britannica* defined it, the term referred largely to religious persuasion. Afterward, many in Britain agreed with Lord Ponsonby's lament that propaganda had injected "the poison of hatred into men's minds by falsehood," a "greater evil in wartime than the actual loss of life."[101] One very real outcome of the visual war in Europe, as Ponsonby's comment illustrates, was the collision between mass culture and politics, an impact clearly seen in the visual war of the years 1914–1918.

Russian Visual Nationhood in the Great War

In January 1916, Vladimir Denisov published a short work entitled *War and the Lubok*.[102] In this examination of the role of the popular image in wartime, Denisov traced the development of this genre in Russian culture and discussed its importance in shaping attitudes. He wrote his work after he observed the extreme popularity of the wartime *lubok* throughout Russia, particularly in the countryside. Echoing similar observations made during the Crimean War and the war in the Far East, he believed that these images had been too successful in their attempts to influence a broad audience. They led, according to Denisov, to increased expectations of a quick victory over the Germans and Austrians.

As Denisov recounts, as soon as Russian troops fired their first shots in 1914, so too did "a hundred thousand brightly colored prints fly from printing presses to the depths of Russia, overtaking newspapers and governmental communications."[103] He asserts that just as "the countryside began to ask what the war was for and what should drive them to fight," images of Germans "in helmets and blue clothes," as well as with "Prussian whiskers" appeared to inform viewers of the conflict. In doing so, he argues, "*lubok* pictures in no small way assisted the war's popularity among the people."[104] Denisov attributes the popularity of the wartime *lubok* to several factors. First, "in the semi-literate countryside," printed materials such as books penetrate only slightly, and "soon are forgotten." Because rumors play a substantial role in how news reaches the countryside, Denisov argues, *lubki* serve as a means by which information reaches a wide number of Russians, for these prints often take the form of legends, making wartime events seem familiar. Furthermore, Russian peasants long have placed popular prints "in the red corner, next to icons" in their huts, and in 1914 they were able to replace prints of older heroes with ones featuring Kozma Kriuchkov, the capture of L'vov, and the crossing of the Carpathians, among other heroic images.[105]

Denisov writes that wars tend to be viewed "in the people's consciousness as worldwide, cosmic events, manifested by Almighty God, who dispatches war like he sends wholesale deaths, famine, earthquakes," and other events.[106] *Lubki*, according to Denisov, because of their long tradition in Russian culture and familiarity among the peasantry, tend to explain wars better than any other source. Whether one agrees with him in this assessment or not, Denisov does offer a compelling argument for how the images of the Great War proved too successful in one very important way. "The successful operations of our troops in the course of the first month of the war gave rich food for the *lubok*," and images appeared trumpeting one "victory" after another.[107] From "the victory of Kozma Kriuchkov" to "the expulsion of the Austrians from the southwest lands": all of the "cheery, colorful news" from the war's first month appeared in the *lubki* and "were delivered across the face of the Russian land." Russians, writes Denisov, saw images where "the enemy runs in masses from the spirited attack of the Cossacks" and "our soldiers." Other prints "ridiculed the cowardice and weakness of the enemy," and villages "laughed at the stupidity of the Kaiser and Franz-Joseph."

For Denisov, these early prints created a sense of quick victory throughout the countryside, and *lubok* publishers fostered this impression by responding to the widespread demand for wartime imagery. According to

Denisov, "more than one thousand [prints] were released by *lubok* publishers," while individual *lubki* reached numbers of "one hundred thousand." After these "excessively and wrongfully boastful" prints did not correspond to realities later in 1914 and throughout 1915, Denisov argues, "the *lubok* [grew] silent," although its content in the first months of the war "reflected the thoughts and feelings of the people."[108] In order to explain why the images of 1914 took the forms they did, Denisov embarks on a brief intellectual journey that traced the history of the wartime *lubok* and how it came to "dictate popular tastes" on the one hand while also responding to demand on the other.[109]

Denisov did not explicitly engage in historical research about Russian national identity in 1916, but his work indirectly sheds light on the nature of Russian patriotic culture and nationhood nonetheless. By tracing how the prints of 1914 drew on religious imagery, in addition to themes from previous Russian wars, Denisov explained why the wartime *lubok* proved to be so popular over the course of one hundred years and five wars. Just one year before revolution engulfed Russia, Denisov concluded, "the *lubok* is destined for a long stay on the wall," for it possesses "many qualities, . . . traditions, and adapts to new contemporary forms."[110] While the setbacks of 1915 had silenced the *lubok,* Denisov believed that the popular print's popularity in the past would continue into the future.

Another contemporary, Gerasim Magula, whose short article on the images of the Great War appeared in 1914, seconded Denisov's conclusions in many ways.[111] Echoing ideas present in peasant observations such as Engelgardt's from the Crimean War, Magula writes that the wartime *lubok* proved so popular in the countryside because of the audience's lack of intelligence. According to Magula, the peasant "is like a child, it is necessary only to catch a hint of the reality" in the print. Despite this negative appraisal of the ability of peasant Russia to understand difficult concepts, Magula admits that the wartime *lubok* appeared everywhere in the countryside, stating that "its place is in the peasant *izba,* with self-made benches, with the red corner and among the icons," and that the peasant calls these popular prints "his pictures," for they "not only decorate his modest dwelling, but raise the idea that they are an outgrowth of his spiritual emotions."[112]

Magula seconds beliefs first expressed by Rovinskii. He writes that the 1851 law affected *lubki* production negatively, claiming that "now *lubki* are simply bad," both in terms of artistic value and connection to the people. Despite his own opinions about these images, Magula notes that *lubok* publishers such as Ivan Sytin make images that retain their popularity, "producing annually people's pictures in the millions." Magula ultimately claims that the *lubki* are "artistic garbage" that have created an "artistic famine," and condemns publishers who "aspire less to spend than to receive money" on their creations.[113] For Magula, such publishers do not "elevate the people" through art, but instead produce images that appeal to the basest emotions of Russians.

Much like the fears of Belokonskii during the Russo-Japanese War, Magula's fears that the wartime *lubok* represents trash stem above all from the fact that these people's pictures proved so successful commercially and influenced the "simple peasant" so significantly. Although his assessment of their value contrasts with that of Denisov, Magula offers similar conclusions, namely that the Great War *lubki* were too successful in shaping attitudes in the countryside. Although Magula and others imply that the overconfidence expressed in the war images may have stemmed from government control, in all likelihood it resulted from the self-censoring of the publishers. By portraying defeats or insignificant skirmishes as victories, publishers like Sytin ensured that their prints would not only pass the censors, but would also sell well. In illustrating the war in this way, however, *lubok* publishers may have undermined the war effort once the conflict wore on.

Other Russians continued to note the appeal of wartime *lubki* in the Russian countryside. A schoolteacher observed in *Russkaia shkola*: "When . . . the book peddler appeared his pictures and booklets (*lubok* and all war) sold out immediately. Which house didn't have pictures about the war? Portraits of Nikolai Nikolaevich, the Belgian King, General Ruzskii and Radko-Dmitriev were popular, and there was at least one in each house."[114] Journalists throughout Russia continued to take note of the appeal of Russia's wartime images, and even commented on how they functioned as newspapers for an illiterate public.[115]

All of these accounts by Russians who lived through the Great War, as well as other recollections,[116] allow the historian to explore recent assertions that Russia lacked a strong sense of nationhood in World War I.[117] Russian wartime culture, and in particular its most important element, the *lubok,* contained themes present in Russian culture for centuries that articulated a specific form of patriotic identity centered on such iconic figures as the Cossack and peasant. In addition to these figures, *lubok* artists and publishers produced images that touted a Russian spirit, in part centered on the Orthodox faith, which attested to Russian military superiority and Russian national identity in general. While these publishers stood at the forefront of the production of the wartime image, the success of the *lubki* depended on their ability to attract buyers. Had the wartime images from 1812 to 1917 not been so popular among a wide range of consumers, they would not have increased in numbers, nor would successful businessmen such as Ivan Sytin have relied on similar themes in their *lubki* from 1877 to 1914. During the Great War, individual printings reached 800,000.[118] The argument that Russia lacked a unifying symbol does not appear as convincing when one takes the long view of Russian wartime culture dating back to 1812, as Denisov did.

What can one conclude about Russian nationhood and patriotic culture during the Great War? The assertion that 1915 marked an important turning point certainly holds up after close scrutiny.[119] *Lubok* publishers did not make many images after the initial wave of popular prints. This suggests two scenarios. Either the demand for new images waned among the Russian population or it did not; instead, the *lubok* publishers could no longer produce the optimistic, confident prints that the censors and consumers alike wanted. As Denisov and Magula claimed, the initial images that touted Russian superiority, much like other European posters from the war, may have proven too successful and inadvertently created a false expectation of quick victories. One report from 1915 claimed that *lubki* publishers had run out of paper and pigment because they had printed so many images.[120] In this case, the wartime *lubok* may have fallen victim to its own success. Wartime propaganda, in other cases, undermined the war effort as much as it aided it. More specifically, the images of the Great War may have contributed to Russians focusing their growing disillusionment with the wartime effort on the person of the tsar and his government.

The tsar had not played a prominent role in wartime imagery since 1877, and many Russians by 1915 believed Nicholas II to be the largest problem both in terms of producing a victory on the battlefield and in alleviating Russia's domestic problems. When Nicholas II assumed command of the Russian army in 1915, he also could be blamed for any further defeats in the war. More importantly, however, Nicholas's absence from the capital left his wife, Alexandra, in an influential position. As a German princess, she became the focus of popular hatred after 1915 in Petrograd, largely through the Russian population's inability to understand her relationship with Grigorii Rasputin. Anti-German rumors and talk of treason dominated all quarters of the capital, ideas fomented by crude caricatures that circulated throughout the city, and these beliefs ultimately played a decisive role in late 1916 and early 1917.[121]

The February Revolution of 1917 can be seen as a patriotic revolution designed to rid Russia of a treasonous government and tsar. The anti-German attitudes spread in part by wartime imagery appeared to have been absorbed by a large percentage of the Russian population, who engaged in various acts of violence against Germans throughout the war.[122] The downfall of the Romanovs and the popular acceptance of their fate in 1917 represented the final act of anti-German activities of the Russian populace in the Great War, and suggest that Russians possessed a sense of nationhood in 1917, however xenophobic this identity was.[123]

Much of the recent work done by other historians of the war support the view that Russians had a strong sense of nationhood. Steve Smith, among others, has argued that historians should examine "national identity in a longer historical perspective" in order to "appreciate the distinctive ways in which the national 'we' was constructed, and the broader social and political implications of its differing constructions." In particular, since Russia "was one of the 'old, continuous nations,'" Smith notes, "the task of constructing national identity was easier than in many countries, since elements from the repertoire of protonational identity could be appropriated and put to new uses."[124] The wartime *lubok* represented one very important medium through which Russian elites—in this case publishers, artists, and censors—attempted to articulate a national and patriotic identity around various themes and symbols.

One of these symbols, the tsar, remained at the fringes of this identity. Smith, in analyzing the diary of A. A. Zamarev, a peasant from a remote village in Vologda, notes that it "not only reveals deep patriotism but surprising knowledge about the course of the war." Zamarev "makes not a single mention of the tsar in his many entries concerning the war."[125] It is best to view 1917 as a struggle to define the meaning of the nation, and that national identity played a decisive role in influencing the outcome of the revolution.[126]

Russian wartime imagery contained similar themes and forms as those from all of the Great War's participants. All the participants produced posters that attempted to build support for the war effort, and all belligerents saw the appearance of national symbols, religious prints, and images ridiculing the enemy.[127] Only in the Russian case, however, has this imagery been termed unsuccessful and used to support a view that Russia in 1917 was unpatriotic and lacked a sense of nationhood. What the Russian experience in the war points to, however, in taking a broader perspective, is the importance of understanding patriotic and national identities as constantly evolving and being redefined. Russian wartime imagery produced visual definitions of Russianness to explain the conflict, and just as this imagery blended in elements of the old in novel ways, so too did Russians in the war respond in numerous ways to their patriotic exhortations.

Why then have historians not viewed the Russian visual experience of the war through a broader lens? Part of the answer rests with the fact that the Bolsheviks, who ultimately emerged as the victors of the revolutionary upheavals that began in 1917, attempted to downplay the importance of the war in favor of a mythical version of the October Revolution. The memory of World War I faded somewhat, and in some cases, as the bulldozing of wartime cemeteries indicates, quite forcefully.[128] Because the war assumed such a role in the eyes of the Soviet leaders, historians both in Russia and the West tended to accept the official version of the war presented by the Bolsheviks. Russia had succumbed to revolution, this version posited, precisely because of its lack of patriotic identity and because of its lack of modernity. Instead, it is possible that patriotic identity peaked in February and then found new outlets by October, after the Bolshevik seizure of power, again a sign of its constantly changing nature.[129] Since the Bolsheviks stressed the importance of the latter event, the patriotism surrounding the former was not emphasized.

Yet recent historical approaches to the study of national identity, along with recent works dealing with Russia in the First World War, suggest a different approach. The continued popularity of the wartime *lubki* through 1915 demonstrates that in a general sense Russians accepted the contents of these images. Russian *lubok* publishers from Sharapov to Sytin enjoyed increased sales in their product right up until 1915, a fact that needs to be weighed seriously in evaluating how a patriotic culture and a national identity were constructed in Russia. Russian elites attempted to articulate a specific national identity from 1812 through the Great War that both appropriated older ideas about Russianness and created new iconic symbols. The ways in which Russians absorbed these ideas contributed to the construction of a Russian nation in the nineteenth century, given the *lubok*'s booming sales and the evidence available regarding its reception.

Vladimir Denisov, whose *War and the Lubok* is discussed above, concluded his book with the following prediction: "The blossoming of *lubok* creativity now has stopped, but not the supply and strength of its creativity. Other days will come and these prints again will depart to all the ends of Russia. It seems, after an involuntary break, after looking back on itself, the rich, splendid blossoming of this unique flower of our art will blossom more magnificently."[130] Although he had no way of knowing about events that would sweep Russia in 1917, Denisov's prediction came true in one way, for the Soviet government would build its visual propaganda upon the foundations laid by the wartime *lubok*.

8

THE **WARTIME** *LUBOK* **AND**
SOVIET VISUAL CULTURE

And in general, the peasant, just like the workers in their mass,
think much more in terms of images than abstract formulas; and
visual illustration, even when a high level of literacy is reached,
will always play a major role for the peasant.
—**Nadezhda Krupskaia** (1923)

• From 19 to 24 February 1913, the Moscow artist Nikolai Dmitreevich
Vinogradov held a *lubok* exhibition in the old Russian capital. Entitled
simply *The First Exhibition of Lubki,* Vinogradov's display represented the
first time that a significant member of Russia's artistic community showcased popular prints as a serious artistic endeavor, and the exhibition can
be considered a milestone in the *lubok*'s history. Russian avant-garde figures such as Mikhail Larionov, Nataliia Goncharova, David Burliuk, and
Kazimir Malevich had begun to adopt a *lubok* style in their works by the
early decades of the twentieth century, and Larionov contributed an essay
about the historical importance of the *lubok* to the catalog for Vinogradov's exhibition.[1] Held just a year before the Great War that saw artists
such as Malevich and Vladimir Mayakovsky produce patriotic *lubki* mock-
ing the Germans, Vinogradov's exhibit marked an important shift among
educated Russians in their approach to popular prints, and it helped to ensure that artists who served the Bolshevik regime would employ the *lubok*
style during the founding years of Soviet visual culture.

This chapter examines the continuing importance of the wartime *lubok*
after 1917. It focuses in particular on the careers of Dmitrii Moor and
Vladimir Mayakovsky, both of whom attended Vinogradov's exhibit, and
both of whom produced popular prints during the Great War. Mayakovsky
and Moor were among the founding fathers of Soviet poster art after 1917,
producing some of the best-known imagery in Soviet history.[2] The images
they produced meant that the wartime *lubok*'s influence continued after
1917, for the themes, style, and propaganda techniques of the Russian
popular print were reproduced in Soviet poster art through the Second
World War. Although the subject of their images changed dramatically in
the wake of 1917, at a basic level their work continued to identify enemies
and persuade the public.

Vinogradov's Exhibit and the Cultural Importance of the *Lubok*

Vinogradov's exhibit came at the end of a series of shows and paintings that began to make use of the *lubok* as a serious artistic form.[3] The early decades of the twentieth century had witnessed Russian neoprimitivists incorporate elements of folk art in their works. For artists such as Wasily Kandinsky, the *lubok* served as a source of inspiration for the use of color schemes he employed in his paintings, and he frequently hung the prints above his workspace.[4] Kandinsky had first encountered the popular print as part of the Tenishev program, when he worked in the Vologda region and was stunned by the number of images he saw in peasant huts.[5] After their encounter with the popular prints, Kandinsky, Larionov, and other Russian avant-garde artists began to scour Moscow's markets and buy as many *lubki* as they could find.[6]

In 1913, around the same time that Vinogradov organized his exhibit, Aleksandr Shevchenko wrote "Neoprimitivism: Its Theory, Its Potentials, Its Achievements," a booklet that served as a manifesto for the new movement. Shevchenko paid particular attention to the importance of the *lubok* as "the most acute, the most direct perception of life," and stated "the simple, unsophisticated beauty of the *lubok*, the severity of the primitive, the mechanical precision of construction, nobility of style, and good color brought together by the creative hand of the artist-ruler—that is our password and our slogan."[7]

Using this idea as a starting point, Larionov painted soldiers and prostitutes and used *lubki* as models, just as Goncharova and Malevich did the same in their paintings of peasants. Larionov, in particular, stated that images such as "The Barber Wants to Cut Off the Old Believer's Beard" and "The Cat of Kazan" inspired his barbershop scenes; and his painting The *"Katsap" Venus* (1912) included a replica of the cat on a wall behind his reclining nude.[8] Larionov also helped organize several exhibitions between 1910 and 1913 that either displayed paintings inspired by *lubki* or the images themselves alongside other examples of folk art. This was the context, a renewed interest in the *lubok*, of Vinogradov's exhibition, which was supported in part by Larionov. In the exhibition catalog, Larionov refers readers first of all to the work of Dmitrii Rovinskii, whose 1881 collection "discovers everything of interest." Larionov then discusses the importance that the *lubok* should have in the development of futurism and other avant-garde art in Russia. Calling the *lubok* "a great art form," Larionov notes that the images have a "timeless character,"[9] and implores artists to adopt their style, for these prints represent a true Russian art form and retain their folk roots.

The exhibit itself displayed not only Russian *lubki*, but also examples of folk prints from China, Japan, Korea, Turkey, France, England, Poland, and Germany, all of which were referred to as *lubki* by Vinogradov.[10] Thus, Vinogradov and Larionov connected the Russian *lubok* to popular prints from around the world in an effort to demonstrate the universality of the folk image and its role in promoting a sense of nationhood. Among the Russian prints, Vinogradov included several wartime *lubki,* including "The Entry of Alexander I into Paris" and "The Capture of Plevna," as well as several Japanese woodblock prints from the Russo-Japanese War.[11] That Larionov and his fellow avant-garde artists paid tribute to Rovinskii, one of the pioneers of *lubok* collectors, was appropriate. One month after Vinogradov's exhibit opened, Larionov debuted his own show, *An Exhibition of Original Icons and Lubok Prints,* which featured 170 *lubki* from his personal collection.[12] Larionov's exhibit focused almost entirely on nineteenth-century images, however, and featured prints such as "Sevastopol" and "The English Attack on the Solovetskii Monastery" from the Crimean War.[13] For Larionov, therefore, *lubki* encompassed all of the "people's pictures" produced after 1851, despite the beliefs of Rovinskii, who claimed that the prints had lost their connection to the people because of tight censorship.

By 1913, Russian artists such as Larionov, Goncharova, and Malevich viewed the *lubok* and its style as a source of inspiration. Goncharova even used the Larionov exhibition to display her own attempts to revive the *lubok.*[14] In the same year, Vladimir Mayakovsky, who attended Vinogradov's display, composed his poem "To Signboards," which he considered to be a "verbal expression of the neoprimitivist delight in this vigorous folk art form."[15] A year later, many of these members of the Russian artistic community would produce their own patriotic wartime *lubki* in an effort to persuade their fellow Russians to support the war effort.[16]

Mayakovsky, Malevich, and Moor in the Great War

On 31 July 1914, the day that Russia declared war on Germany, Mayakovsky climbed to the top of the Skobelev monument in the old Russian capital and shouted patriotic verses.[17] Caught up in the "spirit of 1914" like so many of his artistic contemporaries,[18] Mayakovsky began to compose propaganda pieces for the *lubok* market. As he later recalled: "I reacted with excitement to the war. First I noticed only its decorative and noisy aspects. Did posters on order, and of course very military ones. Then verses."[19]

Mayakovsky's interest in images dated from his childhood. Liudmilla, his sister, noted that as a child young Vladimir loved to peruse Rovinskii's collection of *lubok* prints,[20] and this lifelong fascination with the popular print, combined with the renewed interest generated by the 1913 exhibit, seems to have fueled Mayakovsky's patriotism in 1914. When the Russian government approved of the formation of the publishing house Contemporary *Lubok* in 1914, Mayakovsky offered his services. Among those who also answered patriotic calls to produce images for the publishing house were Aristakh Lentulov and Kazimir Malevich.

Ironically, Mayakovsky's work occurred even as he was being investigated by the tsarist secret police, the Okhrana, who believed him to be "politically unreliable."[21] In October 1914, in response to the investigation, Mayakovsky sent a note to the authorities attesting to his "reliability" and asking for permission to join the Russian army.[22] For evidence, Mayakovsky alluded to his patriotic beliefs, conspicuous in his wartime images. Privately, he wrote "in order to talk about war, it is necessary to see it. I have gone to register as a volunteer."[23] Despite these attempts, however, Mayakovsky's petition was rejected.[24] Thus, at the same time he espoused support for the war through his *lubki* and climbed to the top of the Skobelev monument in an expression of patriotism, the Russian government believed Mayakovsky to be politically unreliable for service in the army.

The images that Mayakovsky and other artists produced fused avant-garde style with the patriotic themes of the war *lubok*. Adopting cultural stereotypes of Germans and Turks present in other images, Mayakovsky produced a print that contained the text, "Near Warsaw and near Grodno we flattened them, Yes, we flattened and crushed the Germans, Even our women can easily kill Prussians *[prusaki]*."[25] The first two panels of the print contained a larger-than-life Russian soldier, long a symbol of Russian national identity, spanking a small German soldier. The second panel is set inside a peasant hut, where a Russian *baba* also fights "Prussians," here depicted as cockroaches and small German soldiers with Prussian helmets.

A second print, illustrated by Malevich and featuring a rhyme by Mayakovsky, is dominated by a fat Wilhelm II surrounded by equally plump troops, all of them wearing Prussian helmets and distinguished by their whiskers.[26] The ditty reads: "Look, look closely, already near the Vistula the Germans have grown swollen, it means they are moping!" Mayakovsky's *lubok* "In the Glorious Forest of Augustus" depicts a Cossack cavalry charging out of the forests near Konigsberg.[27] The Cossacks carry the tricolor Russian flag and chase their frightened German enemies into the Nieman River. Mayakovsky's verse, which accompanied the image that he drew himself, reads, "In the glorious forest of Augustus there are a hundred thousand beaten Germans. The enemy is decimated and then set to floating down the Nieman." Both of these images play on the stereotypes of Germans as unintelligent Prussians that were rampant in Russian wartime culture throughout 1914 and 1915.[28]

Mayakovsky also drew on popular stereotypes of the Turk in his wartime images. One print featured a Cossack, near his horse, shaking his fist at three frightened Turks with distorted features.[29] The largest of the Turks, identified as the sultan himself, drops his hookah and grabs at his comrade next to him, who casts off the Turkish flag out of fear. This image of the cowardly Turk finds further reinforcement in Mayakovsky's verse: "Hey Sultan, sitting in the Porte, don't spoil your mug with such a fight."[30]

8.1 "The Austrian Soldier Marched to Radziwill" A second Malevich print from the war features a Russian peasant woman *(baba)* as the embodiment of the "Russian spirit," easily dispatching with Austrian soldiers who threaten her home. The caption, which rhymes in Russian, reads: "The Austrian soldier marched to Radziwill, but got impaled on a *baba's* pitchfork [*shel avstriets v Radzivily, da popal na bab'i vily*]." Source: Denisov, *Voina i lubok.*

Avant-garde artists like Mayakovsky and Kazimir Malevich also produced patriotic images that featured iconic figures of Russian national identity, such as the peasant and Cossack. The previously mentioned Malevich print, "What a Crash and What a Thunder the Germans are Making Near Lomzha" (Figure 7.6) featured a gigantic Russian peasant, while Malevich's print "The Sausage Eater *[kolbasnik]* Approached Lodz" contained another larger-than-life peasant who thrashes Wilhelm II—the "sausage eater"—and his troops.[31] After welcoming Wilhelm, the peasant easily takes care of the Germans, who "leave with a bruised rear end," in Mayakovsky's words.[32] Another Malevich print (Figure 8.1) depicted a large Russian *baba* easily dispatching a smaller Austrian soldier, suggesting that the Austrians were even weaker than the Germans.[33] The peasant woman impales one soldier with a pitchfork, while other Austrians cower in fear behind the mountains, some even running away. "The Austrian soldier marched to Radziwill," reads his verse, "but got impaled on a *baba's* pitchfork [*shel avstriets v Radzivily, da popal na bab'i vily*]."[34]

While artists such as Lentulov, Mayakovsky, and Malevich worked for the firm Contemporary *Lubok*, other prominent figures such as Dmitrii Moor and Alexander Apsit produced patriotic images for Ivan Sytin's firm.

Apsit, a Latvian who gained respect as an illustrator for journals such as *Rodina* and *Niva* before 1914, turned to illustrating patriotic *lubki* during the first few months of the war.[35] One of his images depicted Germans about to rape two Russian women, while a second panel featured a Russian *starets* blessing his four sons about to go off to battle, presumably to defend the women.[36] A second print entitled "European Food" contained caricatures of the enemy as different foods, with Wilhelm II as a sausage cowering behind a bottle of beer.[37] Apsit also produced two prints that lauded the fighting strength of the Cossack, including one *lubok* devoted to Kozma Kriuchkov.[38]

Like his contemporary Apsit, Dmitrii Moor also worked for large Moscow firms, including Sytin's. His print on Kozma Kriuchkov (Figure 7.2) was one of several sketches Moor produced that featured the heroic exploits of the Cossack.[39] Moor, whose real name was Orlov, was a native of Novocherkassk, the capital of the Don Cossacks. His father had been a Cossack and Moor often dressed in Cossack attire.[40] Moor not only featured traditional patriotic icons such as the Cossack in his wartime images, he also depicted Russian peasant women taking care of German aviators in his print "The *Baba* is Not a Blockhead." In his other *lubki* from 1914, Moor ridiculed the Germans in general and the Kaiser in particular. His "Wilhelm's Cattle" featured the German emperor riding atop his allies, while a Russian Cossack laughed at the motley crew. The *lubok* "How the Devil Grew His Garden" features caricatures of all of Russia's enemies in the style of a *raek* print.[41] The image depicts a potato, a turnip, and mushrooms slowly transforming respectively into Franz Joseph, Wilhelm II, and Turks. Accompanied by verses written for the *raeshnik* by Moor himself, the print suggests that the enemy would not prove too difficult to defeat, and should be considered foolish for having dared invade Russia.

As these examples illustrate, Russian avant-garde artists whose politics by and large leaned toward radicalism nevertheless responded to the outbreak of war in 1914 with unbridled patriotism. Important cultural figures such as Mayakovsky, Malevich—who was busy developing his ideas about suprematism and even finished his famous *Black Square* in 1914—and Aristakh Lentulov, among others, produced numerous *lubki* in the early months of the war. While all of these artists grew weary of the war by 1915, they contributed to its patriotic culture and in the process learned a great deal about the production of popular images.

In Mayakovsky's case, he became despondent by the winter of 1914–1915, writing in his journal, "Disgust and hatred for the war. Ah, close, close the eyes of the newspapers and others. [My] Interest in art at all was gone."[42] His vanished enthusiasm for the war found expression in his poetry of the time, such as "Mama and the Killing of the German Party (1914)," and "War and the World (1916)," an angry, cynically biting commentary on warfare.[43] Rejected by the censors, "War and the World" represented Mayakovsky's total disillusionment with the conflict. Just over a year later, however, Mayakovsky's enthusiasm for art would find a new outlet.

Images of the Russian Civil War, 1917–1921

Although the February Revolution of 1917 resulted in Nicholas II's abdication, it did not end Russia's participation in the Great War. The ensuing power vacuum meant that Russian political parties launched frantic
efforts to persuade Russians and many parties drew on visual sources to
spread their ideas. Russia throughout 1917 was awash in images, as artists
of all kinds and from all political persuasions attempted to capture the
essence of the time.[44] The Provisional Government that emerged as the
driving force behind the renewed war effort of 1917 issued several *lubki*
designed to inform Russians about the makeup of the government and to
mobilize support for its policies. One of these prints, "A Great, Free Russia," featured portraits of all the new ministers in the first Provisional Government, surrounded by a scene of joyous crowds proclaiming their new
freedom outside the Tauride Palace (the headquarters of the Russian
Duma).[45] The Provisional Government also commissioned several war
posters, many of which made use of standard iconographic figures such as
the Russian peasant and soldier. Two of the most famous of these prints—
both of which bore the title "Freedom Loan"—won prizes from a government-
sponsored jury headed by Maxim Gorky.[46]

In addition, political parties as varied as the Socialist Revolutionaries
and the Kadet Party also produced popular images after February 1917,
many of them promoting the Constituent Assembly elections scheduled
for later that year. Viacheslav Polonskii, author of the first important work
on Russian revolutionary poster art, claimed that the prints made by the
SR Party were the most effective in terms of their numbers and artistic
merits, although he also conceded that Kadet posters were also effective.[47]
Other prints portrayed the Bolsheviks as German agents, while the Bolsheviks themselves issued posters that depicted workers and soldiers united in
support of the socialist cause.[48]

The abdication of the tsar also brought Mayakovsky and Moor back to
the task of making popular images. Moor drew the first caricature of
Nicholas II that was allowed into print just days after the tsar's abdication,
appearing in *Utro Rossii* on 8 March 1917.[49] The picture, entitled "Archive
of Tourist Sites," features three "sites" that represent the "old" Russia. The
first, the tsar bell in the Kremlin, had never rung. The second, the tsar
cannon also near Cathedral Square, had never fired. The third "useless" attraction was Nicholas II, depicted as a disheveled, glaring figure with his
hand shoved into his jacket in a Napoleon-like manner. The image thus
linked Nicholas II with other emblems of tsarist rule that had proven useless
—the text notes that these three "don't ring, don't fire, don't rule *[ne
zvonit, ne streliaet, ne tsarstvuet]*." The cartoon attracted letters to the editor, most of them critical of Moor's "disrespectful manner."[50]

Mayakovsky, who also welcomed the February Revolution, displayed
his satisfaction with the tsar's abdication by producing the *lubok* "Forget-

ful Nicholas" (Figure 8.2). A caricature of the tsar, shown dressed in full regalia, is being driven away by a solitary Russian soldier pointing his bayonet.[51] Behind the tsar, the sun shines brightly, its rays illuminating a "new Russia" that includes a factory running smoothly.[52] In the case of both Moor and Mayakovsky, the events of February 1917 had renewed their interest in the effectiveness of the popular image, and both artists used the *lubok* style to produce new prints that welcomed the changes in Russia. Mayakovsky in particular engaged in numerous activities that aimed to use art in order to advance ideas about the "new Russia." He joined or founded several committees after March 1917, among them a movement for "free art," which brought the artist together with Vladimir Denisov, the author of *War and the Lubok*.[53] Moor's and Mayakovsky's prints captured the dominant theme of the images from 1917—hatred directed at the tsar. Between February and October, Nicholas II appeared in dozens of posters, postcards, and popular prints that celebrated his downfall.[54]

The October seizure of power by the Bolsheviks brought a government that would prove extremely interested in the use of imagery to mobilize the masses, in what one historian has termed "the birth of the propaganda state."[55] In the wake of the Great War and the proliferation of its patriotic imagery, the new government took these images seriously. The Soviet regime, led by Lenin himself, shut down *lubok* publishers (particularly Ivan Sytin) because it recognized the influence that patriotic imagery had in the country. The new rulers appropriated the offices, machines, and even artists to found a new Soviet visual culture that would inspire loyalty to the regime. Lenin ordered the "sequestering" of Sytin's printing plants on 28 November 1917, prompting the publisher to catch a train to Petrograd to meet with the Bolshevik leader. After a brief meeting, in which Lenin stated that all of Sytin's businesses would be nationalized, Sytin accepted his fate.[56] Eventually, the Bolsheviks printed their two national dailies, *Pravda* and *Izvestiia,* in Sytin's old newspaper plant in Moscow.

As for the images of Sytin and his fellow publishers, the Soviet government issued a temporary decree that banned the production of *lubki* in November 1917. A year and a half later, in April 1919, the government made this decree permanent. Sytin, however, attempted to persuade the government to allow him to publish new images and *lubok* literature that would espouse ideas acceptable to the Bolsheviks. He won over the Press section of the Moscow Soviet, which wrote Lenin that the *lubok* was "the most accessible" form of reading "for the broad popular masses." Although the *lubok* had promoted "ignorance, superstition, and prejudice" in the past, stated the endorsement, it had been extremely influential and thus could be coopted by the new regime.[57]

The Bolsheviks, however, had their own ideas about producing popular images and did not envision giving Sytin a prominent role. Although he continued to work in a minor capacity for the Soviet regime, the authorities did not allow him to produce any new *lubki*. Instead, the Soviet government

8.2 **"Forgetful Nicholas"** Avant-garde artists who created propaganda prints during the war were among the first to define a "new Russia" that emerged after February 1917. Vladimir Mayakovsky's "Forgetful Nicholas" visually depicts the "victory" of the Russian spirit (embodied in the peasant soldier) over the tsar, Nicholas II. The sun that illuminated the tsar as knight in Figure 7.5 now shines over a "free Russia." Reprinted by permission from the Poster Collection, Hoover Institution Archives

devoted more attention to posters and other forms of persuasion than the tsars had,[58] and centralized the production of all popular imagery, making posters and their contents part of the new "propaganda state." Lenin's regime had no use for Sytin himself, but it did take his work seriously.

The artists who had illustrated some of the most striking *lubki* during the war soon turned their talents to producing images for the Soviet government. Apsit, Moor, and Mayakovsky, among others, helped to establish the new Soviet poster art in the civil war years, and in turn used their *lubok* background to lay the foundations of early Soviet visual culture. Mayakovsky became the driving force behind the special images produced for the Russian Telegraph Agency (ROSTA), which consisted, like *lubki*, of a series of frames accompanied by a rhyming verse.[59] Moor produced over fifty posters during the civil war years, many of them reminiscent of his 1914 *lubki*, while Apsit, who worked for Sytin during the Great War, became the master of the early Soviet poster. In all of these examples, artists who had learned the trade by producing war *lubki* adapted the themes and styles they learned to a new context.

One of the Bolsheviks' primary challenges was to give people a clear depiction of the heroes and villains of the revolution. While the enemies may have changed from foreign armies to internal agents or worldwide capitalism, the purpose of the Soviet poster remained very similar to that of the wartime *lubok*. Using Iurii Lotman's influential essay on binary culture in medieval Russia, Victoria Bonnell contends that early Soviet culture also presented the world in a binary fashion. For the Bolsheviks, "all societies consisted of two basic groups: the collective and individual heroes who advanced the march of history toward a classless society, and their adversaries, the villains or enemies—*vragi*—who tried to prevent the great march forward."[60] Thus the wartime *lubok* performed a similar function by identifying the enemy and contrasting him with iconic "Russians." After 1917, though, enemies were divided into two broad categories: external and internal foes of the Bolsheviks. In addition, Bolshevik poster artists made even more use of allegorical images to illustrate foes such as "imperialism" and "capitalism."[61] The subjects may have changed in Soviet visual culture, but the purpose remained the same as that of the tsarist wartime print.[62]

Apsit's first poster for the Bolshevik regime also turned out to be his best known. "A Year of the Proletarian Dictatorship" appeared in November 1918 and celebrated the first anniversary of the October Revolution. Featuring images of a worker and peasant treading on emblems of the imperial past, these two figures stand before a gateway to a view of workers and peasants celebrating their "prosperity" under the Bolsheviks. Behind the people a huge factory complex displays its vitality by producing smoke that does not quite obscure the bright rays of the sun, another symbol of the new world opened up by the Soviet regime. Identified by Bonnell as "the first major statement of a new image in Bolshevik iconography,"[63] Apsit's poster resembles the wartime *lubok* both in style and content. Apsit recasts the peasant as a symbol of the new Soviet Russia, while also establishing the worker as a new icon. As a sign of his reappropriation of old symbols, Apsit included emblems such as the double-headed eagle standard and tsarist shield beneath the boots of the worker and peasant, replacing these outdated symbols with new ones. In many of his posters from the civil war era, Apsit used peasants and soldiers within the context of the new visual culture.[64] These images proved quite successful: Apsit fled Moscow in late 1919 when Denikin's forces approached the city because he feared being "hanged by the Whites for his posters."[65]

Moor also welcomed the October Revolution and began to seek a means by which he could employ his artistic talents that would "resound on an equal basis with the speech of a political orator."[66] Working for Litizdat, the publishing house established by the Soviet high command, Moor became one of the most productive of all poster artists in the civil war era. He later wrote that he helped to start up the first "agitpoems," "having made them [like] a line of *lubki* of the national type."[67] His 1919 print, "The Tsarist Regiments and the Red Army" (Figure 8.3), also featured

8.3 **"The Tsarist Regiments and the Red Army"** Bolshevik poster artists (many of whom learned their trade by producing tsarist wartime *lubki*) soon reappropriated the visual language of nationhood for the Bolshevik state. This 1919 Dmitrii Moor poster from the civil war period contrasts national symbols from "Before" (on the left, these symbols include Nicholas II, an Orthodox priest, the double-headed eagle, capitalists, and soldiers who fought for these "false ideals") with symbols for "Now" (on the right, factories and new buildings inspire new peasant and worker soldiers to defeat the old army). Reprinted by permission from the Poster Collection, Hoover Institution Archives.

an appropriation of old symbols in the context of the new Soviet system.[68] Issued in a print run of 95,000 copies, the poster, in the words of one scholar, "has particular interest because of its large edition . . . and its elegant application of stylistic devices from both the *lubok* and religious icons."[69] A panel labeled "Before," depicts a caricature of the last tsar surrounded by his supporters, who include an Orthodox priest, a rich capitalist, army officers, and bogatyrs. In front of these symbols of the old regime stand several exhausted army soldiers, clearly worn out from fighting a war for their oppressors. The second panel, labeled "After," depicts gleaming factories and buildings in the background along with rays of sunshine—all designed to symbolize prosperity under the Bolshevik regime. The foreground contains Red Army soldiers, sailors, and two peasants, all of whom brandish bayonets and stand prepared to defend the new order.

In other posters from this era, Moor depicted the new enemy of the Soviet regime, "world imperialism," as a serpent-like beast, a sign of the changing iconography of the enemy.[70] Moor also changed other icons in his Bolshevik posters. His well-known "Have You Enrolled as a Volunteer?"

from 1920, for example, replaced the peasant soldier as a symbol of national identity with the new Red Army soldier. Other Moor posters featured workers and peasants—including peasant workers—in iconlike *lubok*-style images that trumpeted Soviet achievements by 1919.[71] The Bolshevik leaders and the poster artists who worked for them, particularly Moor, also tried to combat the strength of Orthodoxy within Russian culture. War *lubki* had long equated Russianness with Orthodoxy, and Moor attempted to employ similar images that worked counter to this concept. For several years in the 1920s, he drew anti-religious images for journals such as *Bezbozhnik* (The Athiest). Much like the wartime propaganda, however, these drawings may have had unintended effects: Ivan Pavlov, an engraver, recalled that peasants used to put Moor's drawings of saints up in their icon corners and pray to them, oblivious to their satirical intent.[72]

Like Moor, Vladimir Mayakovsky also looked forward to using the experience he gained during the Great War. More than any other poster artist of the civil war era, Mayakovsky and the posters that he produced for the Russian Telegraph Agency drew on the styles and themes of the *lubok*.[73] For Mayakovsky, these and other posters represented the "flowers of the revolution,"[74] while his own creations "meant a nation of 150 million being served by hand by a small group of painters . . . it meant Red Army men looking at posters before battle and going to fight not with a prayer but with a slogan on their lips."[75] Nikolai Vinogradov, the organizer of the first *lubok* exhibit, aided Mayakovsky in making the ROSTA Windows by working as a stenciller.[76]

Once Mayakovsky began work on the windows, in October 1919, he established control over the themes and texts. Mayakovsky himself wrote as many as 90 percent of the six hundred texts in the windows.[77] Initially these windows dealt primarily with the conduct of the civil war, as his print "Help Voluntarily" demonstrates.[78] Using crude drawings that resembled *lubok* prints accompanied by his increasingly famous verses,[79] Mayakovsky called on industry and agriculture to help defeat the White forces, depicted in two panels, with one counter-revolutionary strangling a Russian peasant. Asking, "do you want to work rather than fight?" Mayakovsky points out that vigilance is necessary if Russia's enemies are to be defeated. He returned to this theme in "If We Don't Finish Off the White Guardsmen Completely," in which he included caricatures of Nicholas II, Wrangel, and an Orthodox priest, again making use of images from wartime *lubki*.[80] "Until the Red banner has been strengthened," concluded Mayakovsky, "we can't throw our rifle away."[81]

Fusing *lubok*-style imagery and the verses similar to those he had first written for Contemporary *Lubok* in 1914, Mayakovsky, in his ROSTA Windows, produced "a protocol record of a most difficult three-year period of revolutionary struggle, conveyed by spots of paint and the echoing sound of slogans."[82] His work on the ROSTA Windows fulfilled his earlier promise to display art everywhere, "on the streets, in trams, in factories, in workshops, and in workers' apartments."[83] Contemporaries recalled that the windows drew great crowds wherever they appeared and, according to Mayakovsky, "could bring even a running man to a standstill."[84] At a speech given to the All-Russian Congress of ROSTA Workers in May 1920, Mayakovsky extolled the virtues of visual propaganda:

> [W]e must concentrate all the forces working in our press on the invention of a means whereby the hitting power of our ideas is not weakened by fuzziness and confusion of form. It is clear, comrades, that if the slogans being promoted by us in articles, etc., are not to lose all their impact, if they are to be conspicuous all the time, if they are to command attention from every street wall and from every shop window, it is essential in some way or other to formulate these slogans in a form that does not have a merely transitory significance. Of course, the only way to do this is to apply some art or another for propaganda in more fundamental images. Comrades, this explains ROSTA's partiality for art work, for making posters, displaying windows of satire, etc.[85]

For Mayakovsky, then, Bolshevik propaganda would be most effective and influence a wider audience if produced in visual form, much like the war *lubok*. What he believed had changed somewhat from the tsarist image, though, was the importance of the text. Mayakovsky linked visual propaganda with literacy, and ensured that his rhymes were central to the image as a whole.

The links between the wartime *lubok* and the Soviet poster did not end with Moor, Apsit, and Mayakovsky, although these three former *lubok* artists represent the clearest continuities. Anonymous posters from the civil war period either recast older themes present in the war *lubok* or employed the *lubok* style in service of the new regime. The 1919 print "Long Live the Red Army" features two soldiers on a winged horse flying above the Kremlin, which is in turn encircled by other Red Army soldiers.[86] Stylized like a *lubok*, this print depicts the new heroes flying above and surrounding a long-standing symbol of Russian identity, the Moscow Kremlin. Reinforcing this theme of old and new are fallen capitalists, crowns, and other tsarist symbols resting at the bottom of the print, as well as caricatures of Uncle Sam, John Bull, and Wilhelm II, all of whom flee before the Red Army.

The Petrograd-produced print "The International" also appropriated the style and themes of the war *lubok*.[87] Featuring a worker, a peasant, a soldier, and a sailor standing together in the foreground, the poster also contains new artistic elements such as red banners, communist slogans, army maneuvers, bourgeois elements being chased away, and the lyrics of the "International," all drawn in the style of the former people's print. Finally, V.I. Deni's poster called "The League of Nations" features three fat caricatures of the leading capitalist nations, Britain, France, and the United States, reminiscent of figures from the 1904–1905 war against Japan.[88] At the feet of these three lie a mass of perishing, thin bodies, the victims of the "uniting of all the capitalist countries," as a banner proclaims.[89]

In her study of Soviet political posters from Lenin to Stalin, Victoria Bonnell notes that images of the male worker, the leader, the peasant woman, the capitalist, and others became familiar figures to "nearly every-one who lived in Russia after 1917," making these images icons in their own right.[90] In addition, Bolshevik posters from the civil war period en-gaged in a new form of enmification, and catalogued enemies in order to transform them "into something nonhuman and presenting them in a form that legitimized their destruction."[91] Viacheslav Polonskii com-mented on this function of the Soviet poster when he wrote, "Moor's lith-ographs seldom evoke laughter, but more often hatred, a desire to finish off the enemy, without leaving a trace."[92]

Because Russians in this era had already grown used to a specific visual culture under the old regime, the Bolshevik state appreciated the ability of images to reach a wide number of illiterate people. In 1923, Nadezhda Krupskaia, Lenin's wife, commented that "for the present and the near fu-ture, a peasant can learn to improve his production only if he is taught by visual example."[93] Viacheslav Polonskii was even more specific about the origins of the Soviet political poster, which he claimed "played a big enough role in the history of the proletarian revolution." When dis-cussing the inspiration behind these images, Polonskii wrote that they stemmed "not from pictures that hang in museums, not from book illus-trations that pass from the hands of amateurs, not from frescoes that are accessible for viewing to a few, but the poster *[plakat]* and the *lubok*—millions strong, popular, from the street—closer to a national art."[94] The new gov-ernment placed a great deal of emphasis on this kind of Russian visual propaganda between the years 1918 and 1922, when it produced and dis-tributed more than 7.5 million images. Posters were regularly reviewed in the party newspapers, which proclaimed them "a new and powerful weapon of socialist propaganda, influencing the broadest possible public," while laws passed very early in the Soviet period made it a crime to tear down Bolshevik posters.[95]

The Bolshevik poster's influence, however, was hardly "new," as Polon-skii admitted. Mayakovsky, Moor, and other poster artists in the civil war period reappropriated the themes of the war *lubok* and recast them in the context of a new period of Russian history. Tsarist patriotic culture thus crossed the revolutionary divide of 1917 and helped to inform Soviet culture. The artists used many of the same themes and ideas they had il-lustrated in the Great War: initially the peasant/worker icon, the Red Army soldier, the "spirit" of communism, and anti-Orthodoxy were prevalent in civil war posters in order to counter the influence of church, new enemies, and emblems of the tsarist past. Frida Roginskaia, writing in 1930 for the Soviet Society for Cultural Relations with Foreign Countries (VOKS), made connections between the tsarist wartime *lubok* and the Bolshevik poster. In her article "Soviet Posters and *'Lubok,'*" Roginskaia claims that the reliance on the themes of the tsarist prints may have produced some problems:

> It is the peasant in his millions who is the chief purchaser of the *lubok*. The Soviet *lubok* is therefore faced with the task of carrying Soviet propaganda to the country-side. Here it should be said that the traditional influence of the pre-revolutionary *lubok* is still preventing the successful carrying out of this function. This is particularly true of the battle-piece, for which the same artists who worked on chauvinist publications in the world-war epoch are still found working. But even that devoted to the new life is too often reminiscent of old publications, with their saccharine sentimentality. The influence of the past is also felt in the ethnographical *lubok*. Finally, a very serious defect of our *lubok* is its limited choice of subject matter. Many aspects of industrialization and of the country-side socialist reconstruction are as yet completely untouched in the *lubok*.[96]

As a result of these difficulties, Roginskaia concludes, "there is even a tendency trying to prove that the *lubok* can no longer exist as an independent form of art, but the convenience of the *lubok* as a form of propaganda influencing the broad peasant masses through the agency of graphic art makes this point of view untenable."[97] Thus, the role of the tsarist print and the ways in which artists and consumers alike interpreted these visual sources continued to be contested well into the Stalinist era.

Despite Roginskaia's claims (and fears), the Bolshevik poster differed from the wartime *lubok* in two respects. First was the level of support given by the authorities to the production and distribution of their images. The Bolshevik government's use of the poster transformed it into the kind of propaganda that gave the term a negative connotation. At the same time, Bolshevik leaders rewarded poster artists for their work. Dmitrii Moor, who had once worked for Ivan Sytin, was declared a "hero of the pencil and paintbrush" in 1922 for his posters, which had "raised the fighting spirit" of the Red Army and "lit up the path of struggle."[98] Polonskii later claimed that the civil war poster had proven to be "more powerful than cannon and bullets in achieving the Bolshevik victory."[99]

Second, the Bolshevik poster featured the image of the leader much more than the wartime *lubok* did. Lenin initially sent out contradictory signals about the use of his image, but after an attempt on his life in August 1918, his image began to be featured in state propaganda. By the early months of 1919, Lenin became the subject of several *lubok*-style posters, all of them helping to generate the Lenin cult.[100] Around 1920, Soviet poster artists began to present Lenin as a larger-than-life leader. In a sense, images of Lenin—and later Stalin—took the place of the similarly enhanced heroes of the wartime *lubok* in the Russian visual tradition, a place the tsar had never occupied.[101]

The Great Patriotic War and Soviet Imagery, 1941–1945

When Hitler invaded the Soviet Union on the same day of June that Napoleon had invaded Russia, Russian poster artists had a ready-made comparison to invoke the wartime culture developed ever since 1812. In many ways, the posters produced from 1941 to 1945 represented the final cultural significance of the war *lubok*.[102] By the 1930s, Soviet culture had begun to turn back to the figures and patriotic culture of the tsarist past, a trend that crystallized in the Second World War, known as the Great Patriotic War in Russia.[103] Stalin recast the war in terms of traditional appeals to patriotism, while wartime artists, including Dmitrii Moor, again reappropriated the themes of 1812 to exhort Russians to fight. Soviet culture in the Second World War, as one historian has noted, became predominately Russian, as "the Stalinist leadership deemed the revival of Great Russian traditions and symbols necessary for carrying out the war successfully."[104] Soviet artists mobilized for the war effort made numerous comparisons between 1812 and 1941 in their images, connecting the Patriotic War and its culture to that of the Great Patriotic War.

Soviet propaganda had featured the Nazis as early as the 1920s. After Hitler came to power in 1933, "fascists" became a label applied to all Germans, making use once more of anti-German feelings among the Russian people.[105] When Nazi forces invaded the Soviet Union on 22 June 1941, Soviet propaganda used these sentiments to label the Germans as conquerors and invaders, in the same fashion as the *lubki* of the Great War. Germans were portrayed in Soviet imagery as rapists, savages, butchers, debauchers, and vermin. Several posters from the war depicted Nazi soldiers engaged in various atrocities, including the killing of women and children. Wartime posters also revived the caricature of Germans as Prussians, and Soviet artists depicted Nazi soldiers as fat, mustachioed officers in scenes reminiscent of both World War I prints and images from the Russian civil war (when White officers often appeared as Wilhelmine figures).[106]

Above all, however, the posters of the Second World War, along with Soviet wartime culture in general, represented a revival of Russian nationhood that lasted in some form until the 1991 collapse of the Soviet Union and beyond. Stalin's 1941 radio speech, made as the Nazis approached Moscow, established the tone for this revival:

[T]hese people [Germans] without honor or conscience, with the morality of animals, who have the effrontery to call for the extermination of the great Russian nation, the nation of Plekhanov and Lenin, Belinsky and Chernyshevsky, Pushkin and Tolstoy, Gorky and Chekhov, Glinka and Tchaikovsky,

Sechenov and Pavlov, Suvorov and Kutuzov. The German invaders want a war of extermination against the peoples of the Soviet Union . . . they will have it. Our task now will be to destroy every German to the very last one, who has come to occupy our country. No mercy for the German invaders. Death to the German invaders.[107]

Stalin's speech referred to military figures previously considered taboo in the Soviet Union such as Suvorov and Kutuzov, both of whom had begun to creep into Stalinist culture only in the late 1930s. This proclamation allowed Soviet artists to refer to the Napoleonic invasion of 1812 to an extent not allowed since 1917.

A 1941 poster by V. Milashevskii (Figure 8.4) connected the Napoleonic invasion to the Nazi one, and suggested that Hitler would meet the same fate as the Frenchman.[108] Employing a *lubok* style that further suggested the images of the Patriotic War, the print featured two panels. In the first, labeled "1812," a Russian peasant standing in a snow-covered village stabs Napoleon through with his pitchfork. In the second, marked "1941," a Soviet plane flying over a similar Russian village chases away Hitler, whose legs and arms are distorted to resemble the swastika. The text claims that "the grandfathers took them [the enemy] on pikes *[na piku]*, and today the grandsons take them in an airplane dive *[na pike]*," a play on words also reminiscent of the wartime *lubok*. Much like Milashevskii, Nikolai Dolgorukov drew on *lubok* themes to compare the Nazi invasion to the French. His 1941 "So It Was . . . So It Will Be" featured a Russian bayonet and a pike driving away Napoleon, while Hitler is run through by a larger Soviet bayonet. Both posters appeared shortly after Hitler's army entered the USSR, a testament to how quickly Soviet artists drew on symbols and themes prevalent in Russian visual culture for over a century.

The Kukryniksy, a collective made up of three artists who produced single works, were perhaps the most famous of the Soviet wartime poster artists. The three (Mikhail Kupriianov, Porfirii Krylov, and Nikolai Sokolov—the name of the collective borrowed from their names) had studied together at the Higher Artistic-Technical Studios (VKhUTEMAS) in the 1920s and studied the art of visual propaganda under Dmitrii Moor. After this training, the three began producing popular prints later in the decade.[109] Their work carried many of the traits of both the tsarist wartime *lubok* and the early work of Soviet poster artists such as their teacher Moor. Most of the Kukryniksy posters prior to the Great Patriotic War identified enemies and directed hatred against them, such as their 1930 work "Let's Annihilate the Kulaks as a Class." Their 1932 poster "15 Years of Soviet Power" also directed hatred at the Nazis. In it, the number "15," which resembles the hammer and sickle, squeezes an inhuman German wearing a swastika.

During the war years the Kukryniksy came into their own and produced dozens of posters, prints, and TASS Windows for the Soviet news agency. "We Shall Mercilessly Defeat and Destroy the Enemy" appeared

8.4 "1812 and 1941" The visual nationhood that first found definition in 1812 comes full circle in this print from 1941. Employing a *lubok* style that further suggested the images of the Patriotic War, the poster features two panels. In the first, labeled "1812," a Russian peasant standing in a snow-covered village stabs Napoleon through with his pitchfork. In the second, marked "1941," a Soviet plane flying over a similar Russian village chases away Hitler, whose legs and arms are distorted to resemble the swastika. The text claims that "the grandfathers took them [the enemy] on pikes *[na piku]*, and today the grandsons take them in an airplane dive *[na pike]*," a play on words also reminiscent of the wartime *lubok*. Reprinted by permission from the Poster Collection, Hoover Institution Archives.

shortly after Hitler's invasion and depicted Hitler as a ratlike creature being speared by a Red Army soldier's bayonet. Their poster "Napoleon Was Defeated and That Will Be the Case of the Swelled-Headed Hitler," which also appeared in 1941, cast Hitler as a latter-day Napoleon as it assured viewers that both would meet the same fate. In 1942, during the 130th anniversary of the war against the French, they issued their poster "Not Without Reason All Russia Remembers Borodino Day," which features the main 1812 monument at Borodino undamaged as wolves with Nazi helmets flee before it.[110]

At the same time the Kukryniksy produced posters that dehumanized the enemy while reminding viewers of past military glories, they also created images that featured long-standing ideas about Russian national traits. Their 1941 poster "One Good Turn Deserves Another [*Dolg platezhom krasen*]" features the craftiness of a Russian peasant while facing the Nazis and is reminiscent of images from 1812 and other tsarist wars that attempted to articulate a "Russian spirit." In the first panel, the unarmed peasant doffs his cap to a Nazi officer, who brandishes a gun—the caption reads "during the day the fascist said to the peasant: 'Off with the cap from your head!'" The second panel has the peasant, this time armed as a partisan, cutting off the head of the same officer while he smokes a cigar—"At night he returned with the partisans and took the helmet off with the head."[111]

Other artists produced images that contained similar definitions of a Russian spirit—posters referred to Soviet soldiers as *"bogatyrs"* defending the motherland, including D. Shmarinov's "Forward to the Enemy, Soviet *Bogatyrs*," which featured a Russian medieval knight on horseback holding a Nazi helmet,[112] and Iraklii Toidze's poster "In the Name of the Motherland [*rodina*], Forward *Bogatyrs*," which depicted a knight holding his sword aloft and standing next to a Red Army soldier.[113] Dmitrii Mel'nikov, active as a poster artist since the revolution, worked with Mikhail Andrievskoi to produce the 1941 TASS Window "The Russian People [*Russkii narod*]." In it, the two artists define a timeless bravery and spirit that has characterized Russianness for centuries—separate panels depict military victories over the Teutonic Knights in 1242, the Mongols in 1380, the Prussians in 1760, and the French in 1812, and attributed all of these victories to the valor of the Russian people.[114] Even Dmitrii Moor came out of retirement to produce images such as "How Have You Helped the Front," a replica of his "Have You Volunteered" poster of 1920, establishing a direct biographical link between the posters of the Great Patriotic War and those of the civil war. Mikhail Cheremnykh, who along with Mayakovsky, had been the driving force behind the ROSTA Windows, produced numerous TASS Windows from 1941 to 1945 that drew not only on their civil war predecessors, but on the *lubok* as well. One of these posters, "On the Old Smolensk Road," depicted Napoleon on a sled warning an emaciated Hitler not to go through with his invasion.[115] Finally, the 1941 poster by

Viktor Ivanov "How the *Baby* Took the Fascists Prisoner" revived the image of Russian peasant women as active wartime participants in a way reminiscent of Vasilisa during the French invasion.[116]

Soviet imagery from 1941 to 1945 helped to create new myths about the war even as it popularized the notion that this war was a Great Patriotic War that resembled in its intensity the Patriotic War of 1812. As Richard Stites has shown, Soviet propagandists, "carefully reading the psychology of the wartime masses, constructed new myths and legends and cultural icons designed to draw upon the deep wells of national pride, to substitute emotional themes about the beloved homeland for the drier and more bombastic official patriotism of the prewar period," all in an effort to present the Great Patriotic War as a holy war.[117]

The Soviet government ensured that a revival of the poster took place during the wartime years. The state publishing house of Moscow published 800 posters and a total of 34 million copies.[118] Just as tsarist publishers had flooded the country with visual propaganda, so too did Soviet publishing enterprises. Alexander Werth, the Russian-born correspondent for the BBC during the war, recalled his impressions of Moscow just twelve days after Hitler's invasion:

> On the face of it, Moscow looked perfectly normal. The streets were crowded and the shops were still full of goods. . . . Posters on the walls were being eagerly read, and there were certainly plenty of posters: a Russian tank crushing a giant crab with a Hitler moustache, a Red soldier ramming his bayonet down the throat of a giant Hitler-faced rat—*Razdavit' fascistskuyu gadinu*, it said: crush the Fascist vermin; appeals to women—"Women, go and work on the collective farms, replace the men now in the army!"[119]

Later, Werth would comment in his diary, "there is no longer a dividing line between Soviet and Russian."[120] Werth's comments echo those of Alexander Pasternak's and N. V. Davydov's from the Russo-Japanese and Crimean Wars, respectively. In 1941, just as in the wars of the tsarist period, appeals to nationhood came in the form of visual propaganda. Moreover, in making use of the imagery and themes that they did, Soviet propagandists admitted that pre-1917 symbols still had meaning and could inspire Russians during wartime.[121]

The World of Visual Nationhood in 1941

The explosion of Soviet poster art that took place during the Great Patriotic War, an event that tapped into long-standing cultural myths that had formed the basis of Russian visual nationhood since 1812, found a parallel in the use of posters by all combatants during the Second World War. The Napoleonic era had witnessed a wave of caricatures and popular prints in Europe that defined national identities around a common enemy in order to define "us" and "them." With the outbreak of World War II, the age of visual nationhood that centered on prints reached its apogee. European poster artists, joined this time by American and Asian contemporaries, flooded their countries with prints designed to inspire and to articulate difference. Posters in Russia and elsewhere once again used a common enemy, Germany having replaced France, to reconstruct a sense of nationhood. The images, which had direct links to the Napoleonic-era prints that flooded Europe in the early nineteenth century, represented "battle flags of commercial, cultural, and political rivalries."[122] The war of images that had begun during the time of Napoleon, however, ended during the time of Hitler.

The war led to significant propaganda campaigns in every country—posters joined other forms of media in an effort to exhort people to fight and to unite behind concepts of nationhood. In Britain, for example, posters articulated a visual version of the "people's war" that stressed "English" traits such as stoicism, a sense of humor, determination, and bravery. The 1939 image "*Your* Courage, *Your* Cheerfulness, *Your* Resolution Will Bring Us Victory," for example, identified characteristics deemed "British" by its producers, while a series of posters from 1942 entitled "Your Britain: Fight for It Now" provided numerous visual expressions of British nationhood.[123] After Hitler's invasion of the USSR, British artists, much as they had done during the Napoleonic Wars, borrowed Soviet posters and linked Britain's war to Russia's. The 1942 print, "Russia's Fight is Ours!" contains four Soviet posters, three of them drawn by the Kukryniksy, including "Napoleon Suffered Defeat and That Will Be the Fate of the Swelled-Headed Hitler" (translated for the English audience as "Napoleon Failed and So Will That Blackguard Hitler!").[124]

Jack Werner, an Oxford musician and journalist, published a short book in 1943 that also drew parallels between the propaganda of the Second World War and that of the Napoleonic era. In it, he urges his countrymen to remember the "invasion scare" of 1803 and the images of James Gillray, George Cruikshank, and other British artists who "did much to convey to the reading public the spirit of British resistance to the Tyrant."[125] Werner also paid tribute to the Russian response to Napoleon's invasion of 1812 and commented, "was not Russia [in 1812] Britain's first line of defence, just as she has been since June, 1941?"[126] Just as Britain lampooned Napoleon in caricature, Werner reminded his readers, so too did Russian artists do the same, and even inspired Cruikshank to copy a Russian print, "Russians Teaching Boney to Dance." Ultimately, Werner affirmed that the values of "Britishness" that artists such as Gillray depicted in the nineteenth century applied to the 1940s: "Not even Boney, the terror of the rest of Europe, could deprive John Bull of his high spirits."[127] Werner thus acknowledged that the processes of propaganda and nationhood that had begun with Napoleon, processes that involved a great deal of cultural borrowings between artists from all over Europe, continued well into the twentieth century.

After the Great War, however, more and more Europeans explicitly linked the relationship between popular prints, propaganda, and nationhood. Distrust for propagandistic posters that defined enemies and national characteristics alike grew among consumers throughout Europe. Cyril Bird, the creator of the British wartime poster series "Careless Talk Costs Lives," acknowledged that the British people had developed "a general aversion to reading any notice of any sort" in part because of memories of Great War posters. As a result of this distrust, the British government exerted more effort on wartime propaganda in new media such as radio and film.[128]

In the USSR, propaganda posters designed to exhort Russians against the Nazis made references to themes and stereotypes that had appeared in wartime *lubki* since the Napoleonic invasion, and even adopted the style of the popular print in order to inspire Russians once again to defend their nation. As Victoria Bonnell has argued, the posters of the Great Patriotic War "nearly all made use of visual devices and compositions already familiar to viewers who were old enough to remember propaganda from the Civil War or the First World War." Soviets artist ultimately "returned to the *lubok* format" because "the satirical *lubok* was thought to provide an easy means of communication with broad strata of the population, especially those in the countryside."[129] Soviet uses of propaganda during the Great Patriotic War also included media such as radio and film, but the dominant themes of all this propaganda remained the same as the themes of the Soviet wartime posters—a revival of Russian national identity. Just as artists such as Ivan Terebenev had appropriated names, symbols, customs, common myths, and historical memories in 1812 to articulate a sense of nationhood and create a patriotic culture in the wake of Napoleon's invasion, so poster artists did the same after Hitler invaded the USSR. Once again Russian visual culture served as the means by which artists attempted to popularize notions of nationhood and patriotism. Once again these artists created new myths and new symbols through the use of old ones. Once again Russians from all walks of life encountered these symbols. Just as the images from the Patriotic War served as the foundation for lasting myths, so too did posters from the Great Patriotic War serve the same function.

9 WARTIME CULTURE AND RUSSIAN NATIONAL IDENTITY

Conclusion

• In 1814, *lubok* artists such as Ivan Terebenev praised the Russian tsar, Alexander I, as a divine being who led his nation to triumph over Napoleon. That same year, in July, members of the Senate, the Holy Synod, and the State Council attempted to award Alexander the title "Blessed" *(blagoslovennyi)*, an honor he declined. Poets composed odes to the victorious tsar, monuments such as the Alexander Column in St. Petersburg were commissioned, and thousands of Russians from all walks of life participated in spectacles that celebrated the victory and the tsar's role in it.[1]

One hundred years later, in 1914, *lubok* publishers such as Ivan Sytin rarely included the tsar, Nicholas II, in their patriotic images of the First World War. In one of the few prints that depicted the sovereign, Nicholas performed the mundane task of visiting a hospital to pin an award on a Russian soldier. In the midst of the war, a private in the army called Nicholas "the traitor, [who] drank the blood from our veins." Members of the Russian Duma virtually accused the emperor of treason, and eventually demanded that he abdicate his throne. Crude caricatures of the tsar, his wife, and Rasputin appeared all over Petrograd.

Why did the position of Nicholas II within tsarist patriotic culture differ so drastically from that of his great-great-uncle, Alexander I? The place of the Russian sovereign within wartime culture illustrates that, over the course of one hundred years, the tsar figured less and less in how Russians defined their nation. When Ivan Terebenev and his artistic contemporaries praised Alexander I in their images from 1814, they depicted him as a divine figure commanding his troops. The *lubok* "Alexander I Leads Russian Armies into Paris" presented the tsar triumphantly entering the French capital at the head of his army. Residents of the city surround him and bow before his might, while the text commands readers to "extol him as a Deity, . . . a tsar worthy of all altars." The *lubok* artists who made images like this one established Alexander I as a ruler who had orchestrated the triumph over Napoleon, and in the process they initiated the glorification of the tsar within the myth of 1812.

The years following 1812 brought important changes in the ways that tsars portrayed themselves to the wider public, a shift captured in the wartime *lubki*. Nicholas I, who guarded the use of his image quite carefully, appeared in no prints from the Crimean War. Instead, the war produced numerous *lubki* that praised the bravery of the Russian peasant soldier. Nicholas's brother, Alexander II, by contrast, allowed his image to be used more frequently in wartime culture, and his reign marked an important shift in the representation of the Russian monarch. During the Russo-Turkish War of 1877, for example, Alexander appeared in images such as "God Save the Tsar," and was depicted as taking an active role in the conflict. Alongside this print and others like it, however, Alexander appeared in "The Visit of the Sovereign Emperor to Wounded Russian Soldiers" (Figure 5.2). Here Alexander performs the less-than-divine task of passing out gifts to wounded soldiers. Thus, as these two prints indicate, the tsar's position within Russian wartime culture included illustrations of an active, divine tsar in the mold of Alexander I along with a more passive, mundane ruler.

This latter image dominated Nicholas II's reign and found expression in the prints of the Great War. While Alexander II appeared in many *lubki* in 1877 and 1878, Nicholas II barely featured at all in the years 1914–1915. Ivan Sytin's untitled print from 1914 has Nicholas II visiting a field hospital to inspire his troops to victory and reward them for service. One of only a handful of images that contained Nicholas II in the war—two others were portraits of the tsar and his European allies—this print illustrated that the transition from an active tsar to a passive one within wartime culture was complete. Nicholas II appeared as a lackluster leader in the wartime images, and this fact assured that the tsar did not form an important pillar of patriotic identity.

By contrast to the role of the tsar, that of the Russian peasant in the war *lubki* was remarkably stable between 1812 and 1914. The graphic artists of 1812 lauded the strength of the Russian peasant and used him as a symbol for the Russian nation. The peasant's courage, religious beliefs, and willingness to defend his country served as the basis for numerous images. Larger-than-life depictions of the Russian peasant became standard illustrations in tsarist patriotic culture in 1812 and afterward. Many Russian officers who accompanied peasant soldiers into Paris in 1814 returned home embarrassed that the brave men who had defeated Napoleon remained enserfed, and began to call for their freedom. Similar images that praised the heroic spirit of peasants in the Crimean War contributed to the widespread emancipatory beliefs throughout Russia in the 1850s.

Ivan Terebenev's "The Russian Hercules" (Figure 2.3), for example, featured a gigantic Russian peasant, placed squarely in the center, dispatching five puny French soldiers. The size of this Hercules evokes Russia's vastness, and the puny enemies are easily dealt with by their conqueror. Future prints furthered these constructions. In the Crimean War, Russian publishers placed peasants at the center of their prints depicting heroic deeds, such as Sharapov's *lubok* "Little Russians at Sevastopol," in which two Ukrainian peasant soldiers chat in an embodiment of the collective spirit displayed by the city's defenders. The 1878 image "One, Two, Three!" (Figure 5.3) again contained a gigantic Russian peasant in the center, and again had the hero easily dispatching enemy soldiers. In the 1904 *lubok* "Sitting by the Sea, Waiting for the Right Weather" (Figure 6.4) a larger-than-life peasant holds a cannon at Port Arthur aimed at his puny enemies in Korea. All of these prints included determined, jovial peasants placed in the context of the particular war for which they were created, and all exaggerated the size of their protagonist and contrasted it with a smaller, weaker, enemy. In all of these cases, the peasant was both an important actor in the conflict and a symbol of the Russian nation itself. Unlike other prevalent images of the peasant within Russian culture,[2] the depiction of the muzhik in wartime culture established a clever and powerful symbol that in turn defined Russianness.

During the First World War, moreover, *lubok* artists such as Vladimir Mayakovsky included depictions of larger-than-life peasants in their patriotic prints. Despite the continued belief among many Russians that the peasants were backward and representative of the country's inertia, the muzhik remained an important symbol of Russian nationhood and an integral component of its visual culture. Kazimir Malevich and Mayakovsky collaborated on the print "What a Crash and What a Thunder the Germans are Making near Lomzha" (Figure 7.6), which employed traditional imagery of the Russian peasant in an avant-garde style. This use of the peasant as an iconographic figure of Russianness provided a transition to later, Soviet images of the Russian peasant. When the Bolsheviks seized power several months after Nicholas's abdication, their poster artists, Mayakovsky among them, included the peasant as a symbol of the new Russia. Nicholas II, meanwhile, appeared in far more Soviet wartime images than he ever had during his reign, this time as an emblem of oppression and the antithesis of the new, Soviet, Russia.

The trajectory of the tsar's and the peasant's appearances in wartime culture allows us to reach certain conclusions about the significance of the wartime *lubok* and the national symbols it included. The ebb and flow of the tsar's image within wartime culture illustrates how the Russian monarch, in many ways obsessed about his image, failed to establish a place within the visual patriotism of the nineteenth century. Instead, by the reign of Nicholas II, the tsar had come to be seen by many Russians as an alien part of their nation. The Russian peasant, however, served as a symbol that later artists would employ in their own attempts to articulate a sense of nationhood.[3]

This "victory" of the peasant over the tsar in the wartime *lubki* found expression in Mayakovsky's 1917 *lubok* "Forgetful Nicholas" (Figure 8.2). A peasant soldier, now a part of the new, post-tsarist (but pre-Soviet) Russian army, drives off the former tsar, who drops his scepter. Behind Nicholas, a sign reads: "Out! With your retinue! With your wife and with your mommy!" The verse has the tsar plotting to bind Russians together through service, then have them rot in the field, but reminds the viewer that "yes, he [Nicholas] forgot, by the way, that the soldier was born a worker."[4] For Mayakovsky and his fellow poster artists, the Russian peasant, embodied here by the soldier, has rid the nation of its most powerful internal foe and paved the way for a new society where he can earn a better living. One symbol of Russian identity has been toppled. Another remains.

Mayakovsky's print perfectly captured the evolution of the tsar and peasant in Russian patriotic culture. It demonstrates the importance of images as historical sources. Russian culture has long been a visual one, and Russian artists and publishers turned to the *lubok* during wars in an effort to define what these conflicts were about. In a largely illiterate society, they believed that the traditional Russian image could best express their ideas about Russianness and the enemy. In making use of the *lubok*, Terebenev, Mayakovsky, and others created documents that served as visual narratives of the time. Both then and now their *lubki* allow us to imagine the past more vividly, and their images remain important sources for expressing political ideas and arguments. The Russians who encountered these images and who were inspired by them in turn made the work of Terebenev and others crucial for understanding Russian history and Russian culture.

The importance of visual sources for understanding Russian history does not completely address the wartime *lubok*'s significance. Obviously, the *lubok* illustrates the nature of war and the culture it produces. Wars helped to shape the history of Russia between 1812 and 1945 more than any other events, and historians not only have to grapple with why Russia fought, but also with how wars were presented and understood. The *lubok* was always in high demand during times of war because it often served as the only means for many Russians to understand the conflicts. In addition, *lubki* helped define Russian wartime culture, which in turn shaped notions of Russian nationhood.

Because of this role, the war *lubok* can best be described as propaganda, however dynamic and contradictory its nature. Intended to inspire feelings of unity but subject to tsarist censorship, the genre frequently undermined the war effort. During the Crimean, Russo-Japanese, and First World Wars, the wartime images praised the heroism of Russian soldiers and the Russian spirit, yet these attributes did not lead to victories. The popularity of the *lubok* thus frequently fostered a sense of Russian superiority that could not be matched on the battlefield, and in turn contributed to the crises that affected Russia after these conflicts. Moreover, as Nikolai Davydov (chapter 4) and Alexander Pasternak (chapter 6) alluded to, Russians could not blame their soldiers for defeats, but they did blame their government, which had helped—at least in their minds—to promote these images. In other words, although they were propaganda, wartime *lubki* in the nineteenth century had a subversive function, supporting Philip Taylor's view that propaganda can best be understood as a process for "the sowing, germination, and dissemination of ideas."[5] After the nineteenth century, while retaining the dynamic nature of propaganda, the wartime *lubok* and later the Soviet poster helped to change the way in which the term "propaganda" was understood. Because of the proliferation of prints and other forms of media that fueled first the violence of the Great War and then the violence of the Bolshevik state, for many "propaganda" came to mean something evil. For others, particularly Bolshevik leaders and artists such as Dmitrii Moor and Vladimir Mayakovsky, visual propaganda still had uses in Russia, namely serving the Bolshevik state. The story of the wartime *lubok* thus parallels the story of propaganda, its development and uses, and ultimately its meanings.

Finally, and most importantly, these propaganda images articulated Russian national identity and allowed Russians from a variety of backgrounds to understand this identity. Again, however, the wartime *lubok* had unintended consequences, clearly illustrated by the discussion above. Wartime prints did not regularly feature the tsar, and when he did appear, he was often pictured reviewing troops and visiting hospitals, contrary to the tendency of tsars to see themselves as divine figures. The images of war and the attitudes they helped to crystallize, in other words, contributed to the growing separation between the tsar and the people from 1812 to 1917, a separation that culminated in the February Revolution.[6] The articulation of Russian nationhood found in the war *lubok* did not come simply from government propaganda or an elite effort to mobilize popular support, but sprang from a mix of market demand, popular reception, government acceptance, and publishers' attempts to define Russian nationhood. The Russian national identity that flourished during the nineteenth century found powerful expression in the Russian wartime image.

Yet the importance of the wartime *lubok* did not end in 1917. The Bolsheviks invested a great deal of energy into making their own images. Their posters not only employed artists who had produced patriotic *lubki;* they also featured many of the same themes. Bolshevik poster art again made use of visual sources to articulate propagandistic messages, and the images defined enemies, spread ideas about Soviet identity, and served as visual narratives to events such as the civil war in Russia and the Great Patriotic War. Many of the visual elements had changed since Ivan Terebenev, but in most respects the function remained the same.

NOTES

1—The *Lubok* and Russian Visual Nationhood

1. For more on this subject, see David Brandenberger, *National Bolshevism: Stalinist Mass Culture and the Formation of a Modern Russian National Identity, 1931–1956* (Cambridge: Harvard University Press, 2002); and the essays in Ronald Grigor Suny and Terry Martin, eds., *A State of Nations: Empire and Nation-Making in the Age of Lenin and Stalin* (New York: Oxford University Press, 2001).

2. Joshua Sanborn, *Drafting the Russian Nation: Military Conscription, Total War, and Mass Politics, 1905–1925* (DeKalb: Northern Illinois University Press, 2003), 129.

3. Brandenberger, *National Bolshevism*. As David Hoffmann has argued, Stalin's appeals to Russianness did not necessarily mark a "great break" from socialism, as many commentators have suggested. Hoffmann persuasively argues that the renewed interest in the past and in Russian national identity aimed at creating a socialist state. See Hoffmann, *Stalinist Values: The Cultural Norms of Soviet Modernity, 1917–1941* (Ithaca: Cornell University Press, 2003).

4. The classic account of this mobilization campaign is Peter Kenez, *The Birth of the Propaganda State: Soviet Methods of Mass Mobilization, 1917–1929* (Cambridge: Cambridge University Press, 1985).

5. Jeffrey Brooks, *When Russia Learned to Read: Literacy and Popular Literature, 1861–1917* (Princeton: Princeton University Press, 1985), 62–63. Brooks's pathbreaking work mostly focuses on the *lubok* chapbooks, not on the prints also known as *narodnye kartinki*.

6. E. I. Itkina, *Russkii rizovannyi lubok kontsa XVIII-nachala XX veka* (Moscow: Russkaia kniga, 1992), 44–45.

7. See James Cracraft, *The Petrine Revolution in Russian Imagery* (Chicago: University of Chicago Press, 1997), 305–6; and Alison Hilton, *Russian Folk Art* (Bloomington, IN: Indiana University Press, 1995), 308–9.

8. Toby Clark, *Art and Propaganda in the Twentieth Century: The Political Image in the Age of Mass Culture* (New York: Harry Abrams, 1997), 7.

9. Leonid Ouspensky and Vladimir Lossky, *The Meaning of Icons*, trans. G. E. H. Oalmer and E. Kadloubovsky (Crestwood, NY: St. Vladimir's Seminary Press, 1982), 41. See also the discussion in Vera Shevzov, "Letting the People into Church: Reflections on Orthodoxy and Community in Late Imperial Russia," in *Orthodox Russia: Belief and Faith under the Tsars,* ed. Valerie Kivelson and Robert Greene (University Park: Pennsylvania State University Press, 2003), 59–77, esp. 70–74.

10. Cracraft, *The Petrine Revolution in Russian Imagery;* Dianne Farrell, "Popular Prints in the Cultural History of Eighteenth-Century Russia" (Ph.D. diss., University of Wisconsin, 1980).

11. See Philip Taylor, *Munitions of the Mind: A History of Propaganda from the Ancient World to the Present Day*, 3rd ed. (Manchester: Manchester University Press, 2003); David Welch, "Introduction: Propaganda in Historical Perspective," in *Propaganda and Mass Persuasion: A Historical Encyclopedia, 1500 to the Present*, ed. Nicholas J. Cull, David Culbert, and David Welch (Santa Barbara: ABC-CLIO, 2003), xv–xxi; and Gareth Jowett and Victoria O'Donnell, *Propaganda and Persuasion* (Thousand Oaks: Sage Publications, 1999).

12. The print is reproduced in Vladimir Denisov, *Voina i lubok* (Petrograd: Izd. Novago zhurnala dlia vsiekh, 1916), 1–2.

13. See Catriona Kelly, "Popular Culture," in *The Cambridge Companion to Modern Russian Culture*, ed. Nicholas Rzhevsky (Cambridge: Cambridge University Press, 1998), 125–58, for more on the difficulties facing the historian of Russian culture. Kelly writes that the *lubok* (particularly its visual form, often just called "little pictures" *[kartinki]* by the peasants) had become a rural phenomenon by the turn of the nineteenth century. Before this time, however, the images had largely been confined to the cities in which they were produced. Kelly's work, both in this article and in her other works on Russian cultural studies, has informed my own understanding of Russian culture: see in particular the two volume she edited with David Shepherd, *Constructing Russian Culture in the Age of Revolution, 1881–1940* (Oxford: Oxford University Press, 1998), and *Russian Cultural Studies: An Introduction* (Oxford: Oxford University Press, 1998).

14. See Hans Rogger's seminal *National Consciousness in Eighteenth-Century Russia* (Cambridge: Harvard University Press, 1960) for more on these developments. See also Il'ia Serman, "Russian National Consciousness and Its Development in the Eighteenth Century," in *Russia in the Age of the Enlightenment*, ed. Roger Bartlett and Janet Hartley (New York: St. Martin's, 1990), 40–56. The application of the Russian popular print to nineteenth-century notions of nationhood conforms to the idea of a "national culture before nationalism" discussed in the issue of *Representations* devoted to this theme: see in particular the introduction by Carla Hesse and Thomas Laqueur, *Representations* 47 (Summer 1994): 1–12.

15. D. A. Rovinskii, *Russkie narodnye kartinki*, vol. 1 (St. Petersburg: Tip. Imp. Akademii nauk, 1881); Cracraft, *The Petrine Revolution in Russian Imagery*, 309, states that three-fourths of all images produced from 1750–1799 were nonreligious. Hilton, *Russian Folk Art*, 112.

16. Cracraft, *The Petrine Revolution in Russian Imagery*, 309.

17. See T. C. W. Blanning's brilliant book, *The Culture of Power and the Power of Culture: Old Regime Europe, 1660–1789* (Oxford: Oxford University Press, 2002), which describes this process.

18. See David Bell, *The Cult of the Nation in France: Inventing Nationalism, 1680–1800* (Cambridge: Harvard University Press, 2001).

19. See Maurice Agulhon, *Marianne into Battle: Republican Imagery and Symbolism in France, 1789–1880* (Cambridge: Cambridge University Press, 1981); and Joan Landes, *Visualizing the Nation: Gender, Representation, and Revolution in Eighteenth-Century France* (Ithaca: Cornell University Press, 2001).

20. Linda Colley, *Britons: Forging the Nation, 1707–1837* (New Haven: Yale University Press, 1992). On the role of Napoleon in British culture, see Stuart Semmel, *Napoleon and the British* (New Haven: Yale University Press, 2004); for an outstanding survey of images and the definition of nationhood that surrounded the 1851 Great Exhibition in London, see Jeffrey Auerbach, *The Great Exhibition of 1851: A Nation on Display* (New Haven: Yale University Press, 1999). Both nations also produced popular prints and art works that helped to promote modern imperialism. For France, see Todd Porterfield, *The Allure of Empire: Art in the Service of French Imperialism, 1798–1836* (Princeton: Princeton University Press, 1998); for Britain, see Auerbach, *Great Exhibition*, chap. 6.

21. For more works that examine popular imagery and the articulation of national identity, see Alon Confino, *The Nation as a Local Metaphor: Württemberg, Imperial Germany, and National Memory, 1871–1918* (Chapel Hill: University of North Carolina Press, 1997), chap. 7; Maunu Häyrynen, "The Kaleidoscopic View: The Finnish National Landscape Imagery," *National Identities* 2/1 (2000): 5–19; Rosemary Mitchell, *Picturing the Past: English History in Text and Image, 1830–1870* (Oxford: Clarendon Press, 2000); and Michelle Facos and Sharon Hirsh, eds., *Art, Culture, and National Identity in Fin-de-Siecle Europe* (Cambridge: Cambridge University Press, 2003).

22. Like Sonya Rose, I generally prefer the term "nationhood" to "national identity," although the two are similar. Rose, echoing Rogers Brubaker, argues that "nationhood" captures the idea that nations are "central and protean . . . categor[ies] of modern political and cultural thought, discourse, and practice." See Sonya Rose, *Which People's War? National Identity and Citizenship in Wartime Britain, 1939–1945* (Oxford: Oxford University Press, 2003), 7. It is a measure of how slippery these terms are that, while preferring the term "nationhood," Rose uses "national identity" in the title of her book. Confino has noted "the failure of theory to encompass the malleability of nationhood," for no definition of the term "fully embraces its ambiguous and often contradictory meanings." Confino, *The Nation as a Local Metaphor*, 3. I have taken Confino's warning to heart in this book, and have also been influenced by Simon Franklin and Emma Widdis's writing about Russian national identity. As they state, "much discussion of Russian identity is driven by the belief . . . that the question has an answer, that Russianness is a 'thing' to be located, described, and explained." Franklin and Widdis, by contrast, argue that "identity is not a 'thing' to be objectively described," but "a field of cultural discourse," while "Russian identity is and has been a topic of continual argument, of conflicting claims, competing images, contradictory criteria." Rather than resolve these contradictions, they advocate an approach that allows for an understanding of the "multiple cultural expressions and constructs" as the identity or identities. See Simon Franklin and Emma Widdis, eds., *National Identity in Russian Culture* (Cambridge: Cambridge University Press, 2004), xii.

23. This is the conclusion of Hubertus Jahn, *Russian Patriotic Culture in the First World War* (Ithaca: Cornell University Press, 1995). Jahn writes: "Patriotic imagery reveals that Russians had a pretty clear idea against whom they were fighting in the war, but not for whom and for what. If a nation is a community imagined by its members, as Benedict Anderson convincingly argues, then Russia was not a nation during World War I. There was no commonly accepted national symbolic figure such as Uncle Sam or John Bull or the Deutsche Michel" (173). Jahn further argues that the flag, Orthodoxy, and other symbols failed to create a sense of national consciousness in Russia. *A War of Images* argues that multiple symbols did exist for Russian identity, among them the peasant and the idea of a "Russian spirit," and that these symbols allowed Russians to imagine themselves to be a part of a Russian nation.

24. Brandenberger, *National Bolshevism*, titles his first chapter "Tsarist and Early Soviet Society's Weak Sense of National Identity." In it, he argues that the amorphous nature of Russian national identity before the mid-1930s meant that this sense of nationhood was weak, a weakness he attributes to the tsarist regime's lack of commitment to fostering nationalism. Brandenberger further argues that what united Russians before the 1930s was hatred of an enemy, which he labels an "inarticulate sense of national identity." For me, "amorphousness" describes any national identity and sense of nationhood, while xenophobia remains an important if uncomfortable part of any national imagining.

25. Geoffrey Hosking is the leading scholar of this school of thought. See his *Russia: People and Empire* (Cambridge: Harvard University Press, 1997); and Geoffrey Hosking and Robert Service, eds., *Russian Nationalism Past and Present* (New York: St. Martin's, 1998). In the former book, Hosking states clearly, "*Rossiia* [the name for the empire] obstructed the flowering of *Rus'* [the name for the Russian nation], or if you

prefer it, how the building of an empire impeded the formation of a nation" (xix). Although he allows for "such a thing as a compound national identity," particularly in Britain, Hosking concludes that this sort of national imagining did not occur in Russia, for the tsars did not promote a sense of belonging to the Russian nation and the lack of literacy obstructed the majority of the population from creating an alternative national vision. A Russian scholar who takes a similar view is A. L. Ianov, *Rossiia protiv Rossii. Ocherki istorii russkogo natsionalizma, 1825–1921* (Novosibirsk: "Sibirskii khronograf," 1999). Suny has also written on this subject: "The Empire Strikes Out: Imperial Russia, 'National' Identity, and Theories of Empire," in *A State of Nations*, 23–66. My own view is different, and argues that artists who created wartime culture articulated a sense of nationhood that did not always include the tsar, while illiterate Russians who bought their prints used them as a means of imagining themselves to belong to a Russian nation.

26. Vera Tolz, *Russia: Inventing the Nation* (London: Edward Arnold, 2001). Tolz begins her book with the sentence: "This book studies the ways in which Russian national identity has been constructed through the efforts of intellectuals and politicians from the eighteenth century to the present day." By the next page, after stating that Russia has had problems with constructing a nation, she concludes by stating: "This book seeks to account for the failure of the attempts of Russian intellectuals and politicians to construct a Russian nation, in opposition to the West, while preserving an imperial state and maintaining a particularly close union with other East Slavs." Tolz reaches this conclusion after an attempt to apply contemporary theories on nationalism to the Russian case, a comparison that leads her to conclude that Russian nationhood was "dysfunctional." In many ways, Tolz's book illustrates Confino's warning about the "failure of theory to encompass the malleability of nationhood" (cited in note 22). Tolz writes at length about the multiple ways in which Russians over the centuries have attempted to define Russianness, but concludes that Russia has never been a nation because civic nationalism has never taken hold. I lean toward the view of Paul Bushkovitch (note 33 below), who argues for understanding Russian nationhood on its own terms—the many ways in which Russians articulated a sense of belonging to a Russian nation, however varied these imaginings may be and despite the fact that Russia was not a nation-state in the European sense, points more toward the existence of a Russian nation than against it. For a view similar to Tolz's, see also Hugh Hudson, "An Unimaginable Community: The Failure of Nationalism in Russia during the Nineteenth and Early Twentieth Centuries," *Russian History/Histoire Russe* 26/3 (Fall 1999): 299–314.

27. Brandenberger and Hosking both make this argument: in Hosking's words, "the culmination of this process [a lack of national imagining] was the revolution and civil war of 1917–1921." Hosking, *Russia*, xxvi.

28. N. N. Smirnov et al., eds., *Rossiia i pervaia mirovaia voina (materialy mezhdunarodnogo nauchnogo kollokviuma)* (St. Petersburg: D. Bulanin, 1999), 10.

29. I borrow the term "enmification" from Robert Rieber, ed., *The Psychology of War and Peace: The Image of the Enemy* (New York: Plenum Press, 1991), 5. See also Yulia Mikhailova's appropriation of the term in her article "Images of Enemy and Self: Russian 'Popular Prints' of the Russo-Japanese War," *Acta slavica iaponica* 16 (1998): 30–53.

30. Defining "nation" and "nationalism" has often proven as difficult as explaining their rise and importance. Anthony Smith offers useful definitions of both: he defines "nation" as "a named human population occupying a historic territory or homeland and sharing common myths and memories; a mass, public culture; a single economy; and common rights and duties for all members." Smith states that "nationalism" is "an ideological movement for the attainment and maintenance of autonomy, unity, and identity on behalf of a population deemed by some of its members to constitute an actual or potential 'nation'." Most importantly, Smith views these as "working definitions" that constantly need refinement. See Anthony D. Smith, *The Nation in History: Historiographical Debates about Ethnicity and Nationalism* (Hanover:

University Press of New England, 2000), 3. "National identity," "national consciousness," and "nationhood," while similar, also have proven difficult to define. Ronald Grigor Suny and Geoff Eley, for example, claim that a "fully developed national consciousness" is "one in which national identifications are strong enough to override regional, religious, and even class loyalties for most of the population most of the time, at least in certain kinds of situations [and] tends to require systematic propaganda or political education, normally but not invariably by a centralizing state and its agencies." See Ronald Grigor Suny and Geoff Eley, eds., *Becoming National: A Reader* (Oxford: Oxford University Press, 1996), 9. However, as Alon Confino has written, "nationhood" does not have to be so comprehensive and override so much—"the multifariousness of nationhood is indeed striking: . . . while it is a new historical phenomenon, it is believed to be ancient; while it is part of modernity, it looks obsessively to the past; while it yearns for the past, it simultaneously rejects the past by seeking to construct an improved version of it; while it represents the uniform nation, it tolerates a host of identities within the nation." Confino, *The Nation as a Local Metaphor*, 3. In other words, while defining terms should be an important preoccupation of historians who write about the construction of nationhood, one should keep in mind that terms such as "nation," "nationalism," "national identity," and "nationhood" are themselves contested ones, words that are multifaceted in nature and constantly undergoing redefinition, both at present and over the course of the last two centuries. National identity, as expressed within culture such as the popular print in Russia and elsewhere, does not have to override or be dominant to exist, nor does propaganda have to be total to create it—both are processes, sites of contestation that this study hopes to stress.

31. For a groundbreaking work on Russian patriotic culture and its uses in wartime, see Jahn, *Russian Patriotic Culture in the First World War*.

32. The importance of myths as a crucial means of determining self-image is explored in Geoffrey Hosking and George Schöpflin, eds., *Myths and Nationhood* (New York: Routledge, 1997). Here it is also important to note that the artists and publishers who produced the wartime images already had a sense of national identity, and included personal references to this identity (such as the Polish invasion of 1612, the figure of the peasant, etc.) in their images. For the major works and debates on the formation of national identity, see Benedict Anderson, *Imagined Communities: Reflections on the Origins and Spread of Nationalism*, 2nd ed. (London: Verso, 1991); Eric Hobsbawm, *Nations and Nationalism Since 1780: Programme, Myth, Reality*, 2nd ed. (Cambridge: Cambridge University Press, 1992); Eric Hobsbawm and Terence Ranger, eds., *The Invention of Tradition* (Cambridge: Cambridge University Press, 1983); Ernest Gellner, *Nations and Nationalism* (Ithaca: Cornell University Press, 1983); Adrian Hastings, *The Construction of Nationhood: Ethnicity, Religion, and Nationalism* (Cambridge: Cambridge University Press, 1997); Peter van der Verr and Hartmut Lehmann, eds. *Nation and Religion: Perspectives on Europe and Asia* (Princeton: Princeton University Press, 1999); and Anthony D. Smith, *Myths and Memories of the Nation* (Oxford: Oxford University Press, 1999).

33. Here I follow the work of Paul Bushkovitch, who has argued for understanding both Russian national consciousness and nationalism in general on its own terms. He asserts that Russians of the sixteenth and seventeenth century had a defined sense of national consciousness, "even if it did not take the form as the national consciousness of Pushkin, Alexander III, or Lenin." Bushkovitch observes that most scholars equate national consciousness with political nationalism that appeared after 1789 and concludes that Russian national consciousness evolved along a long and tortuous path from the sixteenth century. See Paul Bushkovitch, "The Formation of a National Consciousness in Early Modern Russia," *Harvard Ukrainian Studies* 10/3–4 (1986): 355–76. Another exception to the general view of Russian national identity, and one that addresses the nineteenth century, is Elena Hellberg-Hirn, *Soil and Soul: The Symbolic*

World of Russianness (Aldershot: Ashgate, 1998). For two insightful works that deal with the contradictions of imperial identities in nineteenth-century Russia, see Theodore Weeks, *Nation and State in Late Imperial Russia: Nationalism and Russification on the Western Frontier, 1863–1914* (DeKalb: Northern Illinois University Press, 1996); and Robert Geraci, *Window on the East: National and Imperial Identities in Late Tsarist Russia* (Ithaca: Cornell University Press, 2001). For more recent works that view Russian national identity in this era on its own terms, see Sanborn's argument about Russian nationalism as a "space of contestation" that allows for a great deal of competing discourse over the nature of the nation. Joshua Sanborn, "The Mobilization of 1914 and the Question of the Russian Nation: A Reexamination," *Slavic Review* 59/2 (Summer 2000): 267–89 and his *Drafting the Russian Nation.* Similarly, Steve Smith contends that "since Russia was one of the 'old, continuous nations,' the task of constructing national identity was easier than in many countries, since elements from the repertoire of protonational identity could be appropriated and put to new uses; at the same time, that repertoire set parameters within which the construction of national identity took place." Steve Smith, "Citizenship and the Russian Nation During World War I," *Slavic Review* 59/2 (Summer 2000): 316–29. Christopher Ely's recent work explores the concept of landscape and Russian nationalism: *This Meager Nature: Landscape and National Identity in Imperial Russia* (DeKalb: Northern Illinois University Press, 2002). A recent collection of essays edited by Simon Franklin and Emma Widdis concludes that the theme of national identity in Russian cultural discourse reveals the "varied, contrasting, perhaps contradictory ways in which Russia and Russianness have been imagined and represented," while acknowledging at least that most Russians had a sense of "national consciousness" by the nineteenth century. See Franklin and Widdis, *National Identity in Russian Culture.*

34. Peter Burke, *Eyewitnessing: The Uses of Images as Historical Evidence* (Ithaca: Cornell University Press, 2001). Confino notes that understanding the reception of cultural works is the most difficult task facing a cultural historian. This book pays a great deal of attention to the reception of the wartime image and the ways in which Russians wrote about, discussed, produced, and reacted to it. For more on the problems of doing cultural history and its reception, see Alon Confino, "Collective Memory and Cultural History: Problems of Method," *American Historical Review* 105/2 (December 1997): 1386–1403. Many historians have used images to advance an iconological argument along the lines suggested by Erwin Panofsky in his seminal work, *Studies in Iconology: Humanistic Themes in the Art of the Renaissance* (New York: Harper and Row, 1939). Panofsky's explanation of reading images has its uses, but in my work, I am not as interested in the changes in motifs, gestures, poses, emblems, and special organization, as Panofsky was. Many scholars of the *lubok* have already done studies in an iconological style, and written about the internal history of the Russian prints. Similarly, I am not adopting a semiotic approach to the *lubok,* although certain aspects of semiotics creep into my account. While the use of color and the relationship between the text and image (both hallmarks of a semiotic approach) do appear briefly in my study, I am more interested in the *lubok* as a document of social views, politics, and power. I thank Matthew Affron for the illuminating discussions on my use of the *lubok.*

35. This argument owes inspiration to the work of B. M. Sokolov, who stresses that pictorial imagery, plot, technique, and the culture of both the buyer and seller are all important in understanding the "artistic language" of the *lubok.* The essence of the popular print, argues Sokolov, is a "creative corruption" *[tvorcheskaia porcha]* in which an amalgam of styles and themes make up the content of the *lubok.* According to Sokolov, *lubki* borrow themes from other cultural genres, and this borrowing helps to alter the meaning of the image. In addition, the reception of the popular print can vary, for individuals may concentrate on the contemporary message in the print, its iconic tradition (if one exists), or another aspect of the image altogether. The *lubok,*

Sokolov argues, is "a poly-traditional product that causes the spectator to provide an active interpretation," a process Sokolov refers to as "the *lubok* game" *[igra s lubkom].* At the same time, what matters most to Sokolov, is that Russians viewed the *lubok* as a part of "their art" and lives. See Sokolov, *Khudozhestvennyi iazyk russkogo lubka* (Moscow: Rossiiskii gos. gumanitarnyi universitet, 1999). For a rich account of the ways in which urban popular culture worked in Russia that focuses on the theater (but also demonstrates the extent to which government, artists, and consumers created this culture), see E. Anthony Swift, *Popular Theater and Society in Tsarist Russia* (Berkeley: University of California Press, 2002).

36. Richard Wortman, in his magisterial work on the "scenarios of power" that each Russian monarch from Peter I to Nicholas II created, also focuses on the propagation of images, myths, and ideas of the Russian nation. Wortman's history explores the rituals and ceremonies surrounding the Russian monarchs in an effort to "understanding the persistence of absolute monarchy in Russia and the abiding loyalty of the nobility" by examining the "ways that these feelings were evoked and sustained." Wortman's work examines nation building from a "top-down" approach—how the monarch and his/her supporters attempted to build loyalty to the figure of the monarch as an embodiment of the nation. My work, while inspired by Wortman's, examines a similar yet competing process from a different perspective—how *lubok* artists and publishers attempted to build loyalty to a Russian nation through their own images and symbols. Wortman's study was published in two volumes: Richard Wortman, *Scenarios of Power: Myth and Ceremony in Russian Monarchy,* 2 vols. (Princeton: Princeton University Press, 1995–2000).

37. Rossiisskii Etnograficheskii Muzei (Russian Ethnographic Museum) REM, *f.* 7 (Etnograficheskoe biuro kn. V. Tenisheva), *op.* 1, *d.* 471, *l.* 2.

38. REM, *f.* 7, *op.* 1, *d.* 1850, *l.* 11; *f.* 7, *op.* 1, *d.* 1433, *l.* 2; and B. M. Firsov and I. G. Kiseleva, eds., *Byt velikorusskikh krest'ian-zemlepashtsev. Opisanie materialov Etnograficheskogo biuro kniazia V. N. Tenisheva (na primere Vladimirskoi gubernii),* (St. Petersburg: Izd-vo Evropeiskogo Doma, 1993), 176. These accounts come from the survey of Russian peasant life sponsored by Prince V. Tenishev in 1897 and 1898. Question number 294 of the "Tenishev program" called on ethnographers to ask about the number and themes of *lubki* in the peasant home. See V. N. Tenishev, ed., *Programma etnograficheskikh svedenii o krest'ianakh tsentral'noi Rossii* (Smolensk: Gub. Tip., 1897), 133.

2—Images of 1812

1. The patriotic outburst in Russia, particularly in the response of the population to Napoleon's invasion, is described in Nadezhda Durova, *The Cavalry Maiden: Journals of a Russian Officer in the Napoleonic Wars,* trans. Mary Fleming Zirin (Bloomington: Indiana University Press, 1988). See also Antony Brett-James, ed., *1812: Eyewitness Accounts of Napoleon's Defeat in Russia* (New York: St. Martin's Press, 1966); A. G. Tartakovskii, ed., *1812 god . . . voennye dnevniki* (Moscow: Sov. Rossiia, 1990); and M. A. Boitsov, ed., *K chesti Rossii iz chastnoi perepiski 1812 goda* (Moscow: "Sovremennik," 1988).

2. From the account in David Saunders, *Russia in the Age of Reaction and Reform, 1801–1881* (London: Longman, 1992), 52.

3. See Amir Weiner, "The Making of a Dominant Myth: The Second World War and the Construction of Political Identities Within the Soviet Polity," *Russian Review* 55 (October 1996): 638–60, and his *Making Sense of War: The Second World War and the Fate of the Bolshevik Revolution* (Princeton: Princeton University Press, 2000). In reference to 1812, the term "Patriotic War" or "Fatherland War" began to be used in Russia shortly after 1812.

4. The exhibit was entitled *1812 g. v karikature. Grafika, khudozhestvennye tkani, voennaia igrushka iz fondov muzeia-zapovednika Borodinskoe pole* and contained many of the *lubki* I discuss below.

5. For a recent, vivid account of these events, see Adam Zamoyski, *Moscow 1812: Napoleon's Fatal March* (New York: HarperCollins, 2004).

6. See Albert Schmidt, "The Restoration of Moscow After 1812," *Slavic Review* 40/1 (1981): 37–48. The fire of Moscow in 1812 destroyed so much of the city, writes Schmidt, that it gave architects and urban planners virtually carte blanche to remake the city in the "neoclassical" style. For more on the social impact of Napoleon's invasion, see Janet Hartley, "Russia in 1812," part 1, "The French Presence in the *Gubernii* of Smolensk and Mogliev," and part 2, "The Russian Administration of Kaluga *Gubernija*," *Jahrbücher für Geschichte Osteuropas* 38 (1990): 178–98; 399–416.

7. Historians have studied the changes in Russian patriotism after 1812 in a variety of ways, but rarely have they focused on popular culture during the war itself and how the myths of the war were disseminated. For more on the cultural reorientation in Russia after 1812, see Peter Christoff, *The Third Heart: Some Intellectual-Ideological Currents and Cross Currents in Russia, 1800–1830* (The Hague: Mouton, 1970), which explores how Russian intellectuals developed their own sense of national identity during the Napoleonic era. A more recent account that explores how the Napoleonic era influenced Russian conservative thought is Alexander Martin, *Romantics, Reformers, Reactionaries: Russian Conservative Thought and Politics in the Reign of Alexander I* (DeKalb: Northern Illinois University Press, 1997). Martin's article on Sergei Glinka also explores how one author (in this case, the editor of *Russian Messenger*, which had 600–700 subscribers in 1812) propagated Francophobic ideas between 1807 and 1813. See Martin, "The Family Model of Society and Russian National Identity in Sergei N. Glinka's *Russian Messenger* (1808–1812)," *Slavic Review* 57/1 (Spring 1998): 28–49. Andrei Zorin's examination of literature and its influence on political ideologies is an exception. Zorin in particular focuses on a variety of patriotic plays, poems, and others texts produced during the Napoleonic Wars, and demonstrates how writers such as Aleksandr Shishkov used the memories of the Polish invasion of 1612 to promote opposition to Napoleon and France before 1812. See Andrei Zorin, *Kormiia dvuglavogo orla . . . Literatura i gosudarstvenaia ideologiia v Rossii v poslednei treti XVIII-pervoi treti XIX veka* (Moscow: NLO, 2002), chaps. 5–7.

8. See *Russian Studies in History* 32/1 (Summer 1993), a special issue devoted to the Russian historiography of the Patriotic War. My use of the term "myth" does not mean to imply that the victory over Napoleon was not in some ways a people's victory. I use myth here in the way that George Schöpflin has outlined in his article, "The Functions of Myth and a Taxonomy of Myths," in *Myths and Nationhood*, ed. Hosking and Schöpflin, 19–35. A myth, as Schöpflin notes, is not identical with falsehood or deception. Historical myths serve several important functions, including a "set of beliefs, usually put forth as a narrative, held by community about itself." While many Russians did fight against Napoleon, the narrative of the "people's victory" with Alexander I as the ultimate leader of this victory became the established story of the Patriotic War promoted in textbooks, monuments, and other sites of memory in the nineteenth century. Molly Wesling also explores the ways in which the victory over Napoleon became the source of a cultural mythology in her book, *Napoleon in Russian Cultural Mythology* (New York: Peter Lang, 2001).

9. John Bowlt, the doyen of Russian art historians, has written that the war of 1812 introduced important changes both in Russian art and Russian caricature. Bowlt views the work of Terebenev, Ivanov, and Venetsianov as caricatures that made use of the *lubok* tradition, thus enhancing their appeal. After 1812, Russian caricature experienced uneven growth. While I agree with Bowlt's assessment of how Terebenev and his contemporaries blended classical training with the *lubok* to produce a powerful set of images from 1812 to 1814, I view these caricatures as *lubki*, ones that transformed this genre in the nineteenth century and paved the way for future explosions of popular prints during wartime. The Russian government viewed the 1812 prints as *lubki* and defined them as such in the 1851 law regulating imagery, as did Dmitrii Rovinskii, who included the 1812 images in his collection of "people's pictures." For the

views of Bowlt and how 1812 transformed the Russian art scene, see Bowlt's two articles, "Russian Painting in the Nineteenth Century" and "Nineteenth-Century Russian Caricature," both in *Art and Culture in Nineteenth-Century Russia*, ed. Theofanis Stavrou (Bloomington: Indiana University Press, 1983).

10. This myth was also popularized through the peep show *(raek)*. Using *lubok*-style prints and stories, peep-show owners *(raeshniki)* broadcast the triumphs of the Russians during 1812 throughout the countryside in the years following the war against Napoleon. Many of these *raeshniki* were former soldiers who had fought against Napoleon and were interested in promoting the idea of a people's victory. See A. F. Nekrylova, *Russkie narodnye gorodskie prazdniki, uveseleniia, i zrelishcha* (Leningrad: Iskusstvo, 1988), 95–125; S. A. Smith, "Citizenship and the Russian Nation During World War I: A Comment," *Slavic Review* 59/2 (Summer 2000): 321.

11. Alexander I's appearance in the *lubki* in 1813–1814 reflected the changing fortunes of the war with Napoleon. Once victory became clear, the tsar began to appear as the architect of this victory.

12. See Colley, *Britons*. Colley notes that the British nation "was an invention forged above all by war," and that Britons defined themselves against the French "other" in a succession of wars against France. Thus, Britons "came to define themselves as a single people not because of any political or cultural consensus at home, but rather in reaction to the Other beyond their shores," 5–6. As Colley's work makes clear, the French under Napoleon served as a source of redefining national identities throughout Europe, including Russia.

13. See A. Kaganovich, *Ivan Ivanovich Terebenev, 1780–1815* (Moscow: Iskusstvo, 1956). See also John Bowlt, "Nineteenth-Century Russian Caricature," 221–236, and "Art and Violence: The Russian Caricature in the Early Nineteenth and Early Twentieth Centuries," *Twentieth Century Studies* 13/14 (December 1975): 56–76. Bowlt notes that the caricatures of Terebenev, Venetsianov, and Ivanov drew heavily on the *lubok* tradition, making them "directly comprehensible to the Russian populace," 227. In addition, the artists of the Patriotic War drew on their academic training, particularly English and even French caricature, to ridicule Napoleon and his troops. Thus, while the work of these artists certainly captured the spirit of the times and helped to articulate ideas about Russian national identity, the artists did not consciously attempt to create an "invented tradition," but produced their images out of a sense of personal patriotism.

14. Kaganovich, *Ivan Ivanovich Terebenev*, 99.

15. Kaganovich, *Ivan Ivanovich Terebenev*, 97, 111.

16. V. A. Vereshchagin, *Russkaia karikatura*. Kn. 2, *Otechestvennaia voina* (St. Petersburg: Tip. Sirius, 1912), 32.

17. Kaganovich, *Ivan Ivanovich Terebenev*, 92–127.

18. Vereshchagin, *Russkaia karikatura*, 58–59. Venetsianov drew a caricature in one edition that depicted a fat Russian bureaucrat lying in bed with his mistress while a line of petitioners waited outside. Although his journal was banned, Venetsianov continued to ridicule the Russian upper class in caricatures before the war, particularly their French manners. See John Bowlt, "Nineteenth-Century Russian Caricature," 229; Rosalind Polly Gray, "The Real and the Ideal in the Work of Aleksei Venetsianov," *Russian Review* 58 (October 1999), 660.

19. Vereshchagin, *Russkaia karikatura*, 62.

20. Vereschagin, *Russkaia karikatura*, 65.

21. Hilton, *Russian Folk Art*, 207–8.

22. Vereshchagin, *Russkaia karikatura*, 77–78.

23. Napoleon had been anathematized by the Russian Orthodox Church as the antichrist as early as 1806, and this view was revived in 1812.

24. Terebenev's Soviet biographer described his images as "a bright page in the history of Russian art" and "serious, effective weapons in the struggle against the

enemy." See Kaganovich, 92–93. Moreover, the fact that Terebenev's caricatures drew on factual events that occurred during the war with Napoleon prompts Kaganovich to state that they "kept a close connection" with the Russian people and thus proved "very popular and effective." Kaganovich's assertion reveals many of the problems inherent in writing about visual sources. He fails to problematize the issue of reception of the *lubki* and just states that they were "popular" without discussing the ways in which Russians viewed the popular images.

25. Gosudarstvennaia Publichnaia Istoricheskaia Biblioteka, Otdel Redkikh Knig (hereafter cited as GPIB ORK), *Papka* 1, "karikatury 1812 goda." This image was one of the first to appear in St. Petersburg.

26. This *lubok* resembles two other Terebenev images. The first, entitled "The Destruction of the Worldwide Monarchy," depicts a Russian peasant and Cossack attacking Napoleon, who flies out of a barrel. See GPIB ORK, *Papka* 1. The second, "The Return Journey, or the Action of the Russian Purgative Powder," depicts a Russian peasant and Cossack on either side of Napoleon. The two humiliate the French emperor, while informing him that he "will soon be off on his old way home," where he will "be able to accurately report the Russian war indemnity." GPIB ORK, *Papka* 1.

27. GPIB ORK, *Papka* 1.

28. Rovinskii, *Russkie narodnye kartinki,* vol. 2, 217.

29. GPIB ORK, *Papka* 2, "Karikatury i allegericheskoe kartinki . . . 1812 godu."

30. GPIB ORK, *Papka* 1. The text also appears in Rovinskii, *Russkie narodnye kartinki,* vol. 2, 158. This particular image appeared in English journals of the time too, as English caricature artists copied Terebenev's original, renaming it "Russians Teaching Boney to Dance," and even included a translation of the original Terebenev text. The English image is reprinted in Kaganovich, *Ivan Ivanovich Terebenev,* 107. See also the image called "The French Traveler in 1812," in which Napoleon, his small stature emphasized, sits crouched on a tiny sled, trying to warm himself from the Russian winter (itself a theme of Russianness). The sled, pulled by a solitary pig, transports Napoleon out of Russia.

31. See the Terebenev image, "Napoleon with S . . . after the Burning of Moscow," which depicts the French emperor's meeting with the devil after the events of 1812. GPIB ORK, *Papka* 1. The text is also in Rovinskii, *Russkie narodnye kartinki,* vol. 2, 153–54.

32. The *lubok* "Napoleon's Triumphal Arrival in Paris," illustrated by Venetsianov, shows the French emperor riding atop a lobster while holding a staff on which hang his "conquests," which consist of one Cossack, a solitary Russian soldier, a puppet, two dead cats, a peasant's cart, two dead birds, a woman's bonnet, and other clothing. GPIB ORK, *Papka* 2. The inclusion of the lobster could be an attempt to parody the Russian fairy tale "The Fox and the Lobster." A similar Terebenev *lubok*, "The Festive Entrance into Paris of the Invincible French Army," further illustrates the costs of Napoleon's campaigns within his own country while poking fun at his self-promotion techniques, this time before a rowdy French crowd. GPIB ORK, *Papka* 2. Rovinskii, *Russkie narodnye kartinki,* vol. 2, 212.

33. GPIB ORK, *Papka* 2. See also the similar *lubok* "Napoleon's Withdrawal from Moscow into Winter Quarters" (GPIB ORK, *Papka* 2). While the image discussed was produced by an unnamed artist, Venetsianov, Terebenev, and Ivanov all produced similar images in the years 1813–1814.

34. GPIB ORK, *Papka* 2. Rovinskii, *Russkie narodnye kartinki,* vol. 2, 189.

35. Burke, *Eyewitnessing,* 43; R. Etlin, ed., *Nationalism in the Visual Arts* (Hanover: University Press of New England, 1991); Albert Boime, *The Unveiling of the National Icons* (Cambridge: Cambridge University Press, 1994); David Matless, *Landscape and Englishness* (London: Reaktion Books, 1998). A similar *lubok* from an unknown artist depicts the French emperor and his troops being driven across the Russian snow by a peasant holding a broom in one hand and a string of carcasses in the other. Entitled "The Russian Peasant [muzhik] Vavil Moroz on the Hare Hunt," the image illustrates the French and Napoleon as rabbits (a symbol for cowards in Russian

lore) and the Russian peasant as an expert "hare hunter." GPIB ORK, *Papka* 2; Rovinskii, *Russkie narodnye kartinki,* vol. 2, 205. See also the *lubok* called "The Chivalrous Journey of Napoleon from Warsaw" and the versions of "The Flight of Napoleon the Great" for similar themes (GPIB ORK, *Papka* 1).

36. Of the 148 *lubki* Rovinskii lists from the Patriotic War, 69 feature Napoleon. See also Terebenev's "A Quarantine for Napoleon after his Return from Russia" and "A Russian Bathhouse." A final example of Terebenev's images of Napoleon, "The Consultation," has French doctors examining Napoleon, whose tongue has changed color because of the lies he has told, whose heart is racing because of the death he has brought to Europe, and who suffers from a fever as a result of his crazy ambitions. All three images are in GPIB ORK, *Papka* 1.

37. GPIB ORK, *Papka* 2.

38. GPIB ORK, *Papka* 2; Rovinskii, *Russkie narodnye kartinki,* vol. 2, 214. Many Poles fought with Napoleon against the Russians in 1812.

39. GPIB ORK, *Papka* 1.

40. GPIB ORK, *Papka* 1; Rovinskii, *Russkie narodnye kartinki,* vol. 2, 158–59.

41. As Molly Wesling has pointed out, this image is historically accurate, although exaggerated. French troops did wear women's clothing during their retreat from Russia for lack of anything else to wear (actions that occurred again in 1941). See Wesling, *Napoleon in Russian Cultural Mythology,* 13. For eyewitness descriptions of French soldiers wearing women's clothes, see *Rossiia pervoi poloviny XIX v. glazami inostrantsev* (Leningrad, 1991), 223, 255, 276, 289.

42. GPIB ORK, *Papka* 1.

43. This print lambasts the Poles who decided to fight with Napoleon rather than with Russia. During 1812, a great number of Poles, particularly from the Duchy of Warsaw, joined Napoleon's Grand Army in hopes that a defeat of Russia would create a new Polish kingdom independent of Russian control. Many Russian memoirs of the war expressed greater hostility toward the Poles who served with Napoleon than toward the French, and used the presence of Polish troops in the Grand Army to question the loyalty of all Poles. The images of Poles among a foreign army invading Russia also conjured up memories of the 1612 Polish invasion during the Time of Troubles. For more on the Polish troops and reaction to them, see Hartley, "Russia in 1812," part 1, 179–80; K. K. Arnol'di, "Frantsuzy v Mogileve-na-Dnepre," *Russkaia starina* 4/8 (1873): 233–37; and Roman Soltyk, *Napoleon en 1812. Mémoires historiques et militaires sur la campagne de Russie* (Paris: n.p., 1836).

44. A. E. Zarin, *Zhenshchiny-geroini v 1812 godu. Ocherki i razskazy iz epochi velikoi otechestvennoi voiny* (Moscow: Izd-vo skl. M. V. Kliukina, 1913), 20–27; Hartley, "Russia in 1812," part 1, 195. Zarin, writing one hundred years later as part of the centenary memories of the war, says, "had Napoleon known of such women he would not have invaded Russia." This caricature of the French found expression in two other *lubki* from 1813. The first, "The French are Frightened by a Goat," from Terebenev, depicts four French soldiers fleeing from a peasant *izba* guarded by a solitary, old peasant woman. The woman frightens the French soldiers away by using a play on the words "goat" and "Cossack" (the Russian words for Cossack, *kazak/kozak*, and goat, *koza*, sound similar). GPIB ORK, *Papka* 2, *Russkie narodnye kartinki,* vol. 2, 195. The second *lubok* that echoes these themes is "Grandmother Kuz'minishna Treats the French Marauders with *Shchi*." This image from an unidentified artist portrays four starving French soldiers eating *shchi*, a Russian cabbage soup, even though it had been poisoned and they find it distasteful. Again the desperation of the French troops, a state in which their Russian experiences has left them, has led them to be fooled by a simple Russian peasant woman. GPIB ORK, *Papka* 1; Rovinskii, *Russkie narodnye kartinki,* vol. 2, 203–4.

45. GPIB ORK, *Papka* 1. This Terebenev image from 1812 was also the subject of a similar print from Ivanov in 1815.

46. GPIB ORK, *Papka* 1; Rovinskii, *Russkie narodnye kartinki*, vol. 2, 160–61.

47. See Ivan Krylov, *Krylov's Fables*, trans. Bernard Pares (New York: Harcourt, Brace, 1927), 29–30.

48. GPIB ORK, *Papka* 1.

49. GPIB ORK, *Papka* 1; Rovinskii, *Russkie narodnye kartinki*, vol. 2, 177. See also Venetsianov's image "*Izgnanie iz Moskvy frantsuzskikh aktris*" (The Expulsion from Moscow of a French Actress) for similar themes, in Rovinskii, *Russkie narodnye kartinki*, vol. 2, 178.

50. See Terebenev's "Carnival, or the Parisian Musician at Shrovetide," "Napoleon Sells by Auction His Stolen Antiques," and the *lubok* from an unnamed artist, "Napoleon's Impertinence," in GPIB ORK, *Papka* 1 and 2; and the Venetsianov images "Activities of the French Women in the Store" and "The French Store for Pomade and Perfumes" in Vereshchagin, *Russkaia karikatura*, vol. 2. Ivan Krylov, the famous fabulist, wrote the comedy *Fashion Shop* in 1806. The play satirized French shopkeepers who cheated Russian customers.

51. Hartley, "Russia in 1812," part 2, 406. See also Domergue's memoirs, *La Russe pendant les guerres de l'Empire (1805–1815). Souvenirs historiques*, vol. 1 (Paris, 1835).

52. Similar trends can be detected in other arts in Russia after Napoleon's invasion. Musical compositions performed in Moscow in 1813 included Steibelt's *Burning of Moscow*, among others, while patriotic plays, folk songs, intermezzos, and satirical sketches dominated Moscow theaters the same year. See Richard Stites, *Serfdom, Society, and the Arts in Imperial Russia: The Pleasure and the Power* (New Haven: Yale University Press, 2005). I thank Richard Stites for sharing with me portions of this work while it was still in manuscript form. In addition to Steibelt's music, the serf composer Stepan Degtiaryov (1766–1813) also composed patriotic odes in the wake of Napoleon's invasion, including *Mnin and Pozharsky, The Liberation of Moscow*, and *Napoleon's Flight*, the last one unfinished.

53. The identification of the Cossack with "Russianness" demonstrates the extent to which Napoleon's invasion altered patriotism and national identity in Russia. Before the invasion, Russian elites tended to identify themselves as western, in many cases emulating French tastes. Cossacks, who lived on the borders of the Russian Empire, had often rebelled against the Russian government, and had participated in the Pugachev rebellion of 1773 in great numbers (Emilian Pugachev himself was a Cossack). Although Cossacks had been integrated into the Russian army in 1775 and served in 1812, as Judith Deutsch Kornblatt argues, they had not yet become "Russian" in the popular imagination. As a result of the war of 1812 and subsequent rethinking of Russian patriotic identity, however, Cossacks began to be depicted as quintessentially "Russian" and as embodiments of Orthodoxy and the "Russian soul." Russian writers began to capture the "Russianness" of the Cossack during the 1820s and 1830s, but the images from 1812 captured these attributes even earlier. For more on the "Cossack myth" in Russian literature, see Kornblatt, *The Cossack Hero in Russian Literature: A Study in Cultural Mythology* (Madison: University of Wisconsin Press, 1992).

54. GPIB ORK, *Papka* 1. Rovinskii entitles the *lubok* "Cossacks Overtake the French Cavalrymen." Rovinskii, *Russkie narodnye kartinki*, vol. 2, 198–199.

55. GPIB ORK, *Papka* 1. It resembles the *lubok* "Russian Hercules from the City of Sychevka" described in Rovinskii, *Russkie narodnye kartinki*, vol. 2, 160.

56. The image is strikingly similar to popular prints from later wars, particularly the Russo-Japanese War of 1904–1905, when several *lubki* featured giant Russians tossing aside small Japanese troops. See particularly "Cossack Petrukha," in GPIB ORK, OIK 1578-a.

57. GPIB ORK, *Papka* 1.

58. See also the Terebenev print "Peasant Taking a Cannon from the French," which features a solitary Russian partisan stealing from the French while they were away. GPIB ORK, *Papka* 1. For more Terebenev images featuring Cossacks and peas-

ants, see, for example, the print "With What Did He Conquer Our Enemy? The *nagaika!*" a print that depicts a solitary Cossack thrashing a French cavalry officer with his whip *(nagaika)*; "The Firmness of the Russian Peasant," which features a single Russian peasant refusing to answer the questions of two French marauders; "The Residents of Vladimir," which presents two peasants, armed with an axe and pitchfork and led by "Peasant Sel'tsa," driving away three French soldiers by crying, "Cossacks!" and "The Cossack Hands Napoleon a Visitor's Pass for a Reciprocal Visit," which depicts a Cossack holding open a door for Napoleon and one of his marshals, giving them a pass to "Moscow" in return for permission to go to Paris. All of these images are in GPIB ORK, *Papka* 1.

59. Orlando Figes, *Natasha's Dance: A Cultural History of Russia* (New York: Metropolitan Books, 2002), 117; A. G. Venetsianov, *Aleksei Gavrilovich Venetsianov. Stat'i, pis'ma, sovremenniki o khudozhnike* (Leningrad: Iskusstvo, 1980), 13.

60. GPIB ORK, *Papka* 1.

61. GPIB ORK, *Papka* 1; Rovinskii, *Russkie narodnye kartinki,* vol. 2, 206. The use of the term "infidel" to describe Catholic French soldiers seems strange. However, as Vladimir Dal' makes clear in his dictionary, the term *"basurman"* although derived from the word for Muslim *(musul'man),* could also mean any foreigner, non-Orthodox person, or person of a different faith. See V. I. Dal', *Tolkovyi slovar' zhivogo velikorusskago iazyka,* t. 1 (St. Petersburg: Izd. T-va M. O. Vol'f, 1903), 134.

62. GPIB ORK, *Papka* 1. Janet Hartley notes that even Napoleon began to believe that he had unleashed a religious war in Russia in 1812. See Hartley, "Russia in 1812," part 1, 186.

63. GPIB ORK, *Papka* 1.

64. GPIB ORK, *Papka* 1; Rovinskii, *Russkie narodnye kartinki,* vol. 2, 180.

65. Kaganovich, *Ivan Ivanovich Terebenev,* 100–101. Kaganovich later claims that Terebenev and his contemporaries "never created caricatures on abstract themes—all of them were closely connected with the concrete facts of international life and the course of military actions," a fact that accounts for the popularity of their images, 117.

66. Terebenev's training, for example, reflected the tensions of Peter the Great's philosophies about culture, Russia, and his capital, tensions seen quite clearly in the academy's teaching. On the one hand, pupils at the imperial art school learned about the techniques, ideas, and styles of western Europe, keeping with Peter's original intentions about westernizing Russia. On the other hand, the Imperial Academy's curriculum consisted almost entirely of copying techniques and attitudes toward art in western Europe (and, under Catherine II's insistence, even sending promising artists to France or Italy). Russian artists and sculptors learned only to imitate the portraits, landscapes, and sculptures of the West, with little attention given over to any native traditions. Built into the curriculum, however, was a stress on Italian classical themes, particularly historical paintings of Roman antiquity. These themes formed part of the training at academies throughout Europe, including the French Academy in Paris. By learning about the heroes of classical Rome such as Junius Brutus and Mucius Scaevola, Terebenev and his fellow students at the academy were exposed to concepts of civic virtue and patriotism. At the time Terebenev studied, the Imperial Art Academy in many ways perfectly embodied the problems of post-Petrine culture in Russia, a culture that wavered between imitation and tradition. For more on the academy, see W. Bruce Lincoln, *Between Heaven and Hell: The Story of a Thousand Years of Artistic Life in Russia* (New York: Viking, 1998); and Elizabeth Valkenier, *Russian Realist Art: The State and Society: The Peredvizhniki and Their Tradition* (Ann Arbor: Ardis, 1977), chap. 1. Christopher Ely discusses how the academy stressed European and not Russian landscapes up to the 1820s in *This Meager Nature.*

67. Mucius Scaevola, surnamed Cordus, became famous when Porsenna, the king of the Etruscans, besieged Rome during the Etruscan wars. Mucius, a patriotic Roman, disguised himself and gained entry into Porsenna's tent. Mistaking

Porsenna's secretary as the Etruscan king, Mucius killed him. When Porsenna asked Mucius why he committed murder, Mucius replied that he was a Roman and had sworn to destroy Porsenna and his men or perish doing so. Out of anger at having failed to accomplish his sworn task, Mucius then plunged his right hand into burning coals without uttering a sound. Porsenna, as legend recounts, was so astonished by the act that he withdrew from Rome. Mucius, who obtained the surname Scaevola because he could no longer use his right hand, had a statue erected in his honor in Rome. The story of Mucius Scaevola appears most famously in Livy's *History of Rome* (book 2, chaps. 12 and 13), where it is cited as an example of Roman patriotism.

68. GPIB ORK, *Papka* 2.

69. GPIB ORK, *Papka* 2; Rovinskii, *Russkie narodnye kartinki,* vol. 2, 208. This 1813 image from Ivanov was clearly drawn from an 1812 Terebenev image of the same title. See Vereshchagin, *Russkaia karikatura,* 153–54. In addition, at least two other *kartinki* recounting the same legend appeared in the years 1813–1814. The tale of a "Russian Scaevola" in 1812 became widespread enough for Russian sculptors to cast figures of a peasant in the process of chopping his arm off—one of the original figures is still on display at the Borodino Panorama Museum in Moscow.

70. GPIB ORK, *Papka* 2.

71. GPIB ORK, *Papka* 2; Rovinskii, *Russkie narodnye kartinki,* vol. 2, 208–9. The legend of Marcus Curtius appears in Livy's *History of Rome,* book 7 chap. 5. It tells of how an enormous cavern once opened up in the Roman Forum "owing either to an earthquake or the action of some other force." When city officials were unable to fill the chasm, they turned to some local seers, who foretold that the city's most prized possession would have to be cast into it. Marcus Curtius, a young soldier who had distinguished himself in battle, declared that nothing was more valuable in Rome than a courageous citizen, and he rode his horse into the pit, which then closed. The tale is used as an illustration of the glory of dying for one's fatherland.

72. GPIB ORK, *Papka* 1.

73. Some popular pictures depicted this native wit by juxtaposing a clever Russian peasant with a group of easily duped French soldiers, such as the "Peasant Pavel Prokhorov," which depicts a Russian peasant dressed as a Cossack standing before five kneeling French soldiers. GPIB ORK, *Papka* 1.

74. GPIB ORK, *Papka* 2. The image "Terent'evna Finishes Off the French Soldier with Shoes without Pardon" illustrates the fighting spirit of a Russian peasant woman, and connects the heroic deeds of the Russian peasant Prokhorov (see note 73 above) directly with Terent'evna, for the two images were often printed together. This image depicts the Russian peasant woman standing over a fallen French soldier, threatening him with her shoes, while the Frenchman begs "Madam, pardon!" Terent'evna boldly proclaims that she is "giving you some advice," claiming that "here is one villain, and here is another infidel who won't regain consciousness."

75. GPIB ORK, *Papka* 2. Rovinskii, Russkie narodnye kartinki, vol. 2, 202.

76. See chaps. 4, 5, 6, and 7 for examples.

77. This association of Russian national identity with faith and the tsar also appears in a proclamation issued by a peasant partisan to his followers in 1812: "You are people of the Russian faith, you are Orthodox peasants! Take up arms for the faith and die for your tsar!" Quoted in Hosking, *Russia: People and Empire,* 134.

78. See the "Spirit of the Fearless Russians," Terebenev's "Napoleon with S . . . after the Burning of Moscow," "The Ural Cossack Sila Vikharev," and "The Russian's Chickens," for examples of images with Orthodox churches in them.

79. See chaps. 4 and 5.

80. Kaganovich, *Ivan Ivanovich Terebenev,* 119–21.

81. Kaganovich, *Ivan Ivanovich Terebenev,* 119–21. I. P. Dreiling, a Riga-born officer in the Russian army that fought at Borodino, recorded in his memoirs that an eagle flew above Kutuzov and his troops on the eve of the battle. According to Dreiling,

"the prince saw it first, bared his head and exclaimed 'Hurrah!'" Dreiling, "Vospominaniia uchastnika voiny 1812 gody" (OPI GIM, *f.* 160, *d.* 309, *ll.* 79–170), reprinted in *1812 god. Vospominaniia voinov russkoi armii iz sobraniia otdela pis'mennykh istochnikov Gosudarstvennogo Istoricheskogo muzeia,* ed. F. A. Petrov (Moscow: "Mysl'," 1991), 373.

82. Other prints that included Kutuzov include Ivanov's 1813 "Kutuzov Rejects the Loristona Peace Offer" and his 1813 "Prince Kutuzov Inspects the Army before the Borodino Battle," both in Gosudarstvennyi Istoricheskii Muzei, Izobrazitel'nyi otdel (hereafter GIM IO).

83. L. Tolstoy, "Neskol'ko slov po povodu knigi 'Voina i mir,'" in *Polnoe sobranie sochinenii v 90 tomakh,* vol. 16 (Moscow: Sov. pisatel', 1955), 9.

84. GIM IO, *Papka* 1204.

85. GIM IO, *Papka* 1204. See also the *lubki* titled "The Defeat of Napoleon outside Paris by the Russian Emperor Alexander I," "The Liberators of Europe," "His Highness Alexander I," "The Entry of the Allies into Paris," and "The Battle of 20 April 1813 led by His Imperial Highness Alexander I," all in GIM IO, *Papka 1204,* for similar expressions of the role of Russia's tsar in orchestrating the victory over the French.

86. GIM IO, *Papka* 1204.

87. See GIM IO, *Papka* 1204, for more *lubki* entitled "The Triumphal Entry of Alexander I into Paris."

88. Jeffrey Brooks also discusses the fusion of representations of the tsar and the Orthodox church into the primary symbol of "Russianness" throughout the nineteenth century. *When Russia Learned to Read,* 214–45.

89. GIM IO, *Papka* 1204.

90. GIM IO, *Papka* 1204. While these images illustrate the growing importance of religion in Alexander's Russia, they stress the tsar's Orthodox background and not his mysticism. As a result of the 1812 invasion, Alexander began a spiritual relationship with Baroness von Krüdener, a woman who preached a form of mysticism. Alexander's conversations with her, and the spiritual crisis brought upon him by Napoleon's invasion, culminated in his call for a "Holy Alliance" among European states in 1815.

91. Wortman, *Scenarios of Power,* vol. I, 215–238. Wortman eloquently writes about the process by which Alexander entered into an alliance with the masses, helping to create the "myth of national sacrifice and unity woven around the events of 1812."

92. GIM IO, *Papka* 1204, "The Ceremonial Entry in Paris of the Sovereign Emperor Alexander I."

93. Wortman, *Scenarios of Power,* vol. I, 222–23. See also GIM IO, *Papka* 1204.

94. Wortman, *Scenarios of Power,* vol. I, 222–23.

95. These image also helped stress, as Wortman notes, the sense of divine mission of the tsar and his army, which had impressed Europe in 1814 and created the "triumphalist myth" of overconfidence in the army that William Fuller argues dominated military thinking for the next few decades in Russia. See Wortman, *Scenarios of Power,* vol. I, 228–29; and William C. Fuller, Jr., *Strategy and Power in Russia, 1600–1914* (New York: The Free Press, 1992), 177–80.

96. The relative absence of the tsar from images of the Russo-Japanese War and the Great War also reflects trends in popular conceptions of nationalism after 1905, when the tsar was less clearly a symbol of Russian national identity. See Sanborn, "The Mobilization of 1914 and the Question of the Russian Nation"; and Seregny, "Zemstvos, Peasants, and Citizenship," 267–315.

97. Karen Hagemann, "Francophobia and Patriotism: Anti-French Images and Sentiments in Prussia and Northern Germany during the Anti-Napoleonic Wars," *French History* 18/4 (December 2004): 404–25. See also Hagemann's monograph, *"Mannlicher Muth und Teutsche Ehre." Nation, Militär, und Geschlecht zur Zeit der Antinapoleonischen Krige Preussens* (Paderborn: F. Schöningh, 2002).

98. Diana Donald, *The Age of Caricature: Satirical Prints in the Reign of George III* (New Haven: Yale University Press, 1996), 7.

99. Donald, *Age of Caricature,* 20–21.

100. Stuart Semmel, *Napoleon and the British* (New Haven: Yale University Press, 2004), 41.

101. Semmel, *Napoleon and the British,* 48.

102. Semmel, *Napoleon and the British,* 50.

103. Semmel, *Napoleon and the British,* 53–54.

104. Bowlt, "Nineteenth-Century Russian Caricature," 222–27.

105. Napoleon became a popular subject for French artists and image makers soon after his exile. For more on his popularity in panoramas and other visual sources, see Maurice Samuels, *The Spectacular Past: Popular History and the Novel in Nineteenth-Century France* (Ithaca: Cornell University Press, 2004).

106. *Sankt-Peterburskie vedomosti,* 8 January 1813, 79. Quoted in Kaganovich, *Ivan Ivanovich Terebenev,* 95.

107. *Russkaia starina* 73 (March 1892): 594–96. Quoted in Kaganovich, *Ivan Ivanovich Terebenev,* 119.

108. Kaganovich, *Ivan Ivanovich Terebenev,* 119.

109. *Russkaia starina* 73 (March 1892): 594–96. The account is reprinted in Kaganovich, *Ivan Ivanovich Terebenev,* 118–19. The doctor spoke Russian and translated the account himself.

110. *Russkaia starina,* 594.

111. *Russkaia starina,* 595. The editor of the journal identified several of the images de la Fliz described as Terebenev's. Although de la Fliz spoke Russian, he did not mention the texts of the images in his account, evidence that the caricatures could be easily interpreted.

112. *Russkaia starina,* 595. De la Fliz entitled the section of his memoirs "The Visit to Graf Pokorskii. The Collection of Caricatures on the French." His memoirs have recently been reprinted in Russia: de la Fliz, *Pokhod Napoleona v Rossiiu v 1812 godu* (Moscow: Nasledie, 2003). The Pokorskii episode is on 126–30.

113. Astolphe de Custine, *Letters From Russia* (New York: New York Review of Books, 2002), 133.

114. Rossiiskii Gosudarstvennyi Istoricheskii Arkhiv (RGIA), *f. 777, op. 27, d. 183, l. 118, no. 183; d. 184, l. 22, no. 137;* M. Peltzer, "Russkaia politicheskaia kartinka 1812 goda. Usloviia proizvodstva i khudozhestvennye osobennosti," in *Mir narodnoi kartinki,* ed. I. E. Danilova (Moscow: Progress—Traditsiia, 1999), 177.

115. See A. G. Tartakovskii, *Russkaia memuaristika i istoricheskoe soznanie XIX veka* (Moscow: "Arkheograficheskii tsentr," 1997) and *1812 god i russkaia memuaristika. Opyt istochnikovedcheskogo izucheniia* (Moscow: Nauka, 1980); and A. V. Buganov, *Russkaia istoriia v pamiati krest'ian XIX veka i natsional'noe samosoznanie* (Moscow: Institut etnologii i antropologii, 1992).

116. See A. G. Tartakovskii, ed., *1812 god v vospominaniiakh sovremennikov* (Moscow: Nauka, 1995), 33–49.

117. Aleksandr Nikitenko, later a well-known censor, was a serf living in the village of Pisarievka during the invasion. He noted that many Muscovites ended up in his village after they had been forced to flee Moscow in 1812. These refugees helped to carry the nationalist message engulfing Russia at the time to the villages. Nikitenko, although only a young boy at the time, could still recite years later a patriotic poem composed by a professor from Moscow, a poem that celebrated Napoleon's defeat and the humiliation of the French at the hands of the Russians. Throughout his reminiscences, Nikitenko refers to "Russia" and "the Russians." Aleksandr Nikitenko, *Up From Serfdom: My Childhood and Youth in Russia, 1804–1824,* trans. Helen Saltz Jacobson (New Haven: Yale University Press, 2001), 70–71.

118. Buganov, *Russkaia istoriia v pamiati krest'ian,* 148–172.

119. Jahn, *Patriotic Culture in Russia During World War I,* 29.

120. A. F. Nekrylova, *Russkie narodnye gorodskie prazdniki, uveseleniia i zrelishcha* (Leningrad: Iskusstvo, 1988), 95–125; A. M. Konechnyi, "Raek v sisteme peterburgskoi

narodnoi kul'tury," *Russkii folklor* 25 (1989): 123–38. See also Catriona Kelly, "Territories of the Eye: The Russian Peep Show (Raek) and Pre-Revolutionary Visual Culture," *Journal of Popular Culture* 31/4 (Spring 1998): 49–74.

121. The building of the Cathedral of Christ the Savior in Moscow, a church originally commissioned by Alexander I but only completed during Alexander III's reign, furthered the construction of the myth of 1812. For more on the fascinating history of this memorial site, see Andrew Genets, "The Life, Death, and Resurrection of the Cathedral of Christ the Saviour, Moscow," *History Workshop Journal* 46 (1998), 72, 86.

122. See chap. 4 for more on Tolstoy, intellectuals, and the *lubok*. See also Kathryn Feuer, *Tolstoy and the Genesis of War and Peace* (Ithaca: Cornell University Press, 1996).

123. For more on Tolstoy's understanding of the *lubok*, see chap. 4.

124. References to popular images appear in book 3, part 1, chap. 19; book 3, part 2, chaps. 17 and 18; and book 3, part 3, chap. 12.

125. Denisov, *Voina i lubok*, 19.

126. The incident occurs in book 3, part 2, chap. 17 of the novel. The image "Korniushka Chikhirin," which appeared on 1 July 1812, is discussed in Vereshchagin, *Russkaia karikatura*, vol. 2, 127; and Rovinskii, *Russkie narodnye kartinki*, vol. 2, 210–12.

127. Leo Tolstoy, *War and Peace*, trans. Louise and Aylmer Maude (Oxford: Oxford University Press, 1998), 891.

128. Information about Rostopchin can be found in his memoirs, and particularly in chap. 5 of Martin, *Romantics, Reformers, Reactionaries*. See also Fedor Vasilevich Rostopchin, *Sochineniia* (St. Petersburg: Izd. A. Smirdina, 1853); *Okh, frantsuzy!* (Moscow: Russkaia kniga, 1992); *Zhurnal iskhodiashchim bumagam kantseliarii Moskovskkago general-gubernatora grafa Rostopchina s iiunia po dekabr' 1812 goda* (Moscow: Tovarishchestvo tip. A. I. Mamontova, 1908); *Rostopchinskiia afishi* (St. Petersburg: A.S. Suvorin, 1904).

129. The nearest parallel was that of the Time of Troubles, when Russians had last faced a powerful invader. The war against Napoleon provoked a wave of reminiscences. These memories led to cultural products that commemorated the Polish invasion, particularly the statue to the "heroes of 1613, Mnin and Pozharsky," erected through public subscription in 1818, and the refashioning of the opera "A Life for the Tsar" by Glinka in 1836. See Wortman, *Scenarios of Power*, vol. I, 232; Zorin, *Korma dvuglavogo orla;* and Thomas Hodge, "Susanin, Two Glinkas, and Ryleev: History Making in *A Life for the Tsar*," in *Intersections and Transpositions: Russian Music, Literature, and Society,* ed. Andrew Wachtel (Evanston: Northwestern University Press, 1998), 3–19.

130. Martin, *Romantics, Reformers, Reactionaries*, 125.

131. Martin, *Romantics, Reformers, Reactionaries*, 128.

132. Martin, *Romantics, Reformers, Reactionaries*, 137. For more on Rostopchin and his broadsheets, see F. V. Rostopchin, *Rostopchinskiia afishi.*

133. See also chap. 4.

134. See chap. 3 for more on this law.

135. See A. F. Koni, "Dmitrii Aleksandrovich Rovinskii," in *Ocherki i vospominaniia. Publichnyia chteniia rechi, stat'i, i zamiatki* (St. Petersburg: A. S. Suvorin, 1906), 588–90.

136. Denisov, *Voina i lubok*, 19–20.

137. Denisov, *Voina i lubok*, 19–21.

138. Again, it is useful to note that the ways in which the *lubki* artists articulated Russian national identity in 1812 corresponded to similar themes in all the arts. See Stites, *Serfdom, Society, and the Arts in Imperial Russia.*

139. Kaganovich, *Ivan Ivanovich Terebenev*, 140; for the china reproductions, see I. A. Ezerskaia and Iu. F. Prudnikov, *Nedarom pomnit vsia Rossiia. Otechestvennaia voina 1812 goda* (Moscow: Sov. Rossiia, 1986).

140. The original Terebenev alphabet book was published in 1815, shortly after his death. It can be found on the internet at: <http://www.museum.ru/museum/1812/English/Library/Azbuka/index.html>

141. Kaganovich, *Ivan Ivanovich Terebenev,* 120. In the midst of the Crimean War, the paper *Sankt-Peterburgskie vedomosti* printed a special dedication to Terebenev and his Patriotic War caricatures, which according to the author, had helped to inspire Russians throughout 1812 and 1813. The author wrote that he remembered viewing Terebenev's images on the shop windows of St. Petersburg, where they always drew a crowd.

142. REM, *f. 7, op.* 1, *d.* 1699, *l.* 4.

143. GPIB ORK.

144. GPIB ORK. The one-hundredth anniversary of the "people's victory" over Napoleon witnessed a number of commemorative *lubki* that again extolled the reasons behind this triumph. See the *lubki* entitled "Napoleon 1812 in Russia" and "Borodino" for examples; GIM IO *Papka* 390. The latter image contained Lermontov's poem of the battle as the text, while the image itself featured a panoramic view of the battle. The former *lubok* depicted the battle for Smolensk, Napoleon on *Poklonnaia Gora,* the retreat of the French emperor, Alexander I, Kutuzov, and Russian peasants and Cossacks fighting at Borodino. Both images, and many commemorative *lubki* like them, also located at GIM, were produced by I. D. Sytin, the subject of chap. 5.

145. See N. G. Miniailo, "Otechestvennaia voina 1812 goda v 'Oknakh TASS' (1941–1945)," in *Stranitsy khudozhestvennogo naslediia Rossii XVI–XX vekov,* ed. E. I. Itkina (Moscow: GIM, 1997), 75–88. See also the Second World War posters from the Russian and Soviet Poster Collection at the Hoover Institution on War, Revolution, and Peace (hereafter cited as RU/SU): RU/SU 2112 ("The Enemies and the Hordes in Great Disarray"), RU/SU 1921.4 ("So It Was, So It Will Be!"), and RU/SU 2129 ("The Lion and the Kitten") are examples of Soviet posters ridiculing Hitler as another Napoleon.

3—Regulating Wartime Culture

1. RGIA, *f. 777, op.* 1, *d.* 205, *ll.* 1–3.

2. Marianna Tax Choldin also argues that an "insidious self-censorship dictated by a sense of what was and was not likely to be tolerated by the government" influenced Russian writers in the nineteenth century. Because of the "fence around the empire" that prevented western ideas from infiltrating Russia, writers had to practice self-censorship in their own works. See Choldin, *A Fence Around the Empire: Russian Censorship of Western Ideas Under the Tsars* (Durham: Duke University Press, 1985), 2.

3. See Rovinskii, *Russkie narodnye kartinki,* vol. 5, 340, for a reprint of the decree.

4. Rovinskii, *Russkie narodnye kartinki,* 340–41.

5. Hilton, *Russian Folk Art,* 109.

6. Cracraft, *The Petrine Revolution in Russian Imagery,* 307–8.

7. Rovinskii, *Russkie narodnye kartinki,* vol. 5, 341.

8. Both of these images can be seen at the Muzei Narodnoi Grafiki (MNG, or Museum of Popular Graphics) in Moscow.

9. The translation is courtesy of Alexander Boguslawski, from his interesting web site on the *lubok* (the two images discussed in this paragraph are both on the site): <http://www.rollins.edu/Foreign_Lang/Russian/Lubok/lubok.html>.

10. Other images promoted Peter's achievements, particularly those that featured the tsar as a latter-day Alexander the Great, Hercules, or Russian *bogatyr'* battling his foes (usually Charles XII of Sweden). See MNG collection and Alison Hilton, *Russian Folk Art,* 110.

11. Robert Crummey, *The Old Believers and the World of the Antichrist: The Vyg Community and the Russian State, 1694–1855* (Madison: University of Wisconsin Press, 1970), xii; Roy Robson, *Old Believers in Modern Russia* (DeKalb: Northern Illinois University Press, 1995), 16.

12. Crummey, *The Old Believers and the World of the Antichrist*, xiii. Dianne Farrell has explored how the Russian government attempted to control Old Believer prints in the eighteenth century, and viewed them as the most potentially harmful images of the time, in her dissertation, "Popular Prints," 30–34, 41–43.

13. Crummey, *The Old Believers and the World of the Antichrist*, xiii.

14. Robson, *Old Believers in Modern Russia*, 88.

15. Dianne Farrell reaches a similar conclusion about censorship of popular prints in eighteenth-century Russia. Before the laws passed in the 1800s, printers could run into trouble with the Holy Synod or the police, and Farrell argues that "the Synod was most concerned with the spread of Old Believer materials; the police most frequently investigated unworthy portraits of members of the Imperial family." Farrell, "Popular Prints," 41.

16. Hilton, *Russian Folk Art*, 112. Sales of Old Believer and other religious prints were particularly strong during Lent.

17. Rovinskii, *Russkie narodnye kartinki*, vol. 5, 343.

18. Rovinskii, *Russkie narodnye kartinki*, vol. 5, 342–43.

19. Charles Ruud, *Fighting Words: Imperial Censorship and the Russian Press, 1804–1906* (Toronto: University of Toronto Press, 1982), 23.

20. Ruud, *Fighting Words*, 24.

21. Rovinskii, *Russkie narodnye kartinki*, vol. 5, 343–44.

22. Marc Raeff, "The Well-Ordered Police State and the Development of Modernity in Seventeenth- and Eighteenth-Century Europe: An Attempt at a Comparative Approach," in *Political Ideas and Institutions in Imperial Russia* (Boulder: Westview Press, 1994), 309–33. It should be noted here that the government did not just target the *lubok* trade—as Raeff and other scholars make clear, Russian officialdom attempted to regulate trade of all kind.

23. M. Peltzer has found that out of 216 total images that appeared either in *lubok* form or as caricatures in the press, 149 were censored properly. See his "Russkaia politicheskaia kartina 1812 goda," 176.

24. This effort broadly falls under the category of "conservative nationalism" set forth by Edward Thaden in his work, *Conservative Nationalism in Nineteenth-Century Russia* (Seattle: University of Washington Press, 1964). Thaden points out that European governments after the French Revolution often attempted to harness nationalism to inculcate loyalty to the state.

25. Kaganovich, *Ivan Ivanovich Terebenev*, 92–127.

26. Peltzer in, "Russkaia politicheskaia kartina 1812 goda," 173–84, notes that the competition between Moscow and St. Petersburg publishers and salesmen led to an intense rivalry. Publishers often reported to the authorities that fellow publishers had circumvented the law in reproducing Terebenev's prints. In another instance, N. I. Grech, the editor of *Syn otechestva*, personally brought an uncensored print he had found to the proper authorities.

27. Ruud, *Fighting Words*, 43.

28. Ruud, *Fighting Words*, 49.

29. Martin, *Romantics, Reformers, Reactionaries*, 6–8. Martin notes that educated Russians after 1812 did not discuss issues that dominated the rest of Europe, such as the power of the established church and state, but instead debated "metaphysical issues such as the national soul, the meaning of history, and the nature of God." Intellectually, the 1812 invasion prompted educated Russians from Nikolai Karamzin to Aleksandr Shishkov to develop what Martin terms a "conservative Russian exceptionalism," which later found expression in Uvarov's concept of "official nationality." One of the ways Russian officials and intellectuals sought to promote this exceptionalism was through censorship.

30. Nicholas Riasanovsky, *Nicholas I and Official Nationality in Russia, 1825–1855* (Berkeley: University of California Press, 1959), 72.

31. Uvarov later stated that he had "like all high society hated Napoleon." Sergei Uvarov, *Stein et Pozzo di Borgo* (St. Petersburg, 1846), 6. Quoted in Cynthia Hale

Whittaker, *The Origins of Modern Russian Education: An Intellectual Biography of Count Sergei Uvarov, 1786–1855* (DeKalb: Northern Illinois University Press, 1984), 36.

32. Andrei Zorin, "Ideologiia 'pravoslaviia-samoderzhaviia-narodnosti': Opyt rekonstruktsii," *Novoe literaturnoe obozrenie* 26 (1997), 81–83. I thank Peter Holquist for bringing this article to my attention. See also Riasanovsky, *Nicholas I and Official Nationality*, 172.

33. One of his liberal friends wrote that he had to convince Uvarov to remain near Moscow and devote himself to his native land in September 1812. See Zorin, "Ideologiia," 84.

34. Whittaker, *Origins of Modern Russian Education*, 36. Uvarov also facilitated the publication of anti-French treatises during this period.

35. Whittaker, *Origins of Modern Russian Education*, 43.

36. It is worth noting that Uvarov remained more comfortable speaking French and German his entire life than Russian, much like many of his aristocratic contemporaries (for example, he composed his patriotic "hymn" to Alexander I in French). Thus, the man responsible for developing the idea of "official nationality," which stressed Russian institutions and Russian particularities, drew on the thinking of German romantics and never felt comfortable speaking Russian. Of course, as we have seen, the artists who drew the patriotic images during the Napoleonic Wars made use of French models of caricature to ridicule the French and to establish iconic figures of Russian national identity.

37. Ruud, *Fighting Words*, 50, 67.

38. Rovinskii, *Russkie narodnye kartinki*, vol. 5, 344.

39. Wortman, *Scenarios of Power*, vol. 1, 298.

40. Wortman, *Scenarios of Power*, vol. 1, 312–13; the terminology is William Fuller's, from his *Strategy and Power in Russia*, 251.

41. Wortman, *Scenarios of Power*, vol. 1, 336, 352.

42. Aleksandr Nikitenko, *The Diary of a Russian Censor*, trans., ed., and abridged by Helen Salz Jacobson (Amherst: University of Massachusetts Press, 1975), 42. For the full Russian version, see A. Nikitenko, *Moia povest' o samom sebie i o tom, "chemu svidietel' v zhizhni byl." Zapiski i dnevniki (1804–1877 gg.)* 2 vols. (St. Petersburg: Tipo-lit. "Gerol'd," 1904–1905).

43. Nikitenko, *Moia povest'*, 61.

44. Nikitenko, *Mois povest'*, 89. Nikitenko had been imprisoned because he allowed two satirical lines about the tsarist army to appear in *Son of the Fatherland*.

45. Ruud, *Fighting Words*, 83–91.

46. Saunders, *Russia in the Age of Reaction and Reform*, 192.

47. Rovinskii, *Russkie narodnye kartinki*, vol. 5, 345.

48. Rovinskii, *Russkie nsrodnye kartinki*, 34–35.

49. Nikitenko, *Diary of a Russian Censor*, 116.

50. Nikitenko, *Diary of a Russian Censor*, 116–21.

51. The experience of 1812 appears to have been a major one for educated and uneducated Russians alike, and suggests a topic for further research. Certainly the wars against Napoleon brought a patriotic response from many corners of Russian society, but the legacies and myths of the war also exerted a profound influence in the decades after 1812. Of those individuals discussed within this chapter alone, Uvarov, Shirinskii-Shikhmatov, and Dmitrii Bludov were profoundly influenced by the war.

52. RGIA, *f.* 1149, *op.* 4, *d.* 46, *ll.* 1–4.

53. RGIA, *f.* 1149, *op.* 4, *d.* 46, *ll.* 1–4. Buturlin himself first proposed this solution.

54. Robson, *Old Believers in Modern Russia*, 17.

55. RGIA, *f.* 1149, *op.* 4, *d.* 46, *ll.* 1–4.

56. RGIA, *f.* 1149, *op.* 4, *d.* 46, *ll.* 1–4.

57. For examples of Old Believer prints from this time, see plates 119–122 in *The Lubok: Russian Folk Pictures, Seventeenth to Nineteenth Century*, ed. Alla Sytova (Leningrad: Aurora Art Publishers, 1984).

58. Sytova, *The Lubok,* 12.

59. See Wesling, *Napoleon in Russian Cultural Mythology,* 84–88. Scholars and church officials continued to investigate "Napoleonists" within Old Believer communities well into the 1870s.

60. RGIA, *f.* 1149, *op.* 4, *d.* 46, *ll.* 7–8.

61. RGIA, *f.* 1149, *op.* 4, *d.* 46, *l.* 9.

62. RGIA, *f.* 1149, *op.* 4, *d.* 46, *l.* 11.

63. RGIA, *f.* 1149, *op.* 4, *d.* 46, *ll.* 13–31.

64. RGIA, *f.* 1149, *op.* 4, *d.* 46, *ll.* 16–20.

65. RGIA, *f.* 1149, *op.* 4, *d.* 46, *l.* 18.

66. RGIA, *f.* 1149, *op.* 4, *d.* 46, *ll.* 19–20.

67. S. A. Klepikov noted in 1939 that *lubok* plates were often used over a long period of time, and that dating plates and dating individual images were two separate matters. See S. A Klepikov, *Lubok* (Moscow: Izd-vo Gos. literaturnogo muzeia, 1939).

68. RGIA, *f.* 1149, *op.* 4, *d.* 46, *ll.* 28–30.

69. RGIA, *f.* 1149, *op.* 4, *d.* 46, *ll.* 34–35.

70. Rovinskii, *Russkie narodnye kartinki,* vol. 5, 356–57.

71. For more on Sytin, see chap. 5.

72. The quote is from E. Gollerbakh, *Istoriia graviury i litografii v Rossii* (Moscow: Gosudarstvennoe izdatel'stvo, 1923), 32; and it appears also in Brooks, *When Russia Learned to Read,* 65.

73. I. A. Golyshev, "Kartinnoe i knizhnoe narodnoe proizvodstvo i torgovlia," *Russkaia starina* 49/3 (1886), 679–81.

74. In addition, lithographic prints were usually hand colored by villagers employed by the publishers. One publisher, for example, employed one thousand peasant women in the village of Nikol'skoe near Moscow. These women painted *lubki* using vegetable dye, lending the prints a primitive appearance that in turn reflected the roots of the popular prints. Brooks, *When Russia Learned to Read,* 65.

75. Brooks, *When Russsia Learned to Read.*

76. For more on this complex relationship between censor and publisher, see chap. 4.

77. I have examined the records of the St. Petersburg committee responsible for censoring lithographic production, the St. Petersburg Censorship Committee, and the Moscow Censorship Committee for evidence of unacceptable images. All the images I discuss in later chapters were carefully listed and bore the proper stamp of the censor, and no patriotic *lubok* failed to pass the censorship board in the Crimean, Russo-Turkish, Russo-Japanese, and Great Wars. The records of the Petersburg Censorship Committee are located in RGIA, *f.* 776, *op.* 29; *f.* 776, *op.* 11; and *f.* 777, *op.* 1. The Moscow Censorship Committee records can be found in the Central State Historical Archive of Moscow (Tsentral'nyi Gosudarstvennyi Istoricheskii Arkhiv Moskvy, hereafter Ts-GIAM), *f.* 31, *op.* 1.

78. I. M. Snegirev, *Dnevnik Ivana Mikhailovicha Snegireva,* vol. 2 (Moscow: Univ. tip., 1904), 25. For more on his life, see chap. 4.

79. Snegirev, *Dnevnik,* 25–30.

80. Snegirev, *Dnevnik,* 30.

81. For more on these images, see chap. 4. These particular prints also were used as part of the *raek* that traveled throughout Russia in the war years.

82. Golyshev, "Kartinnoe i knizhnoe narodnoe proizvodstvo," 682. Golyshev also noted that censors were primarily concerned with images of a spiritual nature, at least through the 1860s, 688–89.

83. In one week of March 1877, for example, the St. Petersburg Censorship Committee arrested a member of the urban lower middle class *(meshchanin)* named Mikhailov and a peasant *(krest'ianin)* named Shitov for publishing pamphlets without submitting them to the censor. Both received a fine, and Mikhailov also spent a day in jail. RGIA, *f.* 776, *op.* 29, *d.* 12, *ll.* 19–23.

84. See, for example, the 1877 attempt of Prince Obolenskii in St. Petersburg, who alerted the St. Petersburg Censorship Committee to the unauthorized use of his portrait in several pamphlets. RGIA, *f. 776, op. 29, d. 12, l. 41.*

85. RGIA, *f. 776, op. 29, d. 13, ll. 24, 26.*

86. TsIAM, *f. 31, op. 1, d. 479, l. 1.* In the same week (the first one in March 1905), the Moscow Committee punished *Moskovskie vedomosti* for publishing details of the disasters in the Far East. RGIA, *f. 31, op. 1, d. 479, l. 5.*

87. Robert Otto, *Publishing for the People: The Firm Posrednik, 1885–1905* (New York: Garland, 1987), 60–90.

88. Louise McReynolds, *The News Under Russia's Old Regime: The Development of a Mass-Circulation Press* (Princeton: Princeton University Press, 1991), 187. Nemirovich-Danchenko later published many of his articles after the 1905 censorship law, as *Vostok i voina* (Moscow: Sytin, 1905).

89. Charles Ruud, *Russian Entrepreneur: Publisher Ivan Sytin of Moscow, 1851–1934* (Montreal: McGill-Queen's University Press, 1990), 70.

90. Ruud, *Russian Entrepreneur,* 148–49. For an example of Sytin's "depressing" stories that landed him a fine in 1915, see TsIAM, *f. 31, op. 3, d. 2205, ll.* 107–8.

91. The term "abolishing ambiguity" comes from Jan Plamper's article, "Abolishing Ambiguity: Soviet Censorship Practices in the 1930s," *Russian Review* 60/4 (October 2001), 543. As Plamper makes clear, Soviet censors obsessed about eliminating any ambiguous meanings in cultural products. For more on the main goals of tsarist censorship, see Ruud, *Fighting Words;* and Choldin, *A Fence Around the Empire.*

4—Consolidating Wartime Culture

1. Tolstoy and a fellow officer submitted plans for a journal called *The War Leaflet,* which would have featured war news from all fronts, lists of decorations and courts-martial, contemporary stories of soldiers' lives, biographies of military personnel, soldiers' songs, and popular articles about warfare. Tolstoy, as he told friends, conceived of the journal as a means by which he could help to maintain the patriotic spirit in the army. Gorchakov approved of the idea, and the plans were sent to Nicholas I, who rejected them because he feared any independently produced materials. For more on this venture, see N. N. Gusev, *Lev Nikolaevich Tolstoi. Materialy k biografii s 1828 po 1855 god* (Moscow: Izd-vo Akademii nauk SSSR, 1954), 495–99; R. F. Christian, ed. and trans., *Tolstoy's Letters,* by Leo Tolstoy, vol. 1, 1828–1879 (New York: Scribner's, 1978), 43–49.

2. Leo Tolstoy, *The Sebastopol Sketches,* trans. David McDuff (New York: Penguin Books, 1986), 109.

3. Tolstoy, *Sebastopol Sketches,* 184.

4. Christian, *Tolstoy's Letters,* vol. 1, 44.

5. He later wrote, "I failed to become a general in the army, but I became one in literature." Quoted in Tolstoy, *Sebastopol Sketches,* 36.

6. For more on this subject, see W. Bruce Lincoln, *The Great Reforms: Autocracy, Bureaucracy, and the Politics of Change in Imperial Russia* (DeKalb: Northern Illinois University Press, 1990); and Ben Eklof, John Bushnell, and Larissa Zakharova, eds., *Russia's Great Reforms, 1855–1881* (Bloomington: Indiana University Press, 1994).

7. Quoted in Robert Edgerton, *Death or Glory: The Legacy of the Crimean War* (Boulder: Westview Press, 1999). For more on the Crimean War's military aspects, see John Curtiss, *Russia's Crimean War* (Durham: Duke University Press, 1979); and William Fuller, *Strategy and Power.*

8. Edgerton, *Death or Glory,* 5.

9. For more on Turkish stereotypes, see chap. 5. For an examination of some of the ways in which Islamic peoples featured in Russian popular culture, see Thomas Barrett, "Southern Living (in Captivity): The Caucasus in Russian Popular Culture," *Journal of Popular Culture* 31/4 (Spring 1998): 75–94.

10. For the use of the term "propaganda," see the discussion below.

11. GIM IO, *Papka* 565 (15 June 1855: A. Vasil'ev; censor N. Fon-Kruze).

12. See, for example, the image "Victorious Don Cossacks in the Crimea," from Sharapov, in GIM, *Papka* 565.

13. GIM IO, *Papka* 564 (November 1855: A. Lavrent'eva).

14. The firm of A. Rudnev printed three portraits of Nicholas I in 1854 and 1855, all of which featured the tsar in various military dress. The prints can be found in the archives of the Helsinki Slavonic Library.

15. GIM IO, *Papka* 221.

16. See Wortman, *Scenarios of Power*, vol. 1, 255–419.

17. See chaps. 5, 6, and 7 for more.

18. GIM IO, *Papka* 561 (E. Khitrovoi).

19. Christian, *Tolstoy's Letters*, 44.

20. "The Heroic Rifleman Stepan Tolstokorov," from Khitrovoi's firm, lauded the selfless act of this Russian soldier, who had climbed up a tree and shot at the enemy in order to protect his comrades. By climbing into the tree, Tolstokorov placed himself dangerously in the line of fire, but again his "coolness" and love for his fellow Russian soldiers helped him undertake the deed. GIM IO, *Papka* 561.

21. See the three images named "The Victory of Andrei Siuzik", from various Moscow printers and all passed by Snegirev, in GIM IO, Papka 558.

22. GIM IO, *Papka* 558. The first was from Shalin, the second Rudnev. All three were passed by the Muscovite censor Flerov.

23. See "The Victory of Private Ivan Ragozhin," from the firm of Sharapov and passed by Snegirev, in GIM IO, *Papka* 559. The image recounts the story of Ragozhin, who fought off a Turkish soldier with his bare hands, remaining at his post as a gunner throughout the battle near Supish.

24. GIM IO, *Papka* 221 (Khitrovoi). The *lubok* was approved on 7 July 1855 by the Moscow censor Fon-Kruze.

25. See Serhii Plokhy, "The City of Glory: Sevastopol in Russian Historical Mythology," *Journal of Contemporary History* 35/3 (July 2000), 381. Plokhy notes that Koshka (whose Ukrainian name is Petro Kishka), appeared in all the books about the siege of Sevastopol published in Ukraine throughout the 1970s and 1980s. Ukrainian historians singled out Kishka for particular praise as a means of challenging what they termed the dominant Russocentric "myth of Sevastopol." For more on how Sevastopol became a site of contestation between local and central government in the Soviet era as a result of the Second World War, see Karl Qualls, "Local-Outsider Negotiations in Postwar Sevastopol's Reconstruction, 1944–53," in *Provincial Landscapes: Local Dimensions of Soviet Power, 1917–1953*, ed. Donald Raleigh (Pittsburgh: University of Pittsburgh Press, 2001), 276–98. The use of the memory of the Crimean War after the Second World War (which in Sevastopol was known as the second great defense of the city) is explored in Karl Qualls, "Imagining Sevastopol: History and Postwar Community Construction, 1942–1953," *National Identities* 5/2 (2003): 123–39.

26. This characterization also found expression in the sermons of Russian priests during the war—Orthodox leaders throughout Russia and in the Crimea frequently portrayed the war as a holy crusade against Islam. For more on the church's response to the war, see Mara Kozelsky, "Orthodoxy Under Fire: Clergy, Sermons, and Christianization during the Crimean War." I thank Mara Kozelsky for sharing her work with me.

27. GIM IO, *Papka* 565.

28. GIM IO, *Papka* 559 (Martianov).

29. "Three *Bunchuks* Send Away the Turks." (Glushkov) also depicts the Turkish sultan as equally cowardly, while "The Victory Gained by General-Lieutenant Prince Androkov Over Thirty Thousand Turkish Troops" (Vasil'ev) reinforces the collective cowardice of the Turks and their leaders. Both images depict the Turkish army fleeing before Russian troops. Finally, the juxtaposition of Turkish culture with Russian culture can also be seen in the image "Our Cossacks as Guests of the Turkish *Mushir*" (Sharapov). All the images are in GIM IO, *Papka* 559.

30. GIM IO, *Papka* 559 (O. Vasil'ev).

31. See the Efimov *lubok* entitled "The Capture of the Turkish Fortress of Kars in Asia, 16 November 1855," and "The English General Williams Under the Orders of the Turkish Mushir-Vasif-Pasha Gives the Fortress of Kars to the Russian Commander Murav'ev, 16 November 1855," both in GIM IO, *Papka* 559.

32. GIM IO, *Papka* 559 (Vasil'ev, approved by Beziushikin in March 1855).

33. "The Entry of Prince Gorchakov into Machin in March 1854" depicts another Russian victory of the Crimean War. The image is in GIM IO, *Papka* 565 (Khitrovoi). M. D. Gorchakov, the focus of this print and one of the most popular Russian generals during the war, also appeared in other *lubki* that praised his troops, who successfully crossed the Danube River in March 1854 to "liberate" Orthodox Slavs. GIM IO, *Papka* 562. See the several images bearing similar titles and themes also located in this folio. Finally, for an insightful account of the ways in which the war affected Russian colonists caught in the war zones, see Nicholas Breyfogle, *Heretics and Colonizers: Forging Russia's Empire in the South Caucasus* (Ithaca: Cornell University Press, 2005) and "Caught in the Crossfire: Russian Sectarians in the Caucasian Theater of War, 1853–1856 and 1877–1878," *Kritika* 2/4 (Fall 2001): 713–50.

34. GIM IO, *Papka* 562 (Zerev, August 1855). For an account of the Solovki Monastery during the war and how the British bombardment soon became enshrined in myth, see Roy Robson, *Solovki: The Story of Russia Told Through its Most Remarkable Islands* (New Haven: Yale University Press, 2004), chap. 12.

35. GIM IO, *Papka* 221.

36. See Christian, *Tolstoy's Letters*, 44.

37. See, among others, the *lubki* "Battle in Kamchatka" (Sharapov, August 1854), "The Victory of the Young Ensign" (Negirev, June 1854), and "The Victory Accomplished near the City of Odessa" (Kuznetsov, May 1854) for examples; all in GIM IO.

38. See Plokhy, "City of Glory," 369–83.

39. GIM IO, *Papka* 221.

40. GIM IO, *Papka* 221.

41. Both quoted in Kozelsky, "Orthodoxy Under Fire." The content of the sermons can be found in this article.

42. The kind of collective spirit in "Sevastopol" appeared in other, lighter *lubki* of the war. "Little Russians at Sevastopol" captures two jovial "little Russian" (a term for Ukrainian) soldiers sitting behind the ramparts of the town. The pair shows no sign of fear or despair with their situation, and instead chat amiably as if nothing could bother them. The text notes that the Ukrainians, one a new recruit and the other a seasoned veteran, are discussing the war. The veteran refers to their common faith and tsar as sources for strength in the battles ahead, words that comfort the younger soldier. GIM IO, *Papka* 221 (Sharapov).

43. GIM IO, *Papka* 565 (Sharapov, 1855).

44. GIM IO, *Papka* 565 (Zernov, August 1855).

45. GIM IO, *Papka* 221.

46. Images like this one and numerous others from the Patriotic War became a standard feature of wartime culture in Russia (and presumably elsewhere). The process of enmification at the heart of wartime images, a process that frequently ridicules and emasculates the enemy, is reinforced through images that stress the strength of one's own army (in this case the Russian) when faced with larger numbers of enemy troops (in this instance French). The victory of the smaller force "proves" the heroism and superiority of Russian troops over a weaker, inferior enemy.

47. GIM IO, *Papka* 221. The text cites *Moskovskie vedomosti*, no. 262 (1854). See also the equally dramatic rendition of a similar event in April 1855, also from Iakovlev, in *Papka* 221.

48. "Events near Sevastopol," a May 1855 *lubok* from the firm of Rudnev, and "The Attack of Anglo-French Troops on Sevastopol on 6 June 1855," also from Rudnev, for example, both in GIM IO, *Papka* 221.

49. "View of the Bombardment of Sevastopol," from Vasil'ev and passed on 18 July 1855, in GIM IO, *Papka* 221.

50. See the untitled *lubok* from Sharapov approved on 22 August 1855 depicting a July skirmish and noting its "model heroism" *[primernem muzhestvom]*, also in *Papka* 221.

51. "View of Sevastopol and the Field of Battle With Konstantin Fortress," a St. Petersburg print from Beketov, in GIM IO, *Papka* 221.

52. Plokhy, "City of Glory."

53. Plokhy, "City of Glory," 370–72.

54. Plokhy, "City of Glory," 373.

55. Plokhy cites the raising of monuments to heroes such as Admiral Nakhimov and other Russian commanders killed during the siege in 1856 as further evidence for the veneration of Sevastopol. Plokhy, "City of Glory," 375.

56. Plokhy, "City of Glory," 376. For an insightful account of how Crimea became a part of the "Russian consciousness" soon after its annexation, see Andrei Zorin, "Krym v istorii russkogo samosoznaniia," *Novoe literaturnoe obozrenie* 31/3 (1998): 123–43. For more on how the war contributed to the importance of Crimea within Russian national consciousness, see Kozelsky, "Orthodoxy Under Fire."

57. Sevastopol is currently a part of the sovereign nation of Ukraine, but has become an important center of debate between Russian and Ukrainian officials in the context of the post-Soviet order. For more on the post-Soviet Sevastopol dispute and its bizarre happenings, see Matthew Brzezinski, *Casino Moscow: A Tale of Greed and Adventure on Capitalism's Wildest Frontier* (New York: The Free Press, 2001), 157–65.

58. The promotion of Sevastopol as an important site can be detected in the recollections of Nikolai Przhevalskii—later famous as the explorer of Inner Asia—who in 1855 at the age of sixteen had one ambition, "to join the heroic exploits of Sevastopol's defenders." Quoted in David Schimmelpenninck van der Oye, "Ex Oriente Lux: Ideologies of Empire and Russia's Far East, 1895–1904" (Ph.D. diss., Yale University, 1997), 17. See also the outstanding book based on this dissertation, *Toward the Rising Sun: Russian Ideologies of Empire and the Path to War with Japan* (DeKalb: Northern Illinois University Press, 2001).

59. The fact that the images of Sevastopol appeared so soon after the actual events they depicted may have helped make the "myth of Sevastopol" more effective. As Peter Burke recounts, the images of the taking of the Bastille that depicted the prison as a symbol of a repressive old regime helped to establish that event as an important myth in France in 1789. Burke, *Eyewitnessing,* 146.

60. "Peterburgskie zametki," *Otechestvennye zapiski* (April 1855), 164.

61. "Peterburgskie zametki," *Otechestvennye zapiski* (May 1855), 75–76; "Peterburgskie zametki," *Otechestvennye zapiski* (June 1855), 125.

62. "Peterburgskie zametki," *Otechestvennye zapiski* (July 1855), 74.

63. N. V. Davydov, *Iz proshlogo* (Moscow, 1914), 62–63.

64. Biographical information on Snegirev comes from the following sources: "Ivan Mikhailovich Snegirev," in *Russkii biograficheskii slovar'*, vol. 19 (St. Petersburg: Izdanie Imperatorskago Russkago istoricheskago obshchestva, 1909), 7–11; A. N. Pypin, *Istoriia russkoi etnografii*, t. 1 (St. Petersburg: Tip. M. M. Stasliulevicha, 1890), 314–29; S. A. Tokarev, *Istoriia russkoi etnografii (dooktiabr'skii period)* (Moscow: Nauka, 1966), 192–97; and the brief information on Snegirev in the archives of the Moscow Censorship Committee: TsGIAM, *f.* 31, *op.* 1, *d.* 121.

65. TsGIAM, *f.* 31, *op.* 1, *d.* 121, *ll.* 2–3.

66. TsGIAM, *f.* 31, *op.* 1, *d.* 121, *ll.* 2–3.

67. Ivan Snegirev, *Lubochnyia kartinki russkago naroda v Moskovskom mirie* (Moscow: v Univ. Tip., 1861).

68. Snegirev dedicated his 1842 work on old Moscow to Emperor Nicholas I. Ivan Snegirev, *Pamiatniki moskovskoi drevnosti, s prisovokupleniem ocherka monumental'noi istorii Moskvy* (Moscow: Tip. A Semena, 1842).

69. Brooks, *When Russia Learned to Read,* 63.

70. Snegirev, *Lubochnye kartinki.*

71. See Snegirev's diary entry from 21 August 1856, when he met with Bludov, who "praised my works" and approved of the publication of his *lubok* study. I. M. Snegirev, *Dnevnik,* vol. 2, 63.

72. I. M. Snegirev, "Russkaia narodnaia galereia ili lubochnye kartinki," *Otechestvennye zapiski* 1822 (no. 30).

73. Snegirev, *Lubochnye kartinki;* Brooks, *When Russia Learned to Read,* 64. See also O. R. Khromov, *Russkaia lubochnaia kniga XVII–XIX vekov* (Moscow: "Pamiatniki istoricheskoi mysli," 1998), 6–16.

74. See Tokarev, *Istoriia Russkoi etnografii,* 316–29.

75. Quoted in "Ivan Mikhailovich Snegirev," *Russkii biograficheskii slovar',* 10.

76. Snegirev, *Lubochnye kartinki,* 1.

77. Snegirev, *Lubochnye kartinki,* 1.

78. Snegirev, *Lubochnye kartinki,* 5.

79. Snegirev, *Lubochnye kartinki,* 133.

80. Snegirev, *Lubichnye kartinki,* 133. Snegirev particularly praised the works of Terebenev, who truly captured the "national spirit" *[dukh narodnyi]* of the time.

81. Snegirev, *Lubochnye kartinki,* 134.

82. The reception of these *lubki* could be as varied as the images themselves; thus, Snegirev (and present-day historians) cannot wholly assert that they served only one function, that of governmental propaganda. However, Snegirev's account does demonstrate that in some respects the popular prints from the Crimean War did contribute to fostering a sense of national belonging.

83. When Snegirev heard about a battle near Sevastopol on 8 September 1854, he noted in his diary that it served as a good omen, for it occurred on the same day as the battle of Kulikovo in 1380, when the Russians had defeated the Mongols. Later that year, after a day's work in the Censorship Committee, Snegirev wrote, "Rescue us, Son of God, from the calumnies of the enemy." After hearing about a large number of enemy losses on 1 November, then approving of more prints, Snegirev wrote, "God, please help the Russian soldiers!" See Snegirev, *Dnevnik,* vol. 2, 26–29.

84. Snegirev, *Lubochnye kartinki,* 136.

85. TsGIAM, *f.* 31, *op.* 1, *d.* 117, *ll.* 17–40.

86. Joseph Watstein, "Ivan Sytin—An Old Russian Success Story," *Russian Review* 30/1 (January 1971), 43.

87. For more on the *ofeni,* see Brooks, *When Russia Learned to Read,* 66, 101–8.

88. Brooks, *When Russia Learned to Read,* 66, 101–8.

89. See, for example, the account of the peddler Mikhaila in chap. 5; also in this source by A. S. Prugavin, *Zarosynaroda i obiazannosti intelligentsii v oblasti.*

90. N. V. Tupulov, ed., *Pol'veka dlia knigi (1866–1916). Literaturno-khudozhestvennyi sbornik, posviashchennyi piatidesiatiletiiu izdatel'skoi deiatel'nosti I. D. Sytina* (Moscow: Sytin, 1916), 15–17.

91. See chap. 5 for more on Sytin's background.

92. *The Eastern Question: A Reprint of Letters written, 1853–1856 Dealing with the Events of the Crimean War,* ed. E. M. Aveling (London: 1897), 535. Quoted in Ulrich Keller, *The Ultimate Spectacle: A Visual History of the Crimean War* (Amsterdam: Gordon and Breach Publishers, 2001), 41.

93. Keller, *Ultimate Spectacle,* 44.

94. Keller, *Ultimate Spectacle,* 188–89.

95. The first quote is from Keller, *Ultimate Spectacle* 123; the second comes from Taylor, *Munitions of the Mind,* 164–65.

96. This is the view of Ulrich Keller, *Ultimate Spectacle,* 157.

97. Taylor, *Munitions of the Mind,* 165.

98. Although Populists did not view the peasants with the disdain that most educated Russians did, Populist authors such as A. S. Prugavin (1852–1918/19) nevertheless

held a negative assessment of the *lubok*. Prugavin believed that "true culture" was rural, and that popular prints, which were produced in Russia's cities, had been corrupted by commercialism, commenting that "a sea of vulgarity, superstition, prejudice, and ignorance of all types" could be found in the *lubki*. See Brooks, *When Russia Learned to Read*, 322–23. Prugavin also claimed that the *lubok* stirred "blood-stained action" among uneducated Russians, particularly during wartime, and thus contributed to peasant support for the regime. Prugavin, *Knigonoshi i ofeni*, vol. 1, 96. See also V. P. Vakhterev, *Vneshkol'noe obrazovanie* (Moscow: n.p., 1894). The view of the *lubok* as vulgar is most apparent in Nikolai Nekrasov's poem "Who Can be Happy and Free in Russia?" The third chapter of Nekrasov's poem, entitled "The Drunken Night," describes the debauchery in peasant Russia during a holiday. One of the stories told in the course of the festivities concerns a peasant named Iakim, who when his hut caught on fire, elected to rush in and save his *lubki* rather than any of his other possessions. See N. A. Nekrasov, *Polnoe sobranie stikhotvorennii v trekh tomakh*, vol. 3 (Leningrad: Sov. Pisatel', 1967), 40–53.

99. Brooks, *When Russia Learned to Read*, 295. For a detailed analysis of how educated society viewed popular literature, see the chapter entitled "The Educated Response," 295–352.

100. Snegirev *(Dnevnik,* vol. 2, 64) records his meeting with Rovinskii on 28 August 1856; Koni, *Ocherki i vospominanie*, 591–92.

101. W. Bruce Lincoln, *In the Vanguard of Reform: Russia's Enlightened Bureaucrats, 1825–1861* (DeKalb: Northern Illinois University Press, 1982).

102. Lincoln, *The Great Reforms*, 110.

103. Rovinskii came into close contact with Russia's appalling prison system, where he personally witnessed numerous abuses. His experiences, as Bruce Lincoln has argued, played an important role in the composition of the new judicial statutes of 1864. See Lincoln, *The Great Reforms*, 110–11.

104. See Koni, *Ocherki i vospominaniia*, 593–94; Koni's memoirs contain a series of portraits of influential people with whom he had intimate contact. His account of Rovinskii runs from 521–624. In addition to Koni's work, see O. B. Vraskaia, "D. A. Rovinskii, ego sovremenniki i posledovateli" in *Narodnaia graviura i fol'klor v Rossii XVII–XIX vv. (k 150–letiiu so dnia rozhdeniia D. A. Rovinskogo)*, ed. I. E. Danilova (Moscow: Sov. khudozhnik, 1976), 5–33.

105. Rovinskii, *Russkie narodnye kartinki*.

106. Koni, *Ocherki i vospominanie*, 588–89.

107. Koni, *Ocherki i vospominanie*, 590.

108. R. F. Christian, ed. and trans. *Tolstoy's Diaries*, vol. 1, 1847–1894 (London: Athlone Press, 1985), 95.

109. Christian, *Tolstoy's Letters*, 45.

110. Toby Clark, *Art and Propaganda in the Twentieth Century: The Political Image in the Age of Mass Culture* (New York: Harry Abrams, 1997), 7.

111. For more on the historical dimensions of propaganda, see Bertrand Taithe and Tim Thornton, eds., *Propaganda: Political Rhetoric and Identity, 1300–2000* (London: Sutton Publishing, 1999); and Robert Jackall, ed., *Propaganda* (New York: New York University Press, 1995).

112. Watstein, "Ivan Sytin," 47; Ruud, *Russian Entrepreneur*, 29.

113. Ruud, *Russian Entrepreneur*, 29.

114. Ruud, *Russian Entrepreneur*, 30–31.

115. See Hilton, *Russian Folk Art*, 245–56; and chap. 8.

116. Many Russian intellectuals began to turn to radical ideas as a result of the widespread belief that heroic Russians had been betrayed by their government in Sevastopol. For more on this process, see Aileen Kelly, "Carnival of the Intellectuals: 1855," in *Toward Another Shore: Russian Thinkers Between Necessity and Chance* (New Haven: Yale University Press, 1998).

117. Plokhy, "City of Glory," 376.

118. Peter Burke also refers to "the work of subversion" that images may perform, even in the "propagation of patriotism." Burke, *Eyewitnessing*, 78–79. The fact that the Crimean images may have served this function illustrates the impossibility of ascribing a single meaning or single function of a given set of images, yet also illustrates just how powerful images can be as historical agents.

5—Depicting the Holy War

1. K. G. Sokol, *Monumenty imperii. Opisanie dvukhsot naibolee interesnykh pamiatnikov imperatorskoi Rossii* (Moscow: GEOS, 1999), 161.

2. In this sense, I agree with Catherine Merridale's assertion that "public memorials, paid for by subscription and approved by the meetings of committees, are the products as well as the bearers of collective memory. If there is no agreed story, it is difficult to conceive of a form in which to embody the past." See Merridale, *Night of Stone: Death and Memory in Twentieth-Century Russia* (New York: Viking, 2001), 308.

3. The best account of the war and its legacies is Bruce W. Menning, *Bayonets before Bullets: The Imperial Russian Army, 1861–1914* (Bloomington: Indiana University Press, 1992), 51–86.

4. Menning, *Bayonets before Bullets*, 52.

5. Menning, *Bayonets before Bullets*, 53.

6. See M. A. Gazenkampf, *Moi dnevnik 1877–1878 gg.* (St. Petersburg: Komissioner voen.-uchebnykh zavedenii, 1908). D. A. Miliutin's letter from February 1877 was reproduced as the second appendix in Mikhail Gazenkampf's diaries from the war.

7. F. V. Greene, *Sketches of Army Life in Russia* (New York: Charles Scribner's Sons, 1880), 14.

8. A. K. Puzyrevskii, *Desiat' let nazad. Voina 1877–1878 gg.* (St. Petersburg: Tip. V.S. Balasheva, 1888), v.

9. Even the composers Modest Mussorgsky and Peter Tchaikovsky glorified the holy war in works of the time. Mussorgsky composed "The Capture of Kars" in 1877, while Tchaikovsky wrote a piece entitled "The Montenegrins Receiving the News of Russia's Declaration of War on Turkey" (now lost) the same year. Richard Taruskin, *Defining Russia Musically: Historical and Hermeneutical Essays* (Princeton: Princeton University Press, 1997), 154.

10. Hans Rogger, "The Skobelev Phenomenon: The Hero and His Worship," *Oxford Slavonic Papers* 9 (1976): 46–78.

11. Skobelev's sister eventually founded the Skobelev Committee, a semiofficial propaganda organization, during the Russo-Japanese War. Nicholas II, recognizing the popularity that Skobelev continued to enjoy, used the committee for official propaganda in World War I. For more, see Jahn, *Patriotic Culture in Russia during World War I*.

12. The images of this war shed a great deal of light on Russian attitudes toward the "Orient" and on the complex relations between Russia and Asia in general. For more on "Russian Orientalism" and its complexities see: Daniel Brower and Edward Lazzerini, eds., *Russia's Orient: Imperial Borderlands and Peoples, 1700–1917* (Bloomington: Indiana University Press, 1997); Geraci, *Window on the East;* Susan Layton, *Russian Literature and Empire: Conquest of the Caucasus from Pushkin to Tolstoy* (Cambridge: Cambridge University Press, 1994); and David Schimmelpenninck van der Oye, "What is Russian Orientalism?" (paper presented at the American Association for the Advancement of Slavic Studies annual meeting, 10 November 2000). For a lively debate over the uses and misuses of Edward Said's work in the Russian context, see Nathaniel Knight's article "Grigor'ev in Orenburg, 1851–1862: Russian Orientalism in the Service of Empire?" *Slavic Review* 59/1 (Spring 2000): 74–100; followed by the exchange between Knight and Adeeb Khalid in *Kritika* 1/4 (Fall 2000): 691–716. My own account of these images mirrors that of Susan Layton's comment that the iconography of the Russo-Turkish War "gave

even illiterate Russians access to the postwar mythology of national victory over Asian fiends." Layton, "Nineteenth-Century Russian Mythologies of Caucasian Savagery," in *Russia's Orient,* ed. Bower and Lazzerini, 95.

13. The wartime images functioned like newspapers in all the wars discussed in this monograph; I just highlight that role in this chapter.

14. GPIB ORK, OIK 1954. The print appeared after 11 November 1876, when the Moscow Censorship Committee approved of this *lubok* from Strel'tsov.

15. GPIB ORK, OIK 1949. The image also came from Strel'tsov's company (11 January 1877).

16. GPIB ORK, OIK 1945. The print was produced by the Moscow firm of A. Abramov.

17. Richard Wortman has noted that Alexander II allowed his image to appear in far more *lubki* than did his father. Popular prints that featured Alexander receiving bread and salt from Moscow workers, dedicating the Millennium Monument in Novgorod, riding with his grand dukes, and even prints celebrating Osip Komissarov, who had allegedly saved Alexander from Dmitrii Karakozov's 1866 assassination attempt, all appeared in the early years of Alexander's reign. Wortman, *Scenarios of Power,* vol. 2, 72–73, 88–89, 100–101, 110–11. According to Wortman, Alexander used his image to try "to show himself acting in concert with his people and taking account of public opinion," (135) a desire that manifested itself during the Russo-Turkish War. Alexander also appeared in prints before the war actually started. The Iakovlev *lubok* "Brotherly Meeting of Three Monarchs" depicts a meeting between the Russian tsar and Wilhelm I, emperor of Germany. Wilhelm holds the hand of the young emperor of Austria, Franz Joseph, a visual depiction of the soon-to-be created Three Emperors' League. Thus, the Russian tsar appeared very early on in these images (unlike in the Crimean War), and reappeared throughout the war. For the only time in nineteenth-century wartime imagery, patriotic *lubki* featured the Russian tsar consistently throughout the war, connecting Alexander II closely to the victory and to Orthodoxy. The print is located at GPIB ORK, OIK 1943. For a second early print that features the tsar, see "A View of the Moscow Troops with the Sovereign Emperor on Theater Square, Moscow," which depicts an impressive review of troops in the heart of the old city, near the Bolshoi Theater (GPIB ORK, OIK 1812. The image is an Iakovlev print).

18. GPIB ORK, OIK 1940. The publisher was Strel'tsov.

19. The first battle *lubok* to appear in the war also reinforced previous concepts of Russian national identity and heroism. In "Caucasian Troops on the Turkish Border," the famed horsemen bravely engaging in battle are led by a general, identified as Terdikasov in the text. Turkish soldiers fall under the bayonets and swords of the Russians, while cannoneers fire on the Turkish troops, who flee before the relentless assault. GPIB ORK, OIK 1788 (Sharapov, 25 April). The text quotes a *Moskovskie vedomosti* report of the first engagement of the war, a battle in a village just across the Turkish border in which the Russian troops took 1,700 prisoners and captured a small citadel.

20. GPIB ORK, OIK 1796 (I. G. Gavrilov, 5 May).

21. See the 18 June Sharapov print of the same name that depicts a similar crossing on 15 June, as well as the five other *lubki* depicting the 3 May fording, all in GPIB ORK, OIK 1793, 1794, 3121, 1842, 3121/27, and 1795. These images call to mind the prints celebrating Gorchakov's crossing of the Danube in the midst of the Crimean War.

22. GIM IO, *Papka* 217.

23. The stereotype of the "cowardly Turk" also appeared in *lubok* chapbooks during the war. The 1878 tale, "Do What You Must" (and two others from the time) can be found in James Von Geldern and Louise McReynolds, eds. *Entertaining Tsarist Russia: Tales, Songs, Movies, Jokes, Ads, and Images from Russian Urban Life, 1779–1917* (Bloomington: Indiana University Press, 1998), 155.

24. GPIB ORK, OIK 1773 (Glushkov, 11 May 1877).

25. GPIB ORK, OIK 1782 (Morozov, 11 June 1877).

26. GIM IO, *Papka* 221 (Petr Akimovich Glushkov, 6 July 1877).

27. Examples include the *lubok* "Capture of the Turkish Fortress of Nikipol," which appeared three days before "The Storming of Nikipol and the Capture of Six Thousand Turkish Prisoners and Two Pashas." The first print is from GPIB ORK, OIK 1776 (Gavrilov, 6 July 1877), the second GIM IO, *Papka* 221 (Morozov). See also the print "Single Combat of the *Vesta* with Turkish Battleships," which reestablished Sevastopol as an important site of Russian heroism. This image depicts a heroic victory near Sevastopol, won over the "real enemy" of the Crimean War, the Turks, an affirmation of the heroic "victory" won at Sevastopol in 1855. GPIB ORK, OIK 1787 (Abramov, 29 July 1877). The August 1877 Sharapov print "Heroic Repulse of the Turks at the Shipka Pass" illustrates one of the most dramatic episodes of the war, the long march from Kishinev to the Shipka Pass (GPIB ORK, OIK 1784). The Strel'tsov print "Russo-Turkish War: The Capture of the Fortress Lovcha, 22 August 1877," using similar language and imagery, depicts numerous Russian troops pouring into the main gates of the battered town. See also the Abramov *lubok* "Capture of Lovcha" and the Iakovlev print "Taking by Storm of the City of Lovcha" in GPIB ORK, OIK 1765, 1770, for similar depictions.

28. GPIB ORK, OIK 1816. The print appeared just five days after the event.

29. Turkish soldiers wore fezzes into battle, and other images from the time captured them—the *Illustrated London News* carried a picture of the defeated Turkish army after Plevna that depicts the Turkish troops in fezzes. The print appeared in the 12 January 1878 edition and is reprinted in Justin McCarthy, *The Ottoman Turks: An Introductory History to 1923* (London: Longman, 1997), 194.

30. The text describes the action, again reported in a newspaper account: "At six in the morning of 19 August 1877 the Turkish troops knocked out our outpost but by 8 o'clock our infantry and artillery had showed itself, after which we launched several successive attacks on the enemy, finally the last crossing brought several hand-to-hand fights that repulsed the troops and our forces hurled back the Turks with massive losses, finishing at 4 in the afternoon."

31. Menning, *Bayonets before Bullets*, 60.

32. Menning, *Bayonets before Bullets*, 60–78.

33. The late summer months also featured images that refocused public attention on the goals of the war. In particular, publishers issued images that depicted Constantinople (in Russian, Tsargrad) and the fortress of Kars as Russian targets. See "View of Constantinople from the Bosphorus," which stresses the fact that the city once had been Orthodox but then in 1453 "the splendid Christian buildings were converted into Muslim ones [*magometanskie*]: such as the famous Cathedral of St. Sophia, which was transformed into a mosque." (GPIB ORK, OIK 1779 [Rudnev, 10 September 1877]). On the fortress of Kars, which Russian troops briefly held in the Crimean War, see the Morozov print entitled simply "A View of the Turkish Fortress of Kars" (GPIB ORK, OIK 1780). With Russian forces bogged down in the Balkans at Plevna, this print focuses instead on the other theater of war, where Russian troops led by M. T. Loris-Melikov attempted to storm the fortress. In spite of heavy Russian losses and inconclusive battles, the Turkish pasha Mukhtiar withdrew from the fort later in September, delivering it to Russia. The Iakovlev print "Third Day's Battle Near Kars," approved on 28 September, further asserts Russian military and cultural superiority over the Turks. While the decisive battle still raged at Plevna, images such as this one reinforced notions of Turkish cowardice, Russian bravery, and Russian military strength. GPIB ORK, OIK 1819.

34. GPIB ORK, OIK 1804 (Sharapov, 12 September 1877).

35. See the Abramov *lubok* also entitled "The Russian Generals" and approved on 20 October in GPIB ORK, OIK 3121/21.

36. See Rogger, "The Skobelev Phenomenon."

37. Skobelev first appeared in the wartime *lubok* during the summer. "Heroes of the 1877 War" contains the portraits of six Russian generals (plus Karl I, the Ruman-

ian prince): Loris-Melikov, P. A. Geiman, Prince Nikolai Nikolaevich, Prince Mikhail Nikolaevich, A. A. Nepokoichitskii, and finally Mikhail Skobelev. See GPIB ORK, OIK 3121/23 (Sharapov, 25 June 1877). Much like the images of the Patriotic War, then, the *lubki* from the Russo-Turkish War featured a popular general in Skobelev, whose name would enter into the pantheon of great Russian military leaders like Kutuzov.

38. GPIB ORK, OIK 1785. This Morozov print appeared on 12 September.

39. An example of the numerous *lubok* portraits of Skobelev is "Lieutenant-General of His Majesty's Suite Mikhail Dmitrievich Skobelev," a Glushkov print from 28 September. In both the language of the text and the portrait of the general, Skobelev is portrayed as quintessentially Russian, a leader who embodies Russian manliness and bravery, known as the "White General" because he always rode a white horse and wore a white uniform on the battlefield, and who provoked suspicion and fear within the Turkish enemy (GPIB ORK, OIK 3121/25).

40. Victory in the Caucasus theater preceded the triumph at Plevna, celebrated in a print called "The Defeat of Mukhtar Pasha's Army." Illustrated by Dmitreev, this print depicts events of 4 October, when the Turks suffered a huge defeat at the hands of Grand Duke Michael, near Kars. This victory in early October began a revival of Russian successes in both fronts of the war, and resulted in the capture of 8,500 prisoners in addition to the 16,000 casualties inflicted on the Turks. GPIB ORK, OIK 1803 (Abramov). See also Menning, *Bayonets before Bullets*, 80.

41. GPIB ORK, OIK 3121/13. With victory more apparent, Alexander II had appeared in several *lubki* during the winter months of 1877. The Strel'tsov print "Presence of the Sovereign Emperor among the Cossack Regiments near the Danube" first appeared on 2 November (GPIB ORK, OIK 3121/15). A Sharapov picture entitled "The Presentation of the Osman Pasha to the Sovereign Emperor" features an austere-looking tsar extending his hand to the Turkish leader, who appears timid. Behind the tsar appear the heroes of Plevna, including Skobelev, while the pasha is flanked by his advisors, all noticeably shorter than the Russians. The tsar accepted the surrender of his enemy, but only after he had seen to his troops, the text notes, and in the company of the hero of Plevna, Skobelev (GPIB ORK, OIK 1948).

42. V. A. Sollugub, *Dnevnik vysochaishchego prebyvaniia za Dunaem v 1877 godu* (St. Petersburg: n.p., 1878), xliii, 114–15; quoted in Wortman, *Scenarios of Power*, vol. 2, 140–41.

43. Wortman, *Scenarios of Power*, vol. 2, 141.

44. For the former, Sharapov's *lubok* "News in Constantinople About the Capture of Plevna" ridicules the Turkish leaders for their lack of fighting prowess (GPIB ORK, OIK 3121/26), and the November print from Strel'tsov entitled "The Son of the Sultan Abdul Hamid" featured the Turkish leader's son awakening from a "dream" in which the Russians had taken Plevna and the Turks had been forced to concede defeat (GPIB ORK, OIK 1956).

45. GIM IO, *Papka* 217.

46. The Turkish fortress of Ardahan was located northwest of Kars and also served as a means of protecting the Caucasian border between Turkey and Russia. The Akhaltsykh Detachment of the Russian army captured the fort on 6 May 1877.

47. While some popular prints contained images of larger-then-life heroes, others depicted joyous Russian peasants receiving the news of the victories. "The Story of the Soldier Ponkrat, Returning from the War," by Abramov's publishing company, contains a scene of Russian peasants receiving news of the war from a returning villager. The text quotes Ponkrat: "it will be a long time that Holy Rus' will remember the days of Plevna, and it will be a long time that the savage enemy will remember the Russian bayonets!"

48. GPIB ORK, OIK 1957 (Sharapov, 11 January 1878).

49. These themes reappear in images dedicated to the Russian capture of Adrianople on 8 January 1878. The Rudnev *lubok* "Occupation by Russian Troops of the

City of Adrianople," approved on 28 January, bears a striking resemblance to the Sofia print. The three Russian generals who led the Balkan campaigns, Gurko, Radetskii, and Skobelev, ride at the head of a long column of Russian troops. Although only Radetskii entered Adrianopole on 8 January, the image links the continued victories of the Russian army after Plevna with all three Russian generals engaged in the march toward Constantinople. The image is in GIM IO, *Papka* 217. For the entry, see Menning, *Bayonets before Bullets*, 78.

50. The Sharapov *lubok* "Entrance of the Great Prince and Chief Commander into San Stefano for the Concluding of the Peace" resembles in many respects prints depicting entrances into Sofia and Adrianople (GIM IO, *Papka* 217). See also a second *lubok*, "The Meeting of His Highness, the Chief Commander Nikolai Nikolaevich and Mahomet-Ali Pasha at the San Stefano Station (near Constantinople)" (in GIM IO, *Papka* 217).

51. GIM IO, *Papka* 217 (Rudnev).

52. Rogger, "The Skobelev Phenomenon," 66.

53. GIM IO, *Papka* 217. The tone of this print is similar to "The Return to the Motherland from the Front," which is set inside a peasant *izba* and features a Russian soldier home from the war embracing his father, while the rest of his large family look on proudly. The joyous welcome the conquering hero receives is reinforced by the brightness and hominess of the interior of the peasant hut, which is adorned by a patriotic *lubok* featuring Alexander II on the far wall (GIM IO, *Papka* 217 [Rudnev]).

54. GIM IO, *Papka* 217. The capture of Plevna produced massive displays in St. Petersburg, prompting the correspondent of the London *Daily News* to write, "I have seen many displays of popular enthusiasm but never have I witnessed a manifestation which impressed me so deeply as the scene in the Kazan Cathedral [on 10 December] . . . It was no picked throng." Quoted in Wortman, *Scenarios of Power*, vol. 2, 141. A second Sharapov print from later in 1878 broadcasts the generosity of the Russian peasant soldier toward his fellow Slavs. Entitled "The Humaneness of the Russian Soldier," the *lubok* is set in a Serbian village after the war and reaffirms the reasons behind the war, its holy nature, and the belief that the Russians "freed" Serbs and other Slavic peoples from Muslim control (GIM IO, *Papka* 217).

55. GIM IO, *Papka* 217 (Abramov).

56. See also "The Atrocities of Bashi-Bazuks and the Circassians upon the Bulgarians," which graphically illustrates how Russians viewed the "Turkish yoke" upon their fellow Slavs and informed Russian viewers of the atrocities committed in the war that angered Europe. The print depicts a number of horrific actions in a Bulgarian town during the war, committed by Muslim Circassians who fought on the Turkish side (GIM IO, *Papka* 217).

57. For more on this subject, see the recent collection edited by James Cracraft and Daniel Rowland, *Architectures of Russian Identity: 1500 to the Present* (Ithaca: Cornell University Press, 2003), particularly the introduction and the articles by Rowland and Richard Wortman.

58. GIM IO, *Papka* 217.

59. GIM IO, *Papka* 217 (Orekhov).

60. The popular prints of 1878 attempted to laud the Russian tsar's role in bringing about the victory. The startling print entitled "Two Unforgettable Victories of Emperor Alexander II" contains separate panels that celebrate the greatest achievements of the tsar's reign. The first depicts the tsar standing on snowy ground in the middle of a peasant village with two huts and a wooden church. Surrounding him are grateful Russian peasants, some of them kneeling. The text at the bottom notes that this image depicts "the freeing of twenty-three million peasants from the bonds of servitude," a reference to Alexander II's freeing of the Russian serfs in 1861. The second panel contains the tsar on a white horse riding at the head of his troops, greeted by foot soldiers waving the imperial flag. On the left, several Serbian peasants kneel in joy before their

Russian hero, and the text claims that the second victory of Alexander II was "the freeing of the Slavs from the Turkish Yoke." As the image makes clear, both of these "victories" occurred on 19 February, seventeen years apart, and it helped to advance the idea that Alexander was a dual liberator (GIM IO, *Papka* 217 [Orekhov, 18 March 1878]).

61. Wortman, *Scenarios of Power,* vol. 2, 143.

62. Buganov, *Russkaia istoriia v pamiati krest'ian.*

63. Cathy Frierson, ed. and trans., *Aleksandr Nikolaevich Engelgardt's Letters from the Country, 1872–1887* (Oxford: Oxford University Press, 1993).

64. Frierson, *Engelgardt's Letters,* 4–7.

65. Frierson, *Engelgardt's Letters,* 6–7.

66. The letter first appeared in the March 1878 edition of the journal, 5–42. The English version can be found in Frierson, *Engelgardt's Letters,* 134–55.

67. Frierson, *Engelgardt's Letters,* 135.

68. Frierson, *Engelgardt's Letters,* 138.

69. Frierson, *Engelgardt's Letters.*

70. Engelgardt expresses disbelief that local peasants "knew" that the Suleiman [sic] had been defeated because "there is nothing in the newspapers yet, but there is always a rumor." Another time Engelgardt notes that the peasants thought that landless peasants would be resettled on Turkish soil after the war. Frierson, *Engelgardt's Letters,* 139–40.

71. Frierson, *Engelgardt's Letters,* 143.

72. I thank Dominic Lieven for bringing this information to my attention.

73. Frierson, *Engelgardt's Letters,* 140.

74. Engelgardt viewed his discussions with peasants as a sign that they did not know what they were talking about, yet even he is forced to ask, "on the other hand, can the muzhik remain indifferent to all of this as he carries the entire burden of the war, which he cannot feel as he hears discussion everywhere about victories, about losses, finding himself, through letters, in close contact with those of his children and brothers who have fallen at Plevna and Kars? We take this inertia and apathy to be indifference toward the cause—but is not this indifference only apparent? . . . Is it possible that everything would be done as it is done if there were no sympathy toward the cause, or, to put it better, a consciousness of the need to do something?" (143). Although Engelgardt continues to have his doubts, we would do well to pay heed to his questions and not assume that the peasants were the "grey masses" he often described. In many respects, Engelgardt's views of the Russian peasantry represents an attempt to "make the peasants backward," described by Yanni Kotsonis in his work, *Making Peasants Backward: Agricultural Cooperatives and the Agrarian Question in Russia, 1861–1914* (New York: St. Martin's, 1999).

75. A. V. Buganov, "Otnoshenie krest'ianstva k russko-turketskoi voine 1877–1878 godov (po materialam poslednei chetverti XIX v.), *Istoriia SSSR* 1987/5 (September/October): 182–89.

76. Buganov, *Russkaia istoriia v pamiati krest'ian.*

77. Buganov, "Otnoshenie krest'ianstva," 182–83.

78. Buganov, "Otnoshenie krest'ianstva," 183.

79. Buganov, "Otnoshenie krest'ianstva," 184–85.

80. Buganov, *Russkaia istoriia v pamiati krest'ian.*

81. Buganov, "Otnoshenie krest'ianstva," 185. The first quote comes from a peasant in the Kaluga province, who in 1900, recounted his role in the fighting of the war a quarter-century earlier; the second from a veteran living in the Iaroslavl region. For examples of peasant huts with *lubki,* see REM, *f. 7, op.* 1, *d.* 471, *l.* 2.

82. Buganov, "Otnoshenie krest'ianstva," 185–86.

83. Buganov, "Otnoshenie krest'ianstva," 187.

84. Buganov, "Otnoshenie krest'ianstva," 188–89.

85. Buganov, "Otnoshenie krest'ianstva," 189.

86. REM, *f. 7, op.* 1, *d.* 471, *l.* 2. For similar observations by other writers working for the Tenishev program, see *op.* 1, *d.* 1850, *l.* 11; *op.* 1, *d.* 1433, *l.* 2; and B. M. Firsov and I. G. Kiseleva, eds., *Byt velikorusskikh krest'ian-zemlepashtsev. Opisanie materialov Etnograficheskogo biuro kniazia V. N. Tenisheva (na primere Vladimirskoi gubernii)* (St. Petersburg: Izd-vo Evropeiskogo Doma, 1993), 176.

87. Wortman, *Scenarios of Power,* vol. 2, 310.

88. K. P. Pobedonostsev, *Pis'ma Pobedonostseva k Aleksandru III* (Moscow: Novaia Moskva, 1925), 109.

89. M. Ch., "Dnevnik ofitsera," in *Sbornik voennykh razskazov sostavlennykh ofitserami-uchastnikami voiny 1877–1878,* ed. V. P. Meshcherskii, vol. 1 (St. Petersburg: Izd. V. Meshcherskago, 1878), 25.

90. M. Ch., "Dnevnik ofitsera," 26.

91. Burke, *Eyewitnessing,* 140–46.

92. Ruud, *Russian Entrepreneur,* 13.

93. Ruud, *Russian Entrepreneur,* 14.

94. See Ben Eklof, *Russian Peasant Schools: Officialdom, Village Culture, and Popular Pedagogy, 1861–1914* (Berkeley: University of California Press, 1986).

95. Ruud, *Russian Entrepreneur,* 14.

96. Ruud, *Russian Entrepreneur,* 15.

97. Ruud, *Russian Entrepreneur,* 17.

98. Ruud, *Russian Entrepreneur,* 18–19.

99. Ruud, *Russian Entrepreneur,* 17.

100. Ruud, *Russian Entrepreneur,* 21–22.

101. Watstein, "Ivan Sytin," 46.

102. I. D. Sytin, *Zhizn' dlia knigi* (Moscow: Kniga, 1978), 37; quoted also in Ruud, *Russian Entrepreneur,* 24. In March 1999, I visited the Sytin Museum in Moscow (Muzei-kvartira I. D. Sytina), located on Tverskaia Street near Pushkin Square. In a lengthy conversation with the director of the museum, N. N. Aleshina, I asked about Sytin's role in developing the themes of his popular pictures. Aleshina responded that Sytin took an active role in developing the contents of his *lubki,* and drew on successful themes from past pictures. Above all, Sytin believed in his ability to articulate themes and images that would be popular among a wide range of Russians, both from his own background and from his experiences in Sharapov's firm. Conversation with N. N. Aleshina, 23 March 1999.

103. Ruud, *Russian Entrepreneur,* 27.

104. Ruud, *Russian Entrepreneur,* 27.

105. TsIAM, *f.* 2316, *op.* 1, *d.* 2, *l.* 22.

106. Ruud, *Russian Entrepreneur,* 33; Prugavin, *Knigonoshi i ofeni,* vol. 1, 289.

107. See the records in TsIAM, *f.* 2316, *op.* 1, *d.* 2, *ll.* 2–17, where Sytin's accountant records the expenses of these supplies in 1900, which ran into the hundreds of thousands of rubles on a yearly basis.

108. TsIAM, *f.* 2316, *op.* 1, *d.* 2, *l.* 2.

109. Sytin, *Zhizn' dlia knigi,* 43.

110. Ruud, *Russian Entrepreneur,* 166.

111. Ruud, *Russian Entrepreneur,* 167. The texts of the speeches appeared in *Russkoe slovo* 42, 21 February 1917.

112. Tupolov, *Pol'veka dlia knigi.*

113. Tupolev, *Pol'veka dlia knigi,* 20.

114. Tupolev, *Pol'veka dlia knigi,* 163–202.

115. Tupolev, *Pol'veka dlia knigi,* 187.

116. See E. A. Malov, "O kreshchenykh tatarakh," *Izvestiia po Kazanskoi eparkhii* (1891), 563. I thank Bob Geraci for bringing this article to my attention.

117. Layton, "Nineteenth-Century Russian Mythologies," 95.

6—Illustrating the Racial War

1. I. P. Belokonskii, "Lubochnaia literatura o iaponsko-ruskoi voine," *Obrazovanie* 13/7 (1904), 80.

2. See also Mikhailova, "Images of Enemy and Self," 30–53. Mikhailova's article focuses on the enmification process inherent in wartime imagery, and she argues that it took a racial tone in the Russo-Japanese War. Although she states that popular prints of the war "were part of an officially sponsored propaganda effort" and that "at the same time they expressed the perception of war and reaction to it not only of the intellectual elite, but of the ordinary people," she offers little evidence to support this view aside from noting that the *lubok* was "closely connected to folklore and images which had existed in the mass consciousness for a long time."

3. I borrow the term "racial war" from John Dower, *War without Mercy: Race and Power in the Pacific War* (New York: Pantheon, 1986). Dower uses the concept of race not as an objective category, but as a category of perception that influenced the Pacific War in numerous ways. For him, stereotypes and racist thinking on both sides contributed to poor military planning, atrocious behavior, and the adoption of extremist policies.

4. Here I do not mean to suggest that imperialism inherently means racism. I merely use the war against Japan and the images produced during the war as sources for examining Russian imperialism. One could easily examine the images from Crimea or the Russo-Turkish War.

5. Racism certainly could be seen as a branch of the "conquistador imperialism" prominent among many Russians at the turn of the century, described aptly by Schimmelpenninck in "Ex Oriente Lux," chap. 1.

6. Nicholas II seems to have held many contradictory beliefs about Japan and the Japanese, having traveled to the country as tsarevich. Despite the scare of an assassination attempt while on tour in 1890, Nicholas commented that he liked Japan. See Schimmelpenninck, "Ex Oriente Lux," 115–28 and his "The Asianist Vision of Prince Ukhtomskii," in *Kazan, Moscow, St. Petersburg: Multiple Faces of the Russian Empire,* ed. Catherine Evtuhov et al. (Moscow: O.G.I., 1997), 188–202. Nicholas's characterization of the Japanese as monkeys in 1904 may have resulted from the growing influence within the court of hawks such as General Alekseev regarding the Russian presence in Manchuria.

7. Menning, *Bayonets before Bullets,* 152.

8. Menning, *Bayonets before Bullets,* 152.

9. Tadayoshi Sakurai, *Human Bullets (NKF-Dan): A Soldier's Story of Port Arthur,* trans. Masujiro Honda and Alice Bacon (Tokyo, 1907), 84.

10. E. K. Nojine, *The Truth about Port Arthur.* Trans. A. B. Lindsay (London, 1908), 256.

11. *Russko-iaponskaia, 1904–1905gg,* vol. I (St. Petersburg, 1910), 290.

12. *Russko-iaponskaia, 1904–1905gg,* vol. I, 153.

13. GPIB ORK, OIK 118-a.

14. GPIB ORK, OIK 1578-a. Approved on 23 March 1904, this print was produced by the Petersburg firm of V. V. Nessler.

15. GPIB ORK, OIK 126-a. Similar language and imagery appears in the March *lubok* from Solov'ev, "The Fighting Song of the Sailors": "to fight with us, monkey, will not be necessary," and "we'll twist your cheeks off without any lead or gun—just by a blow of the fist." GPIB ORK, OIK 2084. See also Rossisskii Gosudarstvennyi Arkhiv Literatury i Iskusstva (hereafter RGALI), *f.* 1931, *op.* 9, *d.* 19.

16. Mikhailova, "Images of Enemy and Self," 42. The word resembles *"makaka,"* or "monkey," which may account for its derogatory use.

17. GPIB ORK, OIK 112-a; RGALI *f.* 1931, *op.* 9, *d.* 24.

18. GPIB ORK, OIK 103-a (a Konovalova image from 4 February).

19. See, for example, the February 1904 print from the Kiev company of I. I. Chokolov entitled "The Attack Near Port Arthur," in GPIB ORK, OIK 3034.

20. "Raeshnik," from V. Ivanov, Petersburg, GPIB ORK, OIK 2288.

21. "The crushing defeat of the Japanese by Cossacks," a Zemstov print from early February that features bloody hand-to-hand fighting; GPIB ORK, OIK 3078. The devious attacks were not limited to Port Arthur, as the *lubok* "Bombardment of Vladivostok" illustrates.

22. GPIB ORK, OIK 127.

23. In addition to the images such as "Cossack Petrukha" and "Well Done, Brave Japan," see "Clash of Russian Cossacks with the Japanese in North Korea" in RGALI, *f.* 1931, *op.* 9, *d.* 24; "Battle near Chemulpo" in RGALI, *f.* 1931, *op.* 9, *d.* 25; and "Battle at Bafangoi" in GIM IO, *Papka* 733, for examples.

24. Dower, *War without Mercy.*

25. Dower, *War without Mercy,* x.

26. Dower, *War without Mercy,* 1–23.

27. Dower, *War without Mercy,* 36–37.

28. V. I. Dal', *Tolkovyi slovar' zhivogo velikorusskago iazyka,* t. 2 (St. Petersburg: Izd. T-va M. O. Vol'f, 1905). The definition quoted the text *"Ish' ikh, kak naslazhivaiutsia, makaki!"* and also stated that the term applied only to the Japanese and not other Asians.

29. GPIB ORK, OIK 130.

30. See, for example, "The Russian Hercules," from 1812.

31. GPIB ORK, OIK 130; Mikhailova, "Images of Enemy and Self," 38–39.

32. GPIB ORK, OIK 3092 (N. N. Nikitenko).

33. GPIB ORK, OIK 3093 (Komarov).

34. GPIB ORK, OIK 3100 (Kh. A. Rumanov).

35. Both Rumanov prints date from August and May 1904, when the war had started to go badly for the Russians. GPIB ORK, OIK 3068, 3101.

36. GPIB ORK, OIK 3071 (Korkin). The other two images of the tsar consisted of a portrait of Nicholas from Komarov and a series of portraits featuring the tsar, General Alekseev, and Kuropatkin from the Petersburg firm of I. V. Evseichik entitled "The Aim of War—the Accession of Peace." GPIB ORK, OIK 3091, 3076.

37. See Wortman, *Scenarios of Power,* vol. 2, 336, 421–35, 439–80, 481. I thank Richard Wortman for his helpful suggestions relating to this subject.

38. GIM IO, *Papka* 733 (The Russian Association). See also the print simply entitled "Russia's War with Japan" that further illlustrates how publishers cast the war in a religious light (GPIB ORK, OIK 2071) (N. N. Sharapov, 10 March 1904).

39. GPIB ORK, OIK 138 (The Russian Association).

40. The reasons why Russians fought, at least as portrayed in wartime imagery, can also be detected in the Sytin print "Russia's War With Japan in 1904: On Land and on Sea." Compared to the images that satirized the Japanese desire to please the Americans and prints that depicted Japanese fleeing from battle, this *lubok* suggests that Russia's cultural strength lay in its traditional symbols of identity (GPIB ORK, OIK 133).

41. See "How I Grieved for You (A Japanese Lament)" from Ivanov; "The Japanese Emperor and his Crafty Well-Wishers" from Kudinev; and "Unfavorable Friends" from Korkin, all in GPIB ORK, and all of them containing caricatures of the British, American, and Japanese relationship.

42. See the discussion by Katerina Clark on Russian attitudes toward Great Britain and the United States in this period, particularly the idea of America as "a sort of bogeyman, the land of pure commercialism, of arrivistes and of a degraded popular culture." Clark, *Petersburg: Crucible of Cultural Revolution* (Cambridge: Harvard University Press, 1995), 56. These attitudes toward the "capitalist powers" had surfaced during the Boxer rebellion, when the Russian press sided more with the Chinese rebels than with Great Britain and Germany. Newspaper editorials railed against the West

and claimed that "Europe is paying the price for its sins," even comparing the rebellion to the "people's war of 1812." For an insightful discussion of these matters, see Schimmelpenninck, *Toward the Rising Sun,* 159–71.

43. GPIB ORK, OIK 124.

44. GPIB ORK, OIK 123; RGALI *f.* 1931, *op.* 9, *d.* 21.

45. Yulia Mikhailova connects the use of the word "nose" in this print to Russian comic traditions such as Gogol's story, and to numerous idioms that use the term in the Russian language. In this case, Russia had made fools of the Japanese *(vodit' za nos)* as well as gotten the better of the Japanese *(uteret' komu-libo nos),* who had stuck their nose where it did not belong. See Mikhailova, "Images of Enemy and Self," 41. See also the "Raeshnik" version of this story from Morozov in GPIB ORK, OIK 128 and RGALI *f.* 1931, *op.* 9, *d.* 25.

46. GPIB ORK, OIK 3070.

47. GPIB ORK, OIK 2080 (Konovalova); Bonnell, *Iconography of Power,* 197–98.

48. GPIB ORK, OIK 103.

49. Karen Petrone has pointed out that the Russian word for "courage" *(muzhestvo),* which appeared numerous times in the *lubki* of 1904–1905, is derived from the root for "man" *(muzh).* Thus the connection between heroism and masculinity is etymologically linked in Russian. See Petrone, "Family, Masculinity, and Heroism in Russian War Posters of the First World War," in *Borderlines: Genders and Identities in War and Peace, 1870–1930,* ed. Billie Melman (New York: Routledge, 1998), 95–120.

50. GPIB ORK, OIK 131 (The Russian Association).

51. GPIB ORK, OIK 1844.

52. A third image, "The Victory of the Medical Student Tarakanov," also acclaims the heroic exploits of a common Russian (GPIB ORK, OIK 1845 [Sytin]), while a final example depicts the heroism of a 13-year-old Russian boy named N. G. Zuev, wounded on 28 March at Port Arthur (GPIB ORK, OIK 3106 [Korkin]).

53. Vasilii Vereshchagin, the famous artist whose memorable paintings of war and the Russian conquest of Central Asia are familiar to all students of Russian culture, also died on board the *Petropavlovsk* with Makarov.

54. The Makarov cult gained such wide currency that the naval ministry, responding to popular pressure, erected a statue in his honor at Kronshtadt, reinforcing the belief that Makarov's death helped to turn the tide of the war, as well as emphasizing his courage and sacrifices for his country. See Sokol, *Monumenty imperii,* 169–70.

55. GPIB ORK, OIK 3009 (A. K. Veierman, 14 April 1904).

56. GPIB ORK, OIK 3031 (Nessler). Prints contained references to other martyrs of the war. A Komarov print entitled "The Death of a Hero" from 2 April 1904 used the death of Admiral Kornilov, who died during the siege of Sevastopol, as a means to link the heroism displayed during the 1850s with the defense of Port Arthur. GPIB ORK, OIK 3083. Prints such as "The Holy Martyr Georgii Pobedonosets in the Far East," "The Heroes of the Far East," and "The Miraculous Courage of the Russian Soldier from the 119th Georgian Cavalry in the Far East" also combine the notions of courage and religion, again providing a stark contrast to the representations of the Japanese enemy. The message in all three is clear—the source of the courage of the Russian soldier, a trait lacking in the enemy, was their faith, both in the Orthodox God and in their cause. GPIB ORK, OIK 3081.

57. GPIB ORK, OIK 3044 (Veiermann).

58. GIM IO, *Papka* 733 (Korkin).

59. Mikhailova, "Images of Enemy and Self," 35.

60. GIM IO, *Papka* 733.

61. GPIB ORK, OIK 3084 (Krovitskii). The heroic defense of Port Arthur more than six months after the war began formed the subject of "Husband and Wife Heroes: General A. M. Stessel and His Spouse Vera Alekseevna Hard at Work in Port Arthur." This print was accompanied with portraits of Stessel, the Russian commander at Port Arthur, and his wife (GPIB ORK, OIK 3075 [Krovitskii, October 1904]).

62. GPIB ORK, OIK 3065 (Morozov, February 1905).

63. GPIB ORK, OIK 113 (Solov'ev, 10 April 1904).

64. For more on these processes, see T. Fujitani, *Splendid Monarchy: Power and Pageantry in Modern Japan* (Berkeley: University of California Press, 1996).

65. Elizabeth De Sabato Swinton, "Russo-Japanese War Triptychs: Chastising a Powerful Enemy," in *A Hidden Fire: Russian and Japanese Cultural Encounters, 1868–1926,* ed. Thomas Rimer (Palo Alto: Stanford University Press, 1995), 114–32. See also De Sabato, *In Battle's Light: Woodblock Prints of Japan's Early Modern Wars* (Worcester: Worcester Art Museum, 1991); Mikhailova, "Images of Enemy and Self," 42–44.

66. Swinton, "Russo-Japanese War Triptychs," 114.

67. Swinton, "Russo-Japanese War Triptychs," 120–21.

68. The term "visual dominance" of Japanese national identity comes from Fujitani, *Splendid Monarchy,* 24–28.

69. Swinton, "Russo-Japanese War Triptychs," 114.

70. Image and text are in Swinton, "Russo-Japanese War Triptychs," 120.

71. See "A Dispatch on the Fighting Between Japan and Russia" and "The First Land Battle" prints in Swinton, "Russo-Japanese War Triptychs."

72. Swinton, "Russo-Japanese War Triptychs," 126.

73. Swinton, "Russo-Japanese War Triptychs," 132.

74. Swinton, "Russo-Japanese War Triptychs," 122. This image also was displayed in the exhibit *A Well-Watched War: Images from the Russo-Japanese Front, 1904–1905,* Arthur Sackler Gallery, Washington, D.C., 1 June - 26 November 2000.

75. Fujitani, *Splendid Monarchy,* 130. For a literary version of the Japanese *yamato-damashii,* or fighting spirit, against the brave Russians, see Sakurai's memoirs of the war, *Human Bullets (Niku-Dan).* In one of his more interesting comparisons, Sakurai compares the capture of Port Arthur to the Russian siege of Plevna during the Russo-Turkish War and the siege of Sevastopol in 1855 (38–41). When interviewing Russian POWs, Sakurai notes that most of them believed the Japanese to be "extremely cruel" and "merciless to those who surrender" (74).

76. Alfred Rieber, "Russian Imperialism: Popular, Emblematic, Ambiguous," *Russian Review* 53/3 (July 1994): 331–35. See also Dietrich Geyer, *Russian Imperialism: The Interaction of Domestic and Foreign Policy, 1861–1914,* trans. Bruce Little (New Haven: Yale University Press, 1977), 186–219.

77. Rieber, "Russian Imperialism," 331.

78. Rieber, "Russian Imperialism," 334–35.

79. The best account of the ambivalent view of Asia before the war and the Asianist vision of people like Esper Ukhtomskii is Schimmelpenninck, *Toward the Rising Sun.*

80. Schimmelpenninck, *Toward the Rising Sun.*

81. See Schimmelpenninck, "The Asianist Vision of Prince Ukhtomskii."

82. Steven Marks, *Road to Power: The Trans-Siberian Railroad and the Colonization of Asian Russia, 1850–1917* (Ithaca: Cornell University Press, 1991).

83. J. N. Westwood, *Russia against Japan: A New Look at the Russo-Japanese War* (London: Macmillan, 1986), 1–4.

84. N. M. Przhevalskii, *Ot Kiakhty na istoki Zheltoi Reki* (St. Petersberg: V. S. Balachev, 1888), 509. Quoted in Schimmelpenninck, *Toward the Rising Sun,* 37. See also Daniel Brower, "Imperial Russia and its Orient: The Renown of Nikolai Przhevalsky," *Russian Review* 53/3 (July 1994): 367–81; Schimmelpenninck, *Toward the Rising Sun,* chap. 2.

85. For Solov'ev's views on the "yellow peril," see Schimmelpenninck, *Toward the Rising Sun,* 82–86.

86. An unlikely and ironic exception was General Kuropatkin (himself a believer in the "yellow peril," however), who later recalled his 1903 visit to Japan: "I saw a beautiful country with a numerous and industrious population. There was activity everywhere. The joie de vivre of the masses, their love of country, and their faith in the

future were great assets. . . . [I]n all the schools of the country military training had an important place, and children and young men took part with pleasure. Military walks involved problems of fieldcraft, deployments, surprise attacks, movements at the double. In every school the study of Japanese history must have helped strengthen patriotism and the conviction that Japan was invincible. The successful wars of Japan were emphasized, and their heroes glorified. The Japanese learned that every Japanese military undertaking had been a success" (quoted in Westwood, *Russia against Japan*, 1).

87. David Schimmelpenninck notes that several intellectual currents formed the basis of Russian imperialism in the Far East, including the racist notions of people such as Nikolai Przhevalskii (a racism Schimmelpenninck compares to that of Arthur de Gobineau), social Darwinism, ideas of a civilizing mission, and beliefs that Russia had a "holy mission" to "reunite" Russia with China. See *Toward the Rising Sun*, part 1.

88. I borrow this expression from Frederick Cooper and Ann Laura Stoler, eds., *Tensions of Empire: Colonial Cultures in a Bourgeois World* (Berkeley: University of California Press, 1997). Cooper and Stoler do not include Russia in their arguments because, in their words, "the colonial pattern of reproducing difference might in theory be mitigated by the geographic possibility of absorption more readily than was the case overseas" (23). However, in many ways the "tensions of empire" they discuss are more evident precisely because of Russia's ambiguous imperial project, which certainly contained notions of incorporation alongside differentiation. For an insightful examination of this process at work in Russia, see Geraci, *Window on the East*. His description of the multiethnic empire as a "homogeneous nation-state in the making" is a particularly useful way of encapsulating these imperial impulses in tsarist Russia. In many respects, the depiction of the Japanese foe as a racially and culturally inferior other betrays the same contradictions in Russian imperialist ideologies that Geraci explores.

89. Cooper and Stoler, *Tensions of Empire*, 10.

90. For more on Russian imperialism in the Far East, and the tensions within the Russian imperial mission, see David Wolff, *To the Harbin Station: The Liberal Alternative in Russian Manchuria, 1898–1914* (Palo Alto: Stanford University Press, 1999), chaps. 1, 4, 5.

91. See, for example, Geyer, *Russian Imperialism*, 220–45.

92. Notable exceptions include Louise McReynolds's work *News Under Russia's Old Regime;* and Jeffrey Brooks's *When Russia Learned to Read*. McReynolds studied the press coverage of the war and the images of the Japanese it contained, and demonstrated that the news did not contain many xenophobic or racist descriptions of the Japanese. Focusing primarily on the coverage in *Russkoe slovo*, one of the most popular St. Petersburg dailies in 1904 and owned by Ivan Sytin, McReynolds counters the claim made by some historians that the press had seized upon Nicholas II's description of the Japanese as "monkeys" *[makaki]* and frequently used the term to describe the enemy. McReynolds states in her careful examination that she never found the term "monkey" in any description of the Japanese. Instead, she distinguishes between popular, racist pamphlets distributed during the war and the editorial positions of newspapers, as Russian editors wrestled with the "yellow peril" and how it "complicated interpretations because of what it implied about minorities in the empire." Jeffrey Brooks's work on popular literature does not address the Russo-Japanese War as directly as does the work of McReynolds, but it does establish an important framework within which to view popular Russian attitudes toward the Japanese after the war. Brooks writes that newspaper reading became common in rural Russia during the war, as peasants gathered around to hear descriptions of the fighting and news from the front. Even more popular than newspapers, war *lubki* provided visual images of the war designed to convey certain messages about the fighting. After the war, Brooks argues, Russian national identity became more "cosmopolitan" in its views, and attitudes toward Japan, which had been racist and xenophobic during the war, changed as a result. See also the appropriate articles in John W. Steinberg et al., eds., *The Russo-Japanese War in Global Perspective: World War Zero* (Leiden: Brill, 2005), particularly the article by Richard Stites.

93. I. P. Belokonskii, "Lubochnaia literatura o iaponsko-russkoi voine," *Obrazovanie* 13/5 (May 1904), 80.

94. Belokonskii, "Lubochnaia literatura." Belokonskii does suggest that the publishers may have been sincere in their attempts to portray the war as a series of "oriental stories."

95. Belokonskii calls the prints monkey and bear stories despite the fact that no images actually featured bears. Instead, he characterizes the prints in a general sense using animal figures that readers could understand: in the case of the Japanese, however, Belokonskii refers to the dominant characterization of the Japanese as they appeared in the prints.

96. Belokonskii, "Lubochnaia literatura," 81.

97. Belokonskii, "Lubochnaia literatura," 81–82.

98. Belokonskii, "Lubochnaia literatura," 86.

99. Belokonskii, "Lubochnaia literatura," 87.

100. Belokonskii, "Lubochnaia literatura," 89.

101. Belokonskii, "Lubochnaia literatura," 90.

102. The image is from GPIB ORK, OIK 116 (Kudinov, March 1904).

103. GPIB ORK, OIK 1577.

104. Belokonskii, "Lubochnaia literatura," 107. The image can be found in GIM IO, *Papka* 734.

105. Belokonskii, "Lubochnaia literatura," 107.

106. Belokonskii, "Lubochnaia literatura," 107.

107. Belokonskii, "Lubochnaia literatura," 111.

108. Belokonskii, "Lubochnaia literatura," 112.

109. Kh. Podborovskii, "Voprosy russko-iaponskoi voiny v sovremennoi derevne," *Vestnik znaniia* 11 (1904): 105–20.

110. Podborovskii, "Voprosy russko-iaponskoi voiny," 120.

111. Frederick McCormick, *The Tragedy of Russia in Pacific Asia,* vol. 2 (New York: The Outing Publishing Company, 1905), 232.

112. McCormick, *Tragedy of Russia in Pacific Asia,* 236.

113. McCormick, *Tragedy of Russia in Pacific Asia,* 239. See also the recollections of A. A. Ignatiev, who fought in the war and noted that rumors abounded in the Far East that the Japanese would cut off the ears and tongues of prisoners. Ignatyev, *A Subaltern in Old Russia,* trans. Ivor Montagu (London: Hutchinson, 1944), 199.

114. McCormick, *Tragedy of Russia in Pacific Asia,* 250–51; 238.

115. The letter was also reproduced in *Cassell's History of the Russo-Japanese War,* vol. 4, 359–60.

116. It is also possible that his change of heart only stemmed from the humiliation of defeat.

117. Alexander Pasternak, *A Vanished Present: The Memoirs of Alexander Pasternak,* trans. Ann Pasternak Slater (San Diego: Harcourt Brace Jovanovich, 1983), 85. In the Russian version of his memoirs, Pasternak calls the posters "narodnye lubki," see his *Vospominaniia* (Munich: W. Fink, 1983), 120.

118. Pasternak, *A Vanished Present,* 87–88.

119. Pasternak, *A Vanished Present,* 88. All of the prints Pasternak mentions are in GIM IO, *Papka* 734. His reference to "spider-like Japs" is only a metaphor that illustrates how the Japanese were depicted as small and swarming, as in the print "In Pursuit of Money." No *lubki* actually illustrated the Japanese as spiders.

120. Pasternak, *A Vanished Present,* 89.

121. Geyer, *Russian Imperialism,* 220–45. Ironically, just as many Russians began to rethink earlier, racist ideas about the Japanese, most Europeans, because of Japan's success against Russia, began to hold much more hostile and racist notions about them. Before the war many European travelers and authors took great pains to portray the Japanese as different from other "Orientals." See Rotem Kowner, "'Lighter Than Yellow, But Not Enough': Western Discourse on the Japanese 'Race,' 1854–1904," *The Historical Journal* 43/1 (2000): 103–31.

122. Brooks, *When Russia Learned to Read,* 235.

123. Russian Silver Age writers such as Andrei Belyi also captured the ambivalent view of Asia that had been present within Russian culture since the 1890s. See Schimmelpenninck's introduction to "Ex Oriente Lux"; and Catherine Evtuhov, "Introduction: The Silver Age as History," in *The Cross and the Sickle: Sergei Bulgakov and the Fate of Russian Religious Philosophy* (Ithaca: Cornell University Press, 1997).

124. David Wells, "The Russo-Japanese War in Russian Literature," in *The Russo-Japanese War in Cultural Perspective, 1904–1905,* ed. David Wells and Sandra Wilson (London: Macmillan, 1999), 109.

125. See Adrian Jones, "Easts and Wests Befuddled: Russian Intelligentsia Responses to the Russo-Japanese War," in *The Russo-Japanese War in Cultural Perspective, 1904–1904* (London: Macmillan, 1999), 135.

7—The Great War in Russian Imagery

1. The notable exception was Norman Stone, *The Eastern Front 1914–1917* (London: Hodder and Stoughton, 1975). Allan Wildman also discussed the effects of the war on Russian soldiers, but viewed it in terms of how it led to revolution. In addition, Wildman argued that "peasant classes generally do not feel an identification with the goals of the larger society or with any such abstractions as the nation, the state, or the empire." See Allan Wildman, *The End of the Russian Imperial Army: The Old Army and the Soldiers' Revolt (March–April 1917)* (Princeton: Princeton University Press, 1980), 37. Hans Rogger's article on Russia in 1914 perhaps exemplifies the predominant historiographical trend the most clearly. His opening sentence reads: "To speak of Russia in 1914 means, inevitably, to think of it in the light of 1917." Hans Rogger, "Russia in 1914," *Journal of Contemporary History* 1/4 (1966), 95.

2. Among these works are Jahn, *Patriotic Culture in Russia during World War I;* Richard Stites, "Days and Nights in Wartime Russia: Cultural Life, 1914–1917," in *European Culture in the Great War: The Arts, Entertainment, and Propaganda, 1914–1918,* ed. Aviel Roshwald and Richard Stites (Cambridge: Cambridge University Press, 1999), 8–31; Petrone, "Family, Masculinity, and Heroism in Russian War Posters of the First World War"; Aaron J. Cohen, "Making Modern Art National: Mass Mobilization, Public Culture, and Art in Russia During the First World War" (Ph.D. diss., Johns Hopkins University, 1998); Sanborn, "The Mobilization of 1914 and the Question of the Russian Nation," 267–89; Seregny, "Zemstvos, Peasants, and Citizenship," 290–315; Peter Gatrell, *A Whole Empire Walking: Refugees in Russia during World War I* (Bloomington: Indiana University Press, 1999); Smirnov, ed., *Rossiia i pervaia mirovaia voina;* Barbara Alpern Engel, "Not by Bread Alone: Subsistence Riots in Russia during World War I," *Journal of Modern History* 69/4 (December 1997): 696–721; Peter Holquist, *Making War, Forging Revolution: Russia's Continuum of Crisis, 1914–1921* (Cambridge: Harvard University Press, 2002); Eric Lohr, *Nationalizing the Russian Empire: The Campaign against Enemy Aliens during World War I* (Cambridge: Harvard University Press, 2003); and Scott Kenworthy, "The Mobilization of Piety: Monasticism and the Great War in Russia, 1914–1916," *Jahrbücher für Geschichte Osteuropas* 52/3 (2004): 388–401.

3. Niall Ferguson, *The Pity of War: Explaining World War I* (New York: Basic Books, 1999).

4. Modris Eksteins, *Rites of Spring: The Great War and the Birth of the Modern Age* (New York: Anchor Books, 1989); Jay Winter, *Sites of Memory, Sites of Mourning: The Great War in European Cultural History* (Cambridge: Cambridge University Press, 1995). The series Studies in the Social and Cultural History of Modern Warfare, under the editorship of Winter, illustrates the broad trends in current historiography concerning the Great War. Of the twenty-two books published (as of August 2005) in the series, only two cover the Eastern Front: the volume edited by Roshwald and Stites

mentioned above, and Vejas Gabriel Liulevicius, *War Land on the Eastern Front: Culture, National Identity, and German Occupation* (Cambridge: Cambridge University Press, 2000), an excellent study that deals with the experience of *German* soldiers. In the case of the Russian experience of the war and how it fits into this historiography, again the wartime *lubok* serves as important source material. Produced by elites, artists, and even a government propaganda agency for the first time between 1914 and 1917, the popular print continued to be consumed by a broad swathe of the Russian population. Moreover, the contents of these images drew on long-standing themes present in Russian patriotic culture since the time of Napoleon. Religious imagery, national symbols, and the stress on heroism embodied in the cult of the bayonet found expression in the popular images of 1914–1917. At the same time, *lubki* catalogued and attempted to explain the differences made evident in the Great War, particularly in the method and modes of fighting. *Lubok* artists and publishers celebrated the heroism of Russian fighter pilots and depicted Cossacks fighting alongside such modern weapons as tanks. Finally, several *lubok* artists adopted an avant-garde style in their patriotic prints during the war, combining their own interest in the *lubok* as a serious artistic genre with the traditions inherent within the wartime prints. In other words, the imagery of the Great War in Russia represented an amalgam of cultural styles that can be termed neither "modern" nor "traditional" in the sense that most historians use them. Instead, the war *lubki* show that the conflict produced a culture that combined many elements and motifs that may best be understood on their own terms and not underneath the rubric of a catch-all definition.

5. Jahn, *Patriotic Culture in Russia during World War I.*

6. Jahn, *Patriotic Culture in Russia during World War I.* Ben Hellman's article on the *lubok* during the First World War, "Pervaia mirovaia voina v lubochnoi literature," in *Rossiia i pervaia mirovaia voina,* ed. Smirnov 303–14, also reaches similar conclusions to Jahn's.

7. See the essays in *European Culture in the Great War,* ed. Roshwald and Stites.

8. That *lubok* publishers should turn to the Germans as the dominant enemy should come as no surprise. Not only had anti-German sentiment revived in Russia during the years leading up to the war, the Germans, as Hubertus Jahn reminds us, had long been the source of national clichés and stereotypes in Russian culture. In the wartime *lubok* alone, German stereotypes date to the Seven Years' War. See Jahn, "Kaiser, Cossacks, Kolbasniks: Caricatures of the German in Russian Popular Culture," *Journal of Popular Culture* (Spring 1998): 109–22. Both the commercial theaters and the Russian circus also staged performances that mocked the Kaiser in the war, and the 1914 film *Wilhelm in the Sultan's Harem* offered a racy depiction. See Stites, "Days and Nights in Wartime Russia," 12, and *Russian Popular Culture,* 34.

9. GPIB ORK, OIK 2649. See also a Postnov print from October 1914 that equates the Kaiser with Napoleon. The text notes that the Kaiser wanted "to be Napoleon," brought war to Russia, and dreamed of "subduing all of Europe." GIM IO, *Papka* 751 (A. F. Postnov, 8 October 1914).

10. For other examples of the comparison between Wilhelm II and Napoleon, see the Mashistov print "The End of Napoleon and Caesar's Career," which likens the Kaiser to the aforementioned generals; and the Shmigel'skii print "Napoleon Acquired Fame near Moscow, Charles XII near Poltava, and We near Warsaw," which compares the early Russian victories in Poland to the previous defeats. The two images are in GPIB ORK, OIK 2684, and OIK 2702.

11. GIM IO, *Papka* 751 (Morozov).

12. GIM IO, *Papka* 751 (Morozov).

13. See also the Mashistov *lubok* "Wilhelm's Damage," which features a caricature of the Kaiser in bed with sheets that contain a map of Europe on them. Wilhelm screams in fear of the Cossack about to run him through, one of the dreams that reveal his madness. GPIB ORK, OIK 2692.

14. GIM IO, *Papka* 751.

15. See also the Rikhter print "Two Friends—The Butcher and His Spouse," which depicts Wilhelm (the butcher) in a sadistic pose with the shadow of "his spouse," the Grim Reaper, behind the Kaiser. GIM IO, *Papka* 751.

16. GPIB ORK, OIK 2727 (Vinogradov, October 1914).

17. This term for cockroach, although spelled differently, nevertheless has its root in the word for "Prussian." The normal word for "cockroach" in Russia is *"tarakan."* See A. G. Preobrazhenskii, *Etimologicheskii slovar' russkogo iazyka* (Moscow: Tip. G. Lissnera i D. Sovko, 1910–1914); and D. N. Ushakov, *Tolkovyi slovar' russkogo iazyka* (Moscow: Gos. in-t "Sovetskaia entsiklopediia," 1939).

18. GPIB ORK, OIK 2661 (Chelnokov).

19. GPIB ORK, OIK 2633; see chap. 8 for more on Mayakovsky's work in the war.

20. Jahn, "Kaiser, Cossacks, and Kolbasniks," 117. For more examples of the wartime characterization of Germans, see *Nashi vragy nemtsy* (Moscow: Sytin, 1914); and P. I. Kovalevskii, S. N. Syromiatkov, and A. M. Mikhailov, *Nashi vragi* (Petrograd: Tip. L. Ia. Ginzburga, 1915).

21. George Mosse, *Toward the Final Solution: A History of European Racism* (Madison: University of Wisconsin Press, 1978). In particular, see chaps. 2 and 3 about stereotypes, racism, and nationalism in the nineteenth century. Mosse also notes that the First World War "revitalized racism in all its forms" (168).

22. Jahn also finds similar figures in his study.

23. GPIB ORK.

24. Leonid Heretz has said that wartime propaganda such as the *lubki* was effective in its intent, claiming that Russian peasants "came to hate Germans (or, more accurately, Wilhelm II as a personification of evil)," largely through the numerous prints devoted to the German emperor. Indeed, Wilhelm as the antichrist proved to be the "dominant and decisive figure" in the "Russian folk consciousness" during the war. See Heretz, "Russian Apocalypse, 1891–1917: Popular Perceptions of Events from the Year of Famine and Cholera to the Fall of the Tsar" (Ph.D. diss., Harvard University, 1993), 291, 303–8.

25. See Petrone, "Family, Masculinity, and Heroism in Russian War Posters."

26. See the publications *"Geroi Kriuchkov" i drugie pesni voiny. Shtabs-Kapitan P. N. Nesterov. Geroi-aviator* (Moscow: Sytin, 1914); *Geroicheskii podvig donskogo kazaka Kuzmy Firsovicha Kriuchkova* (Moscow: P. B. Beltsov, 1914); and *Nashi geroi v sovremennoi velikoi voine* (Moscow: Sytin, 1915). Richard Stites notes that the exploits of Kriuchkov and other early heroes of the war made it to the big screen, in his *Russian Popular Culture*, 34–36. An English translation of one of the Kriuchkov tales can be found in von Geldern and McReynolds, *Entertaining Tsarist Russia*, 379–82.

27. GPIB ORK, OIK 2794 (Korkin). See also the prints of Kriuchkov in RGALI, *f.* 1931, *op.* 9, *d.* 33.

28. The use of a white horse in this print may be an attempt to link Kriuchkov with the "white general" of the Russo-Turkish War, Skobelev, a hero whose cult remained active through the Great War. Karen Petrone points out that one of the popular biographies of Kriuchkov produced in the wake of his mythic status begins with Kriuchkov's grandfather relating to the young Cossack stories of fighting for Russia in the 1877 war, particularly with Skobelev. See Petrone, "Family, Masculinity, and Heroism in Russian War Posters," 100; the tale is from Khristofor Shukhmin, *Slavnyi podvig Donskogo Kazaka Koz'my Kriuchkova* (Moscow: n.p., 1914).

29. GPIB ORK, OIK 2748 (Sytin).

30. For a similar print, see Postnov's 1914 *lubok* "The Bravery of Our Cossack Kriuchkov," which features a large Cossack impaling several Germans, many of whom resemble Wilhelm II and Franz Joseph, on his lance. GPIB ORK, OIK 2648. A Russian reporter who visited the countryside in 1915 reported that peasants complained, "here in the backwoods we can't get any news, just these pictures of a Cossack lifting

up 2 or 3 Germans on his lance." A. N. Faresov, "Otgoloski voiny v derevne" *Istorich-eskii vestnik* (April 1915), 1990. Quoted in Heretz, "Russian Apocalypse," 319.

31. See Petrone, "Family, Masculinity, and Heroism in Russian War Posters."

32. GPIB ORK, OIK 2773.

33. GPIB ORK, OIK 2777.

34. See Petrone, "Family, Masculinity, and Heroism in Russian War Posters," 111–13, for more on Katz, including a reproduction of a *lubok* that featured his exploits.

35. Petrone, "Family, Masculinity, and Heroism in Russian War Posters," 104–5.

36. GPIB ORK, OIK 2677.

37. Petrone, "Family, Masculinity, and Heroism in Russian War Posters," 105. The print "Victory of Sister E. P. Korkina" features the bravery of a Russian woman in a different fashion. The center of the print is dominated by a single Russian nurse, E. P. Korkina, who is treating a wounded Russian soldier. Undaunted by the warfare raging around her, she performs her duties and achieves a victory of her own (RU/SU 322). The image of the heroic nurse defending her motherland also featured prominently in Evgenii Bauer's 1914 film, *Glory to Us, Death to the Enemy*. In the film, a Russian nurse disguises herself as an Austrian in order to spy on the enemy. See Stites, "Days and Nights in Wartime Russia," 19–20; Denise Youngblood, "A War Forgotten: The Great War in Russian and Soviet Cinema," in *The First World War and Popular Cinema, 1914 to the Present,* ed. Michael Paris (New Brunswick: Rutgers University Press, 2000), 174.

38. GPIB ORK, OIK 2660 (Mashistov).

39. GPIB ORK, OIK 2660 (Mashistov). See also Petrone's discussion of this print in "Family, Masculinity, and Heroism in Russian War Posters," 107–8.

40. GPIB ORK, OIK 2676 (Konovalova).

41. Petrone, "Family, Masculinity, and Heroism in Russian War Posters," 109. The translation is Petrone's.

42. The journal *Voina* featured a collection of crude ethnic jokes in one of its 1914 editions that described the Turks as cunning, greedy, and corrupt; while Olga Be-butova's novel *Bloody Half-Moon* (*Krovavyi polumesiats*) from 1915 also depicted the "savage Turk" that had become a standard stereotype within Russian culture. Films regularly showed Turkish atrocities at the front and in Armenia. See Stites, "Days and Nights in Wartime Russia," 20, and *Russian Popular Culture,* 36. To compare these illustrations with Ottoman patriotic political cartoons, see Fatma Müge Göçek, "From Empire to Nation: Images of Women and War in Ottoman Political Cartoons, 1908–1923," in *Borderlines,* ed. Melman, 47–72.

43. See Peter Paret, Beth Irwin Lewis, and Paul Paret, *Persuasive Images: Posters of War and Revolution* (Princeton: Princeton University Press, 1992), 20–26, for examples. For the impact of these prints throughout Europe (except in Russia), the most recent account is Hew Strachan, *The First World War,* vol. 1, *To Arms* (Oxford: Oxford University Press, 2001), 1114–39. For an insightful dissection of the actual atrocities committed by German troops, read John Horne and Alan Kramer, "German 'Atrocities' and Franco-German Opinion, 1914: The Evidence of German Soldiers' Diaries," *Journal of Modern History* 66 (1994): 1–33, and their longer study, *German Atrocities, 1914: A History of Denial* (New Haven: Yale University Press, 2001). To compare these prints with German propaganda images, see William Coupe, "German Cartoons of the First World War," *History Today* 42 (1992): 23–31; and Eberhard Demm, "Propaganda and Caricature in the First World War," *Journal of Contemporary History* 28 (1993): 163–92.

44. GIM IO, *Papka* 751 (Chelnokov).

45. GPIB ORK, OIK 2597 (Kudinov).

46. GPIB ORK, OIK 2802.

47. GIM IO, *Papka* 751.

48. GPIB ORK, OIK 2609.

49. GPIB ORK, OIK 1841.

50. GPIB ORK, OIK 2674.

51. See also the following images: first, the Mashistov print "A Pair of Bay Horses," which features caricatures of Wilhelm, Franz Joseph, and the Turkish leader engaged in various relationships with an obese woman labeled "Germania" (Petrone, "Family, Masculinity, and Heroism in Russian War Posters," 105–6); second, "That Health Is with the Russians, so Death Is with the Germans," which takes the form of a folk tale to tell the story of how a solitary Cossack fooled the enemy (GIM IO, *Papka* 751 [Sytin]); third, the Sytin print, "German Cunning and the Cossack's Native Wit *[smekalka]*" for a similar juxtaposition and folk tale, in GIM IO, *Papka* 751; and fourth, Mashistov's "Tale of a German, a Cossack, and Russian Turpentine" in GPIB ORK, OIK 2658; RGALI *f.* 1931, *op.* 9, *d.* 29.

52. GPIP ORK, OIK 2673 (Korkin).

53. GIM IO, *Papka* 751 (Kosvintsev).

54. Eric Hobsbawm, "Mass-Producing Traditions: Europe, 1870–1914," in *The Invention of Tradition,* ed. Eric Hobsbawm and Terence Ranger (Cambridge: Cambridge University Press, 1983), 276.

55. GIM IO, *Papka* 751.

56. GIM IO, *Papka* 751

57. See Jeffrey Verhey, *The Spirit of 1914: Militarism, Myth, and Mobilization in Germany* (Cambridge: Cambridge University Press, 2000), for how this myth, partly inspired by wartime propaganda, developed in Germany. Two other images that attempted to present a "spirit of 1914" to unite Russians include "War Wives for the Holy Cause," which portrayed a farewell scene at an unnamed Russian train station (GPIB ORK, OIK 2617 [B. V. Kudishov]), and "A Dear, Unexpected Guest," which tells the story of a fictional Russian soldier, a sort of patriotic everyman, who fights at the front and then returns home for leave (GPIB ORK, OIK 2608 [Kazan, December 1914, V. Ermeev and A. Shashabrii]).

58. GIM IO, *Papka* 751.

59. GPIB ORK, OIK 2649 (Postnov).

60. RU/SU 175.

61. See the striking Mashistov print entitled "The Overseas Dragon and the Russian Knight," which also features a *bogatyr'* fighting a dragon whose heads are those of the three enemies, GPIB ORK, OIK 2620.

62. GPIB ORK, OIK 2616 (Chelnokov). See also Bonnell, *Iconography of Power,* 71, where the print is identified as one from the 1904–1905 war.

63. The print "Accord," also presents Russia in a female form, alongside representations of Russia's allies. Russia, named Vera (Faith), stands at the center of this print with Liubov' (Love) representing France and Nadezhda (Hope) England to either side. GPIB ORK, OIK 2614 (Mukharskii). See also Jahn, *Patriotic Culture in Russia,* 24. See also the print "Russia for Justice," which depicts a woman as a medieval *bogatyr'* crushing a two-headed beast that bears the features of Wilhelm and Franz Joseph, discussed in Bonnell, *Iconography of Power,* 71; and Jahn, *Patriotic Culture in Russia,* 25–26.

64. GPIB ORK, OIK 2679.

65. Stites, "Days and Nights in Wartime Russia," 28. See also Kenworthy, "Mobilizing Piety."

66. GPIB ORK, OIK 2615 (Strel'tsov).

67. GPIB ORK, OIK 2868; RU/SU 307 (Kiev, 7 October 1914, N. T. Korchak-Novitskii).

68. See the Sytin print "Victory of the Russian Orthodox Priest," which depicts a priest holding an icon aloft, accompanied by a doctor, a lieutenant, and other soldiers, confronting Austrian soldiers at a bridge, RU/SU 343. Other prints from the war labeled Wilhelm II as the antichrist, just as Terebenev and others had called Napoleon in 1812. See the print entitled "The German Antichrist" featuring Wilhelm riding a wild boar while dogs wearing Prussian helmets devour a goat in RU/SU 736.

69. GIM IO, *Papka* 751 (Sharapov, September 1914).

70. A Petersburg version of this *lubok* that featured the Virgin Mary appearing before Russian troops was printed in a run of 320,000. Hellman, "Pervaia mirovaia voina v lubochnoi literature," 309. Morozov's Moscow firm also produced an image of this occurrence, RU/SU 357. Leonid Heretz states that stories about the appearance of the Virgin Mary at the front circulated widely throughout the countryside, and "Official Russia strove to present the war to the peasants in religious terms." Heretz, "Russian Apocalypse," 315–30, 318.

71. Nataliia Goncharova included a print that depicted the Virgin Mary appearing before Russian troops among the fourteen lithographs she published in 1914. Entitled "The Vision" *(Videnie)*, the image was printed along with several others of a spiritual nature, including "Christian Troops," and "Angels and Airplanes." See Goncharova, *Misticheskie obrazy voiny. 14 [Chternadtsat'] litografii* (Moscow: V. N. Kashin, 1914).

72. Winter, *Sites of Memory, Sites of Mourning*, 65.

73. Winter, *Sites of Memory, Sites of Mourning*, 65. Modern spiritualism found fertile soil in turn-of-the-century Russia, where its practitioners included Dmitrii Mendeleev, among others. See Maria Carlson, "Fashionable Occultism: Spiritualism, Theosophy, Freemasonry, and Hermeticism in Fin-de-Siècle Russia," in *The Occult in Russian and Soviet Culture*, ed. Bernice Glazer Rosenthal (Ithaca: Cornell University Press, 1997), 135–52. For a recent study that demonstrates how all the war's participants viewed it as a holy war, see Stéphane Audoin-Rouzeau and Annette Becker, *14–18: Understanding the Great War* (New York: Hill and Wang, 2002), chap. 5.

74. GPIB ORK, OIK 2612; RU/SU 315 (Sytin).

75. An article that appeared in *Olonetskaia nedelia* in 1914 further clarifies the way in which religion featured during the war. Entitled "How Our Soldiers Die," the article was written by an unnamed "officer" who recounted "an example of our profoundly Christian way of death." Quoted in Merridale, *Night of Stone*, 97–98.

76. GPIB ORK, OIK 2741. Nicholas II appeared alongside Raymond Poincaré, George V, Nicholas I of Montenegro, Albert I of Belgium, Peter I of Serbia, and the leaders of Japan and the United States (sympathetic friends to the Russians).

77. GPIB ORK, OIK 2740. Nicholas is surrounded by René Viviani (French foreign minister), Sergei Sazonov and Edward Grey (Russian and British foreign ministers, respectively), Poincare, George V, Nicholas I of Montenegro, Nikolai Nikolaevich (Russian army commander), Alexander of Serbia, the Serbian premier, and Albert I.

78. GIM IO, *Papka* 751.

79. Stites, "Days and Nights in Wartime Russia," 9. For more on the tsar's absence from wartime culture and its implications, see below.

80. GPIB ORK, OIK 2917 (Morozov).

81. See also the Sofronov print entitled "The Crushing Defeat of the Germans near Warsaw," in GPIB ORK, OIK 2893. The *lubok* features Russian troops, distinguishable by their winter headgear and their bayonet charge, chasing panicky German soldiers through a wooded area outside the Polish city.

82. GPIB ORK, OIK 2941 (Morozov, illustrated by Pavel Iakovlev).

83. Even contemporaries commented on the odd reliance on older methods of fighting in the Great War. Vladimir Littauer, a commander of the Russian Imperial Cavalry in 1914, noted in his memoirs that "the eastern European theater of war during the years between 1914 and 1917 was the last area in the world to witness regular cavalry action of a traditional sort," and stated that "we faced varied bodies of enemy cavalry: 'modernised' Germans, Austrians as conservative as we," and others. For Littauer, "the fighting I remember was rapidly becoming antiquated" by 1914. See Vladimir Littauer, *Russian Hussar* (London: J. A. Allen, 1965), 1.

84. GPIB ORK, OIK 2860 (Korkin).

85. GPIB ORK, OIK 2831; RGALI *f.* 1931, *op.* 9, *d.* 38.

86. GPIB ORK, OIK 2820.

87. Scott Palmer explores the relationship between aviation and military cultures in his work: "Modernizing Russia in the Aeronautical Age: Technology, Legitimacy, and the Structures of Air-Mindedness, 1909–1939" (Ph.D. diss., University of Illinois, 1997), and "On Wings of Courage: Public *Air-Mindedness* and National Identity in Late Imperial Russia," *Russian Review* 54 (April 1995): 209–26.

88. GPIB ORK, OIK 2638.

89. For more on Mayakovsky and others during the war and after, see chap. 8.

90. The text states, "the masses of Germans on foot and on horses travel with guns in the wagons, then Cossacks on the edge scattered the Germans and their guns, and amidst the Cossack hubbub, the enemy train was smashed!" GPIB ORK, OIK 2638.

91. GPIB ORK, OIK 2636.

92. GPIB ORK, OIK 2635.

93. For more on how European artists from all belligerent countries (including Russia) reacted to the war, see Richard Cork, *A Bitter Truth: Avant-Garde Art and the Great War* (Ithaca: Yale University Press, 1994).

94. Paret, Lewis, and Paret, *Persuasive Images,* 12.

95. The words stem from two 1915 recruitment posters, "Step into Your Place," which depicts British men of all classes changing into uniforms and heading toward the front, and "At Neve Chapelle Your Friends Need You—Be a Man," which has British soldiers at the front gesturing toward friends at home.

96. Paret, Lewis, and Paret, *Persuasive Images,* 19.

97. Paret, Lewis, and Paret, *Persuasive Images,* 10.

98. Paret, Lewis, and Paret, *Persuasive Images,* 28.

99. Aviel Roswald and Richard Stites, "Conclusion," in *European Culture in the Great War,* 349.

100. This denial is the subject of Horne and Kramer, *German Atrocities, 1914.*

101. Quoted in Taylor, *Munitions of the Mind,* 196.

102. Denisov, *Voina i lubok.*

103. Denisov, *Voina i lubok,* 1.

104. Denisov, *Voina i lubok,* 1–2.

105. Denisov, *Voina i lubok,* 2–3.

106. Leonid Heretz reaches similar conclusions in his dissertation about peasant reactions to historical events from 1891 to 1917. See Heretz, "Russian Apocalypses."

107. Denisov, *Voina i lubok,* 4.

108. Denisov, *Voina i lubok,* 5.

109. Denisov, *Voina i lubok,* 6.

110. Denisov, *Voina i lubok,* 34.

111. G. Magula, "Voina i narodnye kartiny," *Lukomor'e* 30 (1914): 14–17.

112. Magula, "Voina i narodnye kartiny," 14.

113. Magula, "Voina i narodnye kartiny," 15–16.

114. *Russkaia shkola* 1 (August 1915): 95, quoted in Cohen, "Making Modern Art National," 35.

115. Cohen, "Making Modern Art National," 35–36; see the following articles: *Petrogradskii kur'er* (20 November 1914), 4; *Petrogradskaia gazeta* (21 November 1914), 3; *Sinii zhurnal* (4 September 1914), 12; *Novyi zhurnal dlia vsekh* (December 1915), 42; *Vestnik evropy* 50 (July 1915), 103; and *Iskusstvo i zhizn'* 4 (1915), 54.

116. See, for example, Vera Slavenson's comments in "Voina i lubok," *Vestnik evropy* 7 (1915), in which she wrote "war is the basis on which the *lubok* grows like wild grass, choking other forms of art through its popularity," 91; P. Zhuleev, "Lubochnoe polovod'e," *Russkaia shkola* 1 (August 1915), who called on Russians to fight against the information presented in the wartime imagery; and E. Zviagintsev, "Voina i lubochnaia literatura," *Russkie vedomosti* (12 September 1914), who viewed the popular prints with similar disdain but concluded that their influence was great,

particularly in the countryside, and even ended with the statement that "good popular newspapers are necessary, and good popular books and *lubki* are also necessary."

117. See in particular the discussion about patriotism during the Great War in *Slavic Review* 59/2 (Summer 2000).

118. Cohen, "Making Modern Art National," 35; *Novoe vremia* (18 March 1915), 6; *Vestnik evropy* 50 (July 1915), 92.

119. Denise Youngblood has found that 1915 also marked an important turning point in patriotic film production. From August 1914 until the end of the year, 50 out of 103 films made in Russia concerned the war; by 1916 only 13 out of 500 titles dealt with the war. Youngblood uses this fact to argue that the Russian public became extremely disaffected with the war effort, and that Russia failed to produce "a significant patriotic culture during the Great War," which "must be taken as a significant factor distinguishing Russia from Europe." Youngblood, "A War Forgotten," 188. However, as articles published in the same volume that discuss French and British film production during the war indicate, 1916 proved just as traumatic in those countries too, leading to a decline in the number of patriotic films produced. Where Russia differed from Europe, then, was in the lack of films devoted to the experience of war produced after the conflict ended, largely because the Soviet government downplayed the war in its version of history.

120. *Utro Rossii* (12 October 1916), 2.

121. See Orlando Figes and Boris Kolonitskii, *Interpreting the Russian Revolution: The Language and Symbols of 1917* (New Haven: Yale University Press, 1999), 9–29, for more on the "desacralization of the monarchy" in the war and the role of rumors in bringing about the downfall of the Romanovs.

122. For instance, Russian students painted over German shop signs during the war, a crowd attacked the German embassy in 1914, Russians of German descent adopted Slavic-sounding names, and many instances of Germans being beaten up were reported to the police. See Stites, "Days and Nights in Wartime Russia," 18. In addition to these instances, Germans were designated as alien elements during the war, and the tsarist government actively rounded up Germans (along with other ethnic groups) during the war. See Lohr, *Nationalizing the Russian Empire;* and Gatrell, *A Whole Empire Walking.*

123. Among numerous examples from the time, this view can be detected in a poem written by Fedor Korsun, a private in the Russian reserves. Composed in March 1917, Korsun's ode "On the Old Tsarist Regime" rails against "our tsar, the traitor," his German wife, and how both "kept Russian freedom locked up in chains." Interestingly (or perhaps fittingly), Korsun sent his poem to Ivan Sytin, in hopes that it would be published. Although the poem never appeared, Korsun's thoughts on the state of Russia in March 1917 illustrated the ways in which certain Russians of the time thought of Russia as a nation and the tsar as an unnecessary part of that entity. The poem can be found in Mark Steinberg, ed., *Voices of Revolution, 1917* (New Haven: Yale University Press, 2002), 81–83. See also the letter by a Russian peasant soldier reproduced in Wildman, *End of the the Russian Army,* 113.

124. Steve Smith, "Citizenship and the Russian Nation during World War I," *Slavic Review* 59/2 (Summer 2000), 320. See also in the same issue the articles by Sanborn, "The Mobilization of 1914 and the Question of the Russian Nation"; and Seregny, "Zemstvos, Peasants, and Citizenship," both of which argue that Russia was indeed a nation in the Great War.

125. Smith, "Citizenship and the Russian Nation," 324.

126. Smith, "Citizenship and the Russian Nation," 325–27. Zamarev's diary was published as *Dnevnik totemskogo krest'ianina A. A. Zamareva 1906–1922 gody* (Moscow: Rossiiskaia akademiia nauk, 1995). Some recent work by Russian historians draws similar conclusions: in her study of military censors' summaries, Irina Davidian concludes that the "deep hatred" felt by ordinary soldiers toward the war in 1916 and 1917 "had noth-

ing to do with anti-patriotism or sedition on their part," instead it stemmed from their inability by that point to understand the continuing slaughter, feelings evident throughout Europe at the time. See Davidian, "The Russian Soldier's Morale from the Evidence of Tsarist Military Censorship," in *Facing Armageddon: The First World War Experienced,* ed. Hugh Cecil and Peter Liddle (London: Leo Cooper, 1996), 430.

127. See, among others, Paret, Lewis, and Paret, *Persuasive Images;* and Winter, *Sites of Memory, Sites of Mourning.*

128. Daniel Orlovsky, "Velikaia voina i rossiiskaia pamiat'," in *Rossiia i pervaia mirovaia voina,* ed. N. N. Smirnov, 49–57. See also Merridale, *Nights of Stone,* 98–99, where she states that "the image of the First World War was not developed, for propaganda purposes, in Bolshevik Russia after 1917" and concludes "the collective story of the war was lost in years of mass migration and civil war." For more on the October Revolution as a constructed event, see Frederick Corney, "Rethinking a Great Event: The October Revolution as Memory Project," *Social Science History* 22/4 (1998): 389–414. For an insightful study of the memory of World War I both among Russian émigrés and in the USSR, see Aaron J. Cohen, "Oh, That! Myth, Memory, and World War I in the Russian Emigration and the Soviet Union," *Slavic Review* 62/1 (Spring 2003): 69–86.

129. This parallels similar trends throughout Europe, where war weariness worsened throughout the continent, only to see a new resoluteness in the spring and summer of 1917. See Audoin-Rouzeau and Becker, *14–18,* 59, and chap. 4. While they note that resistance to the war manifested itself in Europe, the authors argue forcefully that the Great War "remained until the end a war defined by consensus."

130. Denisov, *Voina i lubok,* 35–36.

8—The Wartime *Lubok* and Soviet Visual Culture

1. *Pervaia vystavka lubkov, organizovka D. N. Vinogradovym c 19–24 fevralia* (Moscow: n.p., 1913), 3–7. See, for example, the paintings collected in the following: E. F. Kovtun, *Mikhail Larionov, 1881–1964* (Bournemouth: Parkstone Press, 1998); Anthony Parton, *Mikhail Larionov and the Russian Avant-Garde* (Princeton: Princeton University Press, 1993); and Nataliia Goncharova, *Vystavka kartin Natalii Sergievny Goncharovoi, 1900–1913* (Moscow: Khudozhestvennyi salon, 1913).

2. See Stephen White, *The Bolshevik Poster* (New Haven: Yale University Press, 1988).

3. Much of what follows borrows from Alison Hilton's *Russian Folk Art,* 245–56; and E. F. Kovtun, "Narodnoe iskusstvo i russkie khudozhniki nachala XX veka," in *Narodnaia kartinka XVII–XIX vekov,* ed. M. A. Alekseeva and E. A. Mikshina (St. Petersburg: Iskusstvo, 1996), 173–86.

4. See also his 1911 explanation of how the *lubok* color schemes inspired his own: Vasilii Kandinskii, *O dukhovnom v iskusstve* (Moscow: Izd-vo "Arkhimed," 1992).

5. Kandinsky later recalled: "I remember so well how I stopped at the threshold by an unexpected scene. Popular prints were hanging on the walls: a symbolically represented *bogatyr',* and battle scenes looking like a song rendered in color." Quoted in Andrew Nedd, *"Segodniashnii Lubok*: Art, War, and National Identity" (M.A. thesis, University of California, Davis, 1995), 21. I thank Andrew Nedd for sharing his work with me.

6. Pavel Mansurov recounted how he, Larionov, and Kandinsky would hunt for *lubki* together: "more than anything, he [Larionov] and Kandinsky wandered around the markets and looked for peasant *lubok* prints." P.A. Mansurov, "Letter to E.F. Koutun, 28 May 1974" in recipient's archive. Quoted in Kovtun, *Mikhail Larionov,* 81.

7. Aleksandr Shevchenko, *Neo-primitivizm. Ego teoriia, ego vozmozhnosti, ego dostizheniia* (Moscow: n.p., 1913); John Bowlt, ed. and trans., *Russian Art of the Avant-Garde: Theory and Criticism, 1902–1934* (London: Thames and Hudson, 1988), 45. Shevchenko then stated that "primitive art forms—icons, *lubki,* trays, signboards, fabrics of the East, etc.—these are specimens of genuine value and painterly beauty" and

claimed, "for the point of departure in our art we take the *lubok,* the primitive art form, the icon, since we find in them the most acute, most direct perception of life." Interestingly, Shevchenko specifically referred to the Old Believer prints as an example of colorful *lubki* for artists to copy.

8. Hilton, *Russian Folk Art,* 250.

9. *Pervaia vystavka lubkov,* 4–7.

10. I was fortunate enough to view a recreation of the original exhibit while in Moscow in 1999, when the Moscow Art Center displayed the prints under the title, *Vospominaniia o 1–oi vystavke lubkov 1913 goda. Iz kollektsii N. Vinogradova, I. Efimova, i M. Larionova* (Moskovskii tsentr iskusstv, Moscow, 1999).

11. *Pervaia vystavka lubkov.*

12. Kovtun, *Mikhail Larionov,* 82.

13. Mikhail Larionov, *Vystavka ikonopisnykh podlinnikov i lubkov* (Moscow, 1913). For a brilliant examination of the influence of the *lubok* on Larionov's art, see Parton, *Mikhail Larionov,* 77–95.

14. Kovtun, *Mikhail Larionov,* 82–83.

15. Hilton, *Russian Folk Art,* 252. Mayakovsky's poem "Vyveskam" can be found in his *Polnoe sobranie sochinenii v trinadtsati tomakh,* 13 vols. (Moscow: Gos. izd-vo khudozh. lit-ry, 1955), 1:41.

16. While Mayakovsky and Malevich worked for the firm Contemporary *Lubok* in 1914, Goncharova painted several lithographs of her own that were based on icons and the *lubok.* She entitled her series *Mystical Images of War.* See Alison Hilton, "Natalia Goncharova and the Iconography of Revelation," *Studies in Iconography* (Fall 1991): 232–57. The prints themselves can be viewed in Nataliia Goncharova, *Mesticheskie obrazy voiny. 14 [Chternadtsat'] litografii.*

17. Edward Brown, *Mayakovsky: A Poet in the Revolution* (Princeton: Princeton University Press, 1973), 110; Ivan Bunin, *Vospominaniia* (Paris: Vozrozhdenie, 1950), 240. The Skobelev statue later was the first one taken down in Moscow by the Bolsheviks. See Richard Stites, *Revolutionary Dreams: Utopian Vision and Experimental Life in the Russian Revolution* (Oxford: Oxford University Press, 1989), 65.

18. See Ben Hellman, *Poets of Hope and Despair,* for the patriotic responses of the Russian symbolists and for Vasilii Briusov's stint as a war correspondent. Aaron Cohen covers the responses to the war among a wide number of Russian artists in his "Making Modern Art National."

19. Maiakovskii, *Polnoe sobranie sochinenii,* 1:22; Brown, *Mayakovsky,* 109.

20. V. Bakhtin and D. Moldavsky, eds., *Russkii lubok XVII–XIX vv.* (Moscow: Gos. izd-vo izobrazitel'nogo iskusstva, 1962), 12; White, *The Bolshevik Poster,* 3.

21. RGALI, *f.* 336, *op.* 5, *d.* 9, *l.* 2.

22. RGALI, *f.* 336, *op.* 5, *d.* 9, *l.* 14.

23. Maiakovskii, *Polnoe sobranie sochinenii,* 1:22.

24. RGALI, *f.* 336, *op.* 5, *d.* 9, *l.* 20.

25. GPIB ORK, OIK 2633. All of Mayakovsky's wartime *lubki,* long de-emphasized by Soviet biographers, are now on display at the Gosudarstvennyi Muzei V. V. Maiakovskogo in Moscow. See also Mikhail Anikst and Nina Baburina, eds., *Russkii graficheskii dizain, 1880–1917* (Moscow: Vneshsigma, 1997), 141–51. Although biographers did not stress his wartime patriotism, Mayakovsky's 1914 verses were included in collections of his works. See Maiakovskii, *Polnoe sobranie sochinenii,* 1:355–64.

26. GPIB ORK, OIK 2639.

27. GPIB ORK, OIK 2643-l.

28. Velimir Khlebnikov, the Russian avant-garde poet who was conscripted into the Imperial Army in 1916, composed a poem that mocked this Mayakovsky *lubok.* Khlebnikov's verse reads: "The trumpets never squealed a signal for defeat: / 'our comrades, your brothers and sisters, have fallen.' / I'll never be proof against your power— / the cruel equation sings its song. / Nations came unwillingly, swimming / like

Poland into my mansions; / a sweet sight for the crow as it flies, / the banner of the beautiful Savior! / I will never hide behind . . . / Follow him, follow him! / To No-man's-land! / To that green field in *Niemandland,* / beyond the leaden Nieman river, / To Nieman-land, to No-man's land, follow, believer." See Khlebnikov, *Collected Works of Velimir Khlebnikov,* vol. 3, *Selected Poems,* trans. Paul Schmidt (Cambridge: Harvard University Press, 1997), 59–60.

29. RGALI, *f.* 1931, *op.* 1, *d.* 43.

30. A second print features two panels, each with a rhyming verse from Mayakovsky. In the first, a large number of Turkish sailors crowd aboard a ship that flies their national flag. At the bow a Turkish leader points the way toward the Russian port of Sinope, their target. Accompanying the illustration is the text: "the Turks with a half moon were sailing this month." The second panel features a Russian bombardment of the Turk-ish ship. Shells explode around the vessel, while the Turks on board have all fallen into the sea. Mayakovsky's text sardonically notes, "as though the Turks at Sinope have not seen a flood," a reference to previous defeats at the Black Sea fortress. GPIB ORK, OIK 2634.

31. GPIB ORK, OIK 2632.

32. See also Jahn, "Kaiser, Cossacks, and Kolbasniks," 111.

33. GPIB ORK, OIK 2629.

34. See also Bonnell, *Iconography of Power,* 80.

35. White, *The Bolshevik Poster,* 26.

36. Produced for the Muscovite company of E. Chelnokov, the print was enti-tled "Bless Us, Father." GPIB ORK, OIK 2602. Apsit produced at least four more images dealing with alleged German atrocities, all located in the same archive.

37. GPIB ORK, OIK 2688.

38. Both were published by Chernikov: GPIB ORK, OIK 2609 and OIK 2768.

39. White, *The Bolshevik Poster,* 43.

40. White, *The Bolshevik Poster,* 41; Moor, *Ia—Bol'shevik!* (Moscow: Sov. khu-dozhnik, 1967), 7.

41. GPIB ORK, OIK 2686.

42. Maiakovskii, *Polnoe sobranie sochinenii,* 1:23.

43. For the first poem, see Maiakovskii, *Polnoe sobranie sochinenii,* 1:66–67, as well as his other 1914 and 1915 war poems, including "Napoleon and I." "War and the World" [Voina i mir], the same title as Tolstoy's work, features such memorable lines as "Today / no German, / no Russian, / no Turk— / I myself / in a cannibal feast / the bleed-ing skin / from the living world jerk, / gorge myself on its meat. / Continents, carcass-like, on bayonets quiver, / cities in pottery shard-piles laid." See Vladimir Mayakovsky, *Selected Works in Three Volumes* (Moscow: Raduga, 1985), 2:27–54.

44. See V. P. Lapshin, *Khudozhestvennaia zhizn' Moskvy i Petrograda v 1917 godu* (Moscow: Sov. khudozhnik, 1983).

45. GPIB ORK.

46. First prize went to Boris Kustodiev, second to Petr Butchkin. See White, *The Bolshevik Poster,* 15; and *Russkii plakat pervoi mirovoi voiny* (Moscow: Iskusstvo i kul'-tura, 1992), 107–12.

47. Viacheslav Polonskii, *Russkii revoliutsionnyi plakat* (Moscow: Gos. izd-vo, 1925), 21; White, *The Bolshevik Poster,* 15–16.

48. White, *The Bolshevik Poster,* 15–16.

49. *Utro Rossii* (8 March 1917), 6; Moor, *Ia—Bol'shevik,* 9.

50. White, *The Bolshevik Poster,* 43.

51. Gosudarstvennyi Muzei V. V. Maiakovskogo. See also Mayakovsky's 1917 *lubok* "The Reign of Nicholas the Last," which featured a caricature of Nicholas II and Alexandra grabbing vodka and gold coins in *Maiakovskii-khudozhnik* (Moscow: Sovet-skii khudozhnik, 1963), 58.

52. The image of the sun evident in this *lubok* became an important symbol of the Soviet regime, evidenced by the numerous posters that featured sunlight bestowing

knowledge and new life on Russians. See White, *The Bolshevik Poster*, 36; and Apsit's poster "Year One of the Proletarian Dictatorship," discussed below.

53. Lapshin, *Khudozhestvennaia zhizn'*, 334–35.

54. For a representative sample of these images, see Lapshin, *Khudozhestvennaia zhizn'*, chap. 2.

55. Kenez, *The Birth of the Propaganda State*.

56. Ruud, *Russian Entrepreneur*, 173–74.

57. Ruud, *Russian Entrepreneur*, 178.

58. White, *The Bolshevik Poster*, 18.

59. White, *The Bolshevik Poster*, 3.

60. Bonnell, *Iconography of Power*, 187–224.

61. Bonnell, *Iconography of Power*, 187–224. See Iurii Lotman and Boris Uspenskii, "Binary Models in the Dynamic of Russian Culture (to the End of the Eighteenth Century)," in *The Semiotics of Russian Cultural History*, ed. Alexander and Alice Stone Nakhimovsky (Ithaca: Cornell University Press, 1985), 30–66. One does not have to extend Lotman's and Upsenskii's argument to all nineteenth-century culture to agree that the wartime *lubok* established a binary model of classifying enemies.

62. For an insightful account of the changing fortunes of Cossack identity in the twentieth century and how the Cossacks shifted from loyal subjects to potential enemies, see Peter Holquist, "From Estate to Ethnos: The Changing Nature of Cossack Identity in the Twentieth Century," in *Russia at a Crossroads: History, Memory, and Political Practice*, ed. Nurit Schliefman (London: Frank Cass, 1998), 89–123. For more on the "war on signs" that began after 1917 in Russia, see Stites, *Revolutionary Dreams*, 64–68.

63. Bonnell, *Iconography of Power*, 23. The image appears as a full-color plate in Bonnell's work.

64. See his posters "Stand Up for the Defense of Petrograd" (1919), which features a soldier, peasant, and sailor brandishing weapons; "Day of the Wounded Red Army Man" (1919) depicting a soldier treated by a nurse and surrounded by images of his rural background; "To Horse, Proletarian" (1919), which contains a proletarian soldier brandishing a sword; and "To the Deceived Brothers" (1918), featuring a peasant clubbing a five-headed beast that has distorted faces representing tsarism, among others, for example. For these images and more information on Apsit as one of the founders of Soviet poster art, see White, *The Bolshevik Poster*, 26–34.

65. White, *The Bolshevik Poster*, 26.

66. Dmitrii Moor, *Ia-Bolshevik*, 9; White, *The Bolshevik Poster*, 43.

67. Moor, *Ia-Bol'shevik*, 11.

68. RU/SU 520.

69. Bonnell, *Iconography of Power*, 203.

70. Although the enemy had changed considerably here—to imperialism, the form Moor chose to represent this enemy remained similar to the wartime *lubok*, in which Japan and Germany had been illustrated as beasts.

71. See, for example, "Death to World Imperialism" (1919); "What Have You Done for the Front" (1920); "First of May—a Festival of Labor" (1920); and "Soviet Russia Is an Armed Camp" (1919) for examples, in White, *The Bolshevik Poster*, 44–54.

72. White, *The Bolshevik Poster*, 43; I. N. Pavlov, *Moia zhizn' i vstrechi* (Moscow: Iskusstvo, 1949), 260.

73. See Roberta Reeder, "The Interrelationship of Codes in Maiakovskii's ROSTA Posters," *Soviet Union/Union Sovietique* 7 (1980), 29; *Maiakovskii-khudozhnik*, 7.

74. Stephen White, "The Art of the Political Poster," in *Russian Cultural Studies: An Introduction*, ed. Catriona Kelly and David Shepherd (Oxford: Oxford University Press, 1998), 154.

75. White, *The Bolshevik Poster*, 76; Maiakovskii, *Polnoe sobranie sochinenii*, 12:149–58.

76. Kovtun, *Mikhail Larionov*, 81.

77. White, *The Bolshevik Poster*, 67.

78. RGALI, *f. 336, op.* 1.

79. Mayakovsky's ROSTA verses became the source base for numerous children's readers, in much the same way that Terebenev's Patriotic War images served as the basis for a popular alphabet book after 1815. Generations of Soviet school children memorized Mayakovsky's ROSTA verses by heart and in doing so learned about Soviet values. See, for example, Galina Dutkina, *Moscow Days: Life and Hard Times in the New Russia* (New York: Kodansha International, 1996), 3; and Evgeny Steiner, *Stories for Little Comrades: Revolutionary Artists and the Making of Early Soviet Children's Books* (Seattle: University of Washington Press, 1999).

80. RGALI, *f. 336, op.* 1.

81. RGALI, *f. 336, op.* 1; White, *The Bolshevik Poster*, 76.

82. Maiakovskii, *Polnoe sobranie sochinenii*, 12:205.

83. Maiakovskii, "Tolko ne vospominaniia" (1929) in *Polnoe Sobranie* (1961) *Sachinenii* vol. 12, 149–58. Quoted in White, *The Bolshevik Poster*, 76.

84. White, *The Bolshevik Poster*, 114.

85. Mayakovsky, *Selected Works in Three Volumes*, 3:164–65.

86. RU/SU, 2088.

87. RU/SU, 1282.

88. RU/SU, 1968. Ironically, the United States never joined the League of Nations.

89. The Bolsheviks, as Stephen White notes, were not the only ones to use *lubok*-style prints to proclaim their message during the civil war. Numerous White posters depicted White leaders and Bolshevik atrocities in the style of the popular picture in order to persuade Russians to join the anti-Bolshevik campaign. White forces also painted over Bolshevik posters whenever they could and arrested anyone who distributed them. White, *The Bolshevik Poster*, 114–15.

90. Bonnell, *Iconography of Power*, 19.

91. Bonnell, *Iconography of Power*, 197.

92. Polonskii, *Russkii revoliutsionnyi plakat*, 93–94, quoted in Bonnell, *Iconography of Power*, 203.

93. Nadezhda Konstantiaovna Krupskaia, *Pedagogichoskie sochineniia v desiati tomakh*, vol. 7 (Moscow, 1959), 170. Quoted in Bonnell, *Iconography of Power*, 5.

94. Polonskii, *Russkii revoliutsionnyi plakat*, 3.

95. A *Pravda* editorial from October 1918 quoted in White, *The Bolshevik Poster*, 112.

96. F. Roginskaya, "Soviet Posters and 'Lubok,'" *V.O.K.S.* 6/7 (April 1930), 82. I thank Irina Aervitz for this article.

97. Roginskaya, "Soviet Posters and 'Lubok,'" 82.

98. White, *The Bolshevik Poster*. Trotsky himself wrote the declaration honoring Moor.

99. Polonskii, *Russkii revoliutsionnyi plakat*, 76.

100. See Bonnell, *Iconography of Power*, 137–68; and Nina Tumarkin, *Lenin Lives! The Lenin Cult in Soviet Russia* (Cambridge: Harvard University Press, 1983).

101. Bonnell, *Iconography of Power*, 142–43.

102. Poster art had its last heyday in other countries, including the United States, where the Second World War produced such famous poster icons as Rosie the Riveter. In both Russia and the U.S., television and films replaced posters as the primary visual media for depicting warfare.

103. For this process, see David Brandenberger, *National Bolshevism*.

104. Argyrios Pisiotis, "Images of Hate in the Art of War," in *Culture and Entertainment in Wartime Russia*, ed. Richard Stites (Bloomington: Indiana University Press, 1995), 141. Although Soviet culture remained largely Russocentric from 1941 to 1945, the government simultaneously made appeals to a large number of ethnic groups. See Serhy Yekelchyk, "Stalinist Patriotism as Imperial Discourse: Reconciling the Ukrainian and Russian 'Heroic Pasts,' 1939–1945," *Kritika* 3/1 (Winter 2002): 52–80, and

"*Diktat* and Dialogue in Stalinist Culture: Staging Historical Opera in Soviet Ukraine, 1936–1954," *Slavic Review* 59/3 (Fall 2000): 597–624; Kenneth Slepyan, "Their Master's Voice: Radio Moscow's Broadcasts to the Occupied Territories, June 1942–January 1943" (paper presented at the American Association for the Advancement of Slavic Studies annual meeting, 21 November 1999).

105. Pisiotis, "Images of Hate," 141. Between 1939 and 1941, however, when Nazi Germany and Soviet Russia were allies, the Soviet government censored any anti-Nazi references.

106. Pisiotis, "Images of Hate," 142–46. Some actors even referred to the Nazis as *prusaki,* or "cockroaches/Prussians" during the Great Fatherland War.

107. Quoted in Pisiotis, "Images of Hate," 151.

108. RU/SU, 2112.

109. White, *The Bolshevik Poster,* 123.

110. For more information about the Kukryniksy and reproductions of their works, see the excellent website Russian Posters at <http://www.plakaty.ru/authors?id=400&sort=lname>. As the collection indicates, the Kukryniksy remained active well into the 1970s, publishing posters directed at new, cold war enemies for decades after the Great Patriotic War.

111. The image can be found online at <http://www.plakaty.ru/posters?id=1154>. It is also reprinted in *Plakaty voiny i pobedy, 1941–1945* (Moscow: Kontakt-Kul'tura, 2005).

112. RU/SU 2142.

113. RU/SU, 2145. Toidze's poster "The Motherland Calls" became the most well known of all the posters of the Second World War and featured a peasant woman calling on Russians to defend the motherland. Another poster that drew on previous historical events showed Soviet soldiers on the attack, with the ghosts of Russian heroes of 1612 accompanying them in the rear. RU/SU, 2198.

114. Miniailo, "Otechestvennaia voina 1812 goda v 'Oknakh TASS' (1941–1945)," 83–85.

115. Miniailo, "Otechestvennaia voina 1812 goda v 'Oknakh TASS' (1941–1945)," 81. See also Miniailo's article "Otechestvennaia voina 1812 g. i sovetskii plakat perioda velikoi otechestvennoi voiny," in *Bessmertnaia epopeia. K 175-letiiu Otechestvennoi voiny 1812 g. i Osvoboditel'noi voiny 1813 g. v Germanii,* ed. G. B. Moissenko (Moscow: Nauka: 1988), 274–86.

116. RU/SU 2177. The image is also reproduced in Bonnell, *Iconography of Power,* 239.

117. As is well known, Stalin reached a temporary truce with the Orthodox church in 1941. This agreement allowed poster artists to include tsarist figures (mostly military heroes) in their works, and it permitted Soviet citizens to worship in churches again. The truce did not, however, produce any religious imagery in the wartime posters. Stites stresses the idea of holy war to encapsulate the new hatred directed at the Nazi invaders, but also describes how this hatred included elements of the past. Richard Stites, "Introduction: Russia's Holy War," in *Culture and Entertainment in Wartime Russia,* 2. For more on how the "myth of the Great Fatherland War" became the defining myth in the Soviet polity after 1945, see Amir Weiner, *Making Sense of War: The Second World War and the Fate of the Bolshevik Revolution* (Princeton: Princeton University Press, 2001); and Nina Tumarkin, *The Living and the Dead: The Rise and Fall of the Cult of World War II in Russia* (New York: Basic Books, 1994). For the most recent treatment of religion in the war, see Geoffrey Hosking, "The Second World War and Russian National Consciousness," *Past and Present* 175/1 (May 2002): 162–87; and Steven Merritt Miner, *Stalin's Holy War: Religion, Nationalism, and Alliance Politics, 1941–1945* (Chapel Hill: University of North Carolina Press, 2003).

118. Mark Edele, "Paper Soldiers: The World of the Soldier Hero according to Soviet Wartime Posters," *Jahrbücher für Geschichte Osteuropas* 47 (1999), 90.

119. Alexander Werth, *Russia at War, 1941–1945* (New York: Carroll and Graf, 2000), 176–77.

120. Quoted in Brandenberger, *National Bolshevism,* 157.

121. The interest in 1812 that occurred during the Great Patriotic War was not confined to posters—E. V. Tarle's work entitled *Napoleon* (as well as Tarle's studies of the Crimean War, *Nakhimov,* and *The Defense of Sevastopol*) sold well, as did S. Golubev's *Bagration* and V. Kochanov's *Mikhail Kutuzov.* V. Petrov directed the 1943 film *Kutuzov,* one of many that further revived the reputations of tsarist-era heroes, while writers like Konstantin Simonov wrote plays that bore titles such as *The Russian People.* Demand for Tolstoy's *War and Peace* also rose during the war, helping to inspire Sergei Prokofiev to finish his opera version of Tolstoy's novel. In short, as Marietta Shaginian noted in her wartime diary, "demand has developed among ordinary readers for literature concerning our Motherland's heroic past, the people's struggle for their independence, etc." Brandenberger, *National Bolshevism,* 146.

122. Paret, Lewis, and Paret, *Persuasive Images,* ix.

123. A sample of British posters from the war can be found on Paul Výsný's website at St. Andrews University: <http://www.st-andrews.ac.uk/~pv/pv/courses/posters/posters.html>. Philip Taylor notes that the poster stressing "your courage" "merely served to create an 'us and them' attitude," which harkened back to the Great War. Instead, British poster artists soon changed their tune, and made prints "in which the previous gap between soldier and civilian and between politician and public was . . . narrowed." See Taylor, *Munitions of the Mind,* 216.

124. The poster is in John D. Cantwell, *Images of War: British Posters, 1939–1945* (London: H.M.S.O., 1989). Other posters that linked Britian and Russian images included "Cover Your Hair for Safety: Your Russian Sister Does" (date unknown), aimed at British women, 1942's "Maneater," which featured Hitler as a beast gnawing on bones (the print was a Soviet design presented to Lord Beaverbrook), and 1942's "Greetings to the Soviet Heroes. Together We Shall Conquer," which depicted a Red Army soldier and British soldier fighting side by side. The first and second posters come from the Imperial War Museum's collections: IWM PST 3151 and IWM PST 0176, respectively. The third is from the Hoover Institution, UK 3725.

125. Jack Werner, *We Laughed at Boney (or, We've Been Through It All Before): How Our Forefathers Laughed Defiance at the Last Serious Threat of Invasion—by Napoleon: A Striking Parellel with Our Present Position* (London: W. H. Allen, 1943), 62.

126. Werner, *We Laughed at Boney,* 79.

127. Werner, *We Laughed at Boney,* 80.

128. Taylor, *Munitions of the Mind,* 216–17.

129. Bonnell, *Iconography of Power,* 222.

9—Wartime Culture and Russian National Identity

1. Wortman, *Scenarios of Power,* vol. 1, 222–31.

2. See Cathy Frierson, *Peasant Icons: Representations of Rural People in Late Nineteenth Century Russia* (Oxford: Oxford University Press, 1993).

3. For more on how national symbols function, see the articles in Michael Geisler, ed., *National Symbols, Fractured Identities* (Middlebury: Middlebury College Press, 2005). In his introduction, Geisler proposes that we think of national symbols as a "mass media system." Geisler argues that symbols, like mass media, have developed their own modes of articulation (in the Russian case studied here, through popular images, but also other genres such as flags, monuments, etc.), that they establish and maintain a power structure (the peasant as a symbol of Russia's strength and value system), and that they "implicate the individual members of the culture into its value systems." National symbols, in Geisler's view, also can subvert the power structure they are supposed to buttress—the fortunes of the tsar as symbol and the peasant as symbol in Russian wartime imagery support this view. Richard Stites, in his contribution to Geisler's volume, catalogs the numerous Russian national symbols that first emerged in the nineteenth century. See Stites, "Russian Symbols—Nation, People, Ideas," in *National Symbols, Fractured Identities,* 101–17.

4. The verse reads: "'Uzh sgnoiu, skruchu ikh uzh ia!' dumal tsar', razdavshi ruzh'ia. Da zabyl on, mezhdu prochim, chto soldat rozhden rabochim." It can be found in Maiakovskii, *Polnoe sobranie sochinenii*, 1:141.

5. Taylor, *Munitions of the Mind*, 2. Garth Jowett and Victoria O'Donnell also view propaganda as a process, although they see it as a more insidious attempt to "shape perceptions and manipulate cognitions." Jowett and O'Donnell, *Propaganda and Persuasion*, 6.

6. Thus, these images functioned as "national art" in two ways described by Anthony Smith: they crystallized attitudes about the nation and evoked ideas about the national community. See Anthony Smith, "Art and Nationalism in Europe," in *De onmacht van het grote: cultuur in Europe*, ed. J. C. H. Blom, J. Th. Leerssen, and P. de Roy (Amsterdam: Amsterdam University Press, 1993), 64–80.

BIBLIOGRAPHY

Archival Sources

Moscow

GIM IO   Gosudarstvennyi Istoricheskii Muzei, Izobrazitel'nyi otdel (State History Museum, Graphics Department)

Gosudarstvennyi Muzei V. V. Maiakovskogo
(State Museum of Vladimir Mayakovsky)

GPIB ORK   Gosudarstvennaia Publichnaia Istoricheskaia Biblioteka, Otdel Redkikh Knig (State Public History Library, Department of Rare Books)

MNG   Muzei Narodnogo Grafiki (Museum of Folk Graphics)

Muzei-kvartira   I. D. Sytina
(Museum-Apartment of I. D. Sytin)

RGALI   Rossisskii Gosudarstvennyi Arkhiv Literatury i Iskusstva (Russian State Archive of Literature and Art)

     f. 336   V. V. Maiakovskii (Vladimir Mayakovsky)
     f. 1931   plakaty i lubochnye kartiny (posters and *lubok* prints)

TsGIAM   Tsentral'nyi Gosudarstvennyi Istoricheskii Arkhiv Moskvy (Central State Historical Archive of Moscow)

     f. 31   Moskovskii komitet po delam pechati (Moscow Censorship Committee)
     f. 2316   "Tovarishchestvo I. D. Sytina" (I. D. Sytin and Co.)

St. Petersburg

REM   Rossiisskii Etnograficheskii Muzei (Russian Ethnographic Museum)

     f. 7   Etnograficheskoe biuro kn. V. N. Tenishev(Ethnographic Bureau of Prince V. N. Tenishev)

RGIA   Rossisskii Gosudarstvennyi Istoricheskii Arkhiv (Russian State Historical Archive)

     f. 776   Glavnoe upravlenie po delam pechati (Chief Administration on the Publishing Business)

f. 777   Petrogradskii komitet po delam pechati (Peterburgskii tsenzurnyi
           komitet) (Petersburg Censorship Committee)
f. 1149   Departament zakonov, vtoraia gosudarstvennaia kantseliariia
           (Law Department, Second State Chancellery)

Other Archival Sources

RU/SU   Hoover Institution on War, Revolution, and Peace
           (Stanford University)—Russian and Soviet Poster Collection

Helsinki University Slavonic Library—Department of Rare Books

Journals

Etnograficheskoe obozrenie
Istoricheskii vestnik
Lukomor'e
Narod
Niva
Obrazovanie
Otechestvennye zapiski
Rodina
Russkaia starina
Russkii vestnik
Syn otechestva
Teatr i iskusstvo

Published Sources

Agulhon, Maurice. *Marianne into Battle: Republican Imagery and Symbolism in France, 1789–1880*. Translated by Janet Lloyd. Cambridge: Cambridge University Press, 1981.

Alekseeva, M. A. *Graviura petrovskogo vremeni*. Leningrad: Iskusstvo, 1990.

Alekseeva, T. V., ed. *Russkoe iskusstvo XVIII-pervoi poloviny XIX veka. Materialy i issledovaniia*. Moscow: Iskusstvo, 1971.

Aleshina, L. S., et al. *Russkoe iskusstvo XIX-nachala XX veka*. Moscow: Iskusstvo, 1972.

Anderson, Benedict. *Imagined Communities: Reflections on the Origin and Spread of Nationalism*. Rev. ed. London: Verso, 1991.

Anikst, Mikhail, et al. *Russkii graficheskii dizain, 1880–1917*. Moscow: Vneshsigma, 1997.

Armstrong, John. *Nations before Nationalism*. Chapel Hill: University of North Carolina Press, 1982.

Arsh, G. L., V. N. Vinogradov et al., eds. *Russko-turetskaia voina 1877–1878 gg. i Balkany*. Moscow: Nauka, 1978.

Audoin-Rouzeau, Stéphane, and Annette Becker. *14–18: Understanding the Great War*. New York: Hill and Wang, 2002.

Auerbach, Jeffrey. *The Great Exhibition of 1851: A Nation on Display*. New Haven: Yale University Press, 1999.

Baburina, N. I. *Russkii plakat (konets XIX-nachalo XX veka)*. Leningrad: Khudozhnik RSFSR, 1988.

Baiov, A., ed. *Russko-iaponskaia voina v soobshcheniiakh v Nikolaevskoi Akademii General'nogo shtaba*. 2 vols. St. Petersburg: Tip. S. G. Knorus, 1906–1907.

Bakhtin, V. F., comp. *Chastushka*. Moscow: Sovetskii pisatel', 1966.

Bakhtin, V. S. *Russkii lubok XVII–XIX vv.* Moscow: Gos. izd-vo izobrazitel'nogo iskusstva, 1962.

Balmuth, Daniel. *Censorship in Russia, 1865–1905*. Washington, DC: University Press of America, 1979.

Baldina, O. D. *Russkie narodnye kartinki*. Moscow: "Mol. gvardiia," 1972.

Barkhatova, Elena. "'Modern Icon' or 'Tool for Mass Propaganda'? Russian Debate on the Poster." In *Defining Russian Graphic Arts*, edited by Alla Rosenfeld, 132–65. New Brunswick: Rutgers University Press, 1999.

Barrett, Thomas. "Southern Living (in Captivity): The Caucasus in Russian Popular Culture." *Journal of Popular Culture* 31/4 (Spring 1998): 75–94.

Bassin, Mark. *Imperial Visions: Nationalism and Geographical Imagination in the Russian Far East, 1840–1865*. Cambridge: Cambridge University Press, 1999.

Beliaev, N. I. *Russko-turetskaia voina 1877–1878 gg*. Moscow: Voen. izd.-vo., 1956.

Bell, David. *The Cult of the Nation in France: Inventing Nationalism, 1680–1800*. Cambridge, MA: Harvard University Press, 2001.

Belting, Hans. *The Germans and Their Art: A Troublesome Relationship*. New Haven: Yale University Press, 1998.

Billig, Michael. *Banal Nationalism*. London: Sage, 1995.

Blanning, T. C. W. *The Culture of Power and the Power of Culture: Old Regime Europe, 1660–1789*. Oxford: Oxford University Press, 2002.

Bogdanovich, E. V. *Gvardiia russkogo Tsaria na Sofiiskoi doroge 12 Oktiabria 1877 g*. St. Petersburg: Tip. V. Kirshbauma, 1879.

Boime, Albert. *The Unveiling of the National Icons*. Cambridge: Cambridge University Press, 1994.

Boitsov, M. A. *K chesti Rossii iz chastnoi perepiski 1812 goda*. Moscow: "Sovremennik," 1988.

Bonnell, Victoria. *Iconography of Power: Soviet Political Posters under Lenin and Stalin*. Berkeley: University of California Press, 1997.

Bortnevskii, V. G., ed. *Dnevnik Pavla Pushchina (1812–1814)*. Leningrad: Izd-vo Leningradskogo universiteta, 1987.

Bowlt, John. "Art and Violence: The Russian Caricature in the Early Nineteenth and Early Twentieth Centuries." *Twentieth Century Studies* 13/14 (December 1975): 56–76.

———. "Nineteenth-Century Russian Caricature." In *Art and Culture in Nineteenth-Century Russia*, edited by Theofanis Stavrou, 221–36. Bloomington: Indiana University Press, 1983.

———. "Russian Painting in the Nineteenth Century." In *Art and Culture in Nineteenth-Century Russia*, edited by Theofanis Stavrou, 113–39. Bloomington: Indiana University Press, 1983.

Brandenberger, David. *National Bolshevism: Stalinist Mass Culture and the Formation of Modern Russian National Identity, 1931–1956*. Cambridge, MA: Harvard University Press, 2002.

Brett-James, Antony. *1812: Eyewitness Accounts of Napoleon's Defeat in Russia*. London: Macmillan, 1966.

Breyfogle, Nicholas. "Caught in the Crossfire? Russian Sectarians in the Caucasian Theater of War, 1853–1856 and 1877–1878." *Kritika* 2/4 (Fall 2001): 713–50.

———. *Heretics and Colonizers: Forging Russia's Empire in the South Caucasus*. Ithaca: Cornell University Press, 2005.

Brooks, Jeffrey. *Thank You, Comrade Stalin! Soviet Public Culture from Revolution to Cold War*. Princeton: Princeton University Press, 2000.

———. *When Russia Learned to Read: Literacy and Popular Literature, 1861–1917*. Princeton: Princeton University Press, 1985.

Brower, Daniel, and Edward Lazzerini, eds. *Russia's Orient: Imperial Borderlands and Peoples, 1700–1917*. Bloomington: Indiana University Press, 1997.

Brown, Edward. *Mayakovsky: A Poet in the Revolution*. Princeton: Princeton University Press, 1973.

Brzezinski, Matthew. *Casino Moscow: A Tale of Greed and Adventure on Capitalism's Wildest Frontier*. New York: The Free Press, 2001.

Buganov, A. V. "Otnoshenie krest'ianstva k russko-turetskoi voine 1877–1878 godov (po materialam poslednei chetverti XIX v.) *Istoriia SSSR* 1987/5 (September/ October): 182–89.

———. *Russkaia istoriia v pamiati krestian XIX veka i natsional'noe samosoznanie.* Moscow: Institut etnologii i antropologii, 1992.

Buldakov, Vladimir, Sergei Kudryashov, and Genadii Bordiugov. "A Nation at War: The Russian Experience." In *Facing Armageddon: The First World War Experienced,* edited by Hugh Cecil and Peter Liddle, 539–53. London: Leo Cooper, 1996.

Bunin, Ivan. *Vospominaniia.* Paris: Vozrozhdenie, 1950.

Burbank, Jane, and David Ransel, eds., *Imperial Russia: New Histories for the Empire.* Bloomington: Indiana University Press, 1998.

Burke, Peter. *Eyewitnessing: The Uses of Images as Historical Evidence.* Ithaca: Cornell University Press, 2001.

———. *The Fabrication of Louis XIV.* New Haven: Yale University Press, 1992.

———. *Popular Culture in Early Modern Europe.* Aldershot: Ashgate, 1994.

Bushkovitch, Paul. "The Formation of a National Consciousness in Early Modern Russia." *Harvard Ukrainian Studies* 10/3-4 (1986): 355–76.

Cantwell, John D. *Images of War: British Posters, 1939–1945.* London: H.M.S.O., 1989.

Charskaia, Lidiia. *Svoi, ne boites i drugie razskazy iz sovremennykh sobytii.* Petrograd: Knigoizd-vo "Vienok," 1915.

Cherkesova, T. "Politicheskaia grafika epokhi Otechestvennoi voiny 1812 goda i ee sozdateli." In *Russkoe iskusstvo XVIII-pervoi poloviny XIX veka. Materialy i issledovaniia,* edited by T. V. Alekseeva, 11-47. Moscow: Iskusstvo, 1971.

Cherniavsky, Michael. *Tsar and People: Studies in Russian Myths.* New Haven: Yale University Press, 1961.

Choldin, Marianna Tax. *A Fence around the Empire: Russian Censorship of Western Ideas under the Tsars.* Durham: Duke University Press, 1985.

Christian, R. F., ed. and trans. *Tolstoy's Letters.* 2 vols. New York: Scribner's, 1978.

Christoff, Peter. *The Third Heart: Some Intellectual-Ideological Currents and Cross Currents in Russia, 1800–1830.* The Hague: Mouton, 1970.

Chulos, Chris. *Converging Worlds: Religion and Community in Peasant Russia, 1861–1917.* DeKalb: Northern Illinois University Press, 2003.

Clark, J. C. D. "Protestantism, Nationalism, and National Identity, 1660–1832." *The Historical Journal* 43/1 (2000): 249–76.

Clark, Katerina. *Petersburg: Crucible of Cultural Revolution.* Cambridge, MA: Harvard University Press, 1995.

Clark, Toby. *Art and Propaganda in the Twentieth Century.* New York: Henry Abrams, 1997.

Cohen, Aaron J. "Making Modern Art National: Mass Mobilization, Public Culture, and Art in Russia During the First World War." Ph.D. diss., Johns Hopkins University, 1998.

———. "Oh, That! Myth, Memory, and World War I in the Russian Emigration and the Soviet Union." *Slavic Review* 62/1 (Spring 2003): 69–86.

Colley, Linda. *Britons: Forging the Nation, 1707–1837.* New Haven: Yale University Press, 1992.

Confino, Alon. "Collective Memory and Cultural History: Problems of Method." *American Historical Review* 105/2, (December 1997): 1386–1403.

———. *The Nation as a Local Metaphor: Württemberg, Imperial Germany, and National Memory, 1871–1918.* Chapel Hill: University of North Carolina Press, 1997.

Connor, Walker. *Ethnonationalism: The Quest for Understanding.* Princeton: Princeton University Press, 1994.

Cooper, Frederick, and Ann Laura Stoler, eds. *Tensions of Empire: Colonial Cultures in a Bourgeois World.* Berkeley: University of California Press, 1997.

Cork, Richard. *A Bitter Truth: Avant-Garde Art and the Great War.* New Haven: Yale University Press, 1994.

Corney, Frederick. "Rethinking a Great Event: The October Revolution as Memory Project." *Social Science History* 22/4 (1998): 389–414.

Coupe, William. "German Cartoons of the First World War." *History Today* 42 (1992): 23–31.

Cracraft, James. *The Petrine Revolution in Russian Imagery*. Chicago: University of Chicago Press, 1997.

Cracraft, James, and Daniel Rowland, eds. *Architectures of Russian Identity: 1500 to the Present*. Ithaca: Cornell University Press, 2003.

Crummey, Robert. *The Old Believers and the World of the Antichrist: The Vyg Community and the Russian State, 1694–1855*. Madison: University of Wisconsin Press, 1970.

Cull, Nicholas J., David Culbert, and David Welch, eds., *Propaganda and Mass Persuasion: A Historical Encyclopedia, 1500 to the Present*. Santa Barbara: ABC-CLIO, 2003.

Curtiss, John. *Russia's Crimean War*. Durham: Duke University Press, 1977.

Custine, Astolphe de. *Letters From Russia*. New York: New York Review of Books, 2002.

Dal', V. I. *Tolkovyi slovar' zhivogo velikorusskago iazyka*. 4 vols. St. Petersburg: Izd. T-va M. O. Vol'f, 1905.

Danilov, Iu. N. *Rossiia v mirovoi voine 1914–1915 gg*. Berlin: "Slovo," 1924.

Danilova, I. E., ed. *Mir narodnoi kartinki, nauchnoi konferentsii "vipperovskie chtenila-1997."* Moscow: Progress—Traditsiia, 1999.

———, ed. *Narodnaia graviura i fol'klor v Rossii XVII-XIX vv. (k 150-letiiu so dnia rozhdeniia D. A. Rovinskogo)*. Moscow: Sov. khudozhnik, 1976.

Davidian, Irina. "The Russian Soldier's Morale from the Evidence of Tsarist Military Censorship." In *Facing Armageddon: The First World War Experienced*, edited by Hugh Cecil and Peter Liddle, 425–33. London: Leo Cooper, 1996.

Davydov, N. V. *Iz proshlogo*. Moscow: Tip. T-va I.D. Sytina, 1914.

Demm, Eberhard. "Propaganda and Caricature in the First World War." *Journal of Contemporary History* 28 (1993): 163–92.

Denikin, Anton I. *The Career of a Tsarist Officer: Memoirs, 1872–1916*. Translated by Margaret Patoski. Minneapolis: University of Minnesota Press, 1975.

Denisov, V. *Voina i lubok*. Petrograd: Izd. Novago zhurnala dlia vsiekh, 1916.

Dinershtein, E. A. *I. D. Sytin*. Moscow: "Kniga," 1983.

Donald, Diana. *The Age of Caricature: Satirical Prints in the Reign of George III*. New Haven: Yale University Press, 1996.

Dower, John. *War Without Mercy: Race and Power in the Pacific War*. New York: Pantheon Books, 1986.

Durova, Nadezhda. *The Cavalry Maiden: Journals of a Russian Officer in the Napoleonic Wars*. Translated by Mary Fleming Zirin. Bloomington: Indiana University Press, 1988.

Dutkina, Galina. *Moscow Days: Life and Hard Times in the New Russia*. New York: Kodansha International, 1996.

Edele, Mark. "Paper Soldiers: The World of the Soldier Hero According to Soviet Wartime Posters." *Jahrbücher für Geschichte Osteuropas* 47 (1999): 89–108.

Edgerton, Robert. *Death or Glory: The Legacy of the Crimean War*. Boulder: Westview Press, 1999.

Efimova, A., and L. Manovich, eds. *Tekstura: Russian Essays on Visual Culture*. Chicago: University of Chicago Press, 1993.

Eklof, Ben. *Russian Peasant Schools: Officialdom, Village Culture, and Popular Pedagogy, 1861–1914*. Berkeley: University of California Press, 1986.

Eklof, Ben, John Bushnell, and Larissa Zakharova, eds., *Russia's Great Reforms, 1855–1881*. Bloomington: Indiana University Press, 1994.

Eley, Geoff, and Ronald Grigor Suny, eds. *Becoming National: A Reader*. Oxford: Oxford University Press, 1996.

Ely, Christopher. *This Meager Nature: Landscape and National Identity in Imperial Russia*. DeKalb: Northern Illinois University Press, 2002.

Engel, Barbara Alpern. "Not By Bread Alone: Subsistence Riots in Russia During World War I." *The Journal of Modern History* 69/4 (December 1997): 696–721.

Engelgardt, Aleksandr Nikolaevich. *Letters from the Country, 1872–1887.* Edited and translated by Cathy Frierson. Oxford: Oxford University Press, 1993.

Erofeev, N. A. *Tumannyi Al'bion. Angliia i anglichane glazami russkikh (1825–1853 gg.).* Moscow: Nauka, 1982.

Etlin, R., ed. *Nationalism in the Visual Arts.* Hanover: University Press of New England, 1991.

Eventov, I. *Maiakovskii-plakatist.* Leningrad: Iskusstvo, 1940.

Evtuhov, Catherine. *The Cross and the Sickle: Sergei Bulgakov and the Fate of Russian Religious Philosophy.* Ithaca: Cornell University Press, 1997.

Ezerskaia, I. A., and Iu. F. Prudnikov, *Nedarom pomnit vsia Rossiia. Otechestvennaia voina 1812 goda.* Moscow: Sov. Rossiia, 1986.

Facos, Michelle, and Sharon Hirsh, eds. *Art, Culture, and National Identity in Fin-de-Siècle Europe.* Cambridge: Cambridge University Press, 2003.

Farrell, Dianne Ecklund. "Popular Prints in the Cultural History of Eighteenth-Century Russia." Ph.D. diss., University of Wisconsin, Madison, 1980.

Feuer, Kathryn. *Tolstoy and the Genesis of War and Peace.* Ithaca: Cornell University Press, 1996.

Figes, Orlando. *Natasha's Dance: A Cultural History of Russia.* New York: Metropolitan Books, 2002.

———. *A People's Tragedy: A History of the Russian Revolution.* New York: Vintage, 1996.

Figes, Orlando, and Boris Kolonitskii. *Interpreting the Russian Revolution: The Language and Symbols of 1917.* New Haven: Yale University Press, 1999.

Firsov, B. M., and I. G. Kiseleva, eds. *Byt velikorusskikh krest'ian-zemlepashtsev. Opisanie materialov Etnograficheskogo biuro kniazia V. N. Tenisheva (na primere Vladimirskoi gubernii).* St. Petersburg: Izd-vo Evropeiskogo Doma, 1993.

Frank, Stephen, and Mark Steinberg, eds. *Cultures in Flux: Lower-Class Values, Practices, and Resistance in Late Imperial Russia.* Princeton: Princeton University Press, 1994.

Franklin, Simon, and Emma Widdis, eds. *National Identity in Russian Culture.* Cambridge: Cambridge University Press, 2004.

Freedberg, David. *The Power of Images: Studies in the History and Theory of Response.* Chicago: University of Chicago Press, 1989.

Frierson, Cathy. *Peasant Icons: Representations of Rural People in Late Nineteenth-Century Russia.* Oxford: Oxford University Press, 1993.

Fujitani, T. *Splendid Monarchy: Power and Pageantry in Modern Japan.* Berkeley: University of California Press, 1996.

Fuller, William. *Strategy and Power in Russia, 1600–1914.* New York: The Free Press, 1992.

Fyfe, Gordon, and John Law, eds. *Picturing Power: Visual Depiction and Social Relations.* London: Routledge, 1988.

Galaktionov, I. *Lubok. Russkaia narodnyia kartinki. Doklad.* Petrograd: Tip. red. period. izd. M-va finansov, 1915.

Gatrell, Peter. *A Whole Empire Walking: Refugees in Russia during World War I.* Bloomington: Indiana University Press, 1999.

Gazenkampf, M. *Moi dnevnik 1877–1878 gg.* St. Petersburg: Komissioner voen.-uchebnykh zavedenii, 1908.

Geisler, Michael, ed. *National Symbols, Fractured Identities.* Middlebury: Middlebury College Press, 2005.

Gellner, Ernest. *Nations and Nationalism.* Ithaca: Cornell University Press, 1983.

Genets, Andrew. "The Life, Death, and Resurrection of the Cathedral of Christ the Savior, Moscow." *History Workshop Journal* 46 (1998): 63–95.

Geraci, Robert, and Michael Khodarkovsky, eds. *Of Religion and Empire: Missions, Conversion, and Tolerance in Tsarist Russia.* Ithaca: Cornell University Press, 2001.

————. *Window on the East: National and Imperial Identities in Late Tsarist Russia*. Ithaca: Cornell University Press, 2001.

"Geroi Kriuchkov" i drugie pesni voiny. Shtabs-Kapitan P. N. Nesterov: geroi-aviator. Moscow: Sytin, 1914.

Geroicheskii podvig donskogo kazaka Kuz'my Firsovicha Kriuchkova. Moscow: P. B. Beltsov, 1914.

Gillis, John, ed. *Commemorations: The Politics of National Identity*. Princeton: Princeton University Press, 1994.

Glinka, V. M. *Otechestvennaia voina 1812 goda v khudozhestvennykh i istoricheskikh pamiatnikakh iz sobranii ermitazha*. Leningrad: Izd-vo Gos. Ermitazha, 1963.

Gollerbakh, E. *Istoriia graviury i litografii v Rossii*. Moscow: Gosudarstvennoe izdatel'stvo, 1923.

Golovin(e), Nicholas V. *The Russian Army in the World War*. New Haven: Yale University Press, 1931.

Golyshev, I. A. "Kartinnoe i knizhnoe narodnoe proizvodstvo i torgovlia." *Russkaia starina* 49/3 (1886): 679–726.

Gombrich, E. H. *Art and Illusion: A Study in the Psychology of Pictorial Representation*. Princeton: Princeton University Press, 1984.

Goncharova, Nataliia. *Misticheskie obrazy voiny. Chetyrnadtsat' litografii*. Moscow: V. N. Kashin, 1914.

————. *Vystavka kartin Natalii Sergievny Goncharovoi, 1900–1913*. Moscow: Khudozhestvennyi salon, 1913.

Gordienko, I. M. *Iz boevogo proshlogo, 1914–1918 gg*. Moscow: Gos. izd-vo polit. lit-ry, 1957.

Gorelov, A. A. "Otechestvennaia voina 1812 goda i russkoe narodnoe tvorchestvo." In *Otechestvennaia voina 1812 goda i russkaia literatura XIX veka*, edited by V. Iu. Troitskii, 5–57. Moscow: "Nasledie," 1998.

Gorskii, A. A., A. I. Kupriianov, and L. N. Pushkarev. *Tsar i tsarstvo v russkom obshchestvennom soznanii*. Moscow: In-t rossiiskoi istorii RAN, 1999.

Goulzadian, Anne. *L'Empire du Dernier Tsar. 410 cartes postales, 1896–1917*. Paris: Editions Astrid, 1982.

Gray, Camilla. *The Russian Experiment in Art, 1863–1922*. Revised by Marian Burleigh-Motley. London: Thames and Hudson, 1986.

Gray, Rosalind Polly. "The Real and the Ideal in the Work of Aleksei Venetsianov." *Russian Review* 58 (October 1999): 655–75.

————. *Russian Genre Painting in the Nineteenth Century*. Oxford: Oxford University Press, 2000.

Greene, F. V. *Sketches of Army Life in Russia*. New York: Scribner's, 1880.

Greenfeld, Liah. *Nationalism: Five Roads to Modernity*. Cambridge, MA: Harvard University Press, 1992.

Gromyko, M. M. *Mir russkoi derevni*. Moscow: Molodaia Gvardiia, 1991.

Gulin, A. V. "Istoricheskie istochniki v 'Voine i mire' L. N. Tolstogo." In *Otechestvennaia voina 1812 goda i russkaia literatura xix veka*, edited by V. Iu. Troitskii, 344–68. Moscow: "Nasledie," 1998.

Gusev, N. N. *Lev Nikolaevich Tolstoi. Materialy k biografii s 1828 po 1855 god*. Moscow: Izd-vo Akademii nauk SSSR, 1954.

Hagemann, Karen. "Francophobia and Patriotism: Anti-French Images and Sentiments in Prussia and Northern Germany during the Anti-Napoleonic Wars." *French History* 18/4 (December 2004): 404–25.

————. *'Mannlicher Muth und Teutsche Ehre.' Nation, Militär, und Geschlecht zur Zeit der Antinapoleonischen Krige Preussens*. Paderborn: F. Schöningh, 2002.

Hallett, Mark. *The Spectacle of Difference: Graphic Satire in the Age of Hogarth*. New Haven: Yale University Press, 1999.

Hartley, Janet. "Russia in 1812, Part 1: The French Presence in the *Gubernii* of Smolensk and Mogilev." *Jarbücher für Geschichte Osteuropas* 38 (1990): 178–98.

———. "Russia in 1812, Part 2: The Russian Administration of Kaluga *Gubernija.*" *Jahrbücher für Geschichte Osteuropas* 38 (1990): 399–416.

Haskell, Francis. *History and Its Images: Art and the Interpretation of the Past.* New Haven: Yale University Press, 1993.

Hastings, Adrian. *The Construction of Nationhood: Ethnicity, Religion, and Nationalism.* Cambridge: Cambridge University Press, 1997.

Hellberg, Elena. "Folklore, Might, and Glory." *Nordic Journal of Soviet and East European Studies* 3/2 (1986): 9–20.

———. "The Hero in Popular Pictures: Russian *Lubok* and Soviet Poster." In *Populäre Bildmedien,* edited by R. Brednich and A. Hartmann, 171–91. Göttingen: Volker Schmerse, 1989.

Hellberg-Hirn, Elena. *Soil and Soul: The Symbolic World of Russianness.* Aldershot: Ashgate, 1998.

Hellman, Ben. *Poets of Hope and Despair: The Russian Symbolists in War and Revolution, 1914–1918.* Helsinki: Institute for Russian and East European Studies, 1995.

Heretz, Leonid. "Russian Apocalypse, 1891–1917: Popular Perceptions of Events from the Year of Famine and Cholera to the Fall of the Tsar." Ph.D. diss., Harvard University, 1993.

Hilton, Alison. "Natalia Goncharova and the Iconography of Revelation." *Studies in Iconography* (Fall 1991): 232–57.

———. *Russian Folk Art.* Bloomington: Indiana University Press, 1995.

Hobsbawm, E. J. *Nations and Nationalism since 1780: Programme, Myth, Reality.* 2nd ed. Cambridge: Cambridge University Press, 1992.

Hobsbawm, Eric, and Terence Ranger, eds. *The Invention of Tradition.* Cambridge: Cambridge University Press, 1983.

Hodge, Thomas. "Susanin, Two Glinkas, and Ryleev: History Making in *A Life for the Tsar.*" In *Intersections and Transpositions: Russian Music, Literature, and Society,* edited by Andrew Wachtel, 3–19. Evanston: Northwestern University Press, 1998.

Hoffmann, David. *Stalinist Values: The Cultural Norms of Soviet Modernity, 1917–1941.* Ithaca: Cornell University Press, 2003.

Holquist, Peter. "From Estate to Ethnos: The Changing Nature of Cossack Identity in the Twentieth Century." In *Russia at a Crossroads: History, Memory, and Political Practice,* edited by Nurit Schliefman, 89–123. London: Frank Cass, 1998.

———. *Making War, Forging Revolution: Russia's Continuum of Crisis, 1914–1921.* Cambridge, MA: Harvard University Press, 2002.

Horne, John, and Alan Kramer. "German 'Atrocities' and Franco-German Opinion, 1914: The Evidence of German Soldiers' Diaries." *Journal of Modern History* 66 (1994): 1–33.

———. *German Atrocities, 1914: A History of Denial.* New Haven: Yale University Press, 2001.

Hosking, Geoffrey. *Russia: People and Empire, 1552–1917.* Cambridge, MA: Harvard University Press, 1997.

———. "The Second World War and Russian National Consciousness." *Past and Present* 175/1 (May 2002): 162–87.

Hosking, Geoffrey, and George Schöpflin, eds. *Myths and Nationhood.* London: Routledge, 1997.

Hosking, Geoffrey, and Robert Service, eds. *Russian Nationalism Past and Present.* New York: St. Martin's Press, 1998.

Howard, Michael. *The Lessons of History.* Oxford: Oxford University Press, 1991.

Hroch, Miroslav. "From National Movement to the Fully Formed Nation: The Nation-Building Process in Europe." In *Becoming National: A Reader,* edited by Geoff Eley and Ronald Grigor Suny, 60–77. Oxford: Oxford University Press, 1996.

Hubbs, Joanna. *Mother Russia: The Feminine Myth in Russian Culture.* Bloomington: Indiana University Press, 1988.

BIBLIOGRAPHY | 255

Hudson, Hugh. "An Unimaginable Community: The Failure of Nationalism in Russia during the Nineteenth and Early Twentieth Centuries." *Russian History/Histoire Russe* 26/3 (Fall 1999): 299–314.
Iablonovskii, Aleksandr. *Rodnye kartinki.* 3 vols. Moscow: Sytin, 1912–1913.
Ianov, A. L. *Rossiia protiv Rossii. Ocherki istorii russkogo natsionalizma, 1825–1921.* Novosibirsk: "Sibirskii khronograf," 1999.
Ignatyev, A. A. *A Subaltern in Old Russia.* Translated by Ivor Montagu. London: Hutchinson and Co., 1944.
Itkina, E. I. *Russkii risovannyi lubok kontsa XVIII-nachala XX veka.* Moscow: Russkaia kniga, 1992.
Ivanov, E. P. *Russkii narodnyi lubok, s 90 odnots etnymi i 13 krasochnymi reproduktsiiami.* Moscow: Izogiz, 1937.
Jahn, Hubertus. "Kaiser, Cossacks, and Kolbasniks: Caricatures of the German in Russian Popular Culture." *Journal of Popular Culture* (Spring 1998): 109–22.
———. *Patriotic Culture in Russia during World War I.* Ithaca: Cornell University Press, 1995.
Jenks, Andrew. *Russia in a Box: Art and Identity in an Age of Revolution.* DeKalb: Northern Illinois University Press, 2005.
Jones, Adrian. "Easts and Wests Befuddled: Russian Intelligentsia Responses to the Russo-Japanese War." In *The Russo-Japanese War in Cultural Perspective, 1904–05,* edited by David Wells and Sandra Wilson, 134–59. New York: St. Martin's Press, 1999.
Jowett, Garth, and Victoria O'Donnell. *Propaganda and Persuasion.* Thousand Oaks: Sage Publications, 1999.
Kaganovich, A. *Ivan Ivanovich Terebenev, 1780–1815.* Moscow: Iskusstvo, 1956.
Kandinsky, Wassily. *O dukhovnom v iskusstve.* Moscow: Izd-vo "Arkhimed," 1992.
Kantor, A. M. *Dukhovnyi mir russkogo gorozhanina.* Moscow: RGGU, 1999.
Karabanov, N. V. *Otechestvennaia voina v izobrazhenii russkikh pisatelei. Istoricheskaia khrestomatiia so mnozhestvem illustratsii snimkov s kartin russkikh i inostrannykh khudozhnikov i portretov geroev 1812 goda.* Moscow: V. N. Sablin, 1912.
Karshan, Donald. *Malevich, the Graphic Work, 1913–1930: A Print Catalogue Raisonne.* Jerusalem: Israel Museum, 1975.
Kartinki voina russkikh s nemtsami. Petrograd: Sklad izd. u V. I. Uspenskago, 1914–1916?
Kasianova, K. *O russkom natsionalnom kharaktere.* Moscow: Institut natsional'noi modeli ekonomiki, 1994.
Keller, Ulrich. *The Ultimate Spectacle: A Visual History of the Crimean War.* Amsterdam: Gordon and Breach Publishers, 2001.
Kelly, Aileen. *Toward Another Shore: Russian Thinkers between Necessity and Chance.* New Haven: Yale University Press, 1998.
Kelly, Catriona. "Popular Culture." In *The Cambridge Companion to Modern Russian Culture,* edited by Nicholas Rzhevsky, 125–58. Cambridge: Cambridge University Press, 1998.
———. "Territories of the Eye: The Russian Peep Show (Raek) and Pre-Revolutionary Visual Culture." *Journal of Popular Culture* 31/4 (Spring 1998): 49–74.
Kelly, Catriona, and David Sheperd, eds. *Constructing Russian Culture in the Age of Revolution, 1881–1940.* Oxford: Oxford University Press, 1998.
———, eds. *Russian Cultural Studies: An Introduction.* Oxford: Oxford University Press, 1998.
Kenez, Peter. *The Birth of the Propaganda State: Soviet Methods of Mass Mobilization, 1917–1929.* Cambridge: Cambridge University Press, 1985.
Kenworthy, Scott. "The Mobilization of Piety: Monasticism and the Great War in Russia, 1914–1916." *Jahrbücher für Geschichte Osteuropas* 52/3 (2004): 388–401.

Khlebnikov, Velimir. *Collected Works of Velimir Khlebnikov*. Vol. 3, *Selected Poems*. Translated by Paul Schmidt. Cambridge, MA: Harvard University Press, 1997.

Khromov, O. R. *Russkaia lubochnaia kniga, XVII-XIX vekov*. Moscow: "Pamiatniki istoricheskoi mysli," 1998.

Khudushina, I. F. *Tsar', Bog, Rossiia. Samosoznanie russkogo dvorianstva konets XVII-pervaia tret' XIX vv.* Moscow: Institut filosofii RAN, 1995.

Kitromilides, Paschalis. "'Imagined Communities' and the Origins of the National Question in the Balkans." *European History Quarterly* 19/2 (1989): 149–92.

Kizenko, Nadieszda. *A Prodigal Saint: Father John of Kronstadt and the Russian People*. University Park: Pennsylvania State University Press, 2000.

Klepikov, S. A. *Lubok*. Moscow: Izd-vo Gos. literaturnogo muzeia, 1939.

Knight, Alan. "Peasants into Patriots: Thoughts on the Making of the Mexican Nation." *Mexican Studies/Estudios Mexicanos* 10/1 (Winter 1994): 135–161.

———. "Popular Culture and the Revolutionary State in Mexico, 1910–1940." *Hispanic American Historical Review* 74/3 (1994): 393–444.

Knight, Nathaniel. "Grigor'ev in Orenburg, 1851–1862: Russian Orientalism in the Service of Empire?" *Slavic Review* 59/1 (Spring 2000): 74–100.

Knox, Alfred. *With the Russian Army, 1914–1917*. London: Hutchinson and Co., 1921.

Koialovich, M. O. *Istoriia russkogo samosoznaniia*. Minsk: "Luchi Sofii," 1997.

Kolakowski, Leszek. *The Presence of Myth*. Translated by Adam Czerniawski. Chicago: University of Chicago Press, 1989.

Kolonitskii, B. I. *Simvoly vlasti i bor'ba za vlast'. K izucheniiu politicheskoi kul'tury rossiiskoi revoliutsii 1917 goda*. St. Petersburg: Dmitrii Bulanin, 2001.

Konechnyi, A. "Raek v sisteme peterburgskoi narodnoi kul'tury." *Russkii fol'klor* 25 (1989): 123–38.

Konechnyi, A. M., A. V. Leifert, and A. Ia. Aleekseev-Iakovlev, eds. *Petersburgskie balagany*. St. Petersburg: Giperion, 2000.

Koni, A. F. *Ocherki i vospominaniia. Publichnyia chteniia rechi, stat'i, i zamiatki*. St. Petersburg: A. S. Suvorin, 1906.

Kornblatt, Judith Deutsch. *The Cossack Hero in Russian Literature: A Study in Cultural Mythology*. Madison: University of Wisconsin Press, 1992.

Kostin, Boris. *Skobelev*. Moscow: Voen. izd-vo, 1990.

Kotsonis, Yanni. *Making Peasants Backward: Agricultural Cooperatives and the Agrarian Question in Russia, 1861–1914*. New York: St. Martin's, 1999.

Kovalevskii, P. I., S. N. Syromiatkov, and A. M. Mikhailov. *Nashi vragi*. Petrograd: Tip. L.Ia. Ginzburga, 1915.

Kovtun, E. F. *Mikhail Larionov, 1881–1964*. Bournemouth: Parkstone Press, 1998.

Kowner, Rotem. "'Lighter Than Yellow, But Not Enough': Western Discourse on the Japanese 'Race,' 1854–1904." *The Historical Journal* 43/1 (2000): 103–31.

Kozelsky, Mara. "Orthodoxy Under Fire: Clergy, Sermons, and Christianization during the Crimean War." (Unpublished article).

Kozhin, N. A., and I. S. Abramov. *Narodnyi lubok vtoroi poloviny XIX veka i sovremennyi*. Leningrad: Izd. Muzeia Obshchestva pooshchreniia khudozhestv, 1929.

Krylov, Ivan. *Krylov's Fables* Translated by Bernard Pares. New York: Harcourt, Brace, 1927.

Landes, Joan. *Visualizing the Nation: Gender, Representation, and Revolution in Eighteenth-Century France*. Ithaca: Cornell University Press, 2001.

Lapshin, V. P. *Khudozhestvennaia zhizn' Moskvy i Petrograda v 1917 godu*. Moscow: Sov. khudozhnik, 1983.

Larionov, Mikhail. *Vystavka ikonopisnykh podlinnikov i lubkov*. Moscow, 1913.

Layton, Susan. *Russian Literature and Empire: Conquest of the Caucasus from Pushkin to Tolstoy*. Cambridge: Cambridge University Press, 1994.

Lieven, Dominic. *Empire: The Russian Empire and Its Rivals*. New Haven: Yale University Press, 2001.

Lincoln, W. Bruce. *Between Heaven and Hell: The Story of a Thousand Years of Artistic Life in Russia.* New York: Viking, 1998.

———. *The Great Reforms: Autocracy, Bureaucracy, and the Politics of Change in Imperial Russia.* DeKalb: Northern Illinois University Press, 1990.

———. *In War's Dark Shadow: The Russians before the Great War.* New York: Dial Press, 1983.

———. *Passage Through Armageddon: The Russians in War and Revolution, 1914–1918.* New York: Simon and Schuster, 1986.

Littauer, Vladimir. *Russian Hussar: A Story of the Imperial Cavalry, 1911–1920.* Shippensburg, PA: White Mane Publishing Co., 1993.

Lohr, Eric. *Nationalizing the Russian Empire: The Campaign against Enemy Aliens in World War I.* Cambridge, MA: Harvard University Press, 2003.

———. "The Russian Army and the Jews: Mass Deportations, Hostages, and Violence during World I." *Russian Review* 60/3 (July 2001): 404–19.

Lomunov, K. N. "1812 god v 'Voine i mire' L. N. Tolstogo." In *Otechestvennaia voina 1812 i russkaia literatura xix veka,* edited by V. Iu. Troitskii, 321–43. Moscow: "Nasledie," 1998.

Lotman, Iu. M. *Besedy o russkoi kul'ture. Byt i traditsii russkogo dvorianstva (XVIII-nachalo XIX veka).* St. Petersburg: Iskusstvo, 1997.

———. *Universe of the Mind: A Semiotic Theory of Culture.* Translated by Ann Shukman. Bloomington: Indiana University Press, 2000.

Lotman, Iu. M., and Boris Uspenskii. "Binary Models in the Dynamic of Russian Culture (to the End of the Eighteenth Century)." In *The Semiotics of Russian Cultural History,* edited by Alexander and Alice Stone Nakhimovsky. Ithaca: Cornell University Press, 1985.

Magula, Gerasim. "Voina i narodnye kartiny." *Lukomor'e* 30 (1914).

Maiakovskii, Vladimir. *Maiakovskii-khudozhnik.* Moscow: Sovetskii khudozhnik, 1963.

———. *Polnoe sobranie sochinenii.* 13 vols. Moscow: Gosud. Izd-vo Knudozh. Lit-ry, 1955–1961.

———. *Selected Works in Three Volumes.* Moscow: Raduga, 1985.

———. "Tol'ko ne vospominaniia [1927]." In *Polnoe sobranie sochinenii,* vol. 12. Moscow, 1951.

Maier, Charles. *The Unmasterable Past: History, Holocaust, and German National Identity.* Cambridge, MA: Harvard University Press, 1988.

Makine, Andrei. *Requiem for a Lost Empire.* Tranlated by Geoffrey Strachan. New York: Arcade Publishing, 2001.

Maksimov, S. V. *Nechistaia, nevedomaia i krestnaia sila.* St. Petersburg: T-vo R. Golike i A. Vil'borg, 1903.

Malevich, Kazimir. *Malevich: khudozhnik i teoretik.* Moscow: Sov. khudozhnik, 1990.

Mallon, Florencia. *Peasant and Nation: The Making of Postcolonial Mexico and Peru.* Berkeley: University of California Press, 1994.

Malov, E. A. "O kreshchenykh tatarakh." *Izvestiia po Kazanskoi eparkhii* (1891): 555–76.

Marker, Gary. *Publishing, Printing, and the Origins of Intellectual Life in Russia, 1700–1800.* Princeton: Princeton University Press, 1985.

Martin, Alexander. "The Family Model of Society and Russian National Identity in Sergei N. Glinka's *Russian Messenger* (1808–1812)." *Slavic Review* 57/1 (Spring 1998): 28–49.

———. *Romantics, Reformers, Reactionaries: Russian Conservative Thought and Politics in the Reign of Alexander I.* DeKalb: Northern Illinois University Press, 1997.

Martin, Terry. "Modernization or Neo-Traditionalism: Ascribed Nationality and Soviet Primordialism." In *Stalinism: New Directions,* edited by Sheila Fitzpatrick, 348–67. London: Routledge, 2000.

Matless, David. *Landscape and Englishness.* London: Reaktion Books, 1998.

McLeod, Hugh. "Protestantism and British National Identity, 1815–1945." In *Nation and Religion: Perspectives on Europe and Asia*, edited by Peter Van der Veer and Hartmut Lehmann, 44–70. Princeton: Princeton University Press, 1999.

McNeal, Robert. *Tsar and Cossack, 1855–1914*. Oxford: Oxford University Press, 1987.

McReynolds, Louise. "Mobilizing Petrograd's Lower Classes to Fight the Great War: Patriotism as a Counterweight to Working-Class Consciousness in *Gazeta Kopeika*." *Radical History Review* 57 (1993): 160–80.

———. *The News Under Russia's Old Regime: The Development of a Mass-Circulation Press.* Princeton: Princeton University Press, 1991.

Melman, Billie, ed. *Borderlines: Genders and Identities in War and Peace, 1870–1930*. New York: Routledge, 1998.

Menning, Bruce. *Bayonets Before Bullets: The Imperial Russian Army, 1861–1914*. Bloomington: Indiana University Press, 1992.

Merridale, Catherine. *Night of Stone: Death and Memory in Twentieth-Century Russia*. New York: Viking, 2001.

Meshcherskii, V. P., ed. *Sbornik voennykh razskazov sostavlennykh ofitserami-uchastnikami voiny 1877–1878*. Vol. 1. St. Petersburg: Izd. V. Meshcherskago, 1878.

Mezeir, A. V. *1812–1912. Otechestvennaia voina v khudozhestvennykh proizvedeniiakh, zapiskakh, pis'makh, i vospominaniiakh sovremennikov*. St. Petersburg: Sytin, 1912.

Miasoedov, G. "Russkii lubok kontsa XIX-nachala XX veka." In *Illiustratsiia*, edited by G. V. El'shevskaia, 235–50. Moscow: Sov. khudozhnik, 1988.

Mikhailova, Yulia. "Images of Enemy and Self: Russian 'Popular Prints' of the Russo-Japanese War." *Acta Slavica Iaponica* 16 (1998): 30–53.

Miliutin, D. A. *Vospominaniia*. 1919. Reprint, Newtonville, MA: Oriental Research Partners, 1979.

Miller, Fedor Bogdanovich. *Stikhotvoreniia*. Moscow: Tip. F.B. Millera, 1872.

Milner, John. *Art, War, and Revolution in France, 1870–1871: Myth, Reportage, and Reality*. New Haven: Yale University Press, 2000.

Miniailo, N. G. "Otechestvennaia voina 1812 goda v 'Oknakh TASS' (1941–1945)." In *Stranitsy khudozhestvennogo naslediia Rossii XVI-XX vekov*, edited by E. I. Itkina, 75–88. Moscow: GIM, 1997.

Mironov, B. N. *Sotsialnaia istoriia Rossii*. 2 vols. St. Petersburg: D. Bulanin, 1999.

Mirovozrenie i samosoznanie russkogo obshchestva (XI-XX vv). Moscow, 1994.

Mirzoeff, Nicholas, ed. *The Visual Culture Reader*. London: Routledge, 1998.

Mitchell, Rosemary. *Picturing the Past: English History in Text and Image, 1830–1870*. Oxford: Clarendon Press, 2000.

Mitchell, W. J. T. *Iconology: Image, Text, Ideology*. Chicago: University of Chicago Press, 1986.

———. *Picture Theory: Essays on Verbal and Visual Representation*. Chicago: University of Chicago Press, 1995.

Mitrofanova, G. A. "O lubke pro mozhaiskikh krest'ian-partizan 1812 goda." In *Narodnaia graviura i fol'klor v Rossii XVII-XIX vv.*, edited by I. E. Danilova, 199–220. Moscow: Sov. khudozhnik, 1976.

Moissenko, ed., *Bessmertnaia epopeia: k 175-letiiu Otechestvennoi voiny 1812 g. i Osvoboditel'noi voiny 1813 g. v Germanii*. Moscow: Nauka: 1988.

Moon, David. "Peasants into Russian Citizens? A Comparative Perspective." *Revolutionary Russia* 9/1 (1996): 43–81.

Moor, D. S. *Azbuka krasnoarmeitsa*. Moscow: Gos. izd-vo, 1921.

———. *Ia-bol'shevik*. Moscow: Sov. khudozhnik, 1967.

Mosse, George. *Fallen Soldiers: Reshaping the Memory of the World Wars*. Oxford: Oxford University Press, 1990.

———. *The Nationalization of the Masses: Political Symbolism and Mass Movements in Germany from the Napoleonic Wars through the Third Reich*. Ithaca: Cornell University Press, 1991.

————. *Toward the Final Solution: A History of European Racism.* Madison: University of Wisconsin Press, 1978.

Muge Gocek, Fatma. "From Empire to Nation: Images of Women and War in Ottoman Political Cartoons, 1908–1923." In *Borderlines,* edited by Billie Melman, 47–72. New York: Routledge, 1998.

Nashi vragy nemtsy. Moscow: Sytin, 1914.

Nedd, Andrew. "*Segodniashnii Lubok*: Art, War, and National Identity." M.A. thesis, University of California, Davis, 1995.

Nekrasov, N. A. *Polnoe sobranie stikhotvorennii v trekh tomakh.* Leningrad: Sov. Pisatel', 1967.

Nekrylova, A. F. *Russkie narodnye gorodskie prazdniki, uveseleniia, i zrelishcha.* Leningrad: Iskusstvo, 1988.

Nemirovich-Danchenko, Vasilii. *God voiny (dnevnik russkogo korrespondenta) 1877–1878.* St. Petersburg: Novogo vremeni, 1878.

————. *Skobelev. Lichnyia vospominaniia i vpechatlieniia v dvukh chastiakh.* St. Petersburg, 1903.

————. *Vostok i voina.* Moscow: Sytin, 1905.

Neznamov, A. A. *Iz opyta russko-iaponskoi voiny.* St. Petersburg: Izd. P. P. Soikina, 1906.

Nikitenko, Aleksandr. *The Diary of a Russian Censor.* Translated by Helen Saltz Jacobson. Amherst: University of Massachusetts Press, 1975.

————. *Moia povest' o samom sebei o tom, "chemu svidietel' v zhizni byl."* *Zapiski i dnevniki (1804–1877 gg.)* 2 vols. St. Petersburg: Tipo-lit. "Gerol'd," 1904–1905.

————. *Up From Serfdom: My Childhood and Youth in Russia, 1804–1824.* Translated by Helen Saltz Jacobson. New Haven: Yale University Press, 2001.

Norris, Stephen M. "Depicting the Holy War: The Images of the Russo-Turkish War, 1877–1878." *Ab Imperio* 4/2001: 141–68.

————. "Images of 1812: Ivan Terebenev and the Russian Wartime *Lubok.*" *National Identities* 7/1 (March 2005): 1–21.

Otto, Robert. *Publishing for the People: The Firm Posrednik, 1885–1905.* New York: Garland Publishing, 1987.

Ouspensky, Leonid, and Vladimir Lossky. *The Meaning of Icons.* Translated by G. E. H. Oalmer and E. Kadloubovsky. Crestwood, NY: St. Vladimir's Seminary Press, 1982.

Ovsiannikov, Iu. M. *Russkii lubok.* Moscow: Sov. khudozhnik, 1962.

Palmer, Scott. "Modernizing Russia in the Aeronautical Age: Technology, Legitimacy, and the Structures of Air-Mindedness, 1909–1939." Ph.D. diss., University of Illinois, Urbana-Champaign, 1997.

————. "On Wings of Courage: Public *Air-Mindedness* and National Identity in Late Imperial Russia" *Russian Review* 54 (April 1995): 209–26.

Paret, Peter. *Art as History: Episodes in the Culture and Politics of Nineteenth-Century Germany.* Princeton: Princeton University Press, 1988.

————. *Imagined Battles: Reflections of War in European Art.* Chapel Hill: University of North Carolina Press, 1997.

Paret, Peter, Beth Irwin Lewis, and Paul Paret, eds., *Persuasive Images: Posters of War and Revolution from the Hoover Institution Archives.* Princeton: Princeton University Press, 1992.

Parton, Anthony. *Mikhail Larionov and the Russian Avant-Garde.* Princeton: Princeton University Press, 1993.

Pasternak, Alexander. *A Vanished Present: The Memoirs of Alexander Pasternak.* Translated by Ann Pasternak Slater. San Diego: Harcourt Brace Jovanovich, 1984.

————. *Vospominaniia.* Munich: W. Fink, 1983.

Peltzer [Pel'tzer], M. "Russkaia politicheskaia kartina 1812 goda. Usloviia proizvodstva i khudozhestvennye osobennosti." In *Mir narodnoi kartinki,* edited by I. E. Danilova, 173–84. Moscow: Progress—Traditsiia, 1999.

Penzin, Viktor. *Grafika. Monumental'noe iskusstvo. Katalog vystavki.* Moscow, 1989.

Pervaia vystavka lubkov organizovaka D. N. Vinogradovym. Moscow, 1913.

Petrone, Karen. "Family, Masculinity, and Heroism in Russian War Posters of the First World War." In *Borderlines,* edited by Billie Melman, 95–120. New York: Routledge, 1998.

———. "Masculinity and Heroism in Imperial and Soviet Military-Patriotic Cultures." In *Russian Masculinities in History and Culture,* edited by Barbara Evans Clement, Rebecca Friedman, and Dan Healey, 172–93. London: Palgrave, 2002.

Petrov, F. A., et al., eds. *1812 god. Vospominaniia voinov russkoi armii, iz sobraniia otdela pis'mennykh istochnikov Gosudarstvennogo Istoricheskogo muzeia.* Moscow: "Mysl'," 1991.

Pfitzer, Gregory. *Picturing the Past: Illustrated Histories and the American Imagination, 1840–1900.* Washington, D.C.: Smithsonian Institution Press, 2002.

Pisiotis, Argyrios. "Images of Hate in the Art of War." In *Culture and Entertainment in Wartime Russia,* edited by Richard Stites, 141–56. Bloomington: Indiana University Press, 1995.

Plakaty voiny i pobedy, 1941–1945. Moscow: Kontakt-Kul'tura, 2005.

Plamper, Jan. "Abolishing Ambiguity: Soviet Censorship Practices in the 1930s." *Russian Review* 60/4 (October 2001): 526–44.

Plokhy, Serhii. "The City of Glory: Sevastopol in Russian Historical Mythology." *Journal of Contemporary History* 35/3 (July 2000): 369–83.

———. *Tsars and Cossacks: A Study in Iconography.* Cambridge, MA: Harvard University Press, 2003.

Pobedonostsev, K. P. *Pis'ma Pobedonostseva k Aleksandru III.* Moscow: Novaia Moskva, 1925.

Polonskii, V. P. *Russkii revoliutsionnyi plakat.* Moscow: Gos. izd-vo, 1925.

———. "Russkii revoliutsionnyi plakat." *Pechat' i revoliutsiia* 5 (1922).

Polovtsev, A. A., ed. *Russkii biograficheskii slovar'.* St. Petersburg: Izdanie Imperatorskago Russkago istoricheskago obshchestva, 1896–1918.

Porshnova, O. S. *Mentalitet i sotsial'noe povedenie rabochikh, krest'ian, i soldat. Rossiia v period pervoi mirovoi voiny (1914-mart 1918 g.).* Ekaterinburg: UrO RAN, 2000.

Porterfield, Todd. *The Allure of Empire: Art in the Service of French Imperialism, 1798–1836.* Princeton: Princeton University Press, 1998.

Preobrazhenskii, A. G. *Etimologicheskii slovar' russkogo iazyka.* Moscow: Tip. G. Lissnera i D. Sovko, 1910–1914.

Prugavin, V. S. *Ocherki kustarnoi promyshlennosti Rossii po poslednim izsledovaniiam chastnykh lits, zemstve, i kommissii.* Moscow: Tip. N. S. Skvortsova, 1882.

Pushkarev, L. N., ed. *Mirovospriiatie i samosoznanie russkogo obshchestva (XI-XX vv.). Sbornik statei.* Moscow: In-t rossiiskoi istorii RAN, 1994.

Puzyrevskii, A. K. *Desiat' let nazad. Voina 1877–1878 gg.* St. Petersburg: Tip. V.S. Balasheva, 1888.

Pypin, A. N. *Istoriia russkoi etnografii.* 4 vols. St. Petersburg: Tip. M.M. Stasliulevicha, 1890–1892.

Pyrova, N. M. *Otechestvennaia voina 1812 goda v grafike khudozhnikov sovremennikov.* Moscow: GIM, 1990.

Qualls, Karl. "Imagining Sevastopol: History and Postwar Community Construction, 1942–1953." *National Identities* 5/2 (2003): 123–39.

———. "Local-Outsider Negotiations in Postwar Sevastopol's Reconstruction, 1944–53." In *Provincial Landscapes: Local Dimensions of Soviet Power, 1917–1953,* edited by Donald Raleigh, 276–98. Pittsburgh: University of Pittsburgh Press, 2001.

Raeff, Marc. *Political Ideas and Institutions in Imperial Russia.* Boulder: Westview Press, 1994.

Razin, E. A. *Istoriia voennogo iskusstva s drevneishikh vremen do pervoi imperialisticheskoi voiny, 1914–1918 gg.* Moscow: voen. izd-vo, 1940.

Riasanovsky, Nicholas. *The Emergence of Romanticism.* Oxford: Oxford University Press, 1995.
———. *Nicholas I and Official Nationality in Russia, 1825–1855.* Berkeley: University of California Press, 1959.
Rieber, Alfred. "Russian Imperialism: Popular, Emblematic, Ambiguous." *Russian Review* (July 1994): 331–35.
Rieber, Robert, ed. *The Psychology of War and Peace: The Image of the Enemy.* New York: Plenum Press, 1991.
Roberts, Warren. *Jacques-Louis David: Revolutionary Artist.* Chapel Hill: University of North Carolina Press, 1989.
Robson, Roy. *Old Believers in Modern Russia.* DeKalb: Northern Illinois University Press, 1995.
———. *Solovki: The Story of Russia Told through its Most Remarkable Islands.* New Haven: Yale University Press, 2004.
Rogger, Hans. *National Consciousness in Eighteenth-Century Russia.* Cambridge, MA: Harvard University Press, 1960.
———. "The Skobelev Phenomenon: The Hero and His Worship." *Oxford Slavonic Papers* 9 (1976): 46–78.
Roginskaia, F. "Soviet Posters and 'Lubok.'" *V.O.K.S.* 6/7 (April 1930): 79–82.
Rose, Sonya. *Which People's War? National Identity and Citizenship in Wartime Britain, 1939–1945.* Oxford: Oxford University Press, 2003.
Rosenfeld, Alla, ed. *Defining Russian Graphic Arts: From Diaghilev to Stalin, 1898–1934.* New Brunswick: Rutgers University Press, 1999.
———. "The Search for National Identity in Turn-of-the-Century Russian Graphic Design." In *Defining Russian Graphic Arts,* 16–38. New Brunswick: Rutgers University Press, 1999.
———. "The World Turned Upside Down: Russian Posters of the First World War, the Bolshevik Revolution, and the Civil War." In *Defining Russian Graphic Arts,* 121–31. New Brunswick: Rutgers University Press, 1999.
Rosenthal, Bernice Glatzer, ed. *The Occult in Russian and Soviet Culture.* Ithaca: Cornell University Press, 1997.
Roshwald, Aviel, and Richard Stites, eds. *European Culture in the Great War: The Arts, Entertainment, and Propaganda, 1914–1918.* Cambridge: Cambridge University Press, 1999.
Rossiia pervoi poloviny XIX v. glazami inostrantsev. Leningrad: Lenizdat, 1991.
ROSTA Bolshevik Placards, 1919–1921: Handmade Political Posters from the Russian Telegraph Agency. New York: Sander Gallery, 1994.
Rostopchin, F. V. *Okh, frantsuzy!* Moscow: Russkaia kniga, 1992.
———. *Rostopchinskiia afishi.* St. Petersburg: A. S. Suvorin, 1904.
———. *Rostopchinskiia afishi 1812 goda.* St. Petersburg: A. S. Suvorin, 1889.
———. *Sochineniia.* St. Petersburg: Izd. A. Smirdina, 1853.
———. *Zhurnal iskhodiashchim bumagam kantseliarii Moskovskago general-gubernatora grafa Rostopchina s iiunia po dekabr' 1812 goda.* Moscow: Tovarishchestvo tip. A.I. Mamontova, 1908.
Rotberg, Robert, and Theodor Rabb, eds., *Art and History: Images and Their Meaning.* Cambridge: Cambridge University Press, 1988.
Rovinskii, D. A. *Russkiia narodnye kartinki.* 5 vols. St. Petersburg: Tip. Imp. Akademii nauk, 1881–1893.
———. *Russkiia narodnye kartinki atlas.* 4 vols. St. Petersburg: Tip. Imp. Akademii nauk, 1881–1893.
Russkii plakat pervoi mirovoi voiny. Moscow: Iskusstvo i kul'tura, 1992.
Ruud, Charles. *Fighting Words: Imperial Censorship and the Russian Press, 1804–1906.* Toronto: University of Toronto Press, 1982.
———. *Russian Entrepreneur: Publisher Ivan Sytin of Moscow, 1851–1934.* Montreal: McGill-Queen's University Press, 1990.

Russkii lubok. Vystavka iz sobraniia gosudarstvennogo literaturnogo muzeia. Voronezh: GIM, 1988.

Said, Edward. *Orientalism.* New York: Vintage, 1979.

Sakurai, Tadayoshi. *Human Bullets (Niku-Dan): A Soldier's Story of Port Arthur.* Translated by Masujiro Honda and Alice Bacon. Tokyo, 1907.

Salmond, Wendy. *Arts and Crafts in Late Imperial Russia: Reviving the Kustar Art Industries, 1870–1917.* Cambridge: Cambridge University Press, 1996.

Samuels, Maurice. *The Spectacular Past: Popular History and the Novel in Nineteenth-Century France.* Ithaca: Cornell University Press, 2004.

Sanborn, Joshua. *Drafting the Russian Nation: Military Conscription, Total War, and Mass Politics, 1905–1925.* DeKalb: Northern Illinois University Press, 2002.

———. "The Mobilization of 1914 and the Question of the Russian Nation: A Reexamination." *Slavic Review* 59/2 (2000): 267–89.

Sapgir, Kira. *Moskovskiia kartinki/Les images de Moscou. Patrioticheskii lubok.* 5 vols. Moscow: n.p., 1978.

Sbornik soldatskikh pesen. Petrograd: n.p., 1915.

Schama, Simon. *Citizens: A Chronicle of the French Revolution.* New York: Knopf, 1988.

Schimmelpenninck Van Der Oye, David. "The Asianist Vision of Prince Ukhtomskii." In *Kazan, Moscow, St. Petersburg: Multiple Faces of the Russian Empire,* edited by Catherine Evtuhov et al., 188–202. Moscow: O.G.I., 1997.

———. "Ex Oriente Lux: Ideologies of Empire and Russia's Far East, 1895–1904." Ph.D. diss., Yale University, 1997.

———. *Toward the Rising Sun: Russian Ideologies of Empire on the Path to War with Japan.* DeKalb: Northern Illinois University Press, 2001.

———. "What is Russian Orientalism?" Paper presented at the American Association for the Advancement of Slavic Studies Annual Meeting, 10 November 2000.

Schmidt, Albert. "The Restoration of Moscow After 1812." *Slavic Review* 40/1 (1981): 37–48.

Semmel, Stuart. *Napoleon and the British.* New Haven: Yale University Press, 2004.

Semyonova Tian-Shanskaia, Olga. *Village Life in Late Tsarist Russia.* Translated by David Ransel. Bloomington: Indiana University Press, 1993.

Seregny, Scott. "Zemstvos, Peasants, and Citizenship: The Russian Adult Education Movement and World War I." *Slavic Review* 59/2 (2000): 290–315.

Serman, Il'ia. "Russian National Consciousness and Its Development in the Eighteenth Century." In *Russia in the Age of the Enlightenment,* edited by Roger Bartlett and Janet Hartley, 40–56. New York: St. Martin's, 1990.

Sharf, Frederic, and James T. Ulak. *A Well-Watched War: Images From the Russo-Japanese Front, 1904–1905.* Newbury, MA: Newburyport Press, 2000.

Sharpe, Kevin. "Representations and Negotiations: Texts, Images, and Authority in Early Modern England." *The Historical Journal* 42/3 (1999): 853–81.

Shevzov, Vera. "Chapels and the Ecclesial World of Prerevolutionary Russian Peasants." *Slavic Review* 55/3 (Autumn 1996): 585–613.

———. "Letting the People into Church: Reflections on Orthodoxy and Community in Late Imperial Russia." In *Orthodox Russia: Belief and Faith under the Tsars,* edited by Valerie Kivelson and Robert Greene, 59–77. University Park: Pennsylvania State University Press, 2003.

Shevchenko, Aleksandr. *Neo-primitivizm. Ego teoriia, ego vozmozhnosti, ego dostizheniia.* Moscow: n.p., 1913.

Shukhmin, Khristofor. *Slavnyi podvig Donskogo Kazaka Koz'my Kriuchkova.* Moscow: n.p., 1914.

Siljak, Ana. "Rival Visions of the Russian Nation: The Teaching of Russian History, 1890–1917." Ph.D. diss., Harvard University, 1997.

Slepyan, Kenneth. "Their Master's Voice: Radio Moscow's Broadcasts to the Occupied Territories, June 1942–January 1943." Paper presented at the American Association for the Advancement of Slavic Studies Annual Meeting, 21 November 1999.

Slezkine, Yuri. *Arctic Mirrors: Russia and the Small Peoples of the North.* Ithaca: Cornell University Press, 1994.

Smirnov, N. N., ed. *Rossiia i pervaia mirovaia voina. Materialy mezhdunarodnogo nauchnogo kollokviuma.* St. Petersburg: D. Bulanin, 1999.

Smith, Anthony D. "Art and Nationalism in Europe." In *De Onmacht van het Grote: Cultuur in Europa,* edited by J. C. H. Blom et al., 64–80. Amsterdam: Amsterdam University Press, 1993.

———. *Myths and Memories of the Nation.* Oxford: Oxford University Press, 1999.

———. *The Nation in History: Historiographical Debates about Ethnicity and Nationalism.* Hanover: University Press of New England, 2000.

———. *Nationalism and Modernism.* London: Routledge, 1998.

———. "War and Ethnicity: The Role of Warfare in the Formation, Self-Images, and Cohesion of Ethnic Studies." *Ethnic and Racial Studies* 4 (1981): 375–97.

Smith, S. A. "Citizenship and the Russian Nation During World War I: A Comment." *Slavic Review* 59/2 (2000): 316–29.

Snegirev, Ivan. *Dnevnik Ivana Mikhailovicha Snegireva.* 2 vols. Moscow: Univ. tip., 1904–1905.

———. *Lubochnyia kartinki russkago naroda v Moskovskom mire.* Moscow: V. Univ. Tip., 1861.

———. *Pamiatniki moskovskoi drevnosti s prisovokupleniem ocherka monumental'noi istorii moskvy i drevnikh vidov i planov drevnei stolitsy.* Moscow: Tip. A Semena, 1845.

Sandulov, Iu., ed. *Istoriia Rossii. Narod i vlast.* St. Petersburg: Izd.-vo "LAN," 1997.

Sobolev, N. A., and V. A. Artamonov. *Simvoly Rossii.* Moscow: Panorama, 1993.

Sokhriakov, Iu. I. *Natsional'naia ideia v otechestvennoi publitsistike XIX-nachala XX vv.* Moscow: "Nasledie," 2000.

Sokol, K. G. *Monumenty imperii. Opisanie dvukhsot naibolee interesnykh pamiatnikov imperatorskoi Rossii.* Moscow: GEOS, 1999.

Sokolov, B. M. *Khudozhestvennyi iazyk russkogo lubka.* Moscow: Rossiiskii gos. gumanitarnyi universitet, 1999.

Sollugub, V. A. *Dnevnik vysochaishchego prebyvaniia za Dunaem v 1877 godu.* St. Petersburg: n.p., 1878.

Stavrou, Theofanis, ed. *Art and Culture in Nineteenth-Century Russia.* Bloomington: Indiana University Press, 1983.

Steinberg, Mark, ed. *Voices of Revolution, 1917.* New Haven: Yale University Press, 2002.

Steiner, Evgeny. *Stories for Little Comrades: Revolutionary Artists and the Making of Early Soviet Children's Books.* Seattle: University of Washington Press, 1999.

Stephan, John. *The Russian Far East: A History.* Palo Alto: Stanford University Press, 1994.

Stites, Richard, ed. *Culture and Entertainment in Wartime Russia.* Bloomington: Indiana University Press, 1995.

———. "Days and Nights in Wartime Russia: Cultural Life, 1914–1917." In *European Culture in the Great War,* edited by Aviel Roshwald and Richard Stites, 8–31. Cambridge: Cambridge University Press, 1999.

———. *Russian Popular Culture: Entertainment and Society Since 1900.* Cambridge: Cambridge University Press, 1992.

———. *Serfdom, Society, and the Arts in Imperial Russia: The Pleasure and the Power.* New Haven: Yale University Press, 2005.

Stoyle, Mark. "English 'Nationalism,' Celtic Particularism, and the English Civil War." *The Historical Journal* 43/4 (2000): 1113–28.

Strachan, Hew. *The First World War.* Volume 1, *To Arms.* Oxford: Oxford University Press, 2001.

Sunderland, Willard. "An Empire of Peasants: Empire-Building, Interethnic Interaction, and Ethnic Stereotyping in the Rural World of the Russian Empire,

1800–1850s." In *Imperial Russia,* edited by Jane Burbank and David Ransel, 174–98. Bloomington: Indiana University Press, 1998.

Suny, Ronald Grigor. *The Revenge of the Past: Nationalism, Revolution, and the Collapse of the Soviet Union.* Palo Alto: Stanford University Press, 1993.

Suny, Ronald Grigor, and Terry Martin, eds. *A State of Nations: Empire and Nation-Making in the Age of Lenin and Stalin.* Oxford: Oxford University Press, 2001.

Suvorova, K. N., ed. *V. V. Maiakovskii. Opisanie dokumental'nykh materialov, i. "Okna" ROSTA i Glavpolitprosveta, 1919–1922.* Moscow: n.p., 1964.

Swift, E. Anthony. *Popular Theater and Society in Tsarist Russia.* Berkeley: University of California Press, 2002.

Sytin, I. D. *Zhizn' dlia knigi.* Moscow: Kniga, 1978.

Tartakovskii, A. G. *1812 god i russkaia memuaristika: opyt istochnikovedcheskogo izucheniia.* Moscow: Nauka, 1980.

———. *Russkaia memuaristika i istoricheskoe soznanie XIX veka.* Moscow: "Arkheografi-cheskii tsentr," 1997.

———, ed. *1812 god . . . voennye dnevniki.* Moscow: Sov. Rossiia, 1990.

———, ed. *1812 v vospominaniiakh sovremennikov.* Moscow: Nauka, 1995.

Taruskin, Richard. *Defining Russia Musically: Historical and Hermeneutical Essays.* Princeton: Princeton University Press, 1997.

Taylor, Philip. *Munitions of the Mind: A History of Propaganda from the Ancient World to the Present Day.* 3rd ed. Manchester: Manchester University Press, 2003.

Tenishev, V. N., ed. *Programma etnograficheskikh svedenii o krest'ianakh tsentral'noi Rossii.* Smolensk: Gub. Tip., 1897.

Thaden, Edward. *Conservative Nationalism in Nineteenth-Century Russia.* Seattle: University of Washington Press, 1964.

Tokarev, S. A. *Istoriia russkoi etnografii.* Moscow: Nauka, 1966.

Tolstoy, Leo. *Bethink Yourselves!* Translated by V. Tchertkoff. New York: Thomas Y. Crowell, 1904.

———. *Leo Tolstoy's Diaries.* Translated by R. F. Christian. London: Flamingo, 1984.

———. *The Sebastopol Sketches.* Translated by David McDuff. New York: Penguin Books, 1986.

———. *Voina i mir.* 2 vols. Moscow: Sov. pisatel', 1978.

———. *War and Peace.* Translated by Henry Gifford. Oxford: Oxford University Press, 1998.

Tolz, Vera. *Russia: Inventing the Nation.* London: Edward Arnold, 2001.

Tretiakov, N. A. *My Experiences at Nan Shan and Port Arthur with the Fifth East Siberian Rifles.* Translated by A. C. Alford. London: H. Rees, 1911.

Troitskii, V. Iu., ed. *Otechestvennaia voina 1812 goda i russkaia literatura XIX veka.* Moscow: "Nasledie," 1998.

Tumarkin, Nina. *Lenin Lives! The Lenin Cult in Soviet Russia.* Cambridge, MA: Harvard University Press, 1983.

———. *The Living and the Dead: The Rise and Fall of the Cult of World War II in Russia.* New York: Basic Books, 1994.

Tupulov, N. V., ed. *Polveka dlia knigi (1866–1916). Literaturno-khudozhestvennyi sbornik, posviashchennyi piatidesiatilietiiu izdatel'skoi dieiatel'nosti I. D. Sytina.* Moscow: Sytin, 1916.

Ushakov, D. N. *Tolkovyi slovar' russkogo iazyka.* Moscow: Gos. in-t "Sovetskaia entsiklo-pediia," 1939.

Vakhterev, V. P. *Vneshkol'noe obrazovanie.* Moscow: n.p., 1894.

Valkenier, Elizabeth. *Russian Realist Art: The State and Society: The Peredvizhniki and Their Tradition.* Ann Arbor: Ardis, 1977.

Van der Verr, Peter, and Hartmut Lehmann, eds. *Nation and Religion: Perspectives on Europe and Asia.* Princeton: Princeton University Press, 1999.

Vavilov, A. *Zapiski soldata Vavilova.* Moscow, 1927.

Venetsianov, A. G. *Aleksei Gavriilovich Venetsianov. Stat'i, pis'ma, sovremenniki o khudozhnike.* Leningrad: Iskusstvo, 1980.

Vereshchagin, V. A. *Russkaia karikatura.* Vol. 2, *Otechestvennaia voina.* St. Petersburg: Tip. Sirius, 1912.

Verhey, Jeffrey. *The Spirit of 1914: Militarism, Myth, and Mobilization in Germany.* Cambridge: Cambridge University Press, 2000.

Vessel, N. K., ed. *Sbornik soldatskikh, kazatskikh, i matrosskikh pesen.* St. Petersburg: Izd. I. Iurgensona, 1886.

Vevern, Boleslav. *[Shestaia] 6-ia batareia, 1914–1917 gg. Povest o vremeni velikago sluzheniia rodine.* Paris: Tip. Nikishina, 1938.

Voenskii, K. A. *Russkoe dukhovenstvo otechestvennaia voina 1812 goda.* Moscow: Sytin, 1912.

Von Geldern, James, and Louise McReynolds, eds. *Entertaining Tsarist Russia: Tales, Songs, Movies, Jokes, Ads, and Images from Russian Urban Life, 1779–1917.* Bloomington: Indiana University Press, 1998.

———. "Life in Between: Migration and Popular Culture in Late Imperial Russia." *Russian Review* 55/3 (July 1996): 365–83.

Voronina, T. A. "Religioznyi lubok i ego osobennosti v XIX veke." In *Pravoslavnaia zhizn' russkikh krest'ian XIX-XX vekov,* edited by T. A. Listova, 333–60. Moscow: "Nauka," 2001.

Voronovich, N. *Russko-iaponskaia voina. Vospominaniia.* New York: N. Voronovich, 1952.

Vzdornov, G. I. *Istoriia otkrytiia i izucheniia russkoi strednevekovoi zhivopisi XIX v.* Moscow: Iskusstvo, 1986.

Wagner, Peter. *Reading Iconotexts: From Swift to the French Revolution.* London: Reaktion Books, 1995.

Weeks, Theodore. *Nation and State in Late Imperial Russia: Nationalism and Russification on the Western Frontier, 1863–1914.* DeKalb: Northern Illinois University Press, 1996.

Weiner, Amir. "The Making of a Dominant Myth: The Second World War and the Construction of Political Identities within the Soviet Polity." *Russian Review* 55 (October 1996): 638–60.

———. *Making Sense of War: The Second World War and the Fate of the Bolshevik Revolution.* Princeton: Princeton University Press, 2000.

Wells, David, and Sandra Wilson, eds. *The Russo-Japanese War in Cultural Perspective, 1904–05.* New York: St. Martin's Press, 1999.

———. "Paradigms of War in Russian Literature from the Twelfth to the Nineteenth Century" in Wells and Wilson, 86–107.

———. "The Russo-Japanese War in Russian Literature" in Wells and Wilson, 108–133.

Werner, Jack. *We Laughed at Boney (or, We've Been Through It All Before): How Our Forefathers Laughed Defiance at the Last Serious Threat of Invasion by Napoleon: A Striking Parallel with Our Present Position.* London: W. H. Allen, 1943.

Wesling, Molly. *Napoleon in Russian Cultural Mythology.* New York: Peter Lang, 2001.

West, Sally. "The Material Promised Land: Advertising's Modern Agenda in Late Imperial Russia." *Russian Review* 57 (July 1998): 345–63.

White, Stephen. *The Bolshevik Poster.* New Haven: Yale University Press, 1988.

Whittaker, Cynthia Hale. *The Origins of Modern Russian Education: An Intellectual Biography of Count Sergei Uvarov, 1786–1855.* DeKalb: Northern Illinois University Press, 1984.

Wildman, Allan. *The End of the Russian Imperial Army: The Old Army and the Soldiers' Revolt (March–April 1917).* Princeton: Princeton University Press, 1980.

Winter, Jay. "Film and the Matrix of Memory." *American Historical Review* 106/3 (June 2001): 857–64.

———. *Sites of Memory, Sites of Mourning: The Great War in European Cultural History.* Cambridge: Cambridge University Press, 1995.

Wirtschafter, Elise Kimerling. *Social Identity in Imperial Russia.* DeKalb: Northern Illinois University Press, 1997.

———. *Structures of Society: Imperial Russia's "People of Various Ranks."* DeKalb: Northern Illinois University Press, 1994.

Wolff, David. *To the Harbin Station: The Liberal Alternative in Russian Manchuria, 1898–1914.* Palo Alto: Stanford University Press, 1999.

Wortman, Richard. "Publicizing the Imperial Image in 1913." In *Self and Story in Russian History,* edited by Laura Engelstein and Stephanie Sandler, 94–119. Ithaca: Cornell University Press, 2001.

———. *Scenarios of Power: Myth and Ceremony in Russian Monarchy.* Vol. 1, *From Peter the Great to the Death of Nicholas I.* Princeton: Princeton University Press, 1995.

———. *Scenarios of Power: Myth and Ceremony in Russian Monarchy.* Vol. 2, *From Alexander II to the Abdication of Nicholas II.* Princeton: Princeton University Press, 2000.

Yekelchyk, Serhy. "*Diktat* and Dialogue in Stalinist Culture: Staging Historical Opera in Soviet Ukraine, 1936–1954." *Slavic Review* 59/3 (Fall 2000): 597–624.

———. "Stalinist Patriotism as Contested Discourse: Reconciling the Ukrainian and Russian 'Heroic Pasts,' 1939–1945." *Kritika* 3/1 (Winter 2002): 51-80 .

Youngblood, Denise. "A War Forgotten: The Great War in Russian and Soviet Cinema." In *The First World War and Popular Cinema: 1914 to the Present,* edited by Michael Paris, 172–91. New Brunswick: Rutgers University Press, 2000.

Zaionchkovskii, A. M. *Nastupatel'nyi boi po opytu deistvii Generala Skobeleva v srazheniiakh pod Lovchei, Plevnoi (27 i 30 avgusta) i Sheinovo.* St. Petersburg: Tip. S. Kornatovskago, 1893.

Zaitsev, Evgenii. *Voina i mir glazami khudozhnika.* Moscow: TOO "Passim," 1995.

Zamarev, A. A. *Dnevnik totemskogo krest'ianina A. A. Zamareva, 1906–1922 gody.* Moscow: Rossiiskaia akademiia nauk, 1995.

Zamoyski, Adam. *Moscow 1812: Napoleon's Fatal March.* New York: HarperCollins, 2004.

Zarin, A. E. *Zhenshchiny-geroini v 1812 godu. Ocherki i rasskazy iz epochi velikoi otechestvennoi voiny.* Moscow: Izd-vo skl. M. V. Kliukina, 1917.

Zhadova, L. *Malevich: Suprematism and Revolution in Russian Art, 1910–1980.* Translated by Alexander Lieven. London: Thames and Hudson, 1982.

Zolotarev, V. A. *Rossiia i Turtsiia. Voina 1877–1878 gg.* Moscow: Nauka, 1983.

———. *Russko-turetskaia voina 1877–1878 gg. v otechestvennoi istoriografii.* Moscow: Nauka, 1978.

Zorin, Andrei. "Ideologiia 'pravoslaviia-samoderzhaviia-narodnosti.' Opyt rekonstruktsii." *Novoe literaturnoe obozrenie* 26 (1997): 71–104.

———. *Kormia dvuglavogo orla . . . Literatura i gosudarstvennaia ideologiia v Rossii v poslednei treti XVIII - pervoi treti XIX veka.* Moscow: NLO, 2001.

———. "Krym v istorii russkogo samosoznaniia." *Novoe literaturnoe obozrenie* 31/3 (1998): 123–43.

Zorkaia, Neia. *Fol'klor, lubok, ekran.* Moscow: Iskusstvo, 1994.

Exhibitions

1812 g. v karikature. Grafika, khudozhestvennye tkani, voennaia igrushka iz fondov muzeia-zapovednika Borodinskoe pole. Central Museum of the Great Patriotic War (Moscow), 1999.

Pervaia mirovaia . . . prolog XX veka. K 90-letiiu so dnia nachala voiny. State Museum of Russian Political History (St. Petersburg), 2004.

Pod shelest pobednykh znamen. State Museum of Russian Political History (St. Petersburg), 2004.

Vospominaniia o [pervoi] 1-oi vystavke lubkov 1913 goda. Iz kollektsii N. Vinogradova, I. Efimova, i M. Larionova. Moskovskii tsentr iskusstv (Moscow), 1999.

A Well-Watched War: Images From the Russo-Japanese Front, 1904-5. Arthur M. Sackler Gallery (Washington, DC), 2000.

INDEX